W9-BQM-086

Gramley Library
Salem Academy and College
Winston-Salem, N.C. 27108

LITERARY MODERNISM *and* BEYOND

LITERARY MODERNISM *and* BEYOND

THE EXTENDED VISION *and* THE REALMS *of the* TEXT

RICHARD LEHAN

LOUISIANA STATE ✷ UNIVERSITY PRESS

BATON ROUGE

Gramley Library
Salem Academy and College
Winston-Salem, N.C. 27108

Published by Louisiana State University Press
Copyright © 2009 by Louisiana State University Press
All rights reserved
Manufactured in the United States of America
FIRST PRINTING

DESIGNER: *Amanda McDonald Scallan*
TYPEFACE: *Whitman*
PRINTER AND BINDER: *Thomson-Shore, Inc.*

Library of Congress Cataloging-in-Publication Data

Lehan, Richard, 1930-
 Literary modernism and beyond : the extended vision and the realms of
the text / Richard Lehan.
   p. cm.
 Includes bibliographical references and index.
 ISBN 978-0-8071-3388-0 (cloth : alk. paper)
 1. Modernism (Literature) 2. Postmodernism (Literature) I.
Title.
 PN56.M54.L42 2009
 809'.91--dc22

                                          2008028652

The paper in this book meets the guidelines for permanence and
durability of the Committee on Production Guidelines for Book
Longevity of the Council on Library Resources. ∞

Once more for Ann

CONTENTS

VI. POSTMODERNISM AND MASS CULTURE

APPENDIXES

PREFACE

Literary Modernism and Beyond is an introduction, a history, and a critique—a book aimed at the student of literature that organizes literary material in basic ways and yet interprets that material with insights the informed reader might find useful. The primary purpose of this book is to retrieve the meaning of this major cultural movement and its transformations. It provides a summary statement, a retrospective, of this major intellectual and historical movement. It assumes that overlapping concerns make up modernisms—rather than one movement called Modernism—and that these serial elements, when fused, supply a composite picture. This study further assumes that these modernisms rose out of late Romanticism and forms of realism; reached a distinguished realm of achievement with modernists such as Thomas Mann, Marcel Proust, James Joyce, Virginia Woolf, André Gide, Ezra Pound, T. S. Eliot, and Wallace Stevens; and were then transformed by two generations of counterinfluences, what has come to be called postmodernism.

This study provides three contexts: first, it is a historical study of modernism as a generational unfolding; second, it is an in-depth look at the critical transformations the movement underwent; and third, it is a consideration of both the origins of the movement and its re-visionary nature, creating the problem of authenticating a past that is the product of a present perspective, especially when that perspective has created a new textuality.

Modernism can thus best be understood as an unfolding process occurring over roughly three generations: the first stage occurred from about 1890 to 1930, the second from 1930 to the mid-sixties, the third from the sixties to the early nineties and beyond. I highlight several intellectual movements: the rise of structuralism/poststructuralism, the transformation that came with gender and race concerns, and the metamorphosis of modernism when seen as the product of mass/popular culture. The confluence of these three events brought about radical change in a conjectured "original vision," the breakthrough assumptions out of which the modernist movement came into being, the core meaning (or what Wallace Stevens refers to as the "First Idea," the original painting with subsequent paint removed). Every generation views the old through new eyes.

But transformations in the original vision change the "idea" of the text and the way it is to be read. The history of literary modernism—concentrating on such slippage—is the subject of this book.

The early phases of modernism were concerned primarily with aesthetic matters, especially the reach for the beautiful. The emphasis here was upon the idea of self in search of sublimity as the focus moved from an extrinsic to intrinsic realm, from Darwinian to Bergsonian consciousness and creative evolution, which altered the dictates of realism/naturalism. The idea of the beautiful was reinforced by theories of myth and symbol, leading to the idea of spatial form, the universalizing of modernism, the cyclicality of history, and the inevitability of historical decline. These changes were transformed once again by structuralism and poststructuralism and the assumption that the text worked like part of a language system. The next unfolding involved the transformation of the nineteenth-century romance into new forms of realism and then back into postmodern romance, which is partially the product of mass (popular) culture (e.g., the James Bond, Harry Potter novels) and partially the result of a paranoid state of mind (Pynchon) or "systems" worldview (DeLillo). This last change anticipates, along with poststructuralism, the postmodern movement, now a product of mass culture, influenced by gender and race theories, accommodating both elite and popular forms as they relate to crowd psychology.

This study concentrates on the way modernism engaged its era: its rise as literary movement, its transformations under the influence of new critical theories, its radical response to the critical and political influences of the sixties and seventies, and its more recent change stemming from the impress of material culture with a new ideological agenda. That agenda involved a mandate to account for a new cultural diversity and the desire to integrate more popular forms into the modernist canon. The intent here is to be as inclusive as possible. While the configuration of this book promotes a divergent perspective that accommodates comprehensive ways of looking at modernism, I believe that it also supplies a coherent overview of this major literary movement.

Elements of modernism have been critically treated in other books; from 1990 to 1991, eleven books were published on the subject, and these followed a spate of books in the late seventies through the eighties (for specifics, see this volume's bibliographical essay). This book differs from the intent of the others in the way it treats all the elements enumerated above as part of a historical process. In its breadth, it renders other studies of the subject redundant if not obsolete. We have works that consider myth, symbol, and structure, but none to my knowledge that treats the meaning of one in terms of the meaning of the other, or that studies the evolution of modern romance as a product of a revised realism, or that considers the way mass movements have created both a consumer and a popular culture. Such unfolding—mediated by transformations in generational authority and the evolution of textual mandate—resulted in critical changes that redefined the modernist movement and called for its reexamination.

The book is thesis driven to the extent that it contends that modernism is the product of critical and cultural change and the evolution of a changing text. The circumstances, ideas, and beliefs that originally produced modernism have been reconstellated. The impetus for change stemmed from mass-based civilization and market-based economics transforming aesthetic forms of influence. A new consumerism replaced a desire for the sublime. An originary view has been reconfigured to produce a text that is chiefly the end product of criticism itself. The general effect of such change on the idea of modernism has been movement toward the void and forms of nihilism, a gradual sense of diminishment involving historical decline, and a drift toward deferred or suspended meaning, a waiting for what is to happen next.

ACKNOWLEDGMENTS

Since this book extends my previous studies of literary realism and naturalism and the meaning of the literary city, my debt here goes back to those who supported these earlier studies. I am especially grateful for help from the Guggenheim Foundation and for a President's Research fellowship from the University of California. I am also pleased to acknowledge more modest support from the research committee of the academic senate at UCLA.

While the final product may not show it, much of my earlier writing stemmed from drafts that were reworked into core statements and extended in my recent books. Donald Pizer published my essay on European naturalism in his edited book on literary naturalism; Ralph Cohen encouraged some of my earlier thinking on literature and memory when he invited me to participate in a lecture series at the University of Virginia; Edgar Dryden invited me to contribute to a memorial edition of the *Arizona Quarterly*, in homage of Joe Riddel, that helped rekindle thoughts about what is and what is not modernism; and Fred Burwick and Paul Douglass accommodated my preliminary thinking about Bergson in their book on modernism and vitalism. So much of this work reconciled itself to an idea of what literary modernism was and had come to be. These studies found a common denominator in the nature and problematic of transformations within literary movements.

At the LSU Press, my work was fortunate to find the eye of John Easterly, who brought the highest standards of professionalism to vetting this manuscript, and Susan Brady, whose copyediting helped correct my faulty cyclopean eye.

Once again, the research library at UCLA has been unfailingly helpful, and I am especially grateful to those in the circulation department for their many courtesies. Closer to home, in the English department at UCLA, Jeanette Gilkison has been of immense help in processing this manuscript, and Bronson Tran has helped tame a computer that at times had a mind of its own.

As this book's dedication suggests, my greatest debt is to my wife, Ann, whose encouragement and support made an immense amount of work worthwhile.

LITERARY MODERNISM *and* BEYOND

I
MODERNISMS

1 ✢ MODERNISM AND ITS TRANSFORMATIONS

This book builds on two of my previous books: one on literary realism/naturalism, the other on modernism and the theme of the city.[1] The book on literary naturalism was an attempt to understand the events that brought it as a literary movement into being and why those literary elements were transformed in the face of literary modernism, the point at which this book picks up. The book on the city was an attempt to see how the city had become the center of literary activity from the Enlightenment on, and how the historical transformation from an agrarian to urban culture was a major force in understanding literary movements from the Romantic period to postmodernism.

The city book anticipates a study of literary modernism where one of the central tropes involves the artist, or someone who stands in for the artist, as urban viewer. In the tradition of Baudelaire, the quintessential modernist is alone in the crowd. It is the varied consciousness of that viewer that is central to modernist thought. With the rise of structuralism, an emphasis was put on constructed reality at the expense of nature as the mirror of truth. The theme of the city often gives way to the metonym of the crowd and culminates in the attributes we enlist when defining mass culture. The transition from an elitist, intellectual community of like selves to the diversity of mass culture is one of the key elements that led to the transformation of modernism into postmodernism and then to a state of culture beyond.

I

The moderns were trying to adapt to what they saw as the hostile reality of naturalism, and they did this by going to a Romantic theory of the beautiful (aestheticism) and by working inward to theories of consciousness. Modernism began where Nietzsche left off: with consciousness confronting an unmade (godless) universe. That consciousness took many forms, from a Jamesian sense of moral ambiguity, to Bergsonian intuition, to Proustian time spots, to Joycean epiphany, to Hemingway's amour fati kind of neostoicism, all of which were connected within a Nietzschean theory of "perspectivism": the belief that reality stemmed from the way it was perceived, a modernist idea that can be found in Wallace Stevens and Gertrude Stein, among others.

Central to the modernist movement were new ways of thinking about reality: it was a time of radical transformation of philosophical thought. Perhaps the logical starting point here is Schopenhauer and his theory of will and idea. The will for Schopenhauer involved an inner reality: every phenomenon contained an indwelling being, which he related to Plato's Ideas or Forms, universal prototypes that were the object of aesthetic concern. Schopenhauer's theory of inner reality became the basis for Nietzsche's theory of "perspectivism." What was at the center of this chain of association was the belief that there was a hidden meaning within all beings subject to aesthetic discovery or subjective projection—an idea that connected Joyce's epiphanies with Woolf's intuition, Eliot's notion of sensibility, and Pound's theory of the vortex.

II

A desire for a new reality inspired the work of Martin Heidegger (1889–1976), one of the most important spokesmen for a new sense of being. Heidegger was the protégé of Edmund Husserl, and his work anticipated the hermeneutics of Gadamer and the poststructuralism of Derrida and Foucault. His major work was *Sein und Zeit* (*Being and Time*, 1927), which drew heavily upon Nietzsche and Bergson. He rejected a metaphysics of substance for a metaphysics of situation. In the tradition of existentialism, Heidegger maintained that humanity is without essence; human properties unfold as humanity moves from the primitive to the civilized. This view bypassed the narrower view of philosophers such as Descartes, who reduced the self to mind or to technological tools. Our sense of being, of self, is determined in situation. We lose an inauthentic self, the culmination of possibility, when we are drawn into the crowd to play stereotyped roles. Heidegger looked to the ancient Greeks for the model of humanity. He believed that we had been torn from our primal origins, from our defining elements, including language. We bring forth meaning through language, language speaks us, an idea central to poststructural thought. Heidegger's writing after the war involved a repudiation of modern technology, antihumanism as he saw it, in which social efficiency replaced human agency.

Heidegger was in search of Being as a way of organizing the self, not as a manifestation of human essence. Modernism as a state of mind involved a search for an idealized reality—a quest for some kind of presence connected to the unfolding of time. Heidegger's concern was at the heart of modernism, a concern he shared with Virginia Woolf in their belief that mysterious meaning was unlocked in such temporal unfolding. Heidegger insisted that we must engage the world as if it were of our making: the self and the world are existentially inseparable. We can position ourselves in relation to this world in two possible ways. We can bring a creative energy to it and engage its sense of Being, or we can be distracted by it, allow "Being" to give way to "being" and lose our creative drive in everydayness—in the realm of mechanical time and logical relationships. Heidegger believed that we are called back from this realm of everydayness by dread or angst—behind which is the awareness that human time is limited by death. Our dread stems from a sense of nothingness—from seeing the whole structure of being-in-the world as a process of human time culminating in death.

Heidegger saw man as his own creator, in tune with Being or the élan vital—the force of human will working within the restraints of matter and yet expanding those limits. And he saw the modern, mechanical, technological realm—what he referred to as massenmensch (mass-man)—as a real threat to such possibility. Heidegger regretted that we live in a world of forgetfulness— abandoning Being for gadgetry, forsaking what we are and can be. He believed that the understanding of the inner realm of Being involved a consciousness that came close to art and the aesthetic process. Like Nietzsche and Bergson before him, Heidegger moved away from a mechanistic view of humanity subject to immediate stimuli toward humanity as a product of a directing intelligence stemming from human consciousness.

Like many modernists, Heidegger was wary of new technology and the machine. Unlike the naturalists (e.g., Émile Zola and Frank Norris, who accepted the inevitability of the machine), Heidegger believed the machine created a monstrous intrusion between man and nature. Along with Nietzsche and Bergson, Heidegger repositioned the modernist in the industrial age.

Heidegger redefined modern man, making it possible for modernism to replace literary naturalism. His ideas owe much to Edmund Husserl, and they influenced in turn Jean-Paul Sartre. The search for self here starts off as essentialism and ends as existentialism. Many of the ideas that Sartre and Albert Camus advocated were anticipated by André Gide, who believed that values must be found in and then tested by experience, that art must be marshaled to the point that it can revolt against the way bourgeois codes reinforced Christian morality. Gide was opposed to the counterfeit, the falseness, in human behavior that was the product of social forces. If Sartre looked back to Gide, Gide looked back to Nietzsche, Dostoyevsky, Conrad, and Mann. In every case, the backward glance was a look to a new self that freed modern man from the restraints of bourgeois culture.

III

Heidegger's search for the ideal concealed his fear that the modern period was in a process of historical decline, an idea that he shared with a number of other influential moderns, including Oswald Spengler. Such concern masked the equally real fear that beneath surface reality was a moral abyss, that the by-products of modernism (war, imperialism, industrial production, urban slums) were death machines, an idea emphasized by Louis-Ferdinand Céline in *The Journey to the End of the Night* (1932). Samuel Beckett, among others, can be found on this road to nihilism.

The fear of the abyss was intensified for some modernists by their disdain for mass culture. This provoked the elitist stance (the belief in the aristocracy of art) of high modernism (e.g., Pound and Eliot). It also led to a desire to return to some simpler realm of place, whether it was a lost Jeffersonian realm or a primitive Spain, both of which can be found in the writing of John Dos Passos. The modernists could not recapture the old myths, but they celebrated some special moment when the ideal was lost, when cultural decline began. For Pound this happened in the fifteenth century, for Eliot the seventeenth century, for Dos Passos with the defeat of the Jeffersonian vision, for F. Scott Fitzgerald (who often identified with the South of his father) with the rise of an industrialized America after the Civil War, an idea that was turned into a manifesto by the Southern Agrarians.

The common denominator is that these different dates are connected with the rise of urbanism—Renaissance, Enlightenment, or modern urbanism with its diversified culture. The modernist's disdain was embodied in all the by-products of this hyperactive culture: the newspaper with its commodified reality, the crowd as potential mob, and the clerks who ate their dinner out of "tin." The longing for an ideal was really an attempt to fill a philosophical void. The search for the ideal went hand in glove with a growing skepticism, with a palpable sense of emptiness. Modernism involved the contradictory concern of pursuing an ideal at the same time that the culture was giving way to mass culture; it attempted to reconcile bureaucratic reality to a higher meaning, even as philosophical belief was giving way to nihilism. The setting for much of this activity was the city.

A key factor involved the artist (or a substitute for the artist) in the city. Modernism moved from the realms of Romantic nature to the workings of the city. An essential factor here was the historical transformation from an agrarian to urban world. In keeping with the preference of culture over nature and the rise of mass culture, the city was reduced to the metonym of the crowd. Walter Benjamin has discussed the flaneur in his book on Baudelaire's Paris. The flaneur is the spectator who goes to the crowd to be alone, to lose himself within the throng, which as throng involves another form of being human. The flaneur, the spectator as both observer and observed, connects two major themes of literary modernism: the artist and the city combined as the artist in the city. The metaphor of being alone in the crowd is a controlling trope of modernism, just as being lost in the maze becomes a controlling trope of postmodernism.

The artist as social witness, the crowd as state of mind: this intersection is mutually defining. Spectators abound: Tiresias in Eliot's London, Marlow in Conrad's Brussels, and Nick Carraway in Fitzgerald's New York. The artist is the perfect spectator, whether it is Baudelaire or Gide's Edouard or Proust's Marcel in Paris, Mann's Aschenbach in Venice, or Joyce's Dedalus in Dublin. The idea of the crowd is inseparable from the problems of mass culture. A mass demands a master, a situation that questions the merits of democracy and suggests the need for some kind of control—an elite, an intellectual aristocracy, or a strong, perhaps totalitarian, leader.[2]

Modernism subordinated the beauty of nature to the artificial reality of the city. This marked the end of nature as the final source of aesthetic meaning.[3] Aestheticism, one aspect of modernism, celebrated the discovery of the beautiful, often from the perspective of a fledgling artist. The bildungsroman (the transformation of youth) or the künstlerroman (the growth of the artist) satisfied a narrative need from Goethe's Werther to Joyce's Stephen Dedalus, from Balzac's Lucien de Rupemprè and Eugène de Rastignac to Dickens's Pip. The young went to a large city—in Europe, capital cities such as London or Paris—in search of the heightened self. The city that transformed a generation, which in turn changed its world, was Paris at the turn of the twentieth century. During a period of twenty-five years, it brought together an array of talent from many different disciplines.

Henri Bergson made us aware of mental as well as mechanical time. Pablo

Picasso, working with Georges Braque, Juan Gris, and Guillaume Apollinaire, moved beyond postimpressionism to cubism—an artistic way of employing four dimensions, of seeing in more than one perspective. James Joyce applied the same technique to the novel in *Ulysses*, superimposing the heroic time of an ancient hero onto the everyday time of a living man—refining as modernist technique the simultaneity of time present and time past that made the novel possible for Marcel Proust. It is hard to think of a time and place elsewhere that accommodated so much genius, all living at the same time within walking distance of each other, as befell this group in Paris. And out of their separate but conjoined efforts—what one commentator has termed "consilience"—came modernism. This transformation of knowledge changed the way we viewed the world.

Paris became a state of mind, supplying the energy for radical cultural change, bringing together some of the best minds of its era. It attracted Ezra Pound, T. S. Eliot, James Joyce; a bit later Ernest Hemingway and F. Scott Fitzgerald; a bit later Henry Miller, Mina Loy, Jean Rhys, and Hilda Doolittle (H. D.); and later still James Baldwin, Richard Wright, and Chester Himes, to name only a few.[4] An avant-garde challenged the old reality. Surrealism, which could not have come into being without Freud's concept of the subconscious, led to the paintings of Dalí and the plays of Cocteau. Hemingway said that Paris was his Harvard and Yale: he learned there to hone a style from Gertrude Stein, to test literary reality against his own sense of experience, to do with words what Van Gogh and Gauguin had done with paint.

We can ask, why Paris? Why Paris in the first quarter of the twentieth century? One answer is that with the search for new meaning modernism was waiting to happen: a new reality challenged the old in almost every field from physics and biology to philosophy and art. Paris was witness to an intellectual unfolding: the creative imagination, freed from traditional restraints, went beyond itself.

Paris, city of light, was a product of the Enlightenment, that movement of ideas that helped clear the intellectual underbrush. The Enlightenment—with its emphasis upon reason and science—challenged falsehood and superstition, but at the expense of the mythic imagination, as the Romantics well knew. The desire to understand nature turned quickly to a desire to control it, and to use such control to create and sustain wealth and power. The transition from one outmoded system to another can be found within Enlightenment thinkers themselves, as Jefferson and Rousseau reveal.

Rousseau moved original sin from a personal to a collective matter, seeing social man as fallen. Jefferson challenged the old aristocracy in the name of a yeoman hierarchy, an agrarianism that competed with the rise of the new city. Their concerns met and shared common ground in their distrust of crowds and cities, what would eventually become mass culture. Moreover, the belief in progress led to dangerous paradigms—especially a sense of destiny that privileged a nation-state.[5] A sense of destined history could not be reconciled with the evolutionary idea of adaptation; it brought to the forefront the radical individualism of Balzac's Vautrin and Dostoyevsky's Raskolnikov, justifying the forms of power that were to be taken over by the new Caesar/Napoleon figure, anticipating totalitarian coin.

IV

The Enlightenment created a value system that the moderns both accepted and contested. They could accept the Jeffersonian need for a yeoman aristocracy as the means of redeeming Rousseau's fallen society. And they could see the need for mythic belief that went beyond Enlightenment rationalism. For all its virtues, the Enlightenment failed to recognize the power of Dionysus—the power of the irrational—and the way urban disorder could erupt: chaos was "re-presented" in the form of plague, carnival, the crowd/mob, the mysterious stranger. Joyce's Nighttown is to the point here. Joyce's distrust of the Enlightenment followed in great part from Flaubert's distrust of the bourgeoisie. Certainly the Enlightenment thinkers were limited by what they did not know, coming before Darwin and "la bête humaine," before Freud and the idea of the unconscious and repression, before Heidegger's questioning of runaway technology. The Enlightenment was too static for the avant-garde with its desire for radical change, where tradition had to give way to the pragmatic, the old to the new, stable laws to innovation and experiment. Picasso, Breton, Tzara—what use could they make of Enlightenment values?

As a literary response to these matters, modernism was uncomfortable with the main assumptions of both the Enlightenment and Darwinism. The modernists were not yet willing to write off mythic and symbolic reality. They could not reconcile theories of cyclical time and history with a belief in linear evolution and mechanical progress. And finally, they could not accept a mechanistic reality that gave priority to the realm of science and technology at the expense of art and mind, or an idea of humanity based upon a purely mechanistic theory of cognition and of rational motives. Ideas concerning organic form and structuralism (systems theory) rose to usurp the place of the mechanistic meaning.

The challenge came from many directions over a long period of time. Flaubert's *Bouvard et Pécuchet*, for example, satirized bourgeois self-sufficiency, ridiculed the encyclopedic mentality, and suggested that man had minimized rather than enlarged the human self by defining it within such restricted limits. Sir James Frazer (1854–1941) helped catalogue the old myths in a way that allowed James Joyce and T. S. Eliot to see their relevance to modern times. As we know, archaeologists such as Heinrich Schliemann discovered what they believed to be the historic city of Troy and thus fueled an interest in the old mythology as well as a belief in the relevance of the archaeological layering of time.

V

The modernist desire to make it new created an imaginative reality that challenged the status quo: Flaubert and Baudelaire, Stravinsky and Schoenberg, Picasso and Duchamp, Joyce and D. H. Lawrence—all experienced rejection before their work was acknowledged. Different "modernisms" played off each other and created a mutually informing context. Any definition of literary modernism is contingent on the writers chosen to embody the movement. Given varied texts to discuss, different definitions will emerge, or at least different emphases. A way of accommodating this enlarged idea of modernism is to think of it in terms of literary modes rather than literary form. A modal definition assumes a composite Text that is larger than its individual embodiments. A modal definition takes its being from a historical context that highlights shared experience. A novel such as Joyce's *Ulysses* shares much in both technique and subject matter with other modernist texts, but in no way exhausts the modal meaning of a hypothetical larger Text.

Modernism found itself working within concentric circles. Outside the circle of consciousness was a reality with which modernism had to come to terms. The modernists brought to this reality several realms of the text: myth, symbolism, and structure. Modernism was literature at the crossroads: its use of myth competed with a residue of realism; its use of symbols with the literal; its Bergsonian creative evolution worked against Darwin's theory of adaptation and natural selection; and its cyclical history compromised linear meaning and brought causality into question, which in turn worked against a mechanistic reality.

The origins of modernism go back to a belief in a mythic explanation of the universe; from there to a belief in the symbolic nature of the universe; from there to a constructed (i.e., man-made) symbolizing, the beautiful as a product of the imagination; and from there to meaning as structural or paradigmatic unfolding. The move was from nature as the source of meaning to culture as the source of meaning, from the organic nature of form to the relational nature of structure. As we shall see, the differences here mark the drift from modernism to postmodernism, from the search for the ideal to the chaos of the void. As Don DeLillo has observed, all plots tend to move deathward.

VI

Another aspect of modernism concerned the dichotomy between primitivism and civilization. The discussion here involved the difference between nature and culture, and the issue of which was more influential. The question also involved the role technology played in the formation of culture. There was an inconclusive attitude toward the machine, technology, and mass culture; but at its most critical, modernism was elitist, disdainful of mass consumption, and contemptuous of a heterogeneous culture. These qualities are transformed as we move from high modernism to postmodernism. Of major concern in the history of this transition was the place of technology.

Perhaps the most important spokesman on the symbiosis between culture and technology was Marshall McLuhan. Despite the resistance from antitechnology advocates like Heidegger and Lawrence, McLuhan thought of technology as a good thing. His basic premise was that technology extended human capability, facilitated human capacity by accommodating human needs. Tools and implements added dimension to human properties. The technology of writing added dimension to the process of speech, which was transformed in turn by electric media and advanced by the computer, which extended the capacity of the brain. In books like *Understanding Media* (1964), McLuhan reworked basic ideas of Harold Innis, especially as conveyed in his *Empire and Communications* (1950), on the effects of mass media on culture. McLuhan's famous dictum, "the medium is the message," expressed his belief that the way reality was perceived was more important than the content of what was perceived. As we have seen, the idea of "perspectivism" can be traced back to Nietzsche and was basic to the ideas of Heidegger and Freud, Gertrude Stein and Wallace Stevens.

Another important theorist on the subject of culture and technology was Jean Baudrillard, who picked up where McLuhan left off. Baudrillard's theory of simulacra (signs that are copies of other signs and thus without physical referent) was an idea taken directly from McLuhan. McLuhan's "the medium is the message" became, in Baudrillard, "the medium is the model," by which he referred to the way the world was perceived, the way we knew the world, including our sense of self. For Baudrillard, representations of the real precede the real. Simulations no longer refer to real objects but to each other, become

Gramley Library
Salem Academy and College
Winston-Salem, N.C. 27108

self-referential or "hyperreal," to use his word: reality implodes as it is roiled by forms of electric media; a whirl of signs without referent creates its own reality. The tail wags the dog, as signs become the reality. We create the Las Vegas syndrome: the Sphinx looks on the Pyramids, which in turn look on the Statue of Liberty, as history becomes a mélange. Life turns inside out: Disneyland, a system of signs with arbitrary signification, embodies Los Angeles.

VII

Futurists claimed that technology advanced the human race: the machine and its by-products allowed civilization to move ahead in the name of progress. But Sigmund Freud questioned these assumptions: he argued that humanity rested on forms of instinctual behavior. Civilization had gone ahead of evolution, creating a fissure between human nature and social mandates. Civilization had advanced by repressing basic instincts, resulting in modern man being divided from a natural self, continuously frustrated and at odds with oneself.

The more removed individuals are from the workings of nature, the more repressed they become. Modern life in and of itself is more stressful than an existence lived closer to nature. Human desire seeks pleasure, and through pleasure happiness. Technology increases the capacities of life, but at a cost. Advanced communications increase the range of people addressed, but in a more shallow way. Ocean liners and jumbo jets make far-off lands accessible, but at the expense of anxiety over the vulnerability of long-distance travel.

It was an age of anxiety. There was a distrust of the nuclear family and an emphasis upon the personal (when not disguised by implausible theories like Eliot's impersonal poet). A number of the major modernists—Henry Adams, Eliot, Fitzgerald—knew the disruptive effects of mental illness through the disorders of their wives. Eliot captured the prolapsed mind at work in *The Waste Land* ("My nerves are bad tonight. Yes, bad. Stay with me. / Speak to me. Why do you never speak? Speak."). The poem connects personal illness with the effects of postwar ruin, bringing dementia and war trauma into shared context.

Despite their later ideological differences, Carl Jung followed Freud, insisting that symbolism had its origins in primitive thought and that technological man was fast losing contact with symbolic reality, with the residual vitality of the natural world. This idea was shared among a number of the moderns. Henry Adams suggested that the machine (dynamo) existed at the expense of the symbolic imagination (the myth of the Virgin). The loss of an instinctual self became a major theme in the works of D. H. Lawrence. The Southern Agrarians located the cultural ideal in the South, claiming that the industrial revolution contradicted the harmony that came with living on the land. This loss was sexual as well as cultural: Henry James, Edith Wharton, T. S. Eliot gave us inhibited characters (John Marcher, Newland Archer, Alfred Prufrock) who had lost contact with their sexual feelings. Nathanael West saw that these repressed feelings would be exhibited in grotesque ways, eventually expressed in the form of violence as depicted in the ending of *The Day of the Locust,* a theme anticipated by Sherwood Anderson. The grotesque (nature inverted) gave way to the uncanny (the familiar as strange), the source of which for Freud was sexual repression. The primitive became the source for renewed human instinct and mythic meaning.

There was a spectrum of meaning that looked at the primitive-civilization equation in both a positive and negative light, from the positive belief that the land was blessed and that human inventions advanced civilization, to the paradoxical but negative belief that we become less human the more civilized we become. Wallace Stevens believed the imagination could bridge the gulf between our desire for harmony and the reality of cosmic emptiness. A Conradian assumption that there was a degenerative force working in nature—beyond the human will, that controlled both primitive and civilized forms of life—challenged these social attitudes. These conclusions reinforced the various attitudes, both positive and negative, toward imperialism as a foreign-policy option of the nation-state.

VIII

As we move from mythic to symbolic to structural systems, we move through different modes of physical reality, through different forms of intellectual being; we move not just to new ways of talking about literary texts, but to a new idea of the text—to texts that have changed meaning by changing critical/theoretical content and context. The prefix "post" dominates our literary vocabulary today, suggesting that we have moved on, left the past behind, and are now in the realm of that all-sacred territory—the "new."

But there has to be a realm of centered belief for the idea of the "post" to go beyond: there has to be a "post-something." It may be that change is a matter of the return of the repressed, that alternative meanings are built into both our language and paradigms. I believe that the process is more contrived, that critical theory changes literary perspective: we invent the critical prisms through which we describe literary texts. The transformation from one stage to another is a matter of critical mass: at some culmination there is a tipping point in the paradigm, a climax involving a change in literary reality and meaning.

We have located a number of these tipping points. Nabokov, for example, radically revised the aesthetic assumptions of Wallace Stevens and Oscar Wilde; Bergson's creative evolution questioned Samuel Butler's theory of mind, which in turn had questioned Charles Darwin's theory of adaptation; structuralism transformed symbolic reality; the idea of "text" transformed the idea of "form"; cyclical history replaced linear history; nihilism questioned empirical assumptions; Pynchon's use of overblown history with its open-ended conclusions moved the novel toward comic-book reality and the play of cartoon characters that caricatured the goal-directed historical romance. Such movements as gender theory and the Harlem Renaissance were added to the idea of the modern, and popular culture modified modernism as an elitist movement.

These changes radically transformed the foundational or originary basis upon which modernism was built, just as a series of previous changes had transformed the idea of Zola's naturalism, a thesis I develop at length in *Realism and Naturalism: The Novel in an Age of Transition* (2005). The originist assumptions are primarily the product of the writing (i.e., the creative) process; the revisionist tendency is primarily the product of the reading (i.e., the heuristic or critical) process. Interpretive meaning is constantly being transformed, present reality constantly changing critical context, transforming the past. Each generation reinterprets the works of the past, rewriting earlier forms in response to the mandates of its own times. A literary work thus has its origin as "form" before it is transformed into the accreted meanings of "text." Modernist literary assumptions most often stem from the idea of form; postmodern literary assumptions most often stem from the idea of text.

Many of these changes took place as part of the larger transformation occurring with the rise of mass culture in which the boundaries between a popular and an elitist culture were breaking down. The new was often the beneficiary of an unexamined authority, replacing or conflating past readings, even when such readings were not consistent with each other: the new was true; the old was left untold. While such transforming process cannot be avoided (it keeps a subject alive, opens up opportunities for a new generation of commentators by diminishing status quo authority, and encourages new forms of criticism), such avant-garde transformations need to be subject to rearguard scrutiny.

We must not be misled by the belief that the difference between modernism and postmodernism is no more than a changing vocabulary. While modernism and postmodernism share some common ground, the differences are greater than the similarities. The postmodern moves us away from linear time, questions causality, distrusts metanarratives, rejects forms of human (as opposed to mass) consciousness, denies periodization, and repudiates literary movements, deviations that change the critical mass between modernism and postmodernism to the extent that we are dealing with different kinds of literary reality.

There were a number of cultural movements at work independent of high modernism, especially the work of the avant-garde and the Harlem Renaissance, with its literary component and its legitimizing of jazz. And there were other movements that came after the heyday of modernism—such as the rise of gender theory, the feminist movement, and ethnic causes. While all of these activities are important and justify their study, modernism need not be equated with them or reduced to their influence, as is the tendency of recent literary criticism. So much that now passes under the rubric of modernism is really the product of postmodernism, transformed once again by mass-culture phenomena. With the rise of mass culture, a new generation of readers who never knew a different culture has called many of the elitist ideas specific to high modernism into question. Such transformations take us beyond postmodernism, to the realm of a revised postmodernism, a process that justifies critical scrutiny.

Every twenty to thirty years the critical agenda and canon change. The New Criticism took hold in the thirties; structuralism and poststructuralism along with race and gender matters dominated in the sixties and seventies; an interest in popular culture established new critical directions in the nineties and beyond. In this study, we begin with the idea of modernism as a major literary movement that reached its apogee before World War II. Thirty years later, around 1965, a new generation of structural critics began to challenge the major assumptions of literary modernism, destabilizing the movement with their theoretical assumptions. Twenty years after that, this new view of modernism conflated with another view based on theories of mass culture, with its preoccupation with forms of popular activity and commodity appeal. This led to the avalanche of books in 1990–91 that reassessed both the content and the context of the movement.

This review led in turn to three kinds of radical revision, all a matter of changing the literary context. First, the major modernists were reconfigured— for example, T. S. Eliot was connected with such mediums as jazz, and his interest in Jessie Weston and mythic meaning was questioned. Second, under the influence of structuralism and poststructuralism, theories of organic form and symbolic meaning were challenged, as modernism became postmodernism with a different realm of text separate from its origins. And third, another dimension involving such concerns as gender theory and the influence of the Harlem

Renaissance was added to the study of the movement along with an obsession of how life changed under the influence of a new consumerism. This latter movement became connected with mass culture in which an elitist-directed community succumbed to a mass-consumer society.

IX

Modernism owed much to the visual and other arts—especially the contribution of Picasso and the cubists and of Gropius and Le Corbusier in architecture. Picasso and Joyce made use of the archaeological—layers of narrative or spatial meaning superimposed on each other that collapse both time and space in a totally revolutionary way. This method may owe its being to the archaeological work of Heinrich Schliemann (1822–1890), who discovered the layering that connected the modern world with the mythic world of Homer's Troy. If modernism turned to the past—as we find in the works of Joyce, Faulkner, and Pound (with their use of the Ulysses, Absalom, and Homeric myths)—it was to the historical past made mythic, to the layering of past and present events to suggest the simultaneity of historical event, the universality or mythic oneness of time. Such layering added a new dimension to the meaning of character. A character had an archetypal as well as existential meaning, a universal as well as individual being. The universal meaning connected individual characters to prototypical characters such as Faust, Ulysses, Orestes, Oedipus, Absalom, and Christ.

This process of change was often a compilation of contradictions. The modernists went in search of an ideal and found its opposite. The theme of historical decline runs through this period, and it is especially pronounced in America, where theories of the land gave body to the idea of the frontier and the quest West, ideals that were negated by imperial design and the rise of material culture. Modernism as a cultural movement cannot be separated from what can be called "the Great Divide," the transition from an agrarian to an urban world. As we shall see, this call involved two distinct cultural transformations: how a lost agrarianism changed aesthetic and national concerns.

As just suggested, at the core of this system was a basic concern for the land, the belief that the earth was a source of vitality and that the welfare of the nation stemmed from its well-being. To lose the spirit of the land was to lose a state of mind. We can observe obeisance to this belief in George Washington's Farewell Address, the dictates of Jefferson, Emerson and Whitman's idea of a city in the West, the populist politics of William Jennings Bryan, the frontier theory of Frederick Jackson Turner, the western novel of Owen Wister, the land-centered novels of Willa Cather, Scott Fitzgerald's divide between East and West, T. S. Eliot's wasteland depiction, and the regional doctrine of the Southern Agrarians and the Fugitive poets.

The radical change that was taking place in literary genres was paralleled by the radical change taking place in the culture of both Europe and America. After World War I, the American economy went into a slight recession that was followed by an era of almost uninterrupted prosperity, culminating with the stock market crash of 1929 and the international depression that followed. These were years of cataclysmic change. According to the 1920 census, more Americans were living in cities than in rural areas. Frederick Jackson Turner had redefined the frontier based on the census of 1890, but his collection of essays, *The Frontier in American History,* took on additional importance when it was published in book form in 1920. Van Wyck Brooks's *The Ordeal of Mark Twain* (1922) reworked some of these ideas, suggesting that America was culturally divided between the East and the West, between agrarian and industrial realms.

Fitzgerald treated the myth of the land theme by contrasting the American East and West in *The Great Gatsby* (1925). The West still retained a personal element; the East functioned on an impersonal level. While the West had moral superiority over the East, the East embodied the future of America. Fitzgerald brilliantly conveyed the idea that key American ideals and institutions have been exhausted and are located now in a dead past. This was a realm in which the world of the father had broken down. The urban schemes of Meyer Wolfsheim—the product of illegal bootlegging, "bucket" (crooked brokerage) shops, gambling dens, and extortion—had replaced the frontier world of Dan Cody, the product of invested land and individual initiative. Wolfsheim's underworld was an ersatz version of Tom Buchanan's established world, the brokered world where invested money made money. Meanwhile, back in the Dakotas was Mr. Gatz, Gatsby's father, whose yeoman existence was a world apart from life in New York, its humble deficiency putting in motion his son's dream for a more romantic reality. The search for an ideal—at least as embodied by a sense of frontier opportunity—had already been consumed by the past. And although the past had been emptied, it is there Fitzgerald believed we search for the ideal.

Also opposed to the industrialization of America were the Southern Agrarians. In a manifesto entitled *I'll Take My Stand: The South and the Agrarian Tradition* (1930), twelve southerners offered various arguments for the superiority of the South over other regions of America, especially the North, and catalogued what they thought had been lost by the defeat of the South in the Civil War.

While their arguments involved a spectrum of concerns, the common desire was to keep the Jeffersonian tradition alive. But even here it was not clear if they wanted a return to the old aristocracy or to create a new yeoman aristocracy. While twelve authors contributed to *I'll Take My Stand*, Allen Tate's story is typical: he was opposed to industrialization, and he moved from sympathy for the South to an obsession with agrarianism; he wanted to substitute a love of the land for a love of the South. Tate, like the Agrarians in general, was deeply religious and wanted to hold off the secular society.

The Agrarians were also opposed to the abstractions that they felt came as side-effects to the loss of the land: farmers planted seed and harvested their crop, which was then taken as an abstract commodity to a warehouse, where its worth was determined by speculation when it was sold on the commodity market. The process thus moved from the purely concrete (planting and harvesting) to the purely abstract (a commodity sold on speculation). The farmer brought the crop into being; the stock speculator sold the crop without ever having seen or touched it. Capitalism had created a network of abstract systems that led to a detached and remote sense of reality.

The new commercial/industrial order had negated the Jeffersonian vision and the delight of being in harmony with the land. The Agrarians could find solace for their views in Spengler, could find epistemological comfort in Bergson, and could find justification for the rewards of craftsman work in Ruskin. All these benefits were being lost—no longer held together by the myth of the land, the belief that the land was sacred and the source of social stability. The Agrarian movement worked in harmony with the New Criticism: the assumption was that the literary text had an organic unity that paralleled the harmony of living at one with the land. When that unity was broken, the result was a failure of artistic or social achievement.

A visionary war of sorts went on between the southern and New York writers. Two worldviews—one urban, the other agrarian—dueled with each other in novels such as Lionel Trilling's *The Middle of the Journey* and Allen Tate's *The Fathers*. Norman Mailer could be aligned with the New York group; Katherine Anne Porter and Flannery O'Connor were more connected to the southern group. The world divided for both groups around the end of World War I (as previously noted, the census of 1920 revealed more people living in cities than in rural areas), except the New York novelists looked forward from that point, and the Agrarians looked backward.

X

The problems that confronted both groups were now national, not regional. Industrialization and along with it mass culture could not have existed without the reaches of the mass media. Modern man was not only being removed from the land to the city, the suburbs, and later the exurbs; but he was becoming mentally homogenized even as immigration preserved the cliché of the melting pot. What we know and to a great extent what we believe come to us via forms of mass communication. Radio, tabloid newspapers, and film came into being. Pittsburgh's KDKA became the first licensed radio station in America in October 1920, anticipating 576 stations two years later. Tabloid publishing was a British phenomenon until the *New York Daily News* came into being in America. By the mid-twenties New York had three tabloids with a circulation of over 1.6 million.

Another mass medium was film. The movies had begun with the kinetoscope and penny arcade, moved on to the Electric Theatre and the Nickelodeon, and came into their own when director-producers such as D. W. Griffith moved away from the fixed camera and used innovative camera techniques—including the close-up, the long shot, the fade-in and fade-out. Griffith was the father of modern cinema. He discovered Mary Pickford and Lillian Gish and made the first twelve-reel movie, the controversial *The Birth of a Nation,* based on the loss of the status quo after the Civil War and Thomas Dixon's novel glorifying the Ku Klux Klan and the landed South. A new technology in an industrialized America now supplied a nostalgic retrospective of the pre-industrialized land.

The American ideology owed much to Jeffersonian thought. Pound, Faulkner, Fitzgerald, and Dos Passos all regretted the passing of his yeoman vision with its landed aristocracy. Pound was the product of the two contradictory modernisms—European and American. His European interest moved him toward theories of the vortex and the machine-directed futurism of Marinetti; his American interests moved him toward the landed vision of Jefferson. Pound had dreams of a mechanistic future while nostalgically holding to an agrarian past. The land had given up its spiritual meaning in response to the new industrial city and the rise of mass culture. As the land lost its claim to spirituality, a process of historical decline set in, often connected with the workings of the city, an idea that we can find in the works of Oswald Spengler, Henry Adams, Ezra Pound, T. S. Eliot, F. Scott Fitzgerald, Nathanael West, John Steinbeck, and the Agrarian critics, among many others.

This transition came at a time when Enlightenment ideals, especially liberalism with its belief in the priority of individualism, were subject to question, altering a sense of identity and involving a radical revision of literary representation, especially in literary realism. Liberalism had its origins in the "constitutional liberalism" of the seventeenth century, in movements like the Puritan revolt and the American Revolution, which limited the power of monarchical government. In 1892, the Populist Party in America endorsed the implementation of certain progressive government intrusions such as income tax and the rights of organized labor. "Democratic liberalism" built upon this transference of authority and was instrumental in conveying forms of power to women and minorities. But such forms of "people power" had their limits in the face of a growing central government. While big government could act for good (implementing Social Security, the GI Bill, the interstate highway system, Medicare, and other progressive programs), it also moved toward increasing the executive power to determine foreign policy and to declare war, while supporting the influence of a corporate system and the growth of a military-industrial complex. Built into the economy, seemingly a prerequisite of prosperity, was the waste that went with war.

America had lost its pristine innocence. Jeffersonian agrarianism became a lost ideal, especially after the Civil War with the transforming growth of an industrial/urbanized nation. The rise of central government was not merely an American experience; its counterpart could be found in England and Europe, less pronounced perhaps because the transference from the old feudalism to the new authority suggested a less liberal process at work. Nevertheless, the liberal ideal (of, say, John Stuart Mill as well as Jefferson) was now an exhausted ideal located in a remote past.

The meaning of nature and culture was also revised; natural and social law became the product of a constructed (paradigmatic) reality, allowing moral certitude to give way to moral relativity. With the idea of constructed reality came the tenets of postmodernism, which reconceptualized the idea of modernism enough to change its critical mass. Despite those who understandingly wanted to hold on to an older view of modernism, the movement was on the wane; it was now comprehended as a rise-and-fall literary phenomenon with a historical turning point.

2 ❖ "PERSPECTIVISM"

One of the major assumptions of literary modernism was that reality was a matter of the way it was perceived. This was a firm belief of Nietzsche; it dominated much of the literary criticism and the assumptions of the avant-garde, was central to Pater's idea of sensation, and was the foundation of Heisenberg's uncertainty principle. Wallace Stevens made it the basis of his poetry, and Gertrude Stein claimed the major difference between generations stemmed from ways of seeing. "Perspectivism," or realism as a way of seeing, dominated both the literary and the critical canon.

The literary criticism that ran through this period paralleled the literary product. The literary search for an ideal gave way to a critical sense of historical decline, which in its most pronounced form transformed into a new nihilism that allowed writers as different as Louis-Ferdinand Céline and Samuel Beckett to share cosmic doubt, critics as skeptical as Jacques Derrida and Michel Foucault to question the grammatical basis of writing and the philosophical slippage of discourse. The transformations of modernism brought reciprocal change in the cult of personality; individual presence mattered less, was no longer a matter of transparency: no more was the room brightened by the presence of Mrs. Dalloway or the city measured by the wanderings of Leopold Bloom.

The romance of Rider Haggard was revised until it reached the realm of apocalypse that one finds in Pynchon, or in more popular forms such as the James Bond novel, where the protagonist must combat the antagonist who desires to conquer and/or destroy the world. The transformation led to a comic-book reality, good surrounded by evil, a kind of archetypal situation reduced to cartoon expression: one can find it in such popular mass-market products as *Star*

Wars, where Darth Vader is the source of evil, or the Harry Potter novels, where Voldemort embodies that function.

Nineteenth-century forms of the romance tended to merge with forms of myth, often enlisting the supernatural, looking toward distant meaning of the universe and universal truths that lie buried in the remote past. Postmodern forms of the romance moved in the opposite direction toward suspended meaning, the emptiness of the past, or the implausibility of universal conjecture. Built into the postmodern romance is the inverse use of myth that robs it of heightened meaning. Whereas modernism brings various forms of consciousness to bear on reality, postmodernism collapses human consciousness into the culture itself, where it becomes a state of mind like that of the crowd.

The spectrum of cultural meaning found its parallel in the spectrum of human consciousness: the mind functioned on many levels and revealed depths of reality that were assessed in different ways. The rational mind was the source of literal meaning; instinct explained what might be considered subliminal thought; the subconscious explained why rational motives were often undermined by irrational desires and why our everyday thoughts were symbolically transformed in the realm of dreams; the unconscious explained our fascination with the way that archetypal meaning infused a hidden reality; and the collective consciousness dealt with the possibility of a mass mind, a state of public consciousness that preceded and then infused the individual consciousness. From Descartes, to Bergson, to Freud, to Jung, to Lévi-Strauss and Foucault, these were the main modernist concerns involving the human mind, each theorist often emphasizing a different aspect of thought in general.

The confluence of literary phases was neorealism: the work, for example, of Ernest Hemingway, which looked back to the realism of literary naturalism at the same time as it worked in terms of the iceberg theory of language, the narrative practice of leaving unstated motives that work on the character so that the reader has to fill in the ellipses. The assumption is that the text is working on the subconscious of the reader, that language could depict an objective reality and yet appeal in great part to the subjectivity of the reader. Critically not much has been said about neorealism in these terms. The problem involves seeing the new realism as a confluence of modernist movements or phases: the play between Darwin and Bergson; the work of William James's theories of the mind; the influence of the avant-garde, especially of Dada and surrealism; the import of Gertrude Stein's theory of language; and the relevance of Walter Pater's theory of sensation.

Pater's aesthetic beliefs took modernism in two different directions: toward a theory of the beautiful as the end of life, with art as its own justification, and a theory of sensation that moved the concept of self away from empiricism toward an informed subjectivity. As adapted by Joseph Conrad, Pater's theory of sensation led to the impressionism that characterized the work of Stephen Crane and to the active participation of Ernest Hemingway's characters in what was the residue of literary naturalism. Neorealism was, in fact, literary naturalism without its documentation. The benefactors of this blending, besides Hemingway, were F. Scott Fitzgerald, John Dos Passos, Nathanael West, and James M. Cain, whose *The Postman Always Rings Twice* (1934) was a perfect example of literary naturalism devoid of its documentation.

In its use of self-involved, elemental characters, set against a cosmic background of ironic events, neorealism also anticipated literary existentialism. And while it goes back to the Middle Ages and authors such as Rabelais, a discussion of the grotesque is also relevant here. The grotesque involved that aspect of modernism that connected Gogol and Kafka with Sherwood Anderson and Nathanael West, depicting nature working in an inverted way. The grotesque often stemmed from Freud's theory of repressed sexuality, creating an uncanny state of mind in which the familiar becomes strange. When the grotesque led to a fantasy situation that was then treated realistically, it anticipated magic realism. These conflicted concerns led to an ambiguity, often a celebrated ambiguity that went beyond Victorian doubt, enlisting a state of decline that at its most intense suggested the approach of apocalypse.

II

In charting the transition from realism to modernism, we often concentrate on ways of reconciling the self to the rise of a machine society and to the masses of laborers and clerks needed to run an industrial culture. The rise of mass society created a celebrity culture as it diminished the common individual. The idea of the heroic gave way to the comic (Ulysses becomes Leopold Bloom). The artist went in search of a redeeming beauty (Mann's Aschenbach, Gide's Edouard). The new Faust tested his limits (Mann's Faust). The seeker experienced an illuminating moment (Gabriel Conroy's epiphany). An imaginative adolescent invented a romanticized image of self (Fitzgerald's Gatsby). The past informed with the emotion of the present created a state of mind that gave new meaning to physical reality (Proust's time spots). A different artist's perspective (that of Nathanael West's Tod Hackett) saw the frustrations of the crowd degenerate into a riot, a condition intensified by a sense of Western historical decline.

In its origins, modernism was rejected by and in turn rejected middle-class values. In 1863, the Paris Salon rejected works by Manet (*Luncheon on the Grass* and *Olympia*) and Whistler (*Symphony in White No. 1: The White Girl*). Baudelaire's *Les fleurs du mal* (1857) was publicly censored, as were the works of Flaubert. The modernists struck back by satirizing middle-class life. In 1913, fifty years after the Salon des Refuses, the Exhibition of Modern Art, known as the Armory Show, was held in New York, featuring such iconoclastic art as Marcel Duchamp's *Nude Descending a Staircase*. Duchamp's nude was more a celebration of the machine than an erotic depiction of the female form. All of this was in keeping with his celebration of the New York skyline, which he called a work of art, kept alive by demolishing the old and perpetuating the new: "We must learn to forget the past, to live our own lives in our own time." Duchamp redefined art in the bourgeois society by calling attention to its design and practicality rather than to its aesthetic quality. By those standards, an eggbeater was a work of art; so also was a urinal (see Duchamp, *Fountain*, 1917).

As Marjorie Perloff has demonstrated, Duchamp left Paris for New York to avoid the war; there he brought European intervention to the American avant-garde, quickly becoming the center of Walter Arensberg's salon, where his influence reached Man Ray and William Carlos Williams, whose *Kora in Hell* (1920) and *Spring and All* (1923) went beyond Duchamp to incorporate cubist and Dada techniques in an American idiom, "a fusion of Futurist/Dada typography with Romantic lyric subjectivity."[1] E. H. Gombrich argues that cubism is the art form in which representational clues are purposely scrambled to prevent a coherent image of reality. He saw cubism as a radical attempt to depict all facets of an artwork simultaneously, which sets up an interplay of contradictions and negates the illusion of perspective in favor of an instant sensory awareness. The process here is similar to the narrative unfolding of a novel like *The Crying of Lot 49*, in which clues lead to more clues but not conclusions as Oedipa Maas moves from clue to clue but not understanding. There were thus two artistic traditions involving ways of seeing, and each competed with the view of the other. An aesthetic tradition culminated in decadence, and an anti-aesthetic tradition infused the agenda of the avant-garde. A poet such as Ezra Pound has been associated with both traditions, and recent criticism has tried to reconcile the anti-aesthetic tradition with high modernism.

In the same year as the Armory Show, Igor Stravinsky's revolutionary *The Rite of Spring* was performed. Slightly earlier, around 1908, Picasso developed cubism, a new way of seeing in layered or multiple dimensions, and between

1910 and 1912 Wassily Kandinsky moved to abstract painting. In 1914, Gertrude Stein published *Tender Buttons,* which was directly influenced by cubism. Much of this work expressed a conscious disdain for bourgeois values and later a hatred of the war. The work was characterized by deliberate irrationality, a belief in anarchy, and a rejection of the beautiful and of social order. The movement had its American counterpart, composed not only of Walter Arensberg and Man Ray, but also of Alfred Stieglitz and Francis Picabia.

Out of this nihilistic energy came the movement called Dada (a nonsense word) that flourished from 1915 to 1920, provoking a manifesto (1918) by Tristan Tzara. Dada originated in Zurich (1915–16) in the Café Voltaire, greatly in response to the disgust with World War I. In 1917, Dada moved to Berlin, where it took on a more political cast, and to Paris, where it was given intellectual substance by Tzara. The journal *Littérature* (1919–24) became the voice of Dada, publishing such avant-garde spokesmen as André Breton, Louis Aragon, and Paul Éluard. But by 1923, Dada was on the wane, having given way to surrealism.

Surrealism grew out of the Dada movement—out of its fear of rationalism that its adherents felt was responsible for the war. It was based on a theory of how the imagination expressed itself when free of the conscious control of reason and conventions. In 1924, André Breton published the *Surrealist Manifesto,* in which he was saw surrealism connecting conscious and unconscious realms of experience, uniting dream and fantasy with the realm of everyday reality in an absolute reality, a surreality. Major surrealists—reacting against the more formalistic cubist movement, putting emphasis upon free form—were Jean Arp, Max Ernst, René Magritte, Salvador Dalí, and Joan Miró.

Michael S. Bell argues for two forms of surrealism: one (automatism) put the emphasis on the way free-flow images of the subconscious reach consciousness. The other (veristic surrealism) was more analytically grounded in Freud's theory of dreams, in which the dream has symbolic content and gives reality an unconscious meaning. Dalí represented the veristic school, insisting that painting offered a means to understanding the connection between psyche and subconscious. Opposed to Dalí was Picasso, who was closer to the Dada movement and automatic surrealism, connecting a primitive reality to the mysteries of art.

Both Dada and surrealism were avant-garde movements that opposed the commercial-industrial order, especially the rationalism that underpinned modern technology. The avant-garde movement that welcomed the new order was futurism. Futurism was an international movement founded by Filippo Tommaso Marinetti, who published his manifesto *Le futurisme* in 1909 in *Le Figaro,* a Parisian newspaper. Marinetti promulgated the idea of a new art based on the beauty of speed (the automobile was the new god) and the glory of war. Art, he insisted, is "nothing but violence." The futurists praised technology for making the modern world possible and attacked those who enjoyed the advantages of modernism while denouncing the means that made such benefits available.

The futurists celebrated dynamism, energy, and the power of the machine. They rejected the agrarian past for the urban future, welcoming the restlessness of modern life, especially in the city. They glorified electricity, the invention of the electric light by Thomas Edison, and the development of alternating current by Nikola Tesla.[2] Electric light, the telegraph, the telephone, and the automobile—all appeared within a short time of each other. Labor-saving devices allowed the workweek to be reduced from eighty to sixty hours in 1870 and to forty hours by 1910. The futurists believed these new technologies extended the power of modern man, although they were more sympathetic to those investing capital than to the rise of organized labor. But despite their conservative leanings, the rise of labor unions would eventually be an important factor.

The futurists wanted an art of discontinuity and rupture to replace traditional art forms. Pound's vortex theory accommodated Marinetti's theory of futurism, a contradictory alignment given Pound's loathing of the industrial society with its investment capitalism and usury and his belief that society should be grounded on agrarianism. But there was a major difference between Pound and Marinetti: Pound's theory of the vortex was a way of getting to a new poetry that expressed itself through imagery rather than through Romantic statement, while Marinetti's theory of futurism was a celebration of modern technology. Traditional art rested upon conventions that had collapsed at the end of the nineteenth century. The futurists exalted violence and called for the destruction of museums and libraries that preserved the past (anticipating the celebrated burning of the library in William Carlos Williams's *Paterson*). They rejected French cubism as "motionless" but supported the mass production of books. They welcomed the rise of the masses and the authority of the state, moving close to fascism. Working from the same base and asking essentially the same questions, the futurists accepted all that Dada and surrealism rejected, adding a dimension of thought to modernism that attracted relatively few advocates and ultimately would not stand the test of time.

But the story does not end here, and in the last generation the idea of the avant-garde has once again been transformed. Renato Poggioli in *Theory of the Avant-garde* (1962) argued that a theory of the avant-garde depended on how it was chronologically positioned: once established, an avant-garde claim lost its right to that category. As we shall see, Clement Greenberg connected the avant-garde with an industrialized mass culture that produced popular music, soap opera, pulp fiction, B movies, and other popular, mass-produced forms of entertainment. Greenberg called these forms "kitsch," using the German word to suggest their ersatz status, their use of surface meaning devoid of substance (e.g., the use of surrealistic images by advertisers disconnected from their meaning in Freudian/surrealistic consciousness). Poggioli and Greenberg found that the Frankfurt school supported their basic ideas, which depicted mass culture as bogus, the product of institutions (publishing houses, movie studios, news outlets) that put material matters ahead of aesthetic. Originally the avant-garde was opposed to kitsch and mass culture, but eventually products of popular culture became part of the avant-garde, the movement incorporating what it once disdained, a way of seeing that changed diametrically in meaning. What began as an elitist movement was co-opted by the avant-garde before it was co-opted again by mass culture and its kitsch. This radical change in perspective played an important role in the transformation from modernism to postmodernism.

III

The distinction between modernism and postmodernism has been challenged. Some commentators believe postmodernism is a continuation of modernism.[3] The two movements do share common assumptions: the postmodernist's rejection of history and periodicity, the modernist's desire for an inaccessible beauty and the postmodernist's relinquishing of an intractable reality, the formalist/structuralist equation of language and reality, the drift toward a shared nihilism, the postmodernist's preference of the microcosm over the macrocosm, their fondness for self-referentiality. We can find postmodern assumptions at work in the origins of modernism: Gide and Empson, for example, anticipated the postmodern belief in the counterfeit quality of society (the discrepancy between natural impulse and social values) as well as the contention that language is decentered, the product of multiple meaning.

But while modernism and postmodernism shared some of the same concerns, the perspective was often different. Postmodernism, infused by theories of structure, substituted relationship for causality, put greater emphasis upon history as a constructed reality, allowed synchronicity to replace linear history, thought of literature as a system analogous to self-reflexive language, turned reality into paradigms of fiction, and brought to the text a greater sense of play. Postmodernism was far more tolerant of and willing to accommodate mass culture. Most important, postmodernism collapsed personal consciousness into the culture itself, radically changing the very idea of self. The modernist placed emphasis upon individual subjectivity, the postmodernists on mass consciousness.

Shared concerns thus gave way under the different weight placed upon them; in its revised emphasis, postmodernism distinguished itself from what preceded it, just as modernism had distinguished itself from the Romanticism out of which it grew and the literary naturalism to which it was opposed. The claim to conflicted meaning that was essential to poststructuralist deconstruction stemmed in part from every generation rewriting the claims of the past, creating a continued sense of historical contradiction. So much that passes for a re-visionary aspect of modernism is a matter of postmodern transformations.

Today a virtual reality competes with a physical reality. Newspapers and TV decide what is news and then repeat coverage to the exclusion of all other events. When the coverage stops, the all-consuming story falls back into oblivion. As George Orwell has told us, those in political positions have learned that they also can control reality. Every political establishment has its propaganda bureau that helps it control public thought, and this is more true today than it was in the thirties.[4] Consciousness is no longer purely individualistic but has been folded back into the culture itself and is as much a commodity as brand-name cereals and soups (as the paintings of Andy Warhol suggest).

The high modernists anticipated the abuses that mass culture brought. Pound and Eliot looked down upon an industry that encouraged popular culture. In the wake of Matthew Arnold, they argued for tradition (albeit different from Arnold's tradition), wanted a literature of masterpieces that could endure the test of time, each great work a touchstone for the next. Their search for the best that was thought or expressed led to a sense of elitism. The feud over the high and the low concerned a number of major postmodern critics. Adorno and most of the Frankfurt school felt that popular culture was a form of decadence and were wary of the masses, having seen the uses to which they were put in Nazi Germany. While also wary of fascism, critics such as Leslie Fiedler, Fredric Jameson, and Umberto Eco refused to look down on various forms of pop art.

Along with the distinction between an elite and a popular culture, a second issue that divided modernism and postmodernism involved the resulting difference in the nature of consciousness. Descartes believed in a fixed self. Consciousness defined the self, fixing it to an external reality. This idea was challenged as we move in assumption from a Romantic to structuralist theory of language. The Romantic poet celebrated individualism: the visionary ability was personal; the structuralist worked through a language-like system that was anterior to the poet. The difference in emphasis paralleled the change from a society that turned on the individual to a society that turned on the masses.

The transforming influence of structuralism accounts, at least in part, for the substantial difference between modernist and postmodernist consciousness. Modernist consciousness stems from impressionism, the assumption that consciousness is personal, unique to an individual, and thus arbitrary and unpredictable. An example of modern consciousness would be that of Stephen Dedalus in Joyce's *Portrait* as he walks the streets of Dublin superimposing his thoughts of literary matters onto physical places. An example of postmodern consciousness would be that of Mr. Thoth in Pynchon's *The Crying of Lot 49*, who cannot distinguish between signifiers and signified, cannot disentangle tales of his grandfather's experience with the Pony Express from the cartoons that he is watching on TV. As in much of Pynchon's fiction, the point here is both intentionally silly and critically serious: silly in its use of Porky Pig, serious in its belief that the media and other forms of mass communication dominate our consciousness, which is multilayered and diffuse. The postmodern critic collapses consciousness into the culture itself, where it expands beyond the real to what Baudrillard has termed "hyperspace." Consciousness is now as much a public as it is a personal matter; culture speaks us rather than vice versa.

IV

The rise of mass culture transformed the idea of self even further. Gustave Le Bon in *The Crowd* (1895) argued that the crowd altered an individual's state of mind and played into the political purposes of a charismatic leader. Sigmund Freud in his *Group Psychology and the Analysis of the Ego* (1922) held that participation in mass society released deep-seated aggressive impulses, contended that the crowd developed a consciousness and unconsciousness of its own, reduced human motives to primitive instincts, and called atavistic traits into play. Elias Canetti maintained in *Crowds and Power* (1962) that that the crowd created a field of force that pulled the leader into its orbit, the leader embodying rather than directing its destructive energy.

As the crowd became a metonym for the city, social theorists such as Georg Simmel, Max Weber, and Walter Benjamin studied it to get an insight into the urban unconscious, even as the artistic vision became more opaque. Depictions of crowds ranging from those of Zola to those of Nathanael West suggested that the crowd was not a composite of individuals but embodied a separate reality with motivations of its own. This view of the crowd anticipated the mob; dumbed down, its destructive energy was a disorder unto itself.

What thus gets lost in the crowd—personal identity absorbed into the masses, physical presence devoid of individual consciousness—is the individual. Separated by the difference between mass and individual consciousness, the individual is literally alone in the crowd. The rise of mass culture, as a number of recent studies have suggested, effected a major cultural transformation within the modernist movement.[5]

There was a synergy between the literary texts that made up the modernist canon and the critical theory that was used to read those texts. Every critical system is part of a hermeneutical process that allows a different understanding of the same text. Like Wallace Stevens's "Thirteen Ways of Looking at a Blackbird" or "Anecdote of the Jar," each way of seeing gives us a new perspective on the same thing, each creates its own epistemological reality while the composite creates a historical reality.

Much in the modernist doctrine came back to a belief in perspective: reality was a matter of perception. Heisenberg argued that the perspective of the observer was part of the meaning of a scientific experiment; extrapolated, this meant that the critical system brought to a literary work determined its meaning. As the meaning of a text is more complex than its random readings, no one reading can exhaust its meaning or offer a totalizing context. (Spatial form, with the need for a reader to connect layers of time and mythic meaning, especially demands multiple readings.) In the era that constitutes the modern period, neither the text nor the accompanying literary criticism remained stable; both evolved toward a questioning of absolutes, the ontogeny of the text recapitulating the phylogeny of the literary criticism.

As a revision of Romanticism, the early modernist view, both literary and critical, was aesthetic: the work was tested for its search for beauty as in Mann's "Death in Venice." From Baudelaire to Pater, from Henry James to Oscar Wilde, from George Santayana to Wallace Stevens, from Bely to Nabokov, and from Huysmans to Proust, the work was examined under the rubric of "l'art pour l'art," art for art's sake. The search for beauty was a disguised search for the absolute, and there was a religious current to aestheticism. Many of the proponents were Catholic or Catholic converts (Santayana, Huysmans, Tate, Robert Lowell). It was not surprising that T. S. Eliot, the most religious of modern poets, was the cornerstone poet during these years.

As one rereads critics from different generations, one can see that they were often working the same issues, even if their ideas were different; and much of the difference came from collapsing form into language. Saussure led the way, moving us away from the old philology; the Moscow and Prague formalists picked up where he left off; Georg Lukács connected history and class consciousness; Louis Althusser combined structuralism and Marxism in ways that paralleled Kenneth Burke's theory of symbolic action, anticipated in turn by Ernst Cassirer's and Suzanne Langer's theory of symbolic form.

Central to all of these theorists was the transformation from a mechanistic theory of reality to a symbolic theory. Symbolism became a major concern of interest, a touchstone of modernism. F. O. Matthiessen discussed American symbolism as part of an international movement. Charles Feidelson saw it as a more indigenous matter, drawing upon a Puritan heritage.[6] A nineteenth-century symbolic author such as Melville was brought into the modern canon. A novel with the compressed symbolism of Fitzgerald's *The Great Gatsby* became an ur-text, as did Conrad's *Heart of Darkness*, which illustrated the thematic, technical, and narrative elements that ideally constituted a modern work.

The Principles of Literary Criticism (1924), by I. A. Richards, and *Seven Types of Ambiguity* (1931), by William Empson, his student at Cambridge, shifted emphasis to language as the source of reality and literary complexity. Richards believed the emotional power of poetry gave it a being separate from prose, and Empson argued that ambiguity was built within language itself, an idea that anticipated the deconstructionist belief that a multiplicity of meaning infused the word and destabilized language. For example, the word "buckle" in Gerard Manley Hopkins's poem "The Windhover" can mean both "fasten" (as in buckle your belt) and "crumple" (as in the wheel buckled). Literary meaning no longer involved authorial intent, historical and cultural meaning, or reader response. The method emphasized the work as a self-contained, organic form (a product of the literary parts of which it was composed); those literary elements were often a matter of both symbol and rhetoric; and the more complex a work was in theme and technique, the better.

V

Modernism was as much a product of critical systems as it was a purely literary matter. Two of the major assumptions of literary modernism, for example, stem directly from the theory of T. S. Eliot. Eliot's idea of "tradition" substituted "eternal" for chronological order: works from different historical periods could inform each other as the British metaphysical poets informed the French symbolists and vice versa. Literary technique was as much the basis for literary recall as temporal order, and the addition of an original work to the unfolding of tradition altered any ideal order. Another literary preference of Eliot's involved the need of the poem to establish its meaning by going through an image or metaphor. One can speak in prose of love's constancy, but one gives added meaning to the idea when unwavering love is described as "gold to airy thinness beat." Eliot regretted the loss of such meaning in the eighteenth century, when the poetry of Dryden and Pope became more a matter of literal statement than metaphorical unfolding, and he referred to this loss as "the disassociation of sensibility." The desire to ground poetry in metaphor was central to the imagist movement and other methods of technique like Pound's vortex theory. For Eliot, the use of metaphor to carry a poetic idea was not just a new way of "speaking"; it was also a new way of "seeing."

Modernism, in fact, could be considered as a movement involving new ways of seeing, perspectives that involved a combination of new literary ideas. Feminist theory, for example, was best read against the originary views of Virginia Woolf and Simone de Beauvoir. New Criticism was part of a larger critical movement involving earlier theorists such as Viktor Shklovsky, Mikhail Bakhtin, and Roman Jakobson. Kenneth Burke helped shift the emphasis from symbolic form/action to a structuralist/paradigmatic (constructed) literary reality. And Roland Barthes was an agent of change in the revisionary process that let to poststructuralism.

In the fifties, the most common approach to literary studies involved the matter of influences: the emphasis was on the way literary texts built on each other. The New Criticism, with its emphasis upon the autotelic or self-contained text, challenged authorial intention as well as the reader response of the old historicism before it was contested in turn. Structuralism questioned the matter of form. E. D Hirsch's theory of intention disputed Wimsatt and Beardsley's intentional fallacy, and Stanley Fish and Wolfgang Iser restored the interpretative role of the reader.[7] A critical program never stands still and is transformed by a demand for the new. As it changes, it transforms literary reality by instituting new ways of seeing, creating a new canon and new ways of reading it, and by implementing a new order of literary text.

Modernist criticism not only changed the nature of the text, it redirected the modernist move toward the void. Modernism as a literary movement drifted toward philosophical darkness. Such nihilism was part of a larger literary equation.

A Wallace Stevens poem examined the imagination and its pursuit of beauty as it came face to face with the void, at which time the beautiful was reaffirmed. Just as Conrad's Marlow lied to Kurtz's intended about the true nature of reality, Stevens's poetry avoided accepting the inevitability of nihilism by reaffirming the transforming power of the imagination. A tissue of fiction separated modern civilization from a more primitive reality: religion as a source of truth gave way to notions of supreme fiction. Eliot's primary place in the canon gave way to Stevens.

Once reality moved from consciousness to language, structuralism followed. Everything was relational as if part of the same (language) system. From Ferdinand de Saussure to Russian formalism to Lévi-Strauss to the semiotics of Umberto Eco, meaning was constructed, a matter of paradigmatic difference, no longer dependent upon a real world. Structuralism canceled the meaning of author, individual text, history, and reader. The system supplied the meaning. Within every system was a center, whether it be made up of God, self, mind, or the unconscious. The structuralist idea of a center, of logocentrism, brought a response from Jacques Derrida, who objected to the notion of "langue" in which a system of meaning was held together by a unifying concept.

The New Critics read a literary work in terms of its organic form: the assumption was that the parts added up to a coherent whole. The structuralists read the literary work in terms of its paradigmatic homologies: the text was seen as embodying relational rather than organic meaning; the connections between parts were unbonded; lacking adherence, the parts no longer rested on a principle of unity. The change in critical method here involves a radical shift in what is the basis of literary reality, and the transformation marks the difference between modernism and postmodernism.

The modernist drift toward the nihilism beneath civilization (Conrad) or the chaos the imagination could not quite order (Stevens) was now complete. The critical journey here described moves from forms of absolutes (the beautiful), to coherent meaning (the formalist text), to states of mind (phenomenology), to structures of language (structuralism), to finally the chasm that all of these absolutes were trying to fill (deconstruction). As modernism moved from a search for the ideal to a sense of nihilism, as it moved downward to the abyss with its darkness that we encounter in Conrad and Stevens, literary criticism moved in the same direction.

3 ✛ THE MODERNIST EXPERIENCE

Modernism as a literary movement tended to compartmentalize history and literature on the assumption that the historical record was not interchangeable with the literary record. But there is more reciprocity between the two systems than is often acknowledged. A discussion of historical imperialism, for example, anticipates the novels of Conrad, Forster, and Céline and the writing of Orwell, Gide, and Malraux. A discussion of the war anticipates the disillusionment that Ezra Pound's poetry shared with the novels of Fitzgerald and Hemingway. Equally important in such a discussion is what was left out, what in the historical record the modernist failed to consider, and what in the literary record was eclipsed by the historians. This is not to belie the parallel movement between the literary and historical planes: we move from an optimism connected with imperialism to a disillusionment connected with the wars that resulted from imperial conflict to a variety of obfuscations for both. The rise of a mass culture is the phenomenon shared by both history and literature and is one of the subjects modernism addressed as it turned to what was beyond.

I

The politics behind much of literary modernism was that of the political Right with its celebration of ultranationalism. The movement toward the political Right was encouraged by a historical situation that emerged from the nineteenth century. There was first a reaction against Romanticism, which was in part a response to the bloody outcome of the French Revolution and to the rise of liberal and democratic philosophy. Opposed to equalitarian movements was the impetus toward nationalism, reinforced by a theory of the Volk, the celebration of the blood connection of people living off the soil by philosophers like Herder. Inseparable from the belief in nationalism was the cult of the superior individual as embodied in Carlyle's hero, Nietzsche's superman, and a theory of the elite as expressed by Vilfredo Pareto and Gaetano Mosca. Ortega y Gasset in his *Revolt of the Masses* argued for the need of an elite rule in the era of mass movements.

While the aesthetic movement is usually considered nonpolitical, the cult of the artist pointed toward the social need for a cultural elite. Baudelaire rejected democracy. Goethe showed a preference for rule by an aristocracy. Stefan George coupled his dislike for industrialization with an antipathy for democracy. And Oscar Wilde insisted that the pursuit of the beautiful involved the moral superiority of the artist, validating a social elite in the name of art.

Both the cult of the hero and a desire for the rule of an elite played into the role of racial prejudice. Nationalism brought with it the cult of Nordic and Teutonic superiority in both Victorian England and Bismarck's Germany. The notion of racial superiority was spread by nations that believed their imperial efforts were justified in the name of bearing the white man's burden. Charles Maurras and the Action Française and Gabriele d'Annunzio in Italy sympathetically embraced these racial ideas.

A belief in racial supremacy turned into a virulent anti-Semitism—a state of mind that can be found in writers as different as Pound or Eliot and Louis-Ferdinand Céline, whose most famous novel is *Journey to the End of the Night* (1932). Throughout *Journey*, Céline depicted the inability of modern man to sustain altruism in the face of a growing capitalistic-industrial system that elevated production and profit beyond compassion. Perhaps it was the need to find someone to blame for the imperfection of humanity that led Céline to the drastic charge that the Jews were responsible for most social ills. In a rash 300-page pamphlet, *Bagatelles pour un massacre* (1937), he insisted that the Jews were at fault for what was wrong with both capitalism and communism.

France had great trouble putting the Dreyfus affair behind it, and Céline was working an established genre, repeating charges made by such other French writers as Drumont, Vallès, Bloy, Péguy, Daudet, Maurras, and Béraud. Céline argued that the Jewish influence in the United States, Great Britain, and Russia was part of a conspiracy to bring down both France and Germany, and he called for an alliance that would unify these two nations. He brought to his argument an attack on Roosevelt's Jewish sympathies as well as his heavily Jewish cabinet in America, the Jewish basis of Lenin's support in Russia, the Jew as Anglophile, and a questioning of Léon Blum—a Marxist Jew who was recently elected to the position of prime minister in France. France had become a decadent society under the influence of the Jews, and Céline indicted Claudel, Maurois, Proust, and especially Gide.[1]

Céline's experience finds parallels in the career of D. H. Lawrence. France and England shared a sense of decline based on their distrust of the industrial society with its power of alienation, its trust in technology, and its willingness to put profits ahead of human concerns. Lawrence felt that the modern emphasis upon reason separated humanity from a basic consciousness that preceded scientific discovery. Such primitive consciousness was necessary if one was to identify with the physical world. Sir Clifford Chatterley had lost this capacity of empathy; so also had Gerald Crich in *Women in Love,* who, unlike his father, had lost contact with his workers; to him they were inseparable from the machinery he needed to run the mines.

Lawrence moved from the social evils that stemmed from an industrial society to a distrust of mob rule. He connected the liberal approval of the masses with a Jewish state of mind, and he joined the theory of relativity (which, like Wyndham Lewis, he associated with the moral relativism of modernism) with Einstein's Jewishness, claiming the whole liberal-democratic tradition stemmed from Jewish thought. (In his novel *Kangaroo,* the main character's Jewishness is used to illustrate this point.)

A social remedy rested with the need for aristocratic authority, the rise of a superior class, and redemption through the superior person who could go beyond the mechanical restraints of modern society. As John Harrison has claimed, quoting from Lawrence's literary criticism, "Lawrence's views of social leadership are inherently close to the fascist conception of society: 'For the mass of people knowledge must be symbolical, mystical, dynamic. This means you must have a higher, responsible, conscious class and then in varying degrees the lower classes, varying in their degree of consciousness.'"[2]

Where Lawrence stops, Wyndham Lewis begins. In *The Art of Being Ruled* (1926), Lewis claimed that the masses were indifferent to the forms of government by which they were ruled. The rise of an industrial system and the growth of democracy had degraded the masses. Because the masses had abrogated political responsibility, he believed an intellectual class must assume that function. In *The Apes of God* (1930), Lewis contrasted the great person with his imitators. As democracy became stronger and the individual was eclipsed by the masses, intellectual principles were weakened. To be recognized by a mass public, the writer had to lower his standards. Despite the uses that totalitarian forces made of Spengler, Lewis subjected him to attack on the grounds of his Romantic yearning. Lewis felt a cultural decline had set in with the French Revolution. As with the Puritan (Parliamentarian) Revolution, once a supreme authority was eliminated, a culture lost its principle of fixity and a historical slide took place.

In *Time and Western Man* (1927), Lewis attacked proponents of what he called the "time-mind," "the hypostasization and glorification of the concept Time."[3] His main targets of attack involved philosophers and literary artists like Henri Bergson, James Joyce, Gertrude Stein, and Oswald Spengler. But he also included scientists like Einstein for his relativity theory and Whitehead for his theory of organicism. Later he included the impressionist painters, whom he saw as precursors of cubism, futurism, and vorticism. Bergson had postulated an inner force that was moving life toward higher forms (as opposed to the Darwinian belief that such forms were mere adaptations to environment). Einstein proposed a theory of both cosmic and moral relativity. And Joyce supplied metamorphic realism and a Viconian sense of history that universalized time and coupled the heroic (royal) Ulysses with the comic (common) Leopold Bloom. Lewis was especially opposed to Joyce and Stein's favoring simultaneity or a continued present over linear time. He argued that such thinking destroyed the natural movement of a living universe and turned time into a trash heap, a junk pile of accumulated (dead) matter: Joyce has "such a mass of dead stuff hung [on Dedalus and Bloom] that if ever they had any organic life of their own, it would speedily have been overwhelmed in this torrent of matter, of nature-morte."[4]

Joyce's rebuttal came in *Finnegans Wake* when he portrayed Lewis as Professor Jones, who finds in the anthropology of Lévy-Bruhl support for his space-oriented man with his sense of linear time. The exchange suggests the opposition between mythic and scientific thinking. Joyce was unwilling to set the commercial society on a higher plane than the primal society or to merge the day and night world. The "Circe" episode comes late in the evening, releasing from memory the ghosts of the dead, reconciling the living and the dead, infusing order with chaos, adding another dimension to time. At the end of the "Circe" episode, Corny Kelleher, the undertaker and the custodian of the dead, and the policeman, or the custodian of authority, appear. As Bloom is the urban incarnation of Ulysses, so they are incarnations of Dionysus and Apollo.

For Lewis, time was not absolute and had no meaning apart from clock time: time was change, not a universal force driving life before it. He connected the life force with theories of Progress and saw it as part of a liberal attempt to reduce the heroic past to a diminished present. Lewis believed that the aristocracy had lost its authority, its ability to stabilize a culture, and he turned to the idea of the great man for such stability.

Along with *The Art of Being Ruled* and *Time and Western Man,* Lewis wrote *The Lion and the Fox* (1927), a book of Shakespearean criticism that clearly reveals his preference for an authoritarian society. Shakespeare's heroes are great men destroyed by trivial opponents, "who substitute a poor and vulgar thing for the great whole that they have destroyed."[5] Lewis's great man—caught between an ideal world and a time-world—had to be powerful enough to rise beyond the commonality of the masses. This is why Lewis early in his career looked approvingly on Hitler. But while he would revise his opinion of Hitler, he never abandoned his Nietzschean admiration for the great man.

II

If Céline, Lawrence, and Lewis gave us a portrait of the modernist leaning Right, Arthur Koestler supplied a portrait of the modernist leaning Left. Koestler was a product of a changing Europe. His father came from Budapest and his mother from Vienna, and he grew up divided between these Hapsburg cities. His early writing was journalistic, and he operated out of Paris and Berlin when he was not in the Arabian desert or covering the war in Spain. He became a devoted Zionist and spent much time working for the independence of Palestine, at that time a colony of England. When it became clear in the thirties that Palestine would not become a Jewish state, he turned his energies toward communism, becoming a member of the German Communist Party. For seven years he remained faithful to the communist ideal, but when the Stalinist drive to relocate the peasants turned murderous and Soviet participation in the Spanish civil war became more of a contradiction than a cause, his enthusiasm for the party diminished; he eventually abandoned communism as a lost ideal, documenting his disillusionment in two famous works—*Darkness at Noon* (1940) and *The God That Failed* (1949).

Koestler's two-volume autobiography, *Arrow in the Blue* (1952) and *The Invisible Writing* (1954), is a moving account of the modernist period from a political/philosophical/scientific point of view. Koestler witnessed the major premises of nineteenth-century reality in the process of being transformed. From a scientific point of view, space was still noncurved, the world infinite, the mind a rational clockwork. But these assumptions would be challenged with the end to causality, as certainty gave way to probability. Politically, Koestler saw countries and colonies come and go: the Hapsburg dynasty ended with World War I; later

Count Michael Karolyi oversaw Hungary's secession from the Austrian Empire. And the new pursuit of the Promised Land involving first Zionism and then the Communist Party entailed a search for the ideal, a search that, before the Enlightenment (the eighteenth century), involved the idea of God, and after it a pursuit to fill the void.

It was a world held together by force, by a power that was invested in institutions and not always intelligently used by those who exercised it. The transformations brought ideological change; change brought ideological difference; difference subjected dissidents to retribution. No one was safe from the caprice of power: the inquisitor was questioned; the executioner was executed. As Koestler puts it himself: "three out of every four people whom I knew before I was thirty, were subsequently killed in Spain, or hounded to death at Dachau, or gassed at Belsen, or deported to Russia, or liquidated in Russia; some jumped from windows in Vienna or Budapest."[6]

During the Spanish civil war, Koestler himself was arrested in Seville by Franco forces; he was charged with being a Communist spy and held under sentence of death for over four months before he was exchanged for a fascist prisoner. This experience, plus his awareness of events behind the Stalinist purges in Russia, led to such works as *Dialogue with Death* (1942) and *Darkness at Noon* (1940) with its old-line Communist hero, Rubashov, who fought in the October Revolution and Civil War, rose to executive power within the party, only to be accused of political divergence and executed.

As communism developed in Russia, it led to many factions, ideological divisions caused by disagreements over whether or not it was justified to remove the peasants from the land or institute other kinds of collectivism. When some objected on the grounds that the state should uphold, not deny, human benefits, the system tolerated no exception. Koestler's novel depicted the brutality of the Stalin regime, anticipated his own disillusionment with communism, and foreshadowed his resignation from the party. In *Darkness*, Koestler asks the key question: why did faithful members of the party, like Rubashov, confess to incriminating charges that they knew were untrue? Koestler's answer is that they indicted themselves because they did not want to betray the idea of communism; it involved their last service to the party. As Koestler put it himself: "in spite of everything, the Soviet Union still represented our last and only hope on a planet in rapid decay."[7]

Koestler's autobiography is historical testimony from a Leftist point of view of twenties and thirties turmoil: it summarizes the rise and fall of the tenets that made modernism a cultural movement. As Koestler himself said by way of conclusion: "The rise of [a Marxist] Empire was not an edifying story; its decline is. Ultimately, this may be the reason which attracted me to England [where he lived out his life]. I only seem to flourish in a climate of decline, and have always felt best in the season when the trees shed their leaves."[8]

Koestler puts in perspective the ideological currents that run through modernism, revealing why two intelligent adherents of the communist movement could radically disagree over its legitimacy: Jean-Paul Sartre remained loyal to the communist cause while Koestler himself abandoned it. A generation of writers was faced with the same choices: the paths of leading literary and intellectual figures intersected and crossed, and the experiences of some of the major modern writers strangely duplicated each other. Koestler's political and literary activity, for example, brought him in contact with Gide, Malraux, Silone, Mann, and Freud.

Koestler had much in common with André Malraux. Like Koestler, Malraux depicted the Spanish civil war in *L'espoir* (*Man's Hope*, 1937). And while Koestler's experience never involved the Chinese revolution, which was the subject of Malraux's *Les conquérants* (*The Conquerors*, 1928) and *La condition humaine* (*Man's Fate*, 1933), both novelists examined the motives that encouraged revolutionaries to risk their lives in the pursuit of unrealistic political ideals. In *La condition humaine,* Chíen, a Chinese terrorist, and Katov, a Russian revolutionist, both die at the hands of Chiang Kai-shek, who takes control of Shanghai when Moscow orders the Communists to surrender their weapons to Chiang's police. The orders come as a result of a pact between Chiang and the Red forces, a pact that each side is waiting to violate. A false trust, the product of misapplied political power, thus mocks the death of the revolutionaries. The individual brings a blind idealism, an optimism that is belied by the seemingly downward turn of history: man supplies the hope, history the despair. Like Koestler, Malraux—bolstered by the works of Spengler and Frobenius—sees all civilization eventually in a process of decline.[9] The revolutionaries are duped to believe that individual effort matters, when in reality larger forces—political and historical—negate the purpose of human sacrifice: historical forces work independently of individual intention. Such is man's fate.

III

Cumulatively, Céline, Koestler, Malraux, Lawrence, and Lewis supplied an all-too familiar model, and their lives were representative beyond the matter of Céline's racial prejudice: Koestler and Malraux experienced political disillusionment; Lawrence and Lewis expressed a social fear of technology and the machine.

Like Conrad and Gide, Céline went to imperial Africa. Like Hemingway, he was wounded in war and experienced it firsthand as a killing machine. Like Lawrence, he visited America and turned against the anonymity of the metropolis and the impersonality of the machine. And like Theodore Dreiser, John Dos Passos, Edmund Wilson, André Gide, and many others, Céline, Malraux, and Koestler journeyed as "pilgrims" to the Soviet Union to observe firsthand the promise of communism and returned more ambivalent than convinced that it was the new Utopia. Like almost all of the modern writers, they, along with Lawrence and Lewis, experienced an initial momentum that gave way to a sense of radical decline, a topic discussed at length in chapter 9.

Koestler's experience gives us a pattern that comes from the Left. He was in search of a system that would fulfill ideological needs, first connected with Zionism and the hope of an Israeli state in Palestine, and then with the belief that communism could establish class equality, eliminate poverty, bring an end to empire, and facilitate world peace. But all political systems are limited in various ways by imperfect human nature: power is exercised through institutions, but the institutions ultimately rest with an individual subject to cupidity, rapaciousness, and the abuse of power. As a result, Céline's fascism and Koestler's communism were no better than the human element from which they took direction; each brought an equally "false dawn to history." Despite their ideological differences, both the Right and the Left were caught in the spiral of historical decline.

Perhaps this universal sense of disillusionment was connected with the results of war. The aftermath of World War I, fought in the name of democracy, brought an unfavorable reaction to liberal and democratic ideas. The belief that World War I was the war to end all wars was clearly untrue; the belief that World War I would pave the way to global democracy was equally discredited. Hitler inherited a German state in the process of decline. Hitler's strength stemmed from his propaganda machine. He was among the first world leaders who learned how to control and exploit a mass culture. He not only was able to unify the Volk behind his causes; he was able to find a common enemy both at home (the Jews) and abroad (England and the other nations that signed the Versailles Treaty). He had the impressive ability to build his regime on the mistreatment, real and imagined, of the German people after World War I. He called attention to the breakup of the German-speaking coalition, the extreme reparations that stemmed from the Versailles Treaty, and the worldwide depression that he connected to capitalistic manipulations, primarily, he maintained, at the hands of the Jews. Hitler advocated the supremacy of the German people, appealed to the ur-Volk nativist emphasis with its blood-and-soil connections, and attacked egalitarian forms of government.

Democracy was no better than the efficacy of a Congress or a Parliament dependent upon political alignment, often the product of special influence. Both totalitarian and democratic forms of government worked, theoretically at least, to perpetuate the forces of life over death. But even the best in a democratic/capitalistic society sometimes reworked this ideal. For example, the military-industrial complex reversed these priorities. The war industry was a business before it was a system of defense; as a business it promoted a belief in military readiness, demanding a need for a cadre of ideological spokesmen to encourage perpetual desire for war along with wariness dependent upon a demand for up-to-date weapons. The process was circular: the desire for war justified the need for the weapons, and the supply of weapons promoted the desire for war. Both justified the cost and guaranteed sustained runaway military profits. Democracy put authority in the hands of an unpredictable and not always informed elector-ate, who moreover often elected representatives subject to such money interests. Totalitarian systems questioned rule by vote, even as it abused unchecked power. Hitler's desire was for a government of military elite, and many members of the modernist movement—Ezra Pound, T. S. Eliot, Wyndham Lewis, and D. H. Lawrence—were sympathetic to an intellectual equivalent of such an elite.

Much of the resistance to commercial politics stemmed from a distrust of the new industrialism. The medieval church had rejected the idea of a product's value being determined by a market system. Each product had a fair price, inde-pendent of the market, to be determined by the work that produced it. Consent to this idea came from different directions: William Morris and John Ruskin insisted on its validity, as did Karl Marx. Marx objected to the addition of costs brought about by investment capitalism. A surplus profit was added to items, increasing their price beyond the purchasing means of the workers who had brought the goods into being.

Modernism created two contexts: the literary-aesthetic and the social-polit-ical. The major modernists for the most part kept the two categories separate, compartmentalizing one from the other. Despite their disillusionment with World War I and Pound's pro-fascist pronouncements in World War II, the high modernists did not really come to terms with the major atrocities of the Second World War. When we read the late Pound and Eliot, we have no idea that they were writing at one of the bloodiest moments in human history, that 6 million Jews died in the Holocaust, that Stalin murdered about 20 million Russians in the name of peasant relocation and land reform. The ideal society is a product of an organic unity in which life is affirmed over death. Despite the need for such affirmation, the modernists kept literary and political reality separate by affirming that literature (i.e., art) was its own justification, and that such aestheticism was independent of a moral purpose. Such theories as the autotelic (autonomous) text and the reduction of meaning to the workings of language cut off from physical reality eliminated the critical means to come to terms with the atrocities of the outside world.

But once the influence of aestheticism passed, there was a renewed interest in the connection between literature and politics. George Orwell is a representative example. Orwell's intellectual development stemmed from a series of disillusionments. He was disillusioned by imperialism based on his experience as a policeman in Burma. He was disillusioned by communism based on his experience fighting for the popular front in Spain. His sympathy was with Trotsky and not Stalin, whose tactics turned him away from communism to socialism. Orwell had reservations about political remedy from both the Right and the Left. Most important, he saw that the basis for political activity had radically changed. John Stuart Mill's idea of liberty had influenced much nineteenth-century thinking: the individual was free to engage in the arena of ideas, out of which would come Truth. Such a free exchange of individual ideas was no longer available in a world where power determined truth.

Once democracy gave way to the superstate, the idea of individual identity gave way to that of mass identity, the self as a product of the state's power. Most nineteenth-century thought was logocentric—that is, it was held together by centering controlling ideas like democracy. Once logocentrism was challenged, the center could not hold but instead was filled with ideas from each extreme. This curtailed the free exchange of ideas once the state or its surrogate institutions regulated the means by which consciousness (i.e., political reality) came into being. Orwell became a major skeptic when he saw on the Spanish front the discrepancy between events that he had personally experienced and the journalistic accounts of those events. Once controlled, language obfuscated rather than clarified reality, and the obscurity always worked to reinforce an ideology of power.

Another major critic who believed that literature must engage political reality was Jean-Paul Sartre, whose brilliant essays went beyond the aesthetic concerns of the New Criticism and instituted a literature of political responsibility. But the deed had been done. Despite the eventual commitment of Orwell and Sartre, and later Auden, Spender, and Day-Lewis, high modernism (the modernism of

Joyce, Proust, and Woolf) had turned away from the physical world toward an inner reality.

One can argue that this inner world was as much a part of reality as anything outside it, and that is obviously true. And one can further argue that a different literature would not have saved us from a Hitler or Stalin, and that is equally true. But the modernist perspective put the emphasis upon the personal and subjective, limiting the way to assess world events. The modernists rejected naturalism as a literary movement because, among other reasons, it lacked an inner reality, reduced motives to behaviorist theory, and was densely melodramatic—mechanically separating good and evil, which more often than not were inextricably connected. The modernists could not accept such extremes. Thus the modernist eclipsed history: the breech between literary and historical reality became too great to come to terms with one through the other.

Modernism as a literary movement owed its being to a confluence of Continental, British, and American thought. Baudelaire and Flaubert along with literary naturalism transformed by French symbolism were major factors in its development. In England, the Edwardians questioned the values that underpinned the world of Queen Victoria, and the improvisations of Ezra Pound were instrumental in establishing new techniques like imagism and vorticism. Pound was equally instrumental in getting access to the little magazine and introducing in print many young writers who became the major figures in the movement. Hugh Kenner in *The Pound Era* (1971) even goes to the extreme of reducing the idea of modernism to the influence of Pound. One could suggest other primal influences: Gertrude Stein, for example, concentrated on the connection between language and physical reality, working to revise both reality and consciousness by creating a language that perpetuated a continuous present. But the idea that modernism can be reduced to one person's era is misguided. Pound had influence behind the scenes, Stein and Stevens on the fringe, Joyce perhaps more than anyone in the center. But despite the considerable achievement of all of these writers, and many more, modernism in its many guises does not belong to one person.

II
EARLY MODERNISM

4 ✦ THE INWARD TURN

Henri Bergson challenged at the outset the priority of a mechanistic, Darwinian evolution that robbed the universe of a creative unfolding and man of the corresponding creative power of a deep subjectivity within which the mythic, the primitive, and the intuitive could take hold. Both Joyce and Ezra Pound once claimed Flaubert to be the father of modernism, and in an artistic as well as chronological sense they were right. But it was Bergson who created a systematic, rigorous philosophy that became the foundation for modernism. Bergson's philosophy, anticipated by Samuel Butler, was the basis for a new reality.

Among the modernists there was a concentrated move to do away with literary naturalism and to adapt nineteenth-century realism to accommodate a modernist reality. In England the spokesmen for such change were T. E. Hulme and Richard Aldington. Out of these pronouncements came the assumptions that control the fiction of such key modernist novelists as D. H. Lawrence and Virginia Woolf. These assumptions were reinforced by a theory of impressionism that had its origins with Walter Pater and led to the impressionistic method that we find in Joseph Conrad. All of these movements anticipate the method of high modernism, with its use of mythic symbolism and cyclical history. An avant-garde movement sometimes resisted and sometimes complemented these literary transformations.

I

Bergson's deviations from post-Enlightenment optimism occurred in stages. He began his philosophical career as a disciple of Herbert Spencer and a believer in certain fundamental assumptions regarding the material explanation of the universe. Bergson correctly saw that the Enlightenment legacy had left an intellectual construct that gave priority to a mechanical reality and that naturalism and the theory of Darwinian evolution had only extended that reality. Science ultimately relied on the empirical method—on observation and experimentation—as the basis for a system of laws that explain the nature of the universe. Science thus depended on the repetitiveness of nature: nature will continue to repeat the laws that describe it. The categories that make up this scientific discourse were then taken as objectively true. Bergson felt that such "truth" clearly rested on categories of the mind that presumed causality at the heart of nature, a presumption that he felt was a fundamental misconception of how nature worked. Because science cuts us off at an inferior realm of being, Bergson felt the need for an alternative to scientific knowing. We thus end up with two different ways of knowing: one scientific, empirical, logical, abstract, and mechanical; the other subjective, intuitive, and holistic.

Darwinism, in particular, he maintained, relied on "logical" and not "real" connections in nature. Darwin created categories that he believed were descriptive of nature and then established a cause-and-effect relationship between these categories. This in turn created an element of sequence between the categories. Bergson believed that not only were the categories an artificial construct but the sense of evolutionary time that emerged from such a construction was equally artificial.

Bergson rejected both the mechanistic and a teleological view of the universe that had become connected with the theories of evolution. Both bring into play a causality that predetermined a physical unfolding. Teleology (which he called "finalism") was simply an inverted mechanism: it located a determining reality in the future rather than the past, put the emphasis on an internal finality, and gave priority to the controlled nature of "becoming" rather than of "being." Bergson did not deny either the need for scientific discourse or the plausibility of adaptive evolution. But, he insisted, there is a difference between the forces "evolution must reckon with" and other forces, which, as the mechanists claim, "are the directing causes of evolution."[1] Such a conclusion, he claimed, excluded "the hypothesis of an original impetus . . . an internal push that has carried life, by more and more complex forms, to higher and higher destinies" (102).

"An original impetus . . . an internal push"—the belief in an energy, a force, an élan vital at the center of our being was central to Bergson's whole philosophy. Bergson created the divide between an Enlightenment and a modern mentality. Through intelligence, man creates the instruments and tools by which he adapts to and then eventually controls his environment. Intelligence involves an outward-looking process; it examines the material world based on instrumentality and a view toward social order and progress. To understand the inner realm of being, we must turn to intuition, which Bergson defines as "instinct that has become disinterested, self-conscious, capable of reflecting upon its object and of enlarging it indefinitely" (176). Such activity brings into being an aesthetic faculty, which accesses the inner reality of things as pure being rather than as a category or principle of mechanical organization. Bergson views this inner reality as the "being" of time, refers to it as "durée," and connects it with "real" or physical life.

Intelligence turned outward (empiricism) accounts for Enlightenment belief in instrumentality and progress. Intelligence turned inward (intuition) accounts for the modernist belief in an inner, artistic reality inseparable from the essence of being or the realm of form. The penetration of inner reality owes as much to the principles of art as to cognition, because intuition establishes a "sympathetic communication . . . between us and the rest of the living, by the expansion of our consciousness . . . into life's own domain, which is reciprocal interpenetration, endlessly continued creation" (177–78).

Intuitive intelligence is the highest form of cognitive power as well as the force that drives humanity ahead of it. When the weight of this force carries the totality of the past to the moment, we have memory—and the creation of both the universe and the self in Bergson is inseparable from the functioning of intuition and memory. Thus, for Bergson, mind both directs and accesses life. With this idea he undid the notions of mechanism and teleology. He undercut both Enlightenment and Darwinian assumptions. And he gave weight to the modernist belief that art is the highest function of our activity, helped establish the modernist belief that the universe is inseparable from mind and that the self is created out of memory.

II

While it was Bergson who most systematically formulated the modernist theory of time and consciousness, his main ideas were being anticipated by a number of late Victorian and modern writers. Samuel Butler heads this list because he so directly challenged Darwin's theory of evolution and helped formulate a theory of mind-directed evolution that, except perhaps for some of its terminology, is at times startlingly close to Bergson's theories.

In 1872, Butler revised a series of essays and published them as chapters 23 and 24, entitled "The Book of the Machines," in his satire *Erewhon*. Butler was afraid that these chapters had offended Darwin since they were so directly connected to his earlier attack on the idea of natural selection, and he later became convinced that Darwin had found the means to gain revenge. In November 1879, Darwin published *Erasmus Darwin*, a memoir of his grandfather to which he appended a translated essay by a German scholar, Dr. Krause, which had appeared in the February issue of the journal *Kosmos*. Darwin gave the impression that the translation did not vary from the original essay, but when Butler read the essay he found evidence that the essay had been revised, had used material from his *Evolution, Old and New*, and had added a paragraph that he took as a personal attack. When Darwin's explanation failed to satisfy him, Butler broke with him, convinced that Darwin was capable of deception, not only in this project but also in his previous work.

What Butler felt was lacking from Darwin's theory of evolution was a convincing account of mind, especially the way mind works in the matter of memory. Butler felt that the key question here involved identity, or what he called "sameness." We believe that there is continuity between the past and present self, but every cell in the human body is different from the cells there fifty years ago. What holds the self together, Butler insisted, was mind—or, more specifically, memory. Instinct, he claimed, is only inherited memory—that is, memories of actions done repeatedly (he would call them habits) in innumerable past generations. If this were true, then unconscious memory—and not natural selection—was the real clue to heredity. Butler thus insisted that memory went beyond the physical self, that it was inherent in the embryo and reached back to one's parents and foreparents, existing unconsciously within us, supplying motives and structuring heredity, but in ways too remote for us to be aware. The notion of such carryover memory may seem far-fetched to us today, but if we substitute the idea of DNA for personal memory, Butler was not that far removed from the modern belief that bonded in the genes is in fact a memory system passed on from generation to generation.

Butler was so obsessed with these theories of evolution that he gave the better part of his life and his writing to this topic. He rehearsed his initial skepticism about Darwin in *Life and Habit* (1878). Here Butler claimed that the most serious weakness in Darwin's theory was that, while it explained variations that had already taken place, it had no way of seeing those changes as part of a larger pattern of intelligence.[2] Butler's skepticism stemmed from his vast distrust of limiting all reality to the physical realm. The self, he insisted, has a dimension that is not acknowledged by a material definition of man.

The faculty that most established a kind of spiritual dimension for Butler, as it would later for Bergson, was that of memory, which Butler insisted functioned on the level of the unconscious, independent of the material realm of brain and nervous system. Like knowledge and desire, he claimed, "Memory is no less capable of unconscious exercise, and on becoming intense through frequent repetition, vanishes no less completely as a conscious action of the mind than knowledge and volition" (131). Like Bergson, Butler believed that this unconscious power of memory gave a kind of being to the past and helped direct what Darwin saw as the accidental variations of natural selection. At one point, Butler quotes directly from Darwin: "In every living being we may rest assured that a host of long-lost characters lie ready to be evolved under the proper conditions." And then Butler comments: "does not one almost long to substitute the word 'memories' for the word 'characters'?" (196). Here Butler has gone to the heart of the matter. By "characters," Darwin had meant that natural selection is the determining factor in evolution; by "memories," Butler substituted the mind as the determining factor. The two words capsulate the difference between Darwin and Bergson, and Butler had clearly conceptualized that difference before Bergson himself.

Mind then was inseparable from the forms inherent in the flow of time. While Butler did not actually see intuition as the means by which that flow is accessed, he arrived at a parallel idea with his theory of instinct. While Bergson believed that instinct absorbed into intelligence led to intuition, Butler believed that instinct absorbed intelligence; instinct thus becomes for Butler the highest form of intelligence, and he maintained that the mechanical world around us would eventually be absorbed into its realm, that mind would transform the mechanical.[3]

Butler carried these ideas into his literary works. He was so much taken by his theory of hereditary memory that when it came to creating the character of Ernest Pontifex in *The Way of All Flesh*, he described four generations of the family to suggest their mental/emotional continuity. Each generation intuited the same reservations about a religious commitment until Ernest, acting in a way that his father could not, finally makes a break with the past. Throughout the novel, it is Ernest's "unconscious self" that often speaks truths "to which his conscious self was unequal."[4] And because memory has been so internalized in the flow of life, we cannot separate the inner and outer realms of being. This truth is one of the major conclusions by the narrator of the novel:

The trouble is that in the end we shall be driven to admit the unity of the universe so completely as to be compelled to deny that there is either an external or an internal, but must see everything both as external and internal at one and the same time, subject and object—external and internal—being unified as much as everything else. (327)

In his only other significant artistic work, *Erewhon* (1872), Butler once again inserted his major ideas involving evolution. Like Bergson, Butler insisted upon the unity of creation. He maintained, for example, that vegetative and animal life could not be separated from the evolutionary process that brought forth man. Such forms were not separate evolutionary developments but two stages in the same process: "both animals and plants have had a common ancestry," he tells us, "and animals and plants [are] cousins."[5] And there is an intelligence working through such creation, an intelligence that we could better recognize if only individual human mind were not limited in its temporal cycle (246). Furthermore, this intelligence both informs and directs the flux of life; and while the rise of the machine may seem to threaten its integrity, the mind is capable of reconciling mechanical and natural oppositions (222–60). In challenging the mechanistic nature of Darwinian evolution, in insisting that mind (memory) works through the unfolding of time, and in seeing evolution directed by forms of such intelligence, Butler anticipated many of Bergson's major ideas. In fact, only Butler's theory of teleology and his belief that man could absorb the machine separated him from Bergson's final position.

III

D. H. Lawrence takes Bergsonian philosophy even further and in a different direction. There is no question that Lawrence knew the relevant works of Butler and that he had direct knowledge of Bergson's *Creative Evolution*. Lawrence was drawn to these works because they confirmed his belief that organized religion was played out and that an Enlightenment mentality and industrial process was completing the ruination of modern man. He believed that there was an inner self—often identified with a sexual consciousness—from which industrial man had become separated, and all of his major work returned over and over to this theme. In the early works, we see this most forcefully in *The Rainbow* (1915) and its sequel, *Women in Love* (1920), and in the later work in *Lady Chatterley's Lover* (1928) and in his discussion of apocalypse.

Almost all of Lawrence's fiction begins with the consciousness of a woman. In *The Rainbow*, the consciousnesses of Lydia and her daughter, Anna, dominate the first half of the novel, only to be replaced by the consciousnesses of Anna's daughters, Ursula and Gudrun, who will also dominate *Women in Love*. In *The Plumed*

Serpent, the dominant consciousness is that of Kate, and in *Lady Chatterley's Lover,* it is that of Constance Chatterley. A woman also is the dominant presence in "The Fox," "The Man Who Died," and many other Lawrentian short stories or novellas.

The woman in these works begins as a kind of Shavian life force. Often she has lost touch with her inner realm of being and is renewed through sexual activity with a vitalized male. Life passes through the woman, who intuits such natural powers within her. In *The Rainbow,* for example, Lydia became aware that "inside her [was] the subtle sense of the Great Absolute where she had her being."[6] The life force is behind the birth process. As Anna gives birth to Ursula, "She felt so powerfully alive and in the hands of such a masterly force of life, that the bottommost feeling was one of exhilaration" (180). Ursula intuits in a biology class the difference between the vital forces that she feels within her and the mechanical energy that makes up the external world: "She only knew that it was not limited mechanical energy, nor mere purpose of felt-preservation and self-assertion. It was a consummation, a being infinite. Self was a oneness with the infinite" (416–17).

Usually in Lawrence this inner sense of oneness with the infinite is realized through sex. When Anna and Will make love, they are taken to a realm in which they existed "only as an unconscious, dark transit of flame . . . [which] seemed to flow round them" (119–20). The sexual act in Lawrence is repeatedly described in Bergsonian terms with a reality outside of the material realm. Metaphorically, it is the swing of the pendulum (108–9) or the rotation of a great wheel, the stopping of which supplies a motionlessness that takes on the quality of Bergsonian duration—a stillness that "was beyond time, because it remained the same, inexhaustible, unchanging, unexhausted" (135).

Two selves are always at work in Lawrence: an inner self approximates the intuitional realm of Bergsonian being, and an external self participates in mechanical relationships and the routine of everydayness. Failed lovemaking is more than simply bad sex; it is a failure of the inner self to be at one with the creative forces of life. A Bergsonian sense of an inner and outer reality saves Lawrence from the ridiculous when he attempts to make sex into a cosmic act. When Skrebensky tries to make love to Ursula, he cannot break through to her inner self; there is no vital exchange between them; and the Lawrentian love passion—a combination of energy and duration that characterizes the Bergsonian inner self—never comes into being: "She was not there. Patiently she sat under the clock [the reference to mechanical time here is obvious], with Skrebensky holding her hand. But her naked self was away" (300).

The relationship between men and women in Lawrence is supposed to be

mutually dependent and in balance, with one bringing the other into vital consciousness. Birkin tells Ursula: "man had being and woman had being, two pure
beings, each constituting the freedom of the other, balancing each other like
two poles of one force."[7] But this is the ideal in Lawrence's scheme of things, and
often such a balance is never fulfilled. When the outer mechanical self cannot be
broken down, the love affair becomes destructive as one lover tries to dominate
the other, as in the case of Gerald and Gudrun.

But even when the sexual relationship is mutually beneficial, the male element seems more powerful in Lawrence's view. When Birkin referred to Adam
keeping Eve "single with himself, like a star in its orbit," Ursula responds: "There
you are—a star in its orbit! A satellite of Mars—that's what she is to be! There,
there—you've given yourself away!" (142). And Ursula seems to have intuited a
dark Lawrentian truth: the man takes the woman beyond herself, embraces both
her and the life force she embodies, and carries them to a higher plane. The man
is metaphorically the sun; the woman the moon that takes its reflection from the
sun. When Ursula makes love, we are told that the experience was "a dark powerful vibration that encompassed her. She passed away as on a dark wind, far, far
away, into the pristine darkness of paradise, in the original immortality" (426).

If love is inseparable from force in Lawrence, force itself can be subsumed
to the higher power of the unconscious, through which men and women engage
the creative force of the universe. We must "lapse into unknowingness" (37),
Birkin tells Ursula, a process that seems to turn her "dangerous power" into "a
strange unconscious bud of powerful womanhood" (52). If the individual can get
outside the outer, mechanical, totally relational self, he or she can draw upon
the larger power of the universe. Birkin tells us that there is a reality larger than
mankind. Something informs mankind that "can never be lost. . . . After all, what
is mankind but just one expression of the incomprehensible. . . . Let mankind
pass away . . . the creative utterances will not cease" (85). Life works through nature, not humanity. Life passes through women, through the feminine principle,
but a higher reality than mankind is at work. The universe has a greater purpose
than simply that of accommodating man: "it has its own great ends," Birkin tells
us, "man is not the criterion. Best leave it all to the vast, creative, non-human
mystery. Best strive with oneself only, not with the universe" (469).

But the struggle for self is not an easy one. In the process of evolution, the
mind and the senses have become disconnected, the intellectual and the sensual
have become separated, a separation that modern man must reconnect. The
model for such a connection is that of the sensuous African woman, the primi-

tive goddess who often becomes a kind of icon in Lawrentian fiction: "She had thousands of years of purely sensual, purely unspiritual knowledge behind her. It must have been thousands of years since her race had died, mystically: that is, since the relation between the sense and the outspoken mind had broken" (245).

This division within mankind reflects a division within the realms of being: North and South, warm and cold become two allotropic divided realms, and have different moral states of mind connected to them. Northern man is cold and mechanical and has lost contact with his warmer, southern self (embodied by the African goddess). Gudrun and Gerald are connected with the snow. At the end of the novel, Gudrun wants to disappear into the snow, "to climb the wall of white finality," the desire for which is inseparable from death, "the oneness with all . . . the eternal, infinite silence, the sleeping timeless, frozen centre of ALL" (400). This is the realm to which Gerald gives himself.

Just as two forces (the desire for love and power) work within man, two forces work within nature (the force of life and the force of death). The man or woman of mechanical, purely intellectual power draws from the force of death. Gerald cannot escape from his purely industrialized, mechanical world; Loerke, the futuristic artist who suggests Marinetti, embodies a newer version of the same destructive process, and it is to this aspect of him that Gudrun seems drawn. A kind of destructiveness—an apocalyptic urge, an urge to control and dominate—leads all of these people to a metaphorical or a literal death.

Thus, while struggle in Lawrence's fiction is often within the self, it is never limited to that—and the few who find union in the other or in the universe are counterpointed by those who never get beyond struggle and a kind of cosmic death. At some point, the passions relevant to love are overtaken by the passions connected with power. At the end of *Women in Love,* Birkin tells Ursula that her love was not enough for him, that he needed the love of a man (Gerald) as well to sustain him in the larger realm of being. And in *The Plumed Serpent,* Don Carlos, whose primitive energy revitalizes, overpowers, and controls her, brings Kate to a sense of a vital self. Lawrence moves in this novel from this kind of power-in-love to the political power that Don Cipriano taps when he moves to control Mexico. In *Apocalypse,* a book Lawrence was working on near the end of his life, he generalizes on this dichotomy further. Christian religion, he insists, stems from two realities: love and death—that is, a sense of human communion and a sense of an ending, either of the self or the world. But the emotion of love, he claimed, is really subsumed to the emotion of power—and it is a desire to take life to its limits and beyond that ultimately gives the obsession with apocalypse its meaning.

In *Lady Chatterley's Lover,* Lawrence makes final use of many of these ideas. The novel is told against a sense of an ending. The world of the estate, the realm of an older industrial England—all seem to be coming to an end, especially as they are embodied in Sir Chatterley, whose crippled, sexless body and myopic social routine suggest a kind of death-in-life. Constance Chatterley is brought back to vital life by Oliver Mellors, the gamekeeper of the estate, a man whose physically weakened body still pulses with life. Constance and Mellors become outsiders in a conventional world that substitutes manners for sex, conventional thought for an inner consciousness, profit for the embodiment of success, and respectability for happiness. Lawrence does not see the process ending. As Loerke replaces Gerald, a new form of industrialism is replacing Sir Clifford Chatterley. Mrs. Bolton, his servant and purveyor of town gossip, points to more modern forms of industry as well as new processes that "get more money out of the chemical by-products of the coal." She also points to the end of the mines: "They say Tevershall's done, finished; only a question of a few more years, and it'll have to shut down."[8]

There is universal, natural, organic time in Lawrence—a kind of Bergsonian realm that is tapped through the unconscious mind; and then there is a mechanical, historical, clock time, accessed through intellect and logical relationship. The two realms are separate—embody separate states of mind and lead to separate states of being. Like Bergson, Lawrence was never sanguine about where historical time was going:

> This is history. One England blots out another. The mines had made the halls wealthy. Now they were blotting them out, as they have already blotted out cottages. The industrial England blots out the agricultural England. One meaning blots out another. The new England blots out the old England. And the continuity is not organic, but mechanical. (177)

Early in his career, Lawrence had given up on industrial England, which is why he literally went around the world looking for a place where senses and mind, organic and inorganic, sex and work could be brought into harmony. He was trying to find on earth a unity that he believed corresponded to the cosmic unity, the life or creative force that he shared with Bergson. The failure of this quest cannot minimize the urgency that he brought to it, or the sense of importance of Bergsonian reality that he shared with other moderns.[9]

IV

Virginia Woolf's novels peruse the meaning of time. Time in her fiction exists on two levels—the historical and the personal—and there is a constant attempt, always unsuccessful, to find a pattern at work on each level. Some of her fiction is told against the history of England, much against the story of personal lives; but neither national history nor personal lives change the seemingly disordered rush of time, often depicted as the random wash of the waves. The only reality contained within time is death: death is the end product of time, often directly sought, never to be escaped. Characters constantly search for the meaning of their life or that of others, a meaning, if there is one, that lies unfathomed in time, to be canceled by the only reality that can stop time, death itself.

While time is enigmatic, it does have texture. Each moment is weighted, but some moments have more weight than others. Woolf's time spots share some features with Joycean epiphanies and others with Bergsonian durée. While Woolf denied Bergson's influence, affinities connect them. At exactly the point in her career that Woolf's novels become time obsessed, Woolf's sister-in-law, Karin Stephen, wrote *The Misuse of Mind* (1924), one of the first commentaries on Bergson.[10] But even if we take Woolf at her word, we must nevertheless note an affinity of mind between the two. Whereas Woolf never consented to Bergson's claim that there was intelligence—a creative life force, an élan vital—at work in the unfolding of time, like Bergson she thought of time as a force beyond the power of the logical mind to know. Death is the end product of time, but perhaps there is more, an indwelling mystery that makes time the key puzzle of life itself. Thus, in the hope of finding an indwelling meaning and in her distinction between mechanical (moment to moment unfolding) and subjective time (duration), Woolf found common ground with Bergson, and together they extended the idea of time.

Perhaps the clearest insight into such narrative unfolding can be found in *Mrs. Dalloway* (1925), encompassing within a single day the activity of Clarissa Dalloway as she prepares for a dinner party that will bring together old and new friends. Her day is memory-centered as she ponders the meaning of her marriage, the problems of her daughter, and her love for a former suitor. The dinner party is a success, primarily because of Clarissa herself, who holds the group together by something ineffable—a mystery in her presence that, like time, can never be known, only intuited.

In contrast to Mrs. Dalloway's controlling presence is the foreboding appearance of Septimus Smith, a shell-shocked war veteran who contemplates, threatens, and then succeeds at committing suicide. Septimus embodies the reality of death that interrupts Mrs. Dalloway's own sense of time as mysterious unfolding. Mrs. Dalloway and Septimus Smith—two different embodiments of time: one embodies the mystery of ongoing life; the other the reality of death as the end of time. One infuses memory with consciousness, bringing past time into being; the other destroys consciousness, putting an end to time.

Another time-bound novel by Woolf is *To the Lighthouse* (1927), based on Woolf's childhood family vacations on the Isle of Skye in the Hebrides. The Mrs. Dalloway–figure in this novel is Mrs. Ramsay, who holds together her family, composed of her philosopher-husband and their eight children, besides being a central presence for Lily Briscoe, an artist. Once again, time is in flux. Lily unsuccessfully tries to arrest time with her painting.

The main event in the novel involves a boat trip to the lighthouse, which is an obvious symbol of grounded time, since it rises above the waves of the sea. The novel builds to the moment of the journey to the lighthouse, which comes significantly after Mrs. Ramsay has died. James, the youngest son, commands the boat that reaches the lighthouse and wins praise from his otherwise demanding and usually caustic father. The lighthouse and its island become a fixed moment in the sea of life (that is, in time), something to be remembered, a time spot, or what Bergson would call durée. The lighthouse actually takes the place of Mrs. Ramsay; its presence, like her presence, holds the family together, at least temporarily, until the flux of time, like the sea, regains supremacy.

Both *Mrs. Dalloway* and *To the Lighthouse* are modernist novels that bring consciousness and inward meaning to a realistic moment of time. Woolf's *Orlando* (1928) takes us to a different order of fiction. *Orlando,* like so much of Woolf's fiction, functions on two narrative tracks—historical and personal. The historical track takes us from 1588 to the modern metropolis of London in 1928. We visit the realms of King James, King Charles, Queen Anne, and Queen Victoria. The novel begins at a country estate with the arrival by carriage of Queen Elizabeth and ends at the same country estate, now with an airport to accommodate a descending airplane. Against this panorama of events is the story of Orlando, who begins as a young man, changes sex halfway through the novel, and ends as a young woman. In her new embodiment, she visits the court of Queen Anne and participates in the intellectual life that brings her to Addison, Dryden, and Pope. Once in the twentieth century, Orlando marries, and the rest of the novel involves her memories as she searches unsuccessfully for some pattern in her life, now in its extended nature the working of history. That no conclusions emerge emphasize once again Woolf's belief that no meaning is concealed in the flux of time to be intuited or known: time is simply change rather than a flow of cosmic meaning. If there is a meaning to be abstracted from time, it is that while states of mind change from generation to generation, humanity remains much the same.

Another experimental novel by Woolf is *The Waves* (1931), involving six characters whose dramatic monologues pull up from memory their life from childhood to old age and impending death. Their stories are told against a rising and setting sun that parallels their age at the time that they are telling their story. The characters are identified by occupation/avocation or personality type: Bernard is a poet, Neville a scholar, Louis a banker; Jinny, on the other hand, is seen as a hedonist, Rhoda as a depressive, and Susan as a lover of the pastoral life. The presence in the novel that unites them (there is almost always a uniting presence in a Woolf novel) is Percival, who stands for the spirit of England and who dies in India. His death and the suicide of Rhoda cut the circuitry of time. At the end, Bernard struggles to find meaning in their unfolding lives; but, as with Orlando, he finds no pattern beyond individual significance, only the reality of the death symbolized by the waves breaking on a dark shore that awaits them all.

The Years (1937) is Woolf's attempt to rewrite the generational novels like Mann's *Buddenbrooks* and Galsworthy's *Forsyte Saga*. The story involves the Pargiter family seen through several generations. The family is made up of a retired army colonel; his wife, who is dying of cancer; and their three sons and four daughters. While the traditional generational novel depicts the unfolding of events, Woolf's novel is composed mainly of memories that the principal characters retrieve from consciousness. Woolf's novels demand a subjectivity that can hold together the unfolding of time. The oldest daughter, Eleanor, who has become the family caretaker, also becomes the one fixed presence against whom this span of time is measured. She is the Mrs. Dalloway–Mrs. Ramsay–Percival–Orlando figure, aware of each generation as they come and go.

Unlike the traditional generational novel that involves the decline of family fortunes, the Pargiters start off rather shabbily and remain essentially middle class. As the younger generation moves into the professions, marry, and raise their own children, the older generation gets fatter and feebler. As the two generations confront each other, Eleanor asks the residual Woolfian question: is there a pattern, a meaning, behind these lives? Once again, the answer appears to be no.

This conclusion comes symbolically as Eleanor looks out the sun-filled window and sees a couple who have emerged from a taxi, opening a house door with a latchkey, suggesting a possible assignation similar to the affair the Colonel had with his mistress. There appears to be no hidden meaning to life, only random repetition and the change of fashions. One generation repeats the events of the previous generation, including their illicit pursuits; a new day arrives, and life goes on with the flow of time.

Woolf's last novel is *Between the Acts* (1941). As in *Orlando,* the lives of the characters that make up the novel are counterpointed against the history of England. The novel takes its being from the Poinz Hall estate, owned by Bartholomew Oliver and inhabited by his widowed sister, Mrs. Swithin, his son, Giles, and Giles's wife, Isa. The historical element is brought into the novel by Mrs. Swithin's obsession with H. G. Wells's *Outline of History* and by a pageant involving the history of England, written and produced by a Miss La Trobe, a local personality. The pageant covers the historical events of Chaucer's England, beyond to that of Queen Elizabeth, up to the Victorians.

The suggestion is that each of these ages is like the present, except for the dress and other matters of fashion: fashions change while humanity remains much the same. At novel's end, Giles and Isa, whose marriage is at best tenuous, quarrel, make up, and then sleep. Their lives extend the triviality of the past to which they try to bring some profound meaning. Once again, Woolf's novel ends with characters hoping to give some substance to human existence in the face of death.

There was no spokesperson of modernity more critical of the old realism than Virginia Woolf. She was particularly hard on the Arnold Bennett–like novels of saturation, told chronologically, covering generational life rather than the highlights of time. In her essay "Mr. Bennett and Mrs. Brown," she makes the famous statement that "on or about December, 1910, human character changed" (an idea that seemingly contradicts the conclusions of her novels). This was the date that the Edwardian period gave way to the Georgian period. The Edwardians—made up of Arnold Bennett, H. G. Wells, and John Galsworthy—depicted character from the outside, working the realist's conventions of the novel. A character like Mrs. Brown was defined by the kind of house she lived in, the occupation of her husband, the working conditions of his shop, the wages of his employees, the health of her mother, the fate of her children, everything except an inner reality. What Woolf wanted was a state of mind and a specificity of personal detail that defined Mrs. Brown, made her a unique product of life. Her own fiction shifted emphasis away from the physical event, making it essentially either a part of history or of memory, transforming it from physical to mental reality. Like the vitalists, she transformed time-bound reality by allowing it to be changed by the mind.

5 ❖ DECADENCE/AESTHETICISM

I

In France, the reaction to naturalism was called decadence; in England, aestheticism. Both movements were eventually seen as forms of symbolism. All of these terms are twentieth-century constructs of nineteenth-century literary movements; eventually they lost their separate distinctions and were combined into the idea of modernism.

Decadence is both opposed to Romanticism at the same time that it is an extension of Romanticism. It is an aesthetic—that is, literary—way of looking at social depravity. Metaphorically, it can be compared to rotten fruit. The suggestion is that society has taken on the reality of an overripe pear. Decadence foreshadows the idea of degeneration and entropy and anticipates the grotesque. Decadence has to do with the inversion of the creative process, the grotesque with the inversion of nature.

In England, Walter Pater (1839–1894) gave meaning to the idea of decadence. In his conclusion to *Studies in the History of the Renaissance* (1873), he speaks of modernism as a self-fashioning in pursuit of sensations and impressions rather than abstractions: "To burn always with a hard, gemlike flame, to maintain this ecstasy is success in life." His *Marius the Epicurean* (1885) cultivates the pleasures of the mind and spirit. Nineteenth-century British inquiries lie beneath Marius's Roman exterior, and second-century AD Rome conceals the imposition of reference to the late-Victorian British empire. Pater sees a similar kind of superimposition, a layering of memory, in Leonardo's *Mona Lisa*.

Oscar Wilde (1854–1900) continued the connection between French decadence and English aestheticism by modeling *Dorian Gray* (1891) upon *À rebours* (1884) by Joris-Karl Huysmans (1848–1907). Wilde wrote about the city in the "Decay of Lying": "Where if not from the Impressionists, do we get those wonderful brown fogs that come creeping down our streets, blurring the gas-lamps and changing the houses into monstrous shadows?" Wilde's remarks are particularly apt to Joyce's recording Stephen Dedalus's impressions of the city: as Stephen walks through Dublin every place becomes an aesthetic object or text; his impressions are controlled by his sense of art and beauty. Such symbolic thinking takes us to Arthur Symons's *The Symbolist Movement in Literature* (1899), which discussed the French poets' influence upon English poetry. This book had an immense influence on T. S. Eliot, who read it in 1908 when he was at Harvard and through it discovered Verlaine and Corbière.

Before modernism replaced Romanticism, it had to go through the decadent/aesthetic and symbolist experiences: the first created a physical presence so unpleasant that it turned the aesthetic vision inward to escape reality; the second moved to a private, closed mind, shutting out the hostile urban, commercial/industrial world. Under such pressure, the city as a physical place gave way to the city as a state of mind. This process had been long in the making. In England, Hazlitt had shown that Wordsworth's poetry was founded upon an opposition between the natural and the artificial, between the human element and the realm of fashion.

Baudelaire's poetry also worked within the realms of innocence and experience. Throughout was a sense of the fall, a fall that antedated history and consciousness and was comparable to original sin. Such a fall can be understood through art, since it is the artist who "recreates rather than discovers nature."[1] The literary difference between innocence and experience involves the difference between sentiment and sensibility. The move from sentiment to sensibility took Baudelaire close to the Flaubert of *L'éducation sentimentale*, where we move beyond what is natural to what is socially conditioned. The resulting realm of artifice helps explain the self-conscious aspects of *Les fleurs du mal*.

Baudelaire and Eliot were among the few modernists who believed that the industrial city no longer encouraged imaginative coherence. Despite differences in the origin and the substance of their thought, they arrived at conclusions shared by Marx. They all believed that urban disconnection was a by-product of a system of profit and loss; both Baudelaire and Eliot rejected material progress because it led to a cycle of desire, doomed to endless escalation. The city was nature inverted, transformed by the commercial powers of industry (i.e., invested capital).

Thus both Baudelaire and Eliot saw modern man caught in an essentially self-enclosed urban process: the commercial/industrial city became the modern equivalent of Dante's Inferno. Salvation depended upon breaking the circle of materialism. Baudelaire took us to the dandy, and the dandy was the link that connected aestheticism with Nietzsche's overman. Baudelaire believed one could do this by transforming the self as if it were art. T. S. Eliot saw Christ, not the dandy, as the means of escaping material desire. The battle between good and evil turned on a belief in God and Devil. In both cases, nihilism took us one step further and emptied each value system. As a result, we were constantly redefining ourselves against the void. The self as defined against the void is one way of looking at literary modernism; the self as defined against the workings of a mass culture is another. In reality, both concerns are often one and the same.

Arnold Hauser believed aestheticism and impressionism were the axles on which naturalism turned into modernism. Aestheticism, he says, brought impressionism into being and "represents the logical development of naturalism [with its] progress from the general to the particular, from typical to the individual, from abstract idea to concrete, temporally and spatially conditioned experienced. . . . [T]he impressionistic reproduction of reality, with its emphasis upon the instantaneous and the unique, is an important achievement of naturalism."[2] Impressionism, Hauser contends, is primarily the by-product of modern urbanism, the artistic experiment with the city that goes back to Manet:

> At first sight, it may seem surprising that the metropolis, with its herding together and intermingling of people, should produce this intimate art rooted in the feeling of individual singularity and solitude. But it is a familiar fact that nothing seems so isolating as the close proximity of too many people, and nowhere does one feel so lonely and forsaken as in a great crowd of strangers.[3]

Decadence assumed that civilization was exhausted and running down. The drift of nature was toward chaos. Entropy played into the decadent movement. Entropy involves the transition from the systematic to the random, leading to a disordered future. The decadents—and those who followed them—were wary of the future and looked back to an idealized time before the process of decline set in. Aestheticism was an essential part of "the inward turn," the movement of modernism away from physical reality toward subjectivity. As Hauser claimed, the city became the place where engaged artists experienced acute isolation from ordinary people, even as they mingled with the crowd.

Whereas naturalism emphasized the degenerative effects of heredity and environment, modernism softened this unpleasant condition by substituting the quest for the beautiful as the end of art. The movement from primitivism to civilization turned upon a redeeming sense of the beautiful. Alone in the crowd, the artist was subject to urban impressions, a phenomenon already a part of impressionistic art. From the railroad terminal with it rain-glazed lights blinking colorfully in the darkness to the delicate china and silverware to be found on the dinner table, the beautiful was on open display if only one knew how to look. "Perspectivism," the way reality was perceived, was inseparable from the idea of the beautiful.

One's view of reality was infused with ideology. Pound and Eliot felt less comfortable in the crowd, amid the walking dead, than did Baudelaire. But a desire for distance led Baudelaire to explore new poetic possibilities for treating the huge modern metropolis. Most important in this was nostalgia for a spiritual homeland or city that existed beyond the visible world, which explains his obsession with Poe. Such nostalgia accompanied a sense of decay and decline, a Dusk of the Gods, a Dusk of nations "in which all suns and all stars are gradually waning, and mankind with all its institutions and creations is in the midst of a dying world."[4] When this sense of decline was internalized, it led to an impression so strong that it often dominated the way the reality was perceived. Out of this disdain for common experience came the modernists' sense of hierarchy—the willingness to separate themselves from the crowd even to the extent of creating a social elite and approving reactionary forms of power.

II

Wallace Stevens's career took its direction from the tenets of aestheticism. The formative period for this concern came when he was a student at Harvard, which at the turn of the century was the center for such matters in America. Stevens's father, Garret Stevens, was a successful Pennsylvania lawyer, a practical man who took seriously Benjamin Franklin–like resolves. At Harvard, Stevens came under the influence of George Santayana, who carried on the quest of Walter Pater for the beautiful. Stevens's task was to reconcile these two father figures, and he devoted himself to bridging the practical and the beautiful—becoming a successful lawyer while at the same time writing poetry. The challenge involved balancing truth and beauty, reconciling art and life. The pure aesthete would have chosen beauty and art, but Stevens, critical of Pater's passivity, chose beauty and life: his primary concern was to reconcile the beautiful with reality. He was less concerned with justifying art for its own sake than with justifying art by its capacity to enlarge life.[5]

woman questions Christ's divinity: a divinity of "the blood and
divinity that "can come / Only in silent shadows and in dreams."
see that if paradise is reduced to the earth, "The sky will be much
than now"; the earth and sky will become one, the sky no longer a
indifferent blue." Death will no longer be the basis for supernatural
"old chimera of the grave") but will be the basis for the beautiful
mother of beauty"). The beautiful takes its meaning from imper-
m the eclipse of time that gives substance to and makes the moment
temporality that endows "our perishing earth" with the redemptive
beautiful. From a religion based on death as the source of our physi-
and the need for a divine redeemer, we move to the "first idea" of
e source of the beautiful and the need for it as an earthly redeemer.[7]
many modern poets, Stevens saw the need for an indwelling god
ling within the beautiful) rather than a transcendental deity. Stevens's
icipates that of Heraclitus. But instead of physical flux, his thoughts
ns, ideas, and impressions pass through the mind to be concretized
inant presence.[8] He spoke of this search for identity in terms of Pica-
ng many selves: "all of them go back into one of them within him that
tes and makes the design."[9] Stevens's early poetry is a world of changing
exercises in perspective. In "Carlos among the Candles" (1917), a room
s atmosphere each time a candle is lighted. One's identity varies accord-
one's surroundings: reality is determined by a sense of place, a theme he
ains in "The Comedian as the Letter C." Crispin becomes a different poet
moves from Bordeaux, to Yucatan, to the Carolinas.

order to bridge the commercial and artistic realms, Stevens created a
s of poetic masks, anticipating the impersonal poetry that Eliot described
Tradition and the Individual Talent" (1919). Among those masks are the
gher, the fop, and the dandy. He also created a scheme of symbolic meaning:
rs not only flow (or not flow) to the sea, but they suggest Heraclitus's flux.
e color green, along with the sun, embodies the workings of nature; blue,
ng with the moon, the imagination. The drift, however, is downward, and
evens's poetry takes on forms of disintegration. What holds it together, despite
servations about the passivity of aestheticism, are his masks of the aesthete and
andy, which dominate the poetry of *Harmonium*.

In *The Man with a Blue Guitar*, Stevens tried to reconcile aestheticism and
eality by suggesting that the imagination transformed what the mind knows.
The poem works through a series of fixed symbols: nature (green), imagination

When he left Harvard in 1901, S
in the belief that journalism would
literature and life. He took as his m
(1864–1916), who had distinguished
American War (1898), especially the
Rough Riders. The war, which had attr
marily the creation of the press, notably
bought in 1895 by William Randolph He
a circulation war with Joseph Pulitzer's *Ne*
the mundane routine of city reporting cou
and glamour of war. He resigned from the
assistant editor on the *World's Work,* a month

Disillusioned with both the work and the
doned journalism. He enrolled in New York U
in 1903, passed the bar exam in 1904, and beca
accepting a position with the Hartford Accide
1916, where he became executive vice president i
he could compartmentalize the commercial and
commercial contracts by day and poetry about the
His major books of poetry include *Harmonium* (1
Owl's Clover (1936), *The Man with the Blue Guitar* (19
including *Notes toward a Supreme Fiction* (1942), *Esthé*
port to Summer (1947), and *The Auroras of Autumn* (19
(1951) is a volume of essays. His poems were collecte
posthumous edition in 1957. Stevens never outgrew his i
aestheticism of his Harvard years, and he wrote poetry a
imagination's search for the beautiful in the realm of phys

His poetry built upon a number of philosophical assu
rest was his belief in the First Idea, which he thought of in
you take the varnish and dirt of generations off a picture, y
idea. If you think about the world without its varnish and dir
of the first idea."[6] The First Idea is an originary view, a starti
gets built upon it. The First Idea strips away a residue of meani
distracting revisions that have been transformed by new preo
idea is consistent with the thesis of this book: the belief that li
continuously transformed and lose their originary meaning.)

His poem "Sunday Morning" (1915) is an exercise in the

contemplative
sepulcher"—a
She comes to
friendlier the
"dividing and
concern (the
("death is th
manence, fr
precious, th
power of th
cal ending
death as th
Like s
(god dwe
world an
of passi
by a do
sso havi
domina
reality,
chang
ing to
enter
as he
I
serie
in "
bur
riv
Th
al
St
re
d

(blue), reality (sun), light (the transforming power of the imagination). The moon and the guitar change reality, allowing us to see in a different way. "A candle [imagination] is enough to light the world. . . . At night, it lights the fruit and wine / The book and bread, things as they are." Picasso gives us a "picture of ourselves," allows us to see in a new dimension. Poetry is the subject of the poem: from its creation we can abstract a residual absence or a universal revelation. The struggle is between imagination and reality: the guitar cannot "play things as they are" because "Things as they are / Are changed upon the blue guitar." The known (commonplace) of the mind is transformed by the surprises the imagination unfolds. The imagination illuminates reality. Out of it comes the "first idea"—a new way of seeing: "The blue guitar surprises you."[10]

For Stevens, the imagination is the bridge between the chaos of nature and the order of the mind. When the modern seeker gets too close to the reality of chaos, the imagination comes into play and creates a buffer reality that shuts out the void and encourages religion or what might serve as its substitute. As Stevens himself put it, "I ought to say that it is a habit of mind with me to be thinking of some substitute for religion. . . . My trouble, and the trouble of a great many people, is the loss of belief in the sort of God in whom we are all brought up to believe."[11] It is the imagination and what it creates that bridge the difference between traditional religion and the void, fill the cosmic hole and rescue us from the darkness.

Stevens treats this theme again in "The Idea of Order at Key West." The poem begins with a woman singing by the sea. She sings "beyond the genius" of the sea, because the song is not the sea, not even a mask of the sea. The song is distinct from the sea: "it was she and not the sea we heard"; but the song gives meaning to the sea, reconciles it with reality, and endows chaos with order. This transforming process allows the sea to become her song. When the song ends, the poet's world is now embellished in ways that it was not before the song. The lights from the fishing boats on the edge of town are now brighter. Poetry enlightens reality, a phenomenon the poet cannot explain even as he turns to Ramon Fernandez (a French aestheticist whose major work involved theories of meaning through form) for the answer that never comes: the process enshrouds mystery.

In the thirties, Stevens moved briefly from a personal to a communal (mass) form of poetry. He followed a thirties debate between Joseph Wood Krutch and Philip Rahv; Krutch was writing for the *Nation*, Rahv for the *Partisan Review*. Krutch argued that poetry makes life tolerable, allowing us to accept "things as they are." Rahv responded that such aestheticism wiped out the particular historical context, that the masses needed to revolt against "things as they are," not

accept them. Stevens entered the debate himself with his *Owl's Clover.* Responding to an attack on *Ideas of Order* by Stanley Burnshaw, Stevens tried to defend
his aestheticism against the Marxist charges. He argued that political order was
constantly changing, but behind it was sublimity, a sense of the marvelous, that
Marxist thought could not destroy.[12]

Stevens was more interested in aesthetics than politics, and his theory of aesthetics is most clearly outlined in his *Notes toward a Supreme Fiction.* We begin,
he tells us, with the need to turn reality as an abstraction into reality concrete
enough to reveal the first idea. The means for such transference is the poem:

> The poem refreshes life so that we share
> For a moment, the first idea. . . . It satisfies
> Belief in an immaculate beginning.[13]

We know the general (abstract) through the particular and the particular
through poetry, which gives chaos the semblance of order. Poetry supplies a
"blooded" abstraction: the abstract (arrived at by analytic reason) is transformed
by the creative imagination. Such transformation involves change, which
is inseparable from reality and which has its origins in opposites (day/night,
summer/winter, man/woman, imagined/real, music/silence, North/South, sun/
rain, morning/afternoon). Brought to an understanding of the particular, we
take pleasure in reality. Stevens concludes his poem with an idea that is shared
by a number of modernists, including Gertrude Stein: it is this "vast repetition"
that makes for Supreme Fiction. Reality comes down to a general structure of
unfolding particulars. Forms of meaning, including the origin of the beautiful,
involve repetition and constant flux, occur as a matter of process, of becoming
rather than being, creating a continuous present.

After explaining the source of what was "good" in reality, the next step in Stevens's thinking involved explaining what was "bad"—or the origins of "evil." This
he did in *Esthétique du mal.* If *Supreme Fiction* is at the source of pleasure, it also
at the source of pain. To accept reality is to accept both pleasure and pain, good
and evil. Like good, evil is also known through the poetic process, shaped by the
imagination. Stevens's aesthetic vision takes on qualities of existential phenomenology. Like Jean-Paul Sartre, he suggests that the mind/imagination (pour soi)
gives meaning to reality (en soi). This in essence is what *Esthétique du mal* tells
us. The poem's speaker is in Naples, where he realizes that its human thought

that keeps human tragedy alive—that the eruption of Vesuvius with its cata-
strophic human toll would mean nothing disconnected from human awareness:

> Except for us, Vesuvius might consume
> In solid fire the utmost earth and know
> No pain. . . .
> . . . This is a part of the sublime
> From which we shrink and yet, except for us,
> The total past felt nothing when destroyed.[14]

Stevens wrote philosophical poetry based on this aesthetic theory. He believed
that at the center of reality (life as it is lived externally) is an aesthetic process
that is the source of chaos and order, degeneration and the sublime. This process is the barrier reef that saves us from all-consuming doubt, from the dark
void of nihilism. His major assumptions go back to Pater, then beyond Pater to
Baudelaire's engagement with good and evil, and then beyond Baudelaire to the
Romantic idea of the imagination, with its visionary claim and ability to reclaim.
Stevens's aestheticism, like all aestheticism, exalts poetry. For poetry to supply
the Supreme Fiction, to engender the beautiful, the poet must be endowed with
knowledge and ability that the rest of us lack—must be a genius, truly gifted, if not
inspired. The poet becomes the high priest of culture, and poetry becomes a substitute for religion. These are the assumptions that allowed the modernists (or at
least the aesthetes among the modernists) to privilege their work in elitist ways.

III

A poet/novelist who questioned the aesthetic assumptions of modernism even
more than Wallace Stevens was Vladimir Nabokov, whose most celebrated work
was *Lolita* (1957). *Lolita* can be read in a number of ways. The most literal reading
would simply involve Humbert Humbert as pedophile, a seducer of young girls.
A more idealized reading would see him as a character desiring to find a form of
pure innocence or perhaps regain a lost innocence. Humbert's first love, whom
he met on the Mediterranean, was Annabel Leigh, suggesting Poe's theme of lost
love. The loss of this ideal has its cognates in the novel—in, for example, Nabokov's desire to find in America the innocence that was taken from him in Europe, or
Humbert's desire to find in America the innocence that was lost in a material past.

A more aesthetic reading would see Humbert desiring to merge with the permanently beautiful: Lolita as a romantic object of beauty arrested in time. This reading would make the novel a narrative version of Keats's "Ode on a Grecian Urn," the desire for beauty as a permanent state of being:

> Ah, happy, happy boughs! That cannot shed
> Your leaves, nor ever bid the spring adieu
> And, happy melodist, unwearied,
> Forever piping songs forever new;
> More happy love! More happy, happy love!
> Forever warm and still to be enjoy'd
> Forever panting and forever young . . . .
>
> When old age shall this generation waste
> Thou shall remain, in midst of other woe
> Than ours, a friend to man, to whom thou say'st
> "Beauty is truth, truth beauty. . . ."

Lolita can be read as a search for such romantic beauty. As nymph, Lolita becomes the ideal, the beautiful, the perfect desire—all that an artist would strive to attain. Nabokov's *Lolita* shares a sexual content with Mann's "Death in Venice." Both Humbert and Aschenbach find the embodiment of the beautiful in the handsome person of a pre-adolescent child. Both works owe their being (and meaning) to the Romantic tradition of aestheticism. To be more precise, Humbert's moral decadence seems to have its source in literary decadence. When Humbert describes the source of his passion for nymphets, he refers, as we have seen, to Poe's Annabel Lee. The reference to Poe anticipates Humbert's recall of an array of symbolist and decadent French and British poets like Rossetti, Swinburne, Wilde, Beardsley, and Baudelaire. Like Wilde's *The Picture of Dorian Gray*, Lolita is a study in the difference between immorality in life and immortality in art. Humbert wants to immortalize Lolita by arresting time, allowing beauty to subdue morality, realizing in art what he fails to realize in life, an immortality that he and Lolita now share.

Nabokov has given us a complex text and put a number of interpretations at our disposal. Despite the multiple interpretations, one cannot help but consider the novel as also a form of parody. Just how "real" is Lolita as the embodiment of beauty and innocence, as the equivalent of Keats's tableau on the Grecian urn? Lolita proves far from being an object of innocence: she loses her virginity at summer camp at the age of twelve; she seduces Humbert, not vice versa. Her nymphet beauty disappears with time: Lolita is twelve when Humbert meets her, seventeen when they finally part. When last we see her, she is a young woman, now heavy with child, no longer the nymphet, and no more the Romantic embodiment of absolute beauty.

Nabokov is ridiculing Romantic aestheticism, the belief that an idealized beauty can be arrested and made permanent. Humbert's search for beauty is infused with the ugliness of America: Appalachian poverty, industrial landscapes, neon-lighted motels, and cheap roadside diners. The novel suggests that all reality, both beautiful and ugly, functions within limits: that some larger, restraining force is at work. Whatever one's interpretation of this novel, there would be no novel if it had not been written within, or against, the tradition of Romantic aestheticism. Nabokov clearly believes that one cannot perpetuate an idealized past or sustain a Romantic idea of time and beauty against physical reality. *Lolita* parodies the aesthetics of modernism, the second stage of Romanticism. Lolita becomes a caricature of Romantic assumptions: her beauty keeps changing, transformed by time, until the beautiful is proved too fleeting to exist in absolute terms.

But Nabokov's interest in aesthetic ideas does not stop with Humbert and Lolita. He extends this theme in the character of Clare Quilty. The name suggests the words "clearly guilty": he is a second, darker self. Humbert realizes that he has robbed Lolita of her childhood, and in Dostoyevsky fashion he kills off the debased side of his nature. Clare Quilty is a surreal projection of Humbert's guilt: Quilty is a product of his own imagination, working another aesthetic theme to suggest the disparity between art and life. Humbert kills off Quilty, whose imaginative hold on Lolita competes with his own. Humbert must not only compete against physical reality and its threat to absolute beauty, but he must compete against the realm of art that celebrates such beauty, must kill off competing versions of his imagination. Quilty has written a play, *The Enchanted Hunters*, while staying at the Enchanted Hunters hotel, where Humbert has taken Lolita their first night. In the tradition of Oscar Wilde, he argues that life imitates art, that the play orders life. Nabokov refers us to stock literary reality in order to turn his narrative into a Romantic cliché. Humbert triumphs over Quilty the artist by writing his own version of the Lolita story: his own art will triumph over his discordant life and Quilty's version of it. Between life (raw experience) and art (ordered experience) intrudes the passing of time. There may be a pattern built into Humbert's experience of which he is unaware. Writing the novel is his attempt to impose a pattern on time. But the pattern built into time is not identical with that of Humbert's novel. On final analysis, art and life go their different ways, as do Humbert and Lolita at the end of the novel.

Pale Fire (1962) gives us another version of the aesthetic quest. The novel is composed of four elements. There is a foreword by Charles Kinbote, the self-claimed, exiled king of Zembla, who is writing a commentary on a 999-line poem by John Shade. Then there is the poem itself, four cantos, the last line completed by the first line, the poem literally coming full circle. The third component of the work is the commentary itself. This is followed by a glossary of terms and an index of the principal characters. As with *Lolita,* the whole unfolding is a spoof on the relationship between art and reality. The text and the commentary go in two different directions. Instead of illuminating Shade's poem, which is primarily about the death of his daughter, Hazel, the commentary is an extended consideration of Kinbote's exile from Zembla and the pursuit of a hit man, Gradus, who has come to kill him and seemingly killed Shade by mistake.

The work combines two subject matters: there is first an aesthetic concern, dealing with the meaning of the beautiful in the face of death (as in Stevens, "death is the mother of beauty"); and second, there is a political concern, dealing with the displacement that comes with exile. The work begins to take on layers of meaning relevant to Nabokov's past. The appearance of a Russian émigré named Botkin adds complexity to complexity, suggesting that all the elements that make up the story—Kinbote, Zembla, Charles II, Gradus, Shade, the poem—are products of V. Botkin's mind (as indeed they are the products of V. Nabokov's mind).

Each layer of meaning has its own reality: the real and the fictitious, the individual and collective consciousness are hopelessly entwined. For Nabokov reality is too complex, too layered in time, too much the product of our own consciousness, too dependent on the slippage of language, to be known fully. We create our own reality, as Kinbote creates a reality separate from Shade's poem. The aesthetic process involves a quest for the beautiful both in the face of death, the temporality of which gives meaning to beauty, and as a product of a fake reality, the sublimity of which conceals the real. Nabokov's method precludes closure: each link takes the reader deeper into an open-ended chain of events. As with Thomas Pynchon's *The Crying of Lot 49* (Pynchon was Nabokov's student at Cornell), each clue that Oedipa Maas finds simply takes her to the next clue, never to a conclusion. Both Nabokov and Pynchon take us into postmodern reality, into the realm of the indeterminate play involved in physical reality, consciousness, and language—and away from aestheticism.

III
THE REALMS OF THE TEXT

6 ✦ MYTH

Modernism became a distinct literary movement through its special uses of myth, symbolism, and structural thought, which combined with a belief in the cyclicality of time to produce the new narrative technique that became known as spatial form. The uses of these methods transformed both the old realism and literary naturalism; modernism was transformed in turn when the forces of postmodernism, especially the assumptions of poststructuralism and mass culture, brought modernist assumptions into question.

I

Myth had its origins in two sources: nature and human consciousness. Myth is often connected with forms of primitivism because it leads to fundamental (i.e., elemental) explanations of how the universe works. And myth is connected with consciousness on the grounds that it leaves an instinctual residue on human thought. Joseph Campbell describes newly hatched chickens that run for cover when a hawk flies by, even as they are indifferent to the flight of other birds. There seems to be an indwelling fear that alerts the chickens to the threat of hawks. Myth critics argue for the same kind of indwelling meaning in the human mind.

Myth functioned closely in conjunction with religion and offered explanations of cosmic matters. The major myths originated in preliterate societies and were disseminated orally. Primitive people brought the universe to life by endowing its properties with symbolic meaning. In its genesis, myth dealt with supernatural events and gods; legends and saga dealt with more human events. But myths eventually became anthropomorphized. Sir James Frazer in *The Golden Bough* (1890) connected myth with fertility in nature. The mythic meaning of vegetative gods like Demeter and Dionysus, for example, had their origins in the spring and fall equinox and marked the planting and harvesting of the crop, thus connecting the workings of the heavens with the fertility of the land. The well-being of the land became connected to the well-being of the king or tribal leader. The fate of heroes and gods became inextricably mixed as cult meetings examined the Eleusian mysteries of the decay-and-renewal legend involving Demeter, Persephone, and Dionysus, and the Orphic mysteries involved the relationship of Dionysus Zagreus to his father, Zeus. Eventually the stories of royal families usurped legends of the gods: the history of Agamemnon was a family affair, inseparable from the fate of also Menelaus, Clytemnestra, Orestes, and Electra.

Under the influence of the old historicism, the idea of myth was culturally specific: a common use of myth by two different cultures presumed that one culture had influenced the other. But when myths became homologous (similar in structure), they supposedly originated in a shared state of mind or described the same function and thus had no need for causal connection. People from different cultures—for example, the Aztecs and the Mayans—could employ mythic analogues without one culture's myths having transformed the other. Myth was now a matter of archetypal meaning and of shared consciousness. As a product of mind, myth criticism laid the foundation for structuralist criticism: structuralists could think of social concerns as a network of interrelated elements as in a language system, homologous rather than causal in nature.

There seems to be universal meaning connected with major mythic symbols: the sun embodies energy; the moon, imagination (it takes its light from the sun); water, purity; the sea, new life; rivers, the flow of eternal time; garden, paradise; snake, evil; tree, the universe. Colors take on meaning: red, passion; green, hope; blue, spirituality; white, purity; black, death. The hero partakes of mythic experience: the initiation, quest, and sacrifice.

Inherent in all myth are essential elements that take their meaning from human activity. This form of myth usually begins with a violation of the word of God, or with a crime that violates the spirituality of the land, or with the fracturing of a sacred ritual. In each case, an initial harmony is broken (the abduction of Helen provokes hostility between tribes and justifies the need for war; or an Original Sin takes place in a garden of lost innocence; or gold is stolen from the Rhine maidens). These crimes call for the redeeming activity of an avenger or savior (Agamemnon, Christ, Siegfried) who challenges the source of evil (Paris of Troy, the Serpent, Alberich). The antagonist is usually dehumanized, the product of a reckless use of power, often embodying what is inverted or grotesque in nature. The heroic test involves a feat of courage (as Agamemnon demonstrates when he comes to the aid of his younger brother, Menelaus); or a matter of revenge (as Achilles demonstrates when he kills Hector, revenging the death of Patroclus, before he is killed in turn by Paris, revenging the death of Hector); or the righting of a wrong (as when Orestes rights the death of his father, Agamemnon). The acrimony between the participants leads to internecine hostility as when Creon, the uncle of Oedipus, helps Eteocles, son of Oedipus, wrest power by killing Eteocles' brother, Polynices, then denies Polynices proper funeral rites, burying Antigone alive when she defies him by burying her brother. Once the evil impediment is removed, the original order can be restored. In Greek myth, this involves a return to the community as the norm for a restored order; in Christian religion, to a realm of grace as a gift from God (necessary, except for Pelagians, for faith and good works, and conceptualized differently by Calvinists); and in Wagnerian opera the return is to a realm of natural harmony (i.e., a return to what preceded the disrupted order).

Wagner made varied use of these elements in his tetralogy *Der Ring des Nibelungen* (1853–74) in which nature is violated when the Rhine maidens' gold is stolen and "manufactured" into a ring. Wagner created a myth appropriate to that moment of history when an industrial system challenged the values of an agrarian culture. Before we return to lost agrarian innocence, we witness the combat and then the death of Siegmund at the hands of Hunding; Siegfried, his son, is killed later by Hagen. When the spirit of nature (the land) is violated, the mythic hero is needed to help restore (as does Siegfried) the lost balance.

Northrop Frye's theory of mimetic action offered another explanation of the use of myth in modernist literature. Frye believed that realism as a literary mode renewed the narrative cycle and encouraged the return of the mythic. The process was facilitated by Romantic irony, the belief that world meaning is paradoxical and that an ambivalent perspective alone can grasp its contradictory meaning. As Frye put it: "irony descends from the low mimetic: it begins in realism and dispassionate observation. But as it does so, it moves steadily toward myth, and dim outlines of sacrificial rituals and dying gods begin to reappear in it. . . . This reappearance of myth in the ironic is particularly clear in Kafka and Joyce."[1] Frye's argument explains why a number of critics have linked literary naturalism with more heightened narrative types like romance and gothic fiction, which are in turn often linked with each other.[2] Whether nature is confronted directly or in literary terms, myth presupposes that human action takes its origins from a larger realm of archetypal meaning.

II

Conrad, Mann, Joyce, Yeats, Pound, T. S. Eliot, Hart Crane, William Carlos Williams—all heightened their literary work with myth, which in turn endowed it with archetypal elements. Along with its literary application, a number of historical events facilitated the use of myth. Imperial activity kept the primitive sense of a mythic community alive. Archaeologists' finds like those of Schliemann made myth into a modern phenomenon. Works like Frazer's *The Golden Bough* made the ancient myths accessible to the modern imagination. And the plot of the modern romance, often connected to imperial adventure, supplied an equivalent element, transformed the classical version into a popular mode and helped sustain the heightened action that characterized Greek tragedy. The plot of a Rider Haggard romance looks back to a past replete with mythic truths and forward toward cosmic understanding; the plot of a Thomas Pynchon romance looks back to an unfathomable past or forward toward an apocalyptic future.

Primitivism is an important modernist theme and involves an attitude toward nature that subordinates technology and the machine to an elemental realm. Lawrence's *The Plumed Serpent* (1926) involves a quest to find mythic meaning embodied in the ancient Mexican god Quetzalcoatl, whose atavistic and mystical nature has restorative power. Faulkner's "The Bear" is a serpent-in-the-garden study of lost innocence, of what is diminished when nature is turned back on itself. And while Hemingway seldom takes us directly to the mythic situation, his code heroes are sensitive to ritual as a residue of myth, as they define themselves in an enlarged arena, whether it is the bullring or the marlin- and shark-laden sea. Myth and ritual have long taken their being from natural combat.

III

The interest in myth was encouraged by the work in other disciplines, especially anthropology and archaeology. Although an amateur archaeologist, Heinrich Schliemann was instrumental in sustaining interest in ancient culture, especially the history of Troy. Schliemann was born in Neubukow, Germany, the son of a Protestant minister. From childhood, the epics of Homer, especially the *Iliad*, the story of King Menelaus and his ten-year war against Troy, fascinated him.

Schliemann was a very successful businessman: he made a fortune in the export/import business and then added to that fortune when he struck gold in California. Now able to finance an expedition, he visited the islands of Ithaca and Mycenae, the homes of Odysseus and Agamemnon (where he would later successfully dig) before he crossed the sea to Turkey in search of the city of Troy. Using the *Iliad* as his geographical guide, he settled on a hill near the village of Hissarlik as the location of Troy. Excavations started in 1871, at which time Schliemann unearthed eleven cities, each built upon another, the seventh city satisfying him that it was the city of Homer's Troy.

Both the modernist novel and long poem involved a naturalistic plane of reference symbolically held together by a superimposed mythic structure. The literary method here had its parallel in the archaeological discovery of layered cities. The work takes on narrative levels or planes like the layers of Schliemann's Troy. Heinrich Schliemann's discoveries in Troy (1871) and those of Arthur Evans in Crete (Knossos, 1876) had a tremendous influence on the works of writers like d'Annunzio, who in turn, as Jackson Cope has demonstrated, influenced James Joyce.[3]

IV

Of central concern here is the modernists' debt to Bergson, which has to be shared with their debt to Nietzsche. Nietzsche reinforced the mythic method. He had never been able to reconcile Enlightenment reason with mythic truth. As a corrective, he gave priority to Dionysian forces (primordial, orgiastic, chaotic) to the exclusion of Apollonian principles (civilizing, measured, sublime). In *The Birth of Tragedy*, he claimed that Apollonian order gave form to unruly Dionysian energy. The modern tragic vision is Dionysian without the benefit of a return to cosmic order.

Nietzsche supplied the religious basis for the modernist period. He brought to bear pre-Socratic reality, challenging the empiricism/rationalism of the Enlightenment in the name of Dionysus, who triumphs over both Christ and Apollo. While Nietzsche is often connected with the secular drift of modernism, he kept the spirit of religion alive, as did Coleridge with his theory of the secondary imagination in which the artist partakes of God's primary imagination.

Nietzsche's consent to the Dionysus myth, inseparable from the myth of Osiris and Adonis, explained the birth of tragedy. Nietzsche pitted Dionysus against Christ and called himself "the last Disciple or initiate of the God Dionysus." In 1876, Walter Pater published an essay, "A Study of Dionysus," that, like Nietzsche but seemingly independent of him, stressed the need for Dionysian subjectivity as a counter to Apollonian order and control. Nietzsche's prescriptions led to universal time—the repeat of time (what Nietzsche called the eternal return)—

which added another dimension to naturalistic reality. The method not only superimposed the past upon the present but also brought into common focus the primitive and the modern, a device that D. H. Lawrence would later employ.

V

Much of Nietzsche's interest in myth stemmed from his early friendship with Richard Wagner. He was especially interested in a work we have already anticipated, Wagner's *Der Ring des Nibelungen*, a tetralogy on which he had worked for twenty-six years. The four operas are composed of *Das Rheingold* (1853–54), a prelude of sorts; *Die Walküre* (*The Valkyrie*) (1854–56); *Siegfried* (1856–69); and *Die Götterdämmerung* (*The Twilight of the Gods*) (1874). The story involves a cache of gold stolen from the Rhine maidens and forged into a ring by the Nibelung dwarf Alberich. The ring allows its owner to dominate the world. As a result, there is a three-generation struggle to possess the ring, the struggle eventually involving Wotan, the king of the gods. Siegfried wins the ring but is betrayed. Brunhilde, Siegfried's lover and Wotan's daughter, returns the ring, and order is restored.

The alleged sources for the story have been many, including German and Scandinavian myth, Grimm's folk- and fairy tales, and Old Norse Eddas for *Das Rheingold*. The range of interpretation has been large. In its use of the monstrous, it has parallels to *Beowulf*. Peter Kjaerulff, in *The Ringbearers' Diary*, argues that the story has analogues running from Plato's "The Ring of Gyges" to J. R. R. Tolkien's *The Lord of the Rings*, to which today could be added the Harry Potter stories and comic-book reality. Robert Donington, in *Wagner's Ring and Its Symbols*, moves the discussion beyond popular culture to Jungian archetypes. In all of these interpretations, we are brought into contact with a universe in which the laws of nature have been suspended and the ring, swords, and the will of the gods have transforming powers.

A more realistic reading of events is *The Perfect Wagnerite* by George Bernard Shaw, who believes the tetralogy is a socialist critique of the industrial society. Consistent with this reading is the character of Alberich, the embodiment of the industrial process, who is from a mutant species; his attempts to embrace the maidens are at best grotesque. Wotan and Loge descend into the gloomy industrial world of the Nibelungen (H. G. Wells will create a similar monstrous race as industrial deviants from the human race in *The Time Machine*) to confront Alberich, who has substituted greed for love and now controls nature to produce more wealth, which he then turns into more control (power) over the

Nibelungen. *Das Rheingold* ends with the gods preparing to enter their palace, Valhalla, as the Rhine maidens call for the return of their gold.

Die Götterdämmerung marks the end of the false gods and the destruction of Valhalla. The prologue anticipates this when the rope of destiny breaks and the three Fates fall back to earth from which has come and to which returns the treasure that motivated this story from beginning to end. Siegfried dies, Brunhilde is awakened at the beginning and self-sacrificed at the end, the gold is returned, and the land restored; the greedy gods that had entangled three generations in strife are replaced by more enlightened deities.

Wagner's *Ring* infused the modern imagination. Joyce acknowledged it in the Nighttown scenes in *Ulysses,* and Eliot in his use of the Rhine maidens in *The Waste Land.* Central to the myth was the modernist concern with the opposition between a creative and destructive use of the land; both the commercial and the industrial process anticipate a degenerative ending, combining both spiritual and physical decline; and the tetralogy gives birth to Siegfried, whose limited sense of the heroic anticipates a characteristic of modernism. In its use of mythic elements that run from Plato to Tolkien, Wagner's tetralogy captured the archetypal elements that have driven human consciousness before it.

VI

Along with Wagnerian myth, perhaps the most important aspect in the transition from realism to modernism was the formulation of the unconscious, especially as defined by Freud. While Freud was not original in his invention of the concept—the idea can be found in the works of Schopenhauer, William James, von Hartman, Janet, and Binet—he did more than any other contemporary thinker to promote the idea of the subconscious/unconscious vs. consciousness, with the preconscious as a layer separating the two. Such division destabilized Descartes' belief in fixed consciousness, the idea of unified thought ("I think therefore I am"). The Enlightenment reduced reality to the workings of the empirical mind, putting the emphasis upon reason, while Freud put it on association. He believed that our motives stemmed primarily from the subconscious, organized around experiences that left an indelible, albeit suppressed, mental influence.

Freud drove the modern mind forever inward: nothing escaped our unconscious reality; the present was always infused with the past. Characters behave in ways best explained by subconscious rather than conscious motives. Without assumptions of the mind attributed to Freud, the modern novel could never have produced a Proust or Joyce, Virginia Woolf or H. D. Both Greek and Germanic myth depicted chthonic gods infusing the land with vital meaning. Freud transferred the source of this meaning from the land to the human mind.

In *Civilization and Its Discontents* (1930), Freud gave voice to his concern involving the difference between civilization and primitivism. He believed that the more distance we put between our instincts and our reason, the more separated—the more repressed and inhibited—we become. This repression expressed itself as social dissatisfaction. Freud shared Darwin's belief that humanity could not escape its rudimentary animal nature, which we exercise at a price. Man was obviously a sexual animal, motivated often by uncontrolled, militant impulses capable of great destruction, as the devastation of World War I proved. Humanity was in a halfway house, which involved competing motives. The primitive competed with the civilized; the aggressive desires of the individual became even more aggressive when released in mass society. There was thus an essential struggle between the id and the superego, between innate human aggression with its accompanying hostility (and violence) and the more appeasing demands of civilization.

Despite the struggle between competing impulses, Freud believed in the superiority of the primitive over the civilized: the closer we live to the raw workings of desire, the more reconciled to nature we become. Civilization brought frustrating limits to primitive freedom. It was discovered that a person becomes neurotic when he or she cannot tolerate the amount of frustration that society imposes in the name of cultural ideals, and it was inferred from this that reducing those demands would increase the possibility of happiness.[4]

Civilization—the source of beauty, law, and order—had its benefits. Technological advances allowed control over nature, but at a cost: flood channels were turned into canals, but at the expense of the environment; new medicine counteracted disease, but not always without serious side effects. The primitive-civilized equation had an expense factor. The instinctive life involved aggression on the way to self-fulfillment. The end of human desire was pleasure and happiness. But self-fulfillment and happiness were what was repressed as the primitive gave way to the civilized.

Freud spoke of two forces that controlled all life—that of Eros and of Thanatos. Eros was the life force, the sources of the erotic and sexual drive, the source of libidinous energy, the most powerful motivating force in life. Thanatos was a death force, threatening the annihilation of self. Life was a struggle between these two all-powerful forces, with one's well-being dependent on the prevailing of Eros. Freud believed that forms of repression led to a collective neurosis, especially when sexual energy was restrained by the superego. A higher stage of civilized development would involve internalizing such authority until individual authority triumphed over social authority.

Freud further developed this thinking in *The Future of an Illusion* (1927), in which he attacked organized religion as the basis for a collective neurosis by subordinating human instinct to the authority of God as primal father. He pursued these ideas even further in *Moses and Monotheism* (1939), his last major work. God stands in for the right and wrong connected with the community and thus separates man from himself, from the internalizing process that reconciles instinct and authority, the primitive and the civilized.

Carl Jung differs with Freud on mythic meaning by referring myth back to a series of archetypes. Like other Freud disciples, Jung eventually broke with Freud. He picked up on the late-nineteenth-century interest in the similarities between the myths and rituals of primitive people. He argued that the similarities had their source in the deep structures of the human unconscious and were thus intracultural rather than intercultural phenomena, the product of native thought rather than outside cultural influence. These "archetypes" manifested themselves in myth, dreams, and symbolic forms of art, and each culture independently replicated them. The principal archetypes involved the Mask (self), the Shadow (a demonic antiself), the Anima (the feminine side of the male self), and the Animus (the masculine side of the female self). Dichotomies like this led to the theories of the Dark and White Lady as displayed, for example, in the opposition between Becky Sharp and Amelia Sedley in Thackeray's *Vanity Fair*. The Spirit was a more collective archetype embodying human wisdom. Each generation rewrote the stories of the past in ways that made new sense of the archetypes, although the modernists were less attuned to the origins of mythic reality than were more primitive people living directly in contact with the natural world.

Modern man, unable to reconcile the dictates of primitivism with the demands of civilization, was thus emotionally divided: the pull in opposite directions frustrated the fulfillment of self. Freud's work had great similarity to and found common voice with that of D. H. Lawrence and other modernists such as H. D. Like Freud, they perpetuated a continued search for the completion of self—a search for an ideal that was continuously frustrated.

VII

If D. H. Lawrence moved toward Freud, T. S. Eliot found his source of reference in the work of James George Frazer and Jessie Weston and in the Cambridge ritualist school of anthropology, which took Frazer as its model. Eliot showed how modern man had been cut off from the mythic mind and what as a result had been lost. Eliot's source of mythic riches was Frazer's *The Golden Bough* (originally published in 1890; expanded to two volumes in 1892, to thirteen volumes in 1920, and then compressed to one volume in 1922).

Frazer begins his study with the ritual to Diana at Nemi, south of Rome, and then supplied the analogues—the repetitions and duplications—to similar rituals practiced throughout the primitive world. The temple of Diana was located in a grove, centered on a tree with a golden limb (bough). A knight guarded the temple, engaging each invader. The guard ruled until he was killed in combat, at which time his victor became the new guard. The temple was thus always guarded by a knight in his prime, whose well-being depended upon sustaining his strength against perpetual invaders. This ritual was directly related to vegetative myth. The well-being of the land was connected to the well-being of the king or knight.

Most of the analogues Frazer supplied came from interviews he had with explorers or missionaries. What began as a limited study turned into a lifetime, encyclopedic work that covered all aspects of primitive ritual and myth, especially the connection between the human and the chthonic. Central to Frazer's concern was the journey to the underworld and the link between the living and the dead as mediated by the dying king as specifically treated in the Dionysus story, part 5 of volume 1. Frazer's study directly influenced Carl Jung as well as T. S. Eliot, and probably influenced James Joyce, who could find in Irish mythology a world of gods who had been driven underground.

VIII

The Diana ritual was connected to the myth of Dionysus, especially the connection between Dionysus and the goat and the bull. When the corn was planted a goat or bull was sacrificed in the name of Dionysus and the blood sprinkled over the seeds before the supposedly now-fertile earth was closed. If mythic history is to be trusted, Dionysus originated in Crete as a young vegetation god, spread to Asia Minor in the form of the cult of Bacchus (wine), and entered Greece full blown with his maenads and satyrs. In the sixth-century BC, Athens annexed the town of Eleusis with its cult of the black goat. In March of each year, a celebration was held in an arena seating seventeen thousand, during which a chorus recited a song in honor of Dionysus, at which time a goat was sacrificed.

Out of this ritual celebrating the living continuities of nature as well as the nonrational forces of the cosmos came both tragedy and comedy. Each year the major cities held contests celebrating the rituals inherent in tragedy and comedy. For example, among Euripides' papers was a play, *The Bacchae,* which is the story of how Dionysus drove a whole city insane. In the remote past of Thebes there appears a stranger (harbinger of the mysterious stranger and the man-in-the-crowd plot) who claims to be god. He insists that he is the son of Zeus by Semele, which, like Christ, would make him half god, half man. Dionysus, god made flesh and animal made human, thus bridges the divisions of being. The myth seems to satisfy the human need to find continuity from the lowest to the highest forms of possible life and to test the limits of both reason and order. Dionysus leads King Pentheus beyond the order of the tamed, civilized city into the untamed, uncivilized wilderness; there the women, including his own mother, set upon Pentheus and, in their delusional belief that he is a mountain lion, tear him limb from limb.

The Dionysus myth celebrates through the sacrifice of the goat and the bull the fact that in the vegetative process life comes out of death: each spring the dead land renews itself. The sacrifice of the animal constitutes the price that must be paid for the well-being of the land. From animal sacrifice to human sacrifice was the next step. The health of the king was connected to the health of the land. When the king aged or became ill, it was believed that his death and rebirth (in the form of another king) renewed the land. The myth always came back to the well-being of the king, the fertility of the land, and the health of the community.

Both tragedy and comedy, depending on whether the narrative situation works toward hubristic demise or social redemption, have their origin in this myth, as does the realization that reason and order have their human limits. In their belief that the imagination and mind can transform the chaos of reality, both Wallace Stevens and Sigmund Freud gave us an analogue to the myth of rebirth; Mann's Aschenbach, as we shall see, connects the myth with the obsession to find beauty; and in the theme of the carnival and masquerade as well as the theme of the mysterious stranger and the man-in-the crowd, we find modernist counterparts to the Dionysus myth. Indeed, we find in the various counterculture movements—from the mind-altering practices of the hippies and their drug cults to the mayhem of crowd demonstrations—modern expressions of this phenomenon.

IX

Perhaps no group was more influential to the rise of modernism than the Cambridge school of anthropology led by Jane Harrison, Gilbert Murray, and Francis Cornford. Influenced by E. B. Tylor's *Primitive Culture* (1870), their method involved comparative study based on a progressive aspect to history. They believed that myth originated from rituals connected to human activity, such as we have seen with the planting and harvesting of crops. But they insisted that the ritual/myth process was a matter of evolution: each culture went through the same cycle, taking them from magic to religion to science. Gradually each culture moved away from a belief in gods to a more natural explanation of how the universe worked. These ideas had general influence on Yeats, Joyce, Pound, Eliot, and Lawrence.

It all began with the gods. As Gilbert Murray tells us, "the new vegetation God each year is born from the union of the Sky-God and the Earth-Mother . . . the Son of God and a mortal princess."[5] The earth was the source of life, and the personification of its chthonic processes led to the creation of a pantheon of gods, especially in the mold of Dionysus, who, as Murray citing Kretschmer suggests, means "Zeus-the-Son" (Dios/nysos). The heavenly and the earthly interpenetrate: "in the Orphic tradition it is laid down that Zeus yields up his power to Dionysus and bids all the gods of the Cosmos obey him. The mother of Dionysus was Semele, a name that, like Gaia and Rhea, means Earth." The series is not only continuous but also infinite, for on one side Uranus (Sky) was himself the son of Gaia the eternal, and on the other every year a Zeus was succeeded by a Young Zeus.[6]

The Cambridge group believed literature could best be studied as it evolved from primitive ritualism—especially those rituals in keeping with the seasons of the year, spring overcoming the death left by winter, celebrating the victory of life over death. Anthropology became a part of classical studies around 1890, influenced by Jane Harrison's *Mythology and the Monuments of Ancient Athens* (1890) and, as previously noted, James Frazer's *The Golden Bough* (1890). Harrison, perhaps influenced by Émile Durkheim, formulated what was later the shared belief that Greek religion did not begin with the Olympian gods of Homer and Hesiod but with fertility and purification rites. There is a long legacy connected with this idea. Since the means of life (food) came from the earth, mythologically the land was endowed with spiritual meaning, with a life force that gave it the elemental status that we later find in Romanticism.

We have seen how the Southern Agrarians were connected to this theme, and we have also seen why the Southern Agrarians would lean so strongly toward T.

S. Eliot in support of these ideas. Eliot used myth to show how much modern man had lost in moving away from the meaning of the land. Eliot's major sources depicted man in his most elemental contact with the land. The priest was king because he could predict the rise of the river that brought life-giving water. Jessie Weston examined the connection between the meaning of the land and the legends of Tammuz, Adonis, and Christ (to which could be added the stories of Attis, Osiris, Orpheus, and Pan):

> We know that the cult of the god Tammuz, who, if not the direct original of the Phoenician-Greek Adonis, at least represents a common parent deity, may be traced back to 3,000 B.C. . . . . The woes of the land and the folk are set forth in poignant detail, and Tammuz is passionately invoked to have pity upon his worshipers, and to end their suffering by a speedy return. . . . [His] influence is operative, not only in the vernal processes of Nature, as a spring god [note the opening of *The Waste Land*] but in all its reproductive energies.[7]

These mythical elements, which Weston treats in great detail, are incorporated in *The Waste Land*. The Fisher King is a product of this cult of life, as is the Grail legend with its questing knight, especially in the Percival version of Robert de Borron. Eliot's poem is a catalogue of Weston's details. The Percival knight quests across an urban landscape before he arrives at the Chapel Perilous. Eliot superimposed the vegetative myth upon a description of the modern city because he saw the connection between the two. The industrial city destroyed the symbiotic relationship between man and the land, canceled the vegetative fertility of that land—the fertility from which came all life, both physical and spiritual.

X

Eliot's allegiance to the Cambridge school of anthropology stemmed from their emphasis upon ritual and myth as the basis of cultural meaning. The emphasis upon mythic lore supplied narrative grist for the literary imagination. But other schools that would shift emphasis away from ritual and myth were contesting the Cambridge ritualists. Bronislaw Malinowski challenged the Cambridge ritualists by dismissing evolutionary anthropology. He questioned universal meaning and insisted that knowledge must be understood in the social context in which it originated. He rejected the belief that the growth of each culture was the product of a historical model. He believed that each culture fulfilled itself based on its own environment and values (Eskimos have a different attitude toward snow than does a nomadic tribe in the Gobi desert): cultures are different and not analogous to each other.

Such an approach weakened a sense of the mythical. Cultures rose to meet individual social needs rather than satisfy the common needs of a generic, universalized society. Malinowski's anthropology was termed "psychological functionalism" to be distinguished from A. R. Radcliffe-Brown's theory termed "structural functionalism": Malinowski concentrated on the workings of one culture while Radcliffe-Brown worked to establish a pattern that connected cultures. Another variation on this thinking came from Lévy-Bruhl, who opposed the rationalism of Durkheim and concentrated on prelogical and mystical primitive thought. His work anticipated the theories of Lévi-Strauss, who was more interested in the structures of the mind than the structures of culture, especially the binary or oppositional aspects of thinking from which comes meaning (e.g., the red and green of a traffic light signal take their meaning from each other). We have thus moved from the idea of myth as a state of nature to the idea of myth as a state of mind.

XI

T. S. Eliot was the beneficiary of anthropological thinking. Eliot's use of Frazer emphasized archetypal relationships from which we have moved. He believed we must return to such fixed principles if society is to be made new. But Eliot felt myth by itself was not enough, that first we needed to reinterpret myth and then go beyond myth altogether. Eliot combined an interest in both form and myth. His theory of the objective correlative was mainly a formalist principle, guaranteeing that a work's symbolism should engender, support, and justify a work's intended emotion. And his concern with the religious origins of ideas explains his interest in Frazer and Weston, which moved his work toward anthropology.

Eliot's literary criticism, even as it refers to the idea of tradition, is essentially nonhistorical. He thinks of literature as devoid of period or national origin, spread out before him without borders. He then compares works that otherwise would not offer themselves for comparison. This way he is able to see similarities, for example, between French symbolism and metaphysical poetry, between Malarmé and Donne. Eliot thinks of literature as a corpus with each new work altering the whole. As a result, Sophocles is not for us what he was for Aristotle; Shakespeare not what he was for Ben Jonson, Dryden, or Samuel Johnson.

While he was probably unaware of it, Eliot's method, in revising the idea of form, moved the literary text toward structuralist principles.

But Eliot's thinking of literature as having universal dimension also accommodated interest in myth. In his review of Joyce's *Ulysses*, Eliot distinguishes between a narrative method and mythic method. The mythic method establishes a "parallel between contemporaneity and antiquity." It is "a way of controlling, or ordering, of giving a shape and significance to the immense panorama of futility and anarchy which is contemporary history." It is "a step toward making the modern world possible for art."[8]

The supposition here is that layers of temporal meaning run parallel to each other, creating mythic reality (as opposed to the self-generated connection between the whole and the parts at work in organic form). Like Ulysses, Leopold Bloom confronts his wife's suitor, if only in his imagination. In Yeats's "No Second Troy," a Maud Gonne–figure becomes a modern Helen. Pound superimposes the Homeric myths on his *Cantos*. In *The Waste Land*, Tiresias from Thebes foretells events in modern London. In "For the Marriage of Faustus and Helen" (1925), Hart Crane superimposes the heroic world of Faustus and Helen on modern-day New York: Helen rides a streetcar; the Dionysus figure appears on a roof garden with a jazz band; World War I parallels the battle of Troy. In the biblical experiences of Absalom, Faulkner's Thomas Sutpen's story finds its modern equivalent. And when the train "snakes" its way through the wilderness in Faulkner's "The Bear," the reference is to the loss of innocence in the Garden of Eden, the parallel is to what is mutual in ancient and modern rapaciousness that perpetuated the destruction of the pristine wilderness, to destroy in Faulkner's story its heroic dimension (personified by the death of the bear). Along with a new technology, the codes of property have put an end to the new-world garden.

XII

Unlikely as it seems, T. S. Eliot shared a Missouri past with Mark Twain. While their "Missouris" were vastly different places, Eliot bridged the difference by reading Twain's *The Adventures of Huckleberry Finn* in mythic terms, especially Twain's use of the Mississippi River, what Eliot referred to as "a strong brown god" in "The Dry Salvages." Leo Marx has contested Eliot's giving the river mythic status, insisting that the river is literally a river, water in motion, that removes Huck and Jim from a menacing civilization. Eliot sees the river as River, endowed with narrative purpose; Marx sees that purpose as "a facet of [Huck and Jim's] consciousness," which allows rather than embodies their escape. The difference between Eliot's and Marx's interpretations is the difference between the mythic method and organic form.

The mythic method presupposes both cyclical and universal time, the oneness of experience, and thus endows a diminished modern character with qualities from the heroic past. In the mythic system, meaning is determined by the established (that is, historical) meaning of the myth. In the organic system, meaning is stipulative—it depends upon authorial intention: a narrative context that allows the reader to see the symbolic meaning. (As for the formalist's "intentional fallacy," one cannot postulate a "realized" intention until one has postulated an intention.) Organic form depends upon an interpreter making a connection between the whole and the parts; myth is more directly given, relying upon correspondences that stem from nature (personification) and history (heroic legend). The mythic method takes us to the doorstep of structuralism: Eliot's idea of "tradition," as we have just seen, is ripe with structuralist assumptions, especially its claim that all literature is in place, as in a language system, awaiting the modernist's call.

7 ✠ SYMBOL

I

Symbolism as a literary movement shared its being with the cult of the beautiful and l'art pour l'art assumptions. In a commercial age in which science, technology, positivism, and rational thought dominated, it was not surprising to find a counterforce. Along with versions of modernism are versions of symbolism that are undeviating in their ability to transform physical reality and keep the universe alive with mysterious meaning. The idea of symbolism stems from a number of sources: the belief that the universe is a product of symbolic correspondences (Baudelaire's sonnets); the belief that the mythic past or the occult can unfold symbolic meaning (Yeats's *A Vision*); the belief that the artist can create a symbolic universe through the imagination (Rilke). All of these "symbolisms" depend upon the assumption that there is a connection between a literal and metaphoric realm of reality (Pound's imagism).

Most organic theories of the universe depend upon a symbolic system of correspondences. Thoreau gave transcendental expression to his symbolism in *Walden*, where a series of connected symbols suggest the unity of the universe. There is, however, a difference between a cultural symbol and a literary symbol. A historical symbol looks outward to some given meaning, while a literary symbol looks inward: the scarlet letter, the white whale, the pond at Walden, the golden bowl, the lighthouse can mean only what the context of the work from which it is taken allows it to mean; each contains intrinsic meaning.

A literary symbol can be one of two kinds—discontinuous or continuous: the first can be found in imagism or some versions of *symbolisme*, where each image or symbol takes on a meaning of its own in relation to a larger, nonsymbolic meaning; the second can be found in allegory, where the symbols have collective meaning, each symbol extending the symbolism of the whole. Pound's *Cantos* and Eliot's *The Waste Land* would be examples of the first; Spenser's *Faerie Queen* or Bunyan's *Pilgrim's Progress* are examples of the second.

II

Modern literature was primarily a system of discontinuous symbolism. But in its origins it leaned toward a process of systemizing symbolic reference. As we have seen, Arthur Symons's *The Symbolist Movement in Literature* (1899) was of immense influence: Symons chronicled how the French symbolists extended the breakthrough work of Flaubert and Baudelaire. Symons took George Moore's place in mediating the connections between French and British literature. As previously noted, a beneficiary of this legacy was T. S. Eliot, who said of it in 1930, "I myself owe Mr. Symons a great debt: but for having read his book I should not, in the year 1908, have learned of Laforgue or Rimbaud; I should probably not have begun to read Verlaine; and but for reading Verlaine, I should not have heard of Corbière."[1] While less influenced than Eliot, Joyce, as a look at *Chamber Music* reveals, did not escape Symons's influence. And even less influenced than Joyce was Ezra Pound, who reduced the symbol to an image and who saw it as part of a larger language system working as a vortex.

The poets that Symons considers vary in poetic method, and it is therefore not surprising that Symons's consideration of symbolism defines the movement rather loosely. One common element these poets shared seems to be the desire to make the invisible visible and to reach a spiritual realm through access to the preconscious. It is probably not an accident that in the same year that Symons published his book, Freud published his *Interpretation of Dreams* (1899), also an attempt to find symbolic meaning in a state of mind. And it is also probably not accidental that one of the primary influences on Symons's conception of symbolism was William Butler Yeats. As Richard Ellmann has pointed out, "It was W. B. Yeats who seems to have persuaded Symons . . . to see symbolism as the soul's heroic recovery of authority over the body and the material world."[2]

At this time Yeats was experimenting with automatic writing, along with matters mystical and occult, leading to a system of philosophical history that he outlined in his *A Vision*. Both French symbolism and Yeats's symbolism worked on the assumption of connections between the terrestrial and extraterrestrial realms. Yeats also believed that the phases of the moon contained symbolic meaning that included historical reference; his critique of historical periods suggested those of Spengler. Symons dedicated his symbolism book to Yeats, and Yeats dedicated his visionary book to Pound. While the three were separated by what symbolism meant, the dedications nevertheless revealed a chain of modernist interest in symbolic theory and practice.

III

A challenge to Yeats's theory of mystical symbolism was the more empirical work of I. A. Richards. If Yeats embodies what one end of symbolism meant, Richards embodies the other end. In his *The Principles of Literary Criticism* (1924), Richards distinguished between two kinds of language: what he called "pseudo-statement," based on emotive utterances, and "informative statement," based on expository utterances. Richards created two distinct forms of discourse—ideological and emotional—with poetry working the second order, subject to a separate system of belief. His work reinforced assumptions of the New Critics, especially their belief in the self-contained nature of the literary work and the transforming effect of technique that we find in discourse like Mark Schorer's "Technique as Discovery."[3]

At the center of any discussion of modern symbolism is a theory of form. Organic form became the basis of the New Criticism. Every work had a part-to-whole relationship, often reduced to matters of ambiguity, paradox, or irony. The belief in autotelic form dominated the way Western critics read literature from about 1935 to 1970. The concern with form preceded the New Critics and included both the Moscow Linguistic Circle and later the Prague Linguistic Circle. From 1910 to 1920, The Moscow Linguistic Circle listed among its members Boris Eichenbaum (*Theory of the Formal Method*), Viktor Shklovsky (*Theory of Prose*), Vladimir Propp (*Morphology of the Folktale*), and Roman Jakobson (*Linguistics and Poetics*). When formalist criticism was suppressed in Soviet Russia in the early thirties, Jakobson immigrated to Czechoslovakia, where he, along with René Wellek, was connected to the Prague Linguistic Circle.

Important differences separate the New Critics from the Russian formalists. The New Critics put the emphasis upon the self-referential, reinforced by rhetorical elements. They disparaged Romantic poetry and looked to metaphysical poetry of the seventeenth century and contemporary French poetry for their model. The Russian formalists were less interested in the formal properties of an individual work than in the common features that work shared with other literary forms. While the New Critics concentrated on the unfolding of an individual work, the Russian formalists concentrated on the unfolding of literary genres. When these genres were endowed with deep structure, they were infused with layers of meaning, and the symbolic method gave way to structuralism.

The difference between a mechanistic and symbolic theory of reality thus went beyond mere classification systems to become the difference between naturalism and modernism. A symbolic theory of nature found common ground with other theories of modern thought—namely, with that of Bergson, Spengler, Whitehead, Piaget, and the Gestalt psychologists—before it was absorbed into paradigmatic meaning and transformed by structuralism.

IV

Kenneth Burke did not believe symbolic meaning stemmed from a symbolic nature, and he did not believe that symbolic meaning was built into the mind, although the mind was the source of symbolic meaning. Burke believed symbolism worked within a circle of meaning: symbolic meaning was the product of human thought; human thought was the product of language; and language was the product of symbol making and the source of reality. Burke's equating reality with the structures of language (that is, with a constructed, pre-given reality) anticipates paradigmatic thinking and structuralism. He sees language as descriptive of physical reality and as a way of coming to terms with social reality.

The way we define (i.e., symbolize) a problem becomes the way we treat it. For example, if we think that poverty is the result of laziness and ignorance, then there is less that we can do about it than if we think of it as a correctable matter involving education and opportunity. The way we think of human destiny—as determined by DNA and genetic makeup, or as a product of free will and self-fashioning—offers different explanations of the same concern and thus different realities.

We live in a metamorphical, metaphorical, transformational world: all reality is subject to and the product of symbolic naming. The most divergent thought is symbolic. Darwinian evolution and biblical interpretations of creation are equally symbolic: one is based on an evolutionary theory of natural selection and adaptation, the other on a creationist theory of divine intervention and original sin. While both are concerned with the process of change, they offer a different way of understanding and responding to the universe and a different idea of human behavior. The modernists would consider each claim as an aspect of symbolic meaning on the way to symbolic action; the postmodernists would consider such assumptions as homologies on the way to paradigmatic or structural formulation. They both see meaning as pre-given—one source of meaning stemming from the idea of a godhead, the other from the belief in the transformations of physical nature. As starting points, they harbinger totally different conclusions about the meaning of life in the universe.

For Burke (and for modernist thought in general), reality stems from the way it is symbolized. Since our response to a problem is contingent on the way we define it, Burke takes us to the doorstep of pragmatism and the problematic of adaptation. The same idea changes meaning as it changes context. Action is central to Burke's symbolic system, and all action has five components: act, scene, agent, agency, and purpose. A word names the act (i.e., names what took place), and another names the scene (where the act took place); words supply information about the kind of person (agent) who performed the act, the means or instruments used (agency), and the reasons (purpose) for such action.

Although Burke's theory has application to modern pragmatism, it draws its meaning from Aristotle's four causes. (Aristotle's causes involve elements of change and are not causes in the modern, mechanistic sense.) Aristotle's material cause is Burke's scene; the efficient cause is his agent; the final cause is his agency (means) and purpose (end); and the formal cause, which in Aristotle's theory of hylomorphism substantiates all prime matter, is the equivalent of Burke's act. In Aristotle's teleology, everything grows toward an end (an acorn becomes an oak tree, a family a state); each object acts to realize its form, establishing a symbolic transformation between acorn and oak tree, family and state. All growth and social action is thus symbolic: action is equivalent to growth, growth to form, and form to symbol, making action symbolic.

Burke was adept as a synthesizer, brilliant at reclaiming and reformatting influential philosophical and social theories. We have just seen how he adapted Aristotle's four causes to his theory of symbolic action. He would do the same with Marx and Freud, combining their theories and then applying the composite to his own theory of symbolic action. In each case, he believed that the transformation disclosed an essential reality, that one could peel the onion of history and find a stipulated basis for truth at the core.

Such truth often had mythic origins: a primary idea behind Burke's belief is that human motives stem from four central given concerns: hierarchy, guilt, redemption (through sacrifice), and victimage. These elements are at the source of all human relationships. Burke's theory has many different applications. George Orwell, for example, has demonstrated that a system of motives similar to Burke's is at the heart of the imperial experience with its need for hierarchy, demand for sacrifice, residue of guilt, and culmination in both the occupier and occupied as victim. When sacrifice is at the heart of the process, one does not have to look far (T. S. Eliot's Fisher King, William Faulkner's Joe Christmas, Kafka's K.) to see these elements as basic to modern literature. In fact, Kafka's

The Trial (1925) and *The Castle* (1926) offer point-by-point comparisons between Burke's symbolic motives and the human condition as symbolized by Kafka.

Working Freud's theory of the subconscious, Burke takes us to the realm of the gestalt or the linkage of integrated emotional connections stemming from unresolved past experience. For example, the ringing of an iron bar can frighten a child; if the child connects a rabbit with the ringing, that connection can become a component of the fright; the child's subsequent experience with something that links present and past (for example, a fur coat that suggests the rabbit) can result in a similar emotional response. The concerns of childhood and adulthood are thus infused; present time is always imbued with past time. We are the symbolic product of change—both a changing physical and a changing mental reality. Burke's theory of mind has gone once again to the core of a modernist assumption, creating a principle of perspective that we can find at work from Gertrude Stein's theory of repetition to Marcel Proust's time spots.

Burke makes an important distinction between "being" and "becoming," a distinction that allows us to see modernist literature in two distinct aspects. While Aristotle's idea of causality was consistent with Burke's theory of physical unfolding, Burke was not an Aristotelian—far from it. He maintained that his discussion of objects moving toward prescribed (symbolic) ends was metaphorical rather than real. Like Bergson, he rejected both the mechanistic and the teleological. As we have seen, teleology is an inverted mechanism, supplying a determined result in the future instead of the past, emphasizing becoming over being.

The choice was between being and becoming, not the mechanistic or teleological. If we choose to emphasize shifting particularities, we approach human problems historically, as in the philosophies of becoming. The realm of becoming dominated the concerns of the nineteenth century, as illustrated by the thought of Goethe, Hegel, Marx, Darwin, and Nietzsche. The modernists who insisted that reality was a matter of seeing, of perspective rather than being, are Gertrude Stein and Wallace Stevens. If we choose, on the other hand, to emphasize a constancy of human perspective, we move toward Freud. When that constancy takes us to the point of shared assumptions, of similar underlying concerns, we return through symbolism to a philosophy of being[4] The modernists who would fall into this category would be, among others, Heidegger and Virginia Woolf.

Central to Burke's theory of symbolic action is his belief that the symbolic process stems from language rather than from physical reality. "Our concern," he writes, "is primarily with the analysis of language rather than with the analysis of reality. Language being essentially human, we would view human relations in terms of the linguistic instrument."[5] Speech is a system of motives and offers the means of understanding the human situation: "The method would involve the explicit study of language as the 'critical moment' at which human motives take form, since a linguistic factor at every point in human experience complicates and to some extent transcends the purely biological."[6]

Once again, Burke has gone to the heart of a modernist assumption. I. A. Richards and C. K. Ogden had insisted that language creates its own authority and had sponsored the idea of linguistic reality as early as their *The Meaning of Meaning* (1923). Burke is following them by insisting on a context theory. But Burke goes beyond them when he maintains that the universe and not just, say, a poem is the context in which language functions. His belief that we must see the universe in metaphoric and symbolic perspective involves what he calls "perspective by incongruity," a notion taken from Henri Bergson. Bergson claimed that our experience involves incongruity between mind and matter, sensation and thought, flux and stability. These discrepancies reside in the unconscious, which is the source of two kinds of information: the intellect can draw upon this source and create categories that access reality empirically (rationally) from outside; or intuition can draw upon this material and allow feelings that access reality empathetically (emotionally) from within. In either case, we gain insight by seeing one reality in terms of another. Burke points to the incongruent metaphor of man as "Ape-God" as an example of perspective by incongruity. The contradiction helps summarize the metaphorical extremes that have been brought to the idea of man, from man as the Son of God to man as animal. For Burke, then, the world is best accessed through language functioning as metaphor infused with symbolic meaning.

Burke shares his interest in language—rhetoric and grammar, image and symbol—with the New Critics, but he differs from them in seeing the text infused with personal and social (subjective) meaning. He thus reads Milton's "Lycidas" as having a subtheme involving political Restoration. He reads "The Rime of the Ancient Mariner" as Coleridge's way of purging his guilt stemming from his failed marriage and his drug addiction. He reads Shakespeare's *Coriolanus* as symbolizing the fate of the aristocracy at a time when the struggle between patrician and plebian dominated English society. He reads Keats's "Ode on a Grecian Urn" in terms of Keats's bout with psthestic fever in which the sublime is infused with the pathological, the quest for beauty and truth a sublimation of sexuality. Each poem is a symbolic setting relevant to any information system—personal, social, political, economic—that might further inform it. Burke's symbolic action thus moves beyond the figurative meaning of the New Criticism and is on its way to the constructed (paradigmatic) meaning of structuralism.

Burke's theory of symbolism owes much to the element of change, whether it is the change inherent in nature (the caterpillar's transformation into a butterfly or the tadpole's transformation into the frog) or the way that language can change an object by a process of naming or renaming (as when another dimension of meaning is added when a "snake" becomes a "serpent"). But while symbolic reality was embodied in being, Burke insisted that literary form was embodied in becoming. Form, he tells us, "is an arousing and fulfillment of desires. A work has form in so far as one part of it leads a reader [or an audience] to anticipate another part, to be gratified by the sequence."[7] Shakespeare, for example, endows *Hamlet* with form by allowing the audience to anticipate before experiencing the presence of the ghost. Literary form takes on a quality of music, creating and fulfilling emotional expectation. The weakest kind of form stems from pure information. The surprise ending of, say, an O. Henry story loses its effect and the enjoyment of being reread once the ending is known. Our ability to reread a work, and hence its ability to live from one generation to the next (the definition of a "masterpiece"), stems from the "psychology" of form, form as a controlled state of mind.

Lastly, we can begin to see why the matter of causality was diminished in Burke's as well as in modern thought. David Hume had anticipated the question of whether causality was a legitimate attribute of reality, given the difficulty in determining causality, of differentiating between sequence and consequence. More than one factor may be responsible for change (what today might be called "overdetermined"). In an organic system, many elements function simultaneously. Burke points out that given the interdependence of the human body on the heart, lungs, stomach, kidneys, and liver, we cannot talk about one as the cause of the other. Burke points to D. H. Lawrence's amusing observation that a field full of corn makes the sun shine—that is, we can confuse cause and effect. Unfolding reality can be more a matter of process (natural occurrence as a form of change built into a system) rather than of strict causality. (But causality is not always a matter of confused attribution and perhaps should not be so easily dismissed. Historical causes are not to be denied simply because they are sometimes hard to determine.)

As we have seen, myth critics anticipated the rise of structuralism as a heuristic method. Burke, working a symbolic rather than mythic reality, revealed how the symbolic method could duplicate the same process. He began by insisting on the symbolic nature of reality, claiming that symbolic meaning was embodied in language; language could act as its own agency or through memory to draw upon a remembered past and a symbolic present; in both instances this led to a form of symbolism and the possibility of action based on now a paradigmatic (constructed) reality that became the basis for structural meaning with its belief in a network of informing, interrelated elements.

Structuralism is at the source of difference between modernism and post-modernism when the latter disconnects the links in the symbolic (structural) chain. Postmodernism takes us to a ludic house of mirrors (John Barth's *Lost in the Funhouse*) with its referents pointing simultaneously in different directions, or where signs point toward other signs disconnected from physical reality. Post-modernism created a divide between modernist symbolic and physical reality. Myth criticism and symbolic theory were the axles on which literary modernism turned. Structuralism changed all that. Now what we brought to the symbolic mirror was not always what we got back.

8 ❖ STRUCTURE

I

One of the most important transformations in the course of modern criticism can be traced back to Ferdinand de Saussure. His ideas come to us through the notes of his students (their collective work known as "Cours de linguistique générale"), who studied under his tutelage at the University of Geneva between 1907 and 1911. Saussure's theory of language was the basis of Russian formalism and Continental structuralism. It anticipated the work that would be done in both the Moscow and Prague schools and supplied the means by which both myth criticism and symbolic meaning would be transformed.

Saussure's theory of language revised the old historical philology. The old philology emphasized the connection between etymology and objects in nature, studied the evolution of change within groups of languages, and examined their comparative nature—for example, the study of Indo-European languages stressed the similarities between Romance languages or the transformations between and among Anglo-Saxon, Middle English, and modern English. The emphasis was upon cause-and-effect development, the working of change in the evolution of the language. Instead of thinking of language as an entity subject to such historical/causal change, Saussure conceived of language as the product of two relational elements: "langue," or the system of language in general, and "parole," or the individual application of a language element within the system. Each word was a sign, its meaning derived not from etymology (e.g., "salary" from the Latin word for "salt," stemming from the practice of paying Caesar's troops in installments of salt), or from some intrinsic meaning it might have related to nature (e.g., "lunatic" and the belief in the deranging effects of the moon, the Latin word for which is "luna"), but from meaning simply agreed upon by its users (it's "cat" because it's not "bat" or "hat" or "cot" or "cut").

The transition from structuralism as a linguistic system to structuralism as a literary system was a key factor in the transformation from modernism to postmodernism. Structural criticism viewed literature as a second-order system that used language, a first-order system, as its medium. Structuralism took its being from seeing literature as a form of writing (écriture), which expressed meaning through codes or conventions that created a hierarchy of related meaning. Language was an artificial construct, producing its own mode of reality, the product of agreed-upon meaning, removed from nature, constructed within the confines of culture. There were two primary assumptions. First, the signs had both conscious and unconscious meaning, surface and deep structure. Second, they took their meaning from binary opposition within the system and were relational.

Sign systems communicate in two different ways: they function linearly ("the dog bites the boy"); and they function vertically (dog could be replaced by lion or snake). The linear unfolding is called a "syntagmatic" relationship; the vertical unfolding is called a "paradigmatic" relationship. The first functions in terms of the contiguous; the second in terms of substitution. Structuralism accommodated transformations within the system without changing the system. The play between the syntagmatic and the paradigmatic allowed sequence to give way to simultaneity: linear time morphed into universal time, an immediate moment contained all time, an eternal present ("always already") informed the paradigmatic. When extrapolated from linguistics, structuralism put the emphasis upon paradigms that looked inward to a theory of (often unconscious) meaning, to a general system of constructed ideas and shared belief, sometimes taxonomic in purpose. Structuralism was a distinct literary method opposed to mimetic, expressive, and formalist criticism.

One of the most important practitioners of structuralism was Roland Barthes (1915–1980). A literary work for Barthes was a composite of codes, and he contended that a realistic story like Balzac's "Sarrasine" was as conventional (that is, code produced) as any other narrative and drew no more directly upon life than other fictional modes. Barthes insisted that narratives function as if part of a language system controlled by its own inner grammar. Instead of discussing a Balzac story in terms of its individual characteristics—its theme, character and setting, plot and point of view—Barthes read the text in terms of what he called "lexies," producing two hundred pages of commentary on a thirty-page story. Language encoded reality, and there were five codes (a code of action, of puzzles, of fashions, of themes, and of symbols or tropes). While the old concerns of character and plot looked out to a physical reality, Barthes' codes looked in to the language of the text.

Such encoding led to two kinds of texts: the "writerly" text that a reader can rewrite by reading because the codes are still alive, and a "readerly" text that cannot be rewritten in the process of reading because the codes are no longer relevant. Barthes thus emptied realism of meaning by cutting it off from physical reality and by seeing it as encoding signs from a dead past.

II

Saussure's theory of language was applied to other disciplines besides literature, especially under the influence of Claude Lévi-Strauss who saw how it could generate new meaning, revolutionizing the study of anthropology. Instead of looking for "cause-and-effect" connections within a culture, the anthropologist now looked for "kinship" relationships. Reading society as if it were a language, the anthropologist did not have to document how one culture could influence a different culture but could now discover similar meaning in ceremonies separated by the institutions of time and place. They could now see universal (common) elements in human rituals (connected with birth, initiation, courtship, illness, death) and in tribal relationships (customs, fashions, food and how it was cooked, architecture, furniture, landscaping, social hierarchy, political institutions).

We can find a similar change in thought at work in other disciplines such as Marxism. Marx believed that identity was a matter of class-consciousness. He contended that proletariat consciousness embodied the ideal and that history was moving toward a classless society. Under the influence of commentators such as Louis Althusser, Marxist assumptions gave way to structuralism: political ideas were organized on a principle of homology (correspondences stemming from a common source) rather than causality; political reality took on the attributes of language; or as Fredric Jameson would have it, dialectical thinking was "modified" by structuralist assumptions and created a political unconscious.

The same kind of transformation occurred with Freudian thought. Despite their intellectual differences, Freud shared Marx's idea of diffused multiconsciousness. Freud believed that a sense of identity stemmed from early (primarily sexual) experience, often ending in trauma; this process worked the unconscious mind in a system that involved the conscious, unconscious, and preconscious (whose workings were more available to consciousness). Freud's idea of self involved a composition of the id (primal sexual energy), the ego (the drive toward a sense of self), and the superego (conscience). He used the term "primary process" to refer to the work of the id or libido within the unconscious, and the term "secondary process" to refer to the more controlled working of the ego.

Under the influence of Jacques Lacan (1901–1981), Freudian psychology took a structuralist turn. Lacan transformed Freud's ideas from a biological to a linguistic model by substituting symbolic development for physical development. Lacan in effect did away with both Freud's oral and anal stage, substituting sign theory for physical process. Freud's oral stage in child development became Lacan's mirror stage (in which the child can connect the self with its symbolic reflection), and Freud's anal stage became Lacan's symbolic stage (in which the child becomes aware of the connection between signifier and signified, that one thing can symbolize another).

Structural assumptions also transformed other disciplines. Under the influence of Stephen Greenblatt, the literary text was modified by structuralist assumptions, functioned tropologically to display a constructed/timeless history, and became the basis for the new historicism. The world was rife with signs waiting to be read, all part of a new system called semiotics. The physical world becomes an extended text. (If a university center is endowed with buildings devoted to the humanities and the sciences, but then the administration surrounds and dwarfs them with larger, more stately buildings devoted to the professions—business, law, medicine—the architectural transformation "speaks" a change in academic priorities, hierarchies, and values. The landscape is there to be read.)

III

The transition from a structuralist theory of language to a structuralist theory of literary criticism was a matter of extrapolation and turned on the rise of a "constructed" reality. Lacan transformed Freud, and Althusser transformed Marx by submitting their ideas to paradigmatic readings. Paradigmatic reality challenged the priority of form and was contested in turn by Jacques Derrida (1930–2004) and deconstruction. Derrida, more than any other commentator, rejected the centrality of the structuralist method and offered a new way of thinking about the literary text. In a famous essay, "Structure, Sign, and Play in the Discourse of the Human Sciences" (1966), and in two books, *Of Grammatology* (1976) and *Writing and Difference* (1978), Derrida pointed out with an authority that disputed his own distrustful pronouncements that structuralist hierarchy presupposed a critical ability to stand outside and apart from the system and that the superiority of one binary term over another was unearned. Speaking took precedence over writing, for example, based on the gratuitous assumption that speaking involved a presence that was absent in writing. Derrida contended that meaning was always deferred: he questioned the ability of a language system to produce and sustain interpretive authority. He put the binary opposites into play, saw language contingent upon repressed meaning, and challenged both the stability and the centrality of the text. There was nothing outside the text but more text, and the text was unstable.

Derrida contested the authority of structuralism by denying the validity of a center. The center defines the circle without being part of its circumference: it is a point of transcendental presence that gives meaning to the whole. For meaning to be determined, it must be centered, and Derrida challenged its forms: God, langue, origins, and dialectic. Like Nietzsche, he assumed the death of God; he challenged the transcendent signifier that held Saussure's theory of language in place; he queried the idea of origins by questioning Heidegger's desire for a primordial Being, insisting it was a form of nostalgia; and he emptied Marx of historical closure by challenging the synthesis that completed the process of dialectical thinking.

Derrida maintained that structuralism was a form of philosophical totalitarianism with langue as the means of totalizing the system. Once again he attacked the idea of the center, noting that it depended upon binary oppositions—being/nothingness, good/evil, light/dark, nature/culture, speaking/writing, presence/absence—in which the first term had priority over the second. The ability to prioritize was the source of metaphysical authority. When the signs were no longer in fixed relation to a higher meaning, they were in "play," leaving instability (variability) of meaning, limiting systemic reach, removing the linchpin of structuralism.

Derrida doubted the ability of the system to create a stabilizing presence, questioned foundational being, and denied originary meaning. But what Derrida denied as foundational and originary, he brought back when he insisted that there was no meaning outside the text—a claim based on an authority that he should presumably question because it centers meaning, albeit disguised as textuality. Despite his distrust of centers, Derrida creates a center of his own by substituting the idea of the text for the idea of structure, replacing a seamless with an accreted meaning.

Derrida's thinking was both original and influential. While Derrida's early thought was influenced by Jean-Paul Sartre, Sartre questioned the stability of human nature and consciousness, while Derrida went beyond Sartre's doubt and questioned the validity of absolute thinking. Derrida approached forms of meaning with caution but then spoke with an authority he should have logically disclaimed. At the center of his doubt was his insistence that language was a sieve, too porous to hold absolute meaning. His thought involved thesis without synthesis, binary opposition without resolution. The key binary terms were speaking/writing: almost all of Derrida's early concerns involved the nature (the grammar) of writing, especially why the matter of "presence" had allowed speaking to take precedence over writing.

Both as spoken and written, language was unstable. Derrida pointed to words like "pharmakon," which contained contradictory meaning: it can mean both "remedy" and "poison" (when its meaning is not clarified in context). As we have seen, he questioned the idea of "origins," maintaining that the idea of a beginning disappeared into "supplementary" (multiple) meanings. Derrida shrewdly saw how challenging the structure of language supplied a model that justified challenging key disciplines like philosophy and anthropology: how the limits of language set limits to the meaning such disciplines could supply.

Derrida took on a realm of major Western philosophers and cultural critics, from Plato to Lévi-Strauss. His attack on Rousseau caught the spirit of such dissent. He began by questioning Rousseau's claim that writing was the means by which priests and politicians established a power system by instituting (i.e., by inscribing) a system of laws, moving us from nature to civilization, establishing an imaginary realm where good (nature) gave way to evil (society). He found Jacques Lacan's claim equally arbitrary, taking exception to Lacan's equating Poe's "purloined letter" (the hidden as it lies in plain view) to the human unconscious (the hidden realm of the rational mind), seeing both the purloined letter and the unconscious as signifiers (i.e., as the source of hidden meaning). In his *La carte postale de Socrate à Freud et au-delà* (1980), Derrida catalogued the many ways that letters can go astray, suggesting that such instability threw into question Lacan's equation.

Every absolute was subject to the test of Derrida's relative scrutiny. In an essay on Foucault's theory of madness, he pointed to the self-canceling quality of Descartes' cogito as the source of both reason and madness: "Foucault's reading seems to me powerful and illuminating not at the stage of the text which he cites . . . but from the moment . . . when reason and madness have not yet been separated . . . to grasp, once more, the source which permits reason and madness to be determined and stated."[1]

Whereas structuralism found order and meaning in the text, deconstruction contended that language turned against itself; the text undermined surface meaning; a work often canceled itself out with contradictory meaning; repressed meaning altered literal meaning; the grammatical was challenged by the rhetorical when literal and figural meaning upended each other. Derrida believed that "aporia" (propositional confusion) described the working of all language rather than simply naming a singular rhetorical device. Why Derrida's destabilizing theory, often obscurely expressed, had so much influence is a question seldom considered. One is not being unfair in pointing out the difficulty that Derrida's writing presents to even the informed reader. Much of his meaning, at least as translated, is simply impenetrable; and one can see, based on Derrida's own writing, why he might question the coherence and clarity of language in general. But Derrida never deconstructs himself: he presumes that his meaning possesses clarity and stability of meaning that he declines to give to writing in general.

Given the cryptic quality one finds in Derrida's own writing, it is likely that his influence was primarily a product of word-of-mouth information and critical commentary by others.[2] William Empson had argued for the ambiguous nature of language long before Derrida, and in both cases their claim for ambiguity often depended on isolated meaning in a context that otherwise bespoke linguistic clarity. When a passage was fraught with two or more possible meanings, one meaning usually outweighed the others. But despite the limits of Derrida's argument, despite Empson's anticipation of it in terms of the New Criticism, and despite Derrida's obscurity,[3] the moment was ripe for change, and Derrida was its agent. Literary formalism had had its day, and there was a demand for something different. In the radical sixties, the call was for something that challenged authority; an era of perversity demanded a divergent voice; inerrant belief ironically initiated a radical skepticism; and an "up-is-down" philosophy strangely fit the need when it came to challenging prevailing thought.

While the transformation from form to structure and from structure to deconstruction may seem to be a matter of textual authority, it also involved human identity. When Derrida rejected a transcendental signified, he rejected the idea of a human center defining itself against encroaching margins. Once the margins were free to destabilize the center, there was no basis for a stable self-identity, and the Western principle of "metaphysical presence" was challenged. Without a transcendental signifier, reality began to float. Viewed from within a system as unstable as Derrida's system of language, signs no longer anchored meaning: signs no longer pointed toward a redeeming God (as they did for Robinson Crusoe), a redeeming nature (as they did for Wordsworth), a redeeming history (as they did for Hegel), or a redeeming art (as they did for Henry James). Nature had no meaning beyond itself: no teleological purpose (as it had for Aristotle), no meaningful correspondences (as it had for Thoreau), no adaptive evolution involving natural selection (as it had for Darwin), and no dialectical history (as it had for Marx).

Despite his sympathy for Freud, Derrida needed to question the stability of psychoanalytic components, especially Freud's building premise upon premise on the unconscious. Logically, the evolutionary unfolding of Darwin should also have been contested (as perhaps it had when Bergsonian evolution replaced Darwinian evolution in the modernist paradigm). But even Bergson could not offer deconstructionist stability. In questioning the ability of any system to hold meaning in place, Derrida's center gave way to the void. He substituted indeterminacy for determinacy, created a radical nihilism, challenged the authority of Western metaphysics from Plato to Wittgenstein, and established a cult following.

In challenging both a mythic and a scientific center to reality, Derrida opened a hole in time by turning reality into a system of indecipherable dead signs. He took us to the dead end of cultural doubt. If there was meaning in his system, it stemmed from "absence," not "presence," from the ability to undo meaning as a kind of meaning. Moreover, when he questioned the stability of the text, he also questioned, as we have suggested, the stability of human identity. In the center of modernism as a literary movement was the all-important question of what is a text (given the variability of language) and the equally important question of what is a human being (given the variability of identity).

IV

Theories of form and theories of structure involved independent paradigms, offering different ways of looking at literary reality, the belief in form eventually giving way to the belief in structure. Despite Derrida's warnings, the move from a theory of form to a theory of structure revolutionized literary modernism. The text now shared meaning with other texts that were part of the same structure; a system of correspondences (homologies) replaced a belief in mythic/symbolic reality and autotelic form; the text was both a product of the moment (diachronic) and of universal time (synchronic). Structuralism questioned the insulated nature of genre: French symbolism and metaphysical poetry now offered themselves up for comparison; structuralism broke down the tendency to think in historical periods: Victorian forms of skepticism had their modernist equivalent. Disciplines reinforced each other: there could be, for example, Marxist structuralism (Althusser and Jameson), Freudian structuralism (Lacan), and structuralist anthropology (Lévi-Strauss).

A way of grasping the difference between modernism and postmodernism is to see in what way a theory of structuralism changed an "originist" view of modernism. This in turn involves seeing the way Nietzsche was transformed to generate the idea of postmodernism. In the beginning, Nietzsche was doing in Germany what Bergson was doing in France. Nietzsche wanted to return to a natural man but did not want to return to a natural universe because that would simply replicate Rousseau's world, complete with God. So he insisted that man must define himself in relation to a universe without God, to confront the universe as universe. Modernism, as we have suggested, begins here—with man's consciousness confronting an unmade universe. Postmodernism moves one step beyond this and locates consciousness within culture, as originating from without, not within, the mind. Centered meaning gives way to the labyrinth. The labyrinth—a realm where there is no origin or center, where memory is cut off from repetition, where entanglements dominate, where the purity of consciousness, including memory, becomes adulterated—is the perfect metaphor for postmodernism.

Michel Foucault picks up directly from Nietzsche, who challenged both Enlightenment optimism and Christian morality. Once man defines himself in relation to a Godless universe, man becomes the agency of his own being, the product of his own sign system. Foucault's revision created new forms of classification and challenged the authority behind such classification. Madness, for example, was no longer a pathological state but a form of discourse (signification) within a system of discourse, inseparable from other forms of (linguistic) representation. As Nietzsche eliminated God from the universe, Foucault transformed human subjectivity. He moves us from a biological reality to a linguistic reality. For Nietzsche, God is dead; for Foucault, man (at least Rousseau's man) is dead.

Foucault's influence on the transition from modernism to postmodernism was huge despite serious problems with his theory. First, Foucault misleads us when he suggests that he can escape his own subjectivity. His world is not as neutral as he would like it to appear when he is the source of its meaning, creating and defining the epistemes that control the system. He establishes the nature of discourse, chooses the texts and other documents that create that order. Second, Foucault talks about history as fiction; yet once he has created the fiction of the episteme, he enters history as if it were real. He never reconciles this epistemological split: he empties the subject at the beginning of his study only to fill it near the end, as when he does away with the idea of the insane patient only later to see such a patient as worthy of our sympathy. Lastly, Foucault has no way of explaining how we get from episteme to episteme. His scheme not only lacks subject, it also lacks process (sequence/consequence).

Whatever the contradictions, modernism as a literary movement owed its being to the philosophical reality supplied by Nietzsche and Bergson, and postmodernism to the transformation of that reality in the thought of Saussure, Derrida, and Foucault. As we have seen, we can begin a study of modernism with the idea of naturalistic reality (that reality is available to the artist in the same way an experiment is knowable to a scientist in the laboratory), but such an assumption is radically transformed when the modernists substitute a subjective process for this direct meaning, and it is later transformed again when postmodernists collapse modernist subjectivity into the culture itself—that is, into the institutions that hold the culture in place. We move in this transition from physical to subjective reality, to reality as a form of discourse, where objects are relational as in a language system, and where reality gives way to the maze of consciousness, to the labyrinth itself. The discussion here could be extended to include the way structuralism brought new critical systems such as the New Historicism into being.[4]

No one could deny the pervasive influence of structuralist (i.e., Saussure's) theory: it led to transformational grammar (Chomsky), the formalism of the Russian and Prague school (Jakobson), structural anthropology (Lévi-Strauss), myth and folklore criticism (Propp). The idea changed the whole idea of consciousness, questioning formal criticism, replacing archetypal thinking, transforming the idea of myth and symbol criticism. Meaning now worked within a self-enclosed system, outside historical time (i.e., outside periodic influences and causal connections) and moral restrictions, its being determined by its function within a (language-like) system. Whatever Saussure's status today, his initial influence was immense. He changed the order of the mind, transformed the idea of symbol and myth, and revolutionized whole disciplines like linguistics and anthropology. He did away with the New Criticism by questioning the priority of form. Instead of thinking of form in Coleridgian or Kantian terms, we could now think of it as structure that rendered obsolete organic theory and categories of mind.

We can summarize the links among myth, symbol, and structure by seeing them as three steps in the progression from modernism to postmodernism. At the beginning is the influence of myth, the belief that the universe is charged with symbolic meaning embodied in rituals that reinforce myth proper. We can then abstract from such a mythic system an order of symbols as outlined, say, by Kenneth Burke, in which the way we "symbolize" reality becomes that reality, and that reality becomes the basis for heuristic (interpretive) analysis. Once reality becomes a symbolic matter, it is now an order of the mind and can be thought of as a paradigm, grounded in a structuralism in which meaning is inferred on the basis of homology and analogy, a theory of the "organic" giving way to a theory of the "constructed." We thus move from nature as the origin of meaning (through myth), to a theory of symbolism as the basis of (organic) physical reality, to symbolism as a man-made (humanly constructed) reality, to the belief that such constructed reality offers structural (relational) meaning. In sum, nature is subsumed to culture, a physical reality to a constructed reality, causality to homology, temporality to the static time we find in a language system, and periodization to a universal (synchronic) system of time such as our hypothecated language system might allow. In thus transforming myth, we have moved from a mimetic, to an organic, to a constructed reality. As with modernism proper, the movement here is from the natural to the artificial. If there is a meaning to be abstracted, it is that man, not nature, is the source of meaning.

Although Derrida challenged structuralism on a principle as abstract as the idea of a "transcendental signifier," there were more concrete limitations to its implementation: its use of constructed meaning; its dependency upon the subjectivity of a reader; its rejection of nature as a source of meaning—including the rejection of origins, causality, periodicity, evolution, and other forms of meaning. The structuralists contended that meaning was man-made: there was no meaning built into time or nature, despite the overwhelming evidence that supported Darwin's theory of natural selection and adaptation and the rise of DNA and gene theory.

Moreover, the connection between language and history was at best tenuous; a language system is exactly what history is not: a language system has to be complete for it to work, while history (at least the realm of the future) is open-ended and incomplete. The systems supplied the meaning, but the systems themselves privileged the meaning they supplied. For example, Newton's system involving matter in motion is better suited in coming to terms with an ordinary universe than is Heisenberg's indeterminacy system, oriented as it is toward subatomic reality. But Newton's system is demoted in importance when structuralist thinking privileges synchronic over diachronic time, and cultural over biological meaning. Traditional history and biology become the victims of the structuralist inquiry: meaning was now drawn from paradigmatic thinking, not from the historical record or what is directly observable in nature. Knowledge thus becomes the product of the questions we ask: what we bring to a problem is what we get back. We answer what we question: learning is now circular, the product of responding to an echo.

Furthermore, the key assumptions of structuralism did away with narrative movements like realism and naturalism, based as they were on tracing causal connections between character and heredity, character and environment, character and an urban/industrial period of time, and character and biological (Darwinian) teaching. Once the text was reduced to its language, there could be no basis for "realism"—that is, no basis for a literature that looked beyond itself to a historical/physical reality. If there was only text, then there was no justification for a literature of physical representation, for a historical reality separate from textual reality. Literary realism collapsed under its own weight, dismissed for being what it was. Studies of realism and naturalism turned away from seeing the origin of these modes in nineteenth-century empirical thinking and turned toward structuralist (often New Historicist) tropes, usually of an economic nature (the workings of consumerism, the gold standard, machine production) that belied the biological nature of the text.[5]

Structuralists' assumptions were not without further contradiction. The structuralists claimed to be "inside" their own system, subject to its inherent workings, despite the fact that they brought the system into being and were responsible for its components. They privileged culture over nature, cultural paradigms over biological, unconcerned that a physical process such as gravity or entropy had a reality beyond paradigm. Such natural forces prevail in North America as well as South Africa. If they did not, we would not have a different culture; we would have a different universe. Finally, the structuralists postulated a theory of simultaneous time ("always already") that negated chronological sequence, leading to such whimsy as the claim that T. S. Eliot could have influenced Shakespeare.

The structuralists responded to some of these objections. As for questioning causality and periodicity, they maintained that a Kantian epistemology negated Aristotelian or Lockean priorities, that idealism (reality as a product of mind) answered empiricism (meaning based on observation and experience) or rationalism (meaning based on a reasoning process). Meaning (space, time, condition, relationship, modality) inhered as categories of mind, preceding experience and reason, producing a reality independent of causality. If an older historicism privileged cause-and-effect connections, structuralism privileged relational, comparison-and-contrast connections. That structuralism could not come to terms with narrative movements like realism and naturalism was more celebrated than regretted.

While the matter of literary form established a bridge between the Romantics and the structuralists, the two differ in the way they conceptualized the self. As Frank Kermode has demonstrated in *The Romantic Image,* the Romantic poets assumed an individuality that made them a part of their vision, while, as Northrop Frye has pointed out in *The Anatomy of Criticism,* what became the structuralist vision rested on a system distinct from the poet. The structuralist vision subsumed the poet in a way that the modern masses subsumed the individual. The status of the poet was further diminished when the structuralists celebrated the "death" of the poet—that is, when theorists like Roland Barthes removed the poet from critical consideration by emphasizing the unfolding of language and ignoring the function of poet as literary creator.

V

Fredric Jameson played a pivotal role in the transformations from formalism to structuralism (see the bibliographical essay in this volume). His early work involved books that critiqued Continental philosophy: the work of Sartre, the Frankfurt school, Russian formalism, especially the connection between theories of formalism (with its prevailing notion of language as a form of discourse or a self-enclosed system) and structuralism and poststructuralism.[6] His work in this field was also motivated by his desire to find within these systems a space for Marxist thought. He was as determined to demonstrate the workings of Marxist consciousness as he was to come to terms with Marxist history and economics.

In *The Holy Family* (1845), Marx gives us a critique of Eugène Sue's novel *The Mysteries of Paris* (1842–43): he maintains that there is a contradiction between the idealized, Christian consciousness of Sue's hero and heroine and the materialized, social consciousness of Paris under Louis-Philippe. Marx, in other words, felt that a Paris transformed by capitalism could no longer be realistically depicted as having a medieval state of mind. Jameson argued for a cultural consciousness along parallel lines: as capitalism transformed Western culture, so it transformed Western consciousness. The political unconscious thus involves a transformation in the workings of both history and consciousness.

In bringing Marxist thought into sync with structuralism, Jameson was influenced by Louis Althusser (1918–1990). Althusser, the author of *Pour Marx* (1965) and, with Étienne Balibar, of *Lire le capital* (1965), led the attempt to reconcile systems and Marxist thinking, challenging the empiricism of the human sciences in the name of such comparative truths as the laws of production. He saw the topic of production as an ideology shared by Marxist and structuralist theory. This in turn led to a theory of homology, the belief that ideas have common origins or structures. Jameson saw in Continental thought a way to avoid the empiricism of the Anglo-American tradition. As he put it himself, "Althusser's program for a structural Marxism must be understood as modification within the dialectical tradition, rather than a complete break with it, a kind of genetic mutation in which some wholly new Marxism emerges that has no relationship at all to the classical categories in which dialectical philosophy has been couched."[7]

In *The Political Unconscious* (1981), Jameson distinguished between realism and modernism: realism moved toward individual experience, modernism toward universal experience. Jameson actually went beyond modernism in his intent to penetrate the text's political unconscious, to reveal the historical contradictions and social conflicts that the text had repressed. History was revealed in the subtext. Buried in the historical record of modernism were ideological transformations that constantly renewed the modernist vision. Based on Althusser's notion of homology, Jameson could now see (Marxist) history and language (structuralism) as theoretically compatible, the end product of which produced a shared cultural consciousness, or what Jameson called the "political unconscious."[8]

But in combining Marxist and structuralist thought, Jameson radically revised the Marxist idea of history. He begins his *The Political Unconscious* with the words "always historicize!"[9] And with ideas like Althusser's theory of production in mind, Jameson has insisted that a literary work has its ideological roots in history, especially in the history of modern capitalism. But he can no longer uphold traditional Marxist history, no longer support a linear (cause-and-effect) connection between events, a correspondence between historical happening and Marxist assumptions, especially the belief in a dialectical resolution to historical antitheses. What he wants is a textual history: instead of history preceding the text, he suggests that the text precedes history—that history comes to us through forms of textuality, through literary constructs (as practiced by the structuralists) from which a sense of history can be abstracted. Jameson engages in binary activity, dialectic without synthesis. Like the structuralists, he works the paradigmatic to the extent that he privileges, perhaps unintentionally, the synchronic over the diachronic. What we get is a radical revision—Althusser's structuralist Marxism.

In combining structuralism and Marxism, Jameson created a hybrid reality: he preserved the Marxist sense of periodicity (capitalism evolving through a commercial stage, imperial or monopoly stage, and late or global stage), while he jettisoned principles of causality and dialectic that had been the basis for Marxist history. Jameson superimposed Marxist concerns on to literary concerns. In discussing, say, literary realism, he could then access the subject through "Marxism" (realism as a product of imperialism, production, or mass consumption) or through "culture" (realism as a product of literary consciousness). What he ends up with is a Marxism that, like structuralism, proceeds relationally—that is, by comparison and contrast rather than by cause and effect. Jameson transformed Marxism from a political philosophy with a revolutionary purpose to a critical system with a heuristic (interpretive) agenda.

Just as the masses have absorbed the individual in a theory of mass culture, a theory of structure has absorbed Marxist thought. Whereas Marx's thought accommodated nineteenth-century reality, structuralist thought better accommodates twentieth-century reality, now a product of mass culture and of revised ideas like that of production. Moreover, the structuralist idea of language co-opted—that is, diminished—a sense of self. We are born into the language that shapes reality; the language speaks us rather than vice versa. When a sense of mass culture precedes the self, consciousness becomes inseparable from that culture. When a system of language precedes the self, consciousness becomes inseparable from language. In both instances, the systems co-opt a traditional sense of self, destroy Descartes' subject, cogito and all.

Like Georg Lukács and Louis Althusser, Fredric Jameson has been tremendously influential in redefining modernism in relation to the evolution of capitalism, claiming a parallelism between the development of the novel and the evolution of capitalism. He connects the rise of realism with the origins of market (commercial) capitalism, modernism with the rise of monopoly capitalism (imperialism), and postmodernism with the rise of late capitalism (characterized by the expansion of the state, bureaucratization, dominated by the multinational corporation or global capitalism). Discussions of realism/naturalism now emerge from theories of consumerism, modernism from discussions of imperialism, postmodernism from globalization.

Jameson has been influential in a number of other ways. His interest in mass culture also involved his closing the gap between high and low (popular) modernism. And in bringing language and consciousness into a common context with the stages of capitalism, and capitalism into context with an evolving narrative, he formulated a new way of discussing matters like narrative. Along with Althusser, he encouraged the postmodern movement by which structuralism dominated the shift away from organic literary form. And again, along with Althusser, he revised Marxist's notions of history, questioning causality and dialectical process, substituting the idea of text for the idea of traditional history, seeing the literary work as the prism through which to interpret political history. In a more remote, less asymmetrical way, he helped transform a traditional view of history into what was to become, under the influence of Stephen Greenblatt, the New Historicism. The influence of structuralism revised the discipline of anthropology, encouraging Lévi-Strauss's comparative (relational) approach to cultures. And, finally, it led to Bertalanffy's systems theory of biology that information unfolds in loops of relational meaning. The influence of structuralism would have been greater if its authority had not been challenged by Jacques Derrida in the sixties, and if the academic world had not given rise to competing theory (e.g., American studies, cultural studies, feminist studies, African American studies, Chicano studies, and gay studies).

IV
TIME AND SPACE

9 ✣ TIME/HISTORY

I

The Old and New Testaments' use of time involved linear unfolding, time as a process of movement from the moment of creation to Augustine's City of God or the biblical prophecy of apocalypse. Flaubert radically revised biblical time by superimposing in *Salammbo* (1862) one order of space and time (Carthage at the time of the Punic Wars) on another order of space and time (Paris in the Second Empire). Flaubert's method would become essential to modernism, anticipating Joyce's Homeric theme in *Ulysses* and Picasso's use of cubism. Pound in the *Cantos* and Eliot in *The Waste Land* would also superimpose ancient themes onto modern reality, as did William Carlos Williams in *A Voyage to Pagany* and *Kora in Hell*.

The way time unfolds determines our view of essential matters. Time connected to the workings of the universe is one way of looking at myth; time as repetition suggests its oneness or universality; time as the history of a nation-state involves a sense of destiny; and time as the unfolding of personal meaning takes us to epiphany. Time is usually processed chronologically. The modernist emphasis upon the simultaneity of events, however, led to a belief in the cyclicality of history. The belief in cyclical history goes back to the ancients—to Egypt, Greece, and Rome. It was based in part on the observation that the universe worked in circular terms: the sun rose and set and then rose again; the seasons of the year repeated each other: each spring brought renewed life.

Whitman and Tolstoy offered two contradictory ways of looking at time and history. Both saw history as a force, as a form of destiny. But Whitman believed the crowd embodied the spirit of that destiny: out of the crowd stepped an ensemble of heroes to help fulfill national destiny, a destiny that Whitman connected with the promise of the land as America moved west. Tolstoy, on the other hand, thought that history was too complex, too connected to the workings of inscrutable causes to be understood or to be controlled by an individual or even a group of individuals, no matter how gifted. History was more an anonymous matter. Tolstoy believed in forces, but they were impersonal forces, among them the direction offered by the aristocracy working the landed estate. As different as Whitman and Tolstoy were in defining history, they put trust in the power of the land to help direct the unfolding of history, as did others like Zola, who also celebrated the power inherent in the land in novels like *La terre* and *Germinal*. But at the same time as the modernists saw the land as a redemptive historical force, they anticipated the inevitability of historical decline as the land succumbed to an encroaching industrial system.

There was still another way that the modernists conceptualized history. Language, devoid of chronology, existed in a simultaneous state, to be called into play as needed. T. S. Eliot's idea of "tradition" anticipated certain aspects of structuralism: all literature was available at once with each new literary product changing the existing alignment: "tradition" brought all literature simultaneously into being, common access overriding chronology. Metaphysical poetry and French symbolism shared critical context. Once the modernists went beyond the limits of chronological time, they created a philosophy of history that both justified and clarified time as "spatial form." The most important theorists consulted were Vico, Nietzsche, and Oswald Spengler; the most important response came from Wyndham Lewis.

II

Giambattista Vico (1668–1744) maintained that civilization passed through three stages—theocracy, aristocracy, and democracy—before giving way to anarchy. These stages worked in conjunction with three ages: an age of the gods, an age of heroes, and an age of men. Vico also referred to them as historical realms: the primitive, the semi-historic, and the historic. The age of the gods was characterized by rites of religion and put the emphasis upon the family. At the center was the patriarchal family, which controlled the priests who curbed the natural brutality of the tribe by recourse to mythology and threats of intervention from supernatural powers. The age of heroes saw the emphasis shift to a social order that was created by marriage, which led to emerging class rule and alliances of families that created an oligarchy and sustained order by implementing a host of unjust laws. And the age of men saw the lower classes gain power and control, an event that initiated a process of decline and burial, the disintegration of the state. The age of men was engendered by class conflict: plebian demands generated civil rights, and a legal system implemented those rights. But democracy as a process was too susceptible to special interests, which led to corruption and eventually the dissolution of the state. The cycle ended with the state falling from conquest from without or disintegration from within, followed by a reversion to barbarianism and the cycle repeated. The *ricorso* saw a return to a more primitive condition, at which time the process started over but at a more heightened beginning than in the previous cycle. The movement was from the simple to the more complex, a drift toward perfection without reaching it.

The first turn in the cycle took place before the Trojan War, the second during the Trojan War, and the third at the time Athens and Rome became republics. The reflux, or the *ricorso*, occurred with the fall of Rome, whereby civilization gave way to a new barbarianism, which led to a new age of feudal or medieval heroes, which in turn was replaced by the Enlightenment democracies that Vico thought he was observing in his own day. The more recent reflux brought with it a commercial paralysis and moral decadence from which modernism seemed unable to extricate itself.

Vico's *New Science* was an attack on Descartes' reduction of meaning to purely human terms. Vico extended the perspective and looked at humanity through language and myth. Descartes' conclusions stemmed from observation; Vico's from the construction of historic process that explained the evolution from the barbaric to the civilized: there was "*corso e ricorso*" in every society that moved from barbarian to civilization and then back again. The process was analogous to the development of the individual from birth, to growth and maturity, to decay and death.

Vico's theory of history had more influence in the nineteenth century than it did in his own time. One reason was that the German Romantics were sympathetic to its organic principles. Eventually Spengler would be one of Vico's benefactors. Another reason stems from the fact that Vico saw growth from what looked like a classical period to Enlightenment, at which point time reversed itself, an idea that would be of interest to historians who had just passed through what they termed Enlightenment. The modernist who made most use of Vico was James Joyce, as we shall see in chapter 10. According to Richard Ellmann, Joyce was reading Vico as early as 1913, and Vico's beliefs take on historical relief when Joyce's superimposes the mythic world of Homeric heroes onto the commercial world of modern Dublin.

III

In *Thus Spake Zarathustra*, Nietzsche outlined his theory of the eternal return, his belief that history was circular and that everything had already happened and will continue to happen for an eternity. The eternal return works on the assumption that there is infinite time and a finite number of events, so that events are bound to recur. In infinite time, every combination of events will eventually unfold. This idea anticipates a key assumption of the structuralists—namely, the belief in "always already," that chronology does not apply because events can be summoned in any sequence; every combination of time is possible right now. The idea was not original with Nietzsche: Heinrich Heine, whom Nietzsche knew well, was probably his source. Nietzsche believed that the universe was in a persistent state of flux, in constant change and becoming, devoid of mechanistic laws to be obeyed, lacking an end toward which it was working. What unfolds is not a matter of "law" but of "power relationships" between forces.

Nietzsche affirmed life against death through this pattern of eternal return: life renewed itself as energy, was formed and released in a tragic rhythm of rise and fall, day and night, joy and pain, happiness and sadness. He believed that the great man (the Caesar figure) had the moral right to fulfill himself regardless of the cost to others: all that proceeded from power was good. He demanded that the strong man claim the rights the state had reserved for itself: the authority to execute, imprison, tax, and spy. He wanted a visionary who had the courage to act against church and state in the name of a new man. The race would develop when the strong man had control. Napoleon embodied this idea: his triumphs renewed the empire; his defeats brought national decline.

IV

Embedded in Oswald Spengler's famous two-volume work, *The Decline of the West* (1918, 1922), is a theory of both Romantic and of entropic history. Spengler discussed three cultures that have experienced the process of growth and decay: the Apollonian, the Magian, and the Faustian, which was being replaced by a new era of modern Caesars. Each of these cultures was independent of the other; their destiny was inborn; the similarity of their history revealed a common process at work and not a causal connection between them. Each culture had its own forms of being, which "arise, ripen, decay and never return." Given the cyclicality of history, we have correspondence between seasons of the year and historical eras. In one culture, Homer marked spring, as did the northern sagas in a corresponding culture; among the ancients, Plato and Aristotle embodied winter, as did Goethe and Kant among the premoderns.

Kenneth Burke points out that Spengler's "morphology of history" rests on Nietzsche's theories of decadence and on eternal recurrence. Spengler used Nietzsche to work out his theory of the contemporaneous, things existing at corresponding historical stages in different cultures. Thus "the pre-Socratic of the sixth and fifth centuries of the [ancient] culture would be contemporaneous with Galileo, Bacon, and Descartes in Western culture; Socrates would be 'contemporaneous' with the French Encyclopedists, Hellenism with Schopenhauer and Nietzsche." Such a method made it possible to speak of "Arabian Puritanism," converting a term that had meaning in one historical context to apply to another. Kenneth Burke called this search for historical correspondences, which Spengler and Yeats shared with Nietzsche, "perspective by incongruity."[1]

Spengler's theory of history has many analogues. Yeats himself points to the correspondences between his *A Vision* and Spengler's *Decline:* "correspondences too great for coincidence between most of his essential dates and those I had received before the publication of his first German edition." Yeats believed that Spengler's "main source [was] in Vico, and that half of the revolutionary thought of Europe are a perversion of Vico's philosophy," including the works of Marx and Sorel. Yeats also pointed to common ground between his *A Vision* and the historical speculation of Henry Adams, "where I found some of the dates I had been given and much of the same interpretation."[2]

Yeats's theory mediates between Nietzsche's idea of eternal return and Spengler's theory of the rise and fall (birth, growth, decline) of "living" historical periods, twenty-eight in all to correspond to the monthly phases of the moon. Yeats's theory rests upon a complicated system of gyres and moon phases. The theory of gyres, based in great part on a belief in the antithetical nature of history, gives us the principle of eternal return; the phases of the moon give us the historical specifics in which the "turning" phase of the ancient gyres corresponds to phase 1 on the modern gyres. This leads to Yeats's anticipation of historical decline based on an elaborate system of correspondence between ancient and modern reality.[3]

Yeats returned to the theme of decline throughout his poetry. It can be found emphatically in poems like "The Second Coming" (1919), which he wrote in the aftermath of World War I, at a time of unrest in Ireland, the world having just experienced the fall of the czars in Russia, accompanied by the displacement of the aristocracy, the class in which he placed his political hopes. After an eight-line introduction made up of philosophical aphorisms suggesting the disruption of the natural order ("The falcon cannot hear the falconer"), Yeats takes us to the political heart of the poem, insisting that there is no way the modernist center can hold. The Second Coming will not involve a new Christ figure as Messiah, but instead a shape with lion body and head of man: "a rough beast, its hour come" will emerge from the sands of the desert; such a creature "slouches towards Bethlehem to be born." Yeats takes us beyond Spengler's decline to the inevitability of world apocalypse.

Like Yeats's, Spengler's list of historical correspondences between the ancient and modern world was quite elaborate. In terms of ancient man, Greek culture gave way to Roman civilization. If Pericles marked an historical beginning point, Alexander was a turning point, and the rise of Julius Caesar and his followers a terminal point. Modern history offered parallels. If Charlemagne marked a beginning point, Napoleon was a turning point in Western culture, and his passing anticipates the coming of the new Caesars. The turning point of each culture marks the passing of control from the landed aristocracy to an urban money-center.

Faustian man finds himself longing for the unattainable, has no sense of limits, allows his imagination to soar like his Gothic cathedrals to encompass the idea of infinity, his painting to make use of distant perspective, his music to expand into such forms as the fugue, and his adventures to be long distant. When Faustian man lingered into the modern, he was transformed by the Enlightenment, which brought with it the limits of the empirical (experiential) and the need for quantitative measurement. Man, no longer at one with the land, moved to the city, which had become a money-center. The rise of a new breed of money brokers transformed the Old World.

Spengler believed that the process of maturity gave way to decline when culture gave way to civilization—that is, when we move from a landed to an urban society, which he saw as the natural giving way to an artificial process. Such polarities as destiny and causality, countryside and city, are the very heart of Spengler's theory. As a people move away from the natural rhythms of the land, their sense of instinct is replaced by reason, their sense of nature and myth by scientific theory, and their sense of natural marketplace (barter and exchange) by abstract theories of money.

"Race has roots," Spengler insisted. "Race and landscape belong together." With the rise of ethnic diversity, what is organic and homogeneous to a culture breaks down. All of these factors are responsible for the move from culture to civilization, at which point a process of cultural decline takes over. At a crucial point, Faustian expansiveness gives way to a new set of limits, Romantic history to the entropic.

V

Henry Adams was a mechanist: he believed that reality was constituted by matter in motion; for every action there was a reaction; we could not have wealth without poverty, health without sickness, strength without weakness. History operated in terms of laws: we do not create a national identity; we discover it. There is no order built into nature; matter is in flux. There is only the illusion of order, but this illusion can organize and energize a society (here Adams anticipates Wallace Stevens).

Adams's world breaks in two: there is the medieval world made up of the Virgin, religion, art, feeling, and characterized by a feminine principle; and there is the modern world constituted by the dynamo, science, technology, reason, and characterized by a male principle. In the age of the dynamo, the compelling illusion is democracy (Adams points to the doctrines of the Founding Fathers, Paine, and Walt Whitman). In his novel *Democracy,* he asks the central question: Is democracy able to supply the controlling illusion for the nineteenth and twentieth centuries as the idea of the Virgin did for the sixth to the sixteenth centuries? The answer was clearly no.

In his novel, Adams depicted a character named Carrington, who is an eighteenth-century idealist like George Washington, whose views are doomed. Opposed to Carrington is Senator Silas Ratcliffe, who acts in the name of putative ideals: his ends are always defensible, but his means are corrupt. Adams concludes that ideals cannot remain pure in the face of corrupting political power. Senator Ratcliffe is not a sympathetic character, but he appears to be a realist; he is contrasted to Carrington, who is the voice of meaningless honor based on traditions of a dead past; he is also opposed to Madeline Lee, who is fascinated by power but shocked by how it works.

Adams came to believe that democracy simply led to organized advocacy groups. Power structures rose and perpetuated privilege. Behind the noble ideas and principles of a democracy was blatant self-interest embodied by lobbyists. Adams admired eighteenth-century idealists like Jefferson. But Jefferson, an antifederalist opposed to big government, did more to perpetuate intrusive government (e.g., the Louisiana Purchase, his capitulation to John Marshall over the reach of the Supreme Court in *Marbury v. Madison,* his use of the embargo against England) than any other president at that time. History involved ego in conflict with power: history for Adams was a determinant that negated individual will.

Adams came to believe that democracy marked the end of the modern era, that it was subject to its own inner workings, as the ocean (its symbol) was subject to the working of the tides. The tensions in history—man against nature, democracy against special interests, Federalist against Republican, America against Europe—had become more pronounced. Democratic man was succumbing to imperialistic and then technological man: science, reason, and multiplicity would triumph over religion, feeling, and unity. Adams developed these ideas in *Mont-Saint-Michel and Chartres* and *The Education of Henry Adams*. At this point in history, there was a transformation of identity, the end of innocence, a change in human meaning: the individual relied less on emotion and more on reason, abandoned religion for science, art for technology, and surrendered an inner sense of unity to an outer-world sense of multiplicity. Niagara Falls became a key symbol of the particles of life emptying with undirected energy into a void.

Adams had written a biography of Albert Gallatin, Jefferson's secretary of the treasury, and was researching the history of Jefferson and Madison when he was writing *Democracy:* he saw clearly stamped into time a process whereby the unfolding of history was beyond the control, the will, of an individual. Gallatin's life was depicted as a struggle between the illusion of democracy and the reality of self-interest, with self-interest winning out. Adams came to believe in natural forces that operate mechanically through men. As we have seen, he believed that a fragmenting process was going on, an idea that he treated symbolically through the Niagara Falls metaphor in *Esther*.

In his history of Jefferson and Madison, he argued that political ideals have no meaning until they have a force behind them, especially military force; this creates the currents of history and diminishes the individual. History was now destiny: individual choice and desire, the working of the will, had been nullified by circumstance. In moving toward this idea, Adams was sharing belief with Carlyle, Tolstoy, and Spengler. If the modernists believed in cyclical history, they also believed that time was gaining power—a phenomenon that they internalized. Like a runaway train on a steep decline, history was gaining force as it went, creating a new reality, the product of uncontrolled momentum. Transformed was a sense of the past, now the repository of exhausted ideals like the integrity of the individual (an idea Adams would share with the moderns in general, especially F. Scott Fitzgerald).

Adams anticipated Pound, Eliot, Wallace Stevens, and Fitzgerald. He questioned the efficacy of individual will, and he gave voice to a sense of force that the moderns had to accommodate or repudiate. He believed in historical eras or periods, more-or-less self-contained and working themselves toward destined ends through the push and pull of inward forces that transformed the country and dissipated its energy. Adams believed that history reached a high point with eighteenth-century ideas of democracy. But democracy was doomed: its ideals were illusions, and forces within would destroy it. These are ideas he worked out in detail in his history of Jefferson and Madison and in his gold-conspiracy essay, a work that shared sentiment with Ezra Pound.

Adams demythologized an era. He saw the Middle Ages preserving its sense of unity by refusing to see its own contradictions—by creating a saving illusion. William of Chapeaux and Abelard represented two extreme positions (realist and nominalist), both of which led to solipsism, pantheism, and heresy. Aquinas never healed this division. In fact, his own ideas were more pantheistic than he cared to realize. But the idea of the Virgin had offered a way out, a unifying state of mind.

Adams believed in force, energy, and power. His "Dynamic Theory of History" became a credo. Out of this credo came stock figures of American culture: the fated idealist who is defeated by a materialist world (Gatsby, Thomas Sutpen, Jim Burden), the person of paralyzed will (John Marcher, Newland Archer, Prufrock), and (anticipating Wallace Stevens) the person with redeeming imagination. Medieval man had the illusion of unity: he could accept the Virgin because he did not know the dynamo, did not know the reality of uncontrolled, blind force.

VI

Like both Spengler and Adams, Ezra Pound believed each culture functioned in relation to historical laws. Pastoral cultures gave way to agrarian societies, which perpetuated craftsmen. Such communities reached a moment of perfection in the city-states of Athens, Rome, Florence, the America of Adams and Jefferson, and the Italy of Mussolini. But with the passing (although sometimes the encouragement) of the enlightened leader, these states gave way to empire, and the expansion that followed brought about total corruption—corruption of the people, their arts, their morals. Each culture had a realm of energy, which the enlightened leader must know how to use. In keeping with this theory of the vortex, Pound believed that the key was to use that energy centripetally, drawing it into a vital center, as opposed to using it centrifugally, allowing it to spin off.

Pound illustrated his theory of historical process beginning with the fate of Florence and the Medici. Florence was an ideal community that reached its completion in the quattrocento and then began to decline under the pressures of expansion, its own and its neighboring states (Pound cites the expansion that came with Columbus's voyages and with the Reformation, which encouraged the usury that the Church had opposed). This led to the Holy Roman Empire, the rise of the bourgeoisie, and the abuses of the aristocracy. It reached its climax with the French Revolution, which turned back upon itself. Napoleon could have led the Revolution in a more positive direction, but he also succumbed to imperial expansion. The American Revolution of 1776 was a new beginning. Jefferson and Adams could have reestablished the promise of fifteenth-century Florence, but Hamilton defeated them. The tragic end came with the Civil War and the triumph of industry, finance capitalism, credit economy, and runaway technology over a pre-industrial society.

Pound's key to history turned on a theory of money. He felt that money should reflect the exact worth of a good as a manufactured item. Finance capitalism added another dimension to the production of goods: interest payments were now added to the costs of materials and labor; a surplus profit raised the price of goods beyond their worth, outpricing them to the labor force that brought them into being: "the power to purchase can never (under the present system) catch up with the prices at large."[4] Under capitalism, the usurer makes more money than the artisan, violating the spiritual relationship between man and his work. The usurer is behind the drive for expansion—behind imperialism, war, and technology. Pound believed that every society went into decline once usury was the controlling principle: "Wars are provoked in succession, deliberately, by the great usurers, in order to create debts, to create scarcity, so that they can extort the interest on these debts, so that they can raise the price of money . . . . completely indifferent to the human victim, to the accumulated treasure of civilization, to the cultural heritage."[5]

Pound's ideas had roots in basic American thought. He was following Franklin and Jefferson, who, in the tradition of the French physiocrats, believed that the agrarian was the most legitimate way of life because it allowed human work to turn the wilderness into property and bring forth new forms of wealth. This was clearly better than making money through contractual or legally contrived forms of business—such as through mortgages, tenant farming, indentured servitude, or outright serfdom. To transform the wilderness through human labor was among the highest of human pursuits and gave integrity to both the land and its value as property.

Pound's theory of economics was the basis for his literary theory, especially his belief that literary well-being depended upon the economic health of a country. Language was a vital, living matter: corrupt society and you also corrupt language. Pound's desire for imagistic poetry, a literature of concrete ideas, paralleled his desire for a concrete money system: just as there should be immediate meaning between a poetic image and what it reflected, so there should be a one-to-one relationship between money and the value of goods. The poet and the carpenter were both artisans. When the artisan's work lost its integrity and became only a means to the usurer's end, then a culture could not produce an honest artist like Michelangelo or Dante.

Pound's belief in cyclical history was consistent with his theory of the vortex: all events are caught in the swirl of time. Like nature, history was a living process; and like history, material objects had a form of life. "As God animated the tree, the artisan animated a desk. God is in the world or nowhere, creating continually in us and around us. This creative principle is everywhere. . . . In so far as man partakes of this creative process does he partake of the divine."[6]

While Pound had formulated his key ideas before he encountered Spengler, *The Decline of the West* reaffirmed those beliefs.[7] Like Spengler, Pound believed in the organic nature of culture, that each culture had its own unfolding (what he called its "Kulturmorphologie") even as its general development was subject to the laws of history. But most important to Pound was Spengler on the decline of culture. As previously noted, Spengler believed each culture had an existence like a plant, that it grew, ripened, decayed, and vanished. Following Nietzsche, Spengler distinguished between a culture in its prime and in a later stage, which he termed "civilization": "the most external and artificial states of which a species of developed humanity is capable." Civilization was an abstract form of culture. With the rise of civilization, one lost contact with nature: barter gave way to money, the land to mortgages, myth to science, craft to technology, and the process of decline began. Pound was genuinely interested in what became Spengler's formula involving culture/civilization, ideas that were reinforced by the cyclical theories of Frobenius and Brooks Adams.

But what Pound wanted in economics and literature (that is, in culture), the modern world could no longer supply. He wanted in an age of industrial hierarchy to return to an Emersonian sense of self-reliance, in an era of the megalopolis to return to Thoreau's harmony with nature, in an age of the machine to return to Jefferson's yeoman farmer, and in an age of national banks to a money system based upon the worth of individual work. Pound never addressed the problems of mass culture because he never recognized mass culture for what it was. He wanted to reduce the complexity of the modern world to the simplicity of the city-state, to accommodate a mass culture as if it were ancient Athens with a population of thirty thousand. So long as capitalism prevailed, there would be investment capital and the interest that went with it. Pound was unrealistic in suggesting that America could turn back to the world of Jefferson. He was equally misled when he put his faith in the ability of the strong man like Mussolini to rise ideally above the masses.

VII

While Pound turned to economic theory for cultural remedy, T. S. Eliot turned to religious explanations. They both felt that the seeds of decline were implanted in the West, and they drank from the same well of prophetic gloom: both shared an interest in Spengler, while Pound was also drawn to the warnings of Henry Adams of the *Education* (1917) and Eliot toward the jeremiads of Hermann Hesse of *Blick ins Chaos* (1920), which Eliot refers to in *The Waste Land*. Hesse believed that an uncivilized state of being lay dormant in culture, and when it awakened it would release the spirit of Dostoyevsky's Karamazovs, the primitive spirit of the East, especially of Asia, which would conflict with the more rational (civilized and repressed) culture of the West. Both Spengler and Hesse believed in the inevitable decline of the West: Spengler feared the influence of the new industrial urbanism; Hesse warned of an emerging Dionysianism.

In *The Waste Land*, Eliot makes use of an archaeology of history, the super-imposition of one layer of time upon another. One can reconstruct the history of the city from Athens through to modern London. There is first the cast of characters: Tiresias (Athens), Christ (Jerusalem), Cleopatra (Alexandria), Marie Larisch (Vienna), and Queen Elizabeth (London). London is the center of the poem, both high-society and low-society London: the London of pubs, bordellos, of comic opera, of cheap flats where Tiresias witnesses passionless seduction, to more lavish flats with the picture of Philomel on the wall and ether-soaked handkerchiefs that hint of neurasthenia, to Lower Thames Street and the church of Magnus Martyr—the creation of Christopher Wren, a holy icon fragile as re-ligious belief to the extent that it was on the list for demolition at the time Eliot was writing the poem—to Billingsgate, the London fish market, suggesting the Fisher King or Christ the fisher of men, whose desired presence here contrasts with his unrecognized presence on the road to Emmaus.

In earlier drafts of *The Waste Land*, Eliot uses as a subtitle "He do the Police in different voices," a reference to Betty Higden in Dickens's *Our Mutual Friend*, where a street waif named Sloppy, whom she has adopted, reads the papers to her, simulating the character's voice he is depicting. At some point in his composition, Eliot may have been trying to do much the same in his poem—which would explain the broad range of class differences in the poem—only to discover that such an intention was beyond his ability. What we have instead is a history of Western civilization as it existed in Eliot's mind. Eliot depicts history as a state of mind through the unfolding of his principal characters: each character is an "objective correlative" of a social situation. We move from urban incarnations—Tiresias, the women in the pub, the neurasthenic woman, the young man carbuncular and his lady typist—to activity on the desert where the voice of thunder inhabits the rain clouds. The poem incarnates Eliot's idea of tradition as an effluence of references from Western civilization that create a universal state of mind by collapsing historical events into each other, as Eliot collapses the Punic Wars into World War I. It is the reader who completes the poem by reading it as spatial form—that is, by bringing together the fragments that infuse meaning out of what is otherwise verbal chaos. The technique can be traced back to Flaubert, but Eliot discovered it in Joyce, describing the process in his famous review of *Ulysses*.

Eliot does not write poetry of statement; his images carry poetic meaning: the reader activates the poem's content. One must decipher Eliot's poetic details, a process Eliot shared with the metaphysical poets and French symbolists, the loss of which he referred to as the "dissociation of sensibility," the break in technique that changed the nature of English poetry in the seventeenth century. Eliot created his own vortex technique by repositioning poetry of sensibility with Joycean use of mythic history; he created a symbolic reality, a spatial form that universalized time and brought with it new forms of meaning.

In *The Waste Land*, Eliot depicts London emerging from these fragments as a fraught state of mind. London was next on the list of failed empires, Eliot's "falling towers" (Jerusalem, Athens, Alexandria, Vienna, London), capitals that were historically exhausted when they became overextended in response to imperial demands. Postwar London is the center of the poem as it reaches out to both historical and mythical forms of damnation and redemption: the rape of Philomel, the conversion of Augustine, the song of the Rhine maidens, the questing knight's journey to the Chapel Perilous, the death of Phlebas, anticipating the death and resurrection of Christ, and the many other episodes that Pound recommended be deleted from the finished poem. The past empties into the present, seeking order from chaos, redemption from historical decline.

As Eliot's city lost touch with the land, with the psychic nourishment of nature, the loss of redeeming water brought on desert drought, and an entropic process brought on an urban wasteland. Eliot depicts emptiness in cluttered space and loneliness in the crowd. Is there a way out? The answer is left suspended. A materialistic city looks for the means of religious redemption. The historical slope is downward; the mythical arch upward, offering hope.

The way out of the industrial wasteland would not to be easy. Eliot shared a fear of the dynamo with Adams (motors and horns bring Sweeney to Mrs. Porter), the belief that modern society was on a destructive path with history now that the machine had fragmented an agrarian society previously unified by a controlling myth. In *After Strange Gods* (1933), first delivered as a series of lectures at the University of Virginia, Eliot tells his mostly homogeneous audience that culture is more readily available to them than to a diversity of people that one might find in New York. Eliot was probably thinking of the fact that four of the first five presidents of the United States were from Virginia (Washington, Jefferson, Madison, Monroe), and that a Jefferson aristocracy founded on a society of yeoman farmers (that is, a state that combined elite leadership and redeeming labor) was more of a possibility there than elsewhere in America, even in the thirties. What Eliot wanted was a culture of "like selves." As an ideal, such a culture was more likely to be found in an agrarian society (despite Eliot's own preference for city living) than in the diversity that came with the industrial and urban revolution, an assumption that explains his own sense of displacement by the Boston Irish, embodied in his ugly depiction of Apeneck Sweeney.

In the chorus II from *The Rock*, Eliot gives us his summary of what went wrong in modern history:

> Then [we] could set about imperial expansion
> Accompanied by industrial development.
> Exporting iron, coal and cotton goods
> And intellectual enlightenment
> And everything, including capital
> And several versions of the Word of GOD:
> The British race assured of a mission
> Performed it, but left much at home unsure.[8]

Eliot's early poetry, especially *The Waste Land*, depicted the decay of an industrial society. Like Baudelaire's Paris, Eliot's London is a city of the walking dead—the spiritually dead in life, the mechanized dead in a commercial/industrial world. April is the cruelest month because spring brings returned life to those who do not want it. Eliot brought the same concern to the study of primitive society that he brought to the study of decadent ones. He felt something vital had been lost in the transition from one to the other, and he was sensitive to the literary catalogue of which he was a part.

Eliot was building upon Baudelaire, who had bridged the modern urban and primitive realms. Closer to him in time was James Thomson, who supplied a Dante-like equivalent of the city as hell in "The City of Dreadful Night." The deleterious effects of empire were forever present. Even the most rational of men, Sherlock Holmes, confronted the irrational as it stemmed from imperial corners, or encountered the unpredictability of nature even in London. As Conan Doyle put it himself, Sherlock Holmes of London is set against a world that precedes civilization: even in London he must "recognize the price of those great elementary forces which shriek at mankind through the bars of his civilization, like untamed beasts in a cage."[9]

As Robert Crawford has amply documented, Eliot's early reading was taken up with anthropological works such as Durkheim's *The Elementary Forms of Religious Life* (1915), E. B. Tylor's *Primitive Culture* (1891), and F. B. Jevons's *Introduction to the History of Religion* (1896). Eliot's reading in modern anthropology led to two conclusions: the energy of the primitive society had given way to the ennui of modern society, and the modern society was now characterized by the dead in life, the detritus of an industrial society, conclusions consistent with Spengler's theory of Western decline.

VIII

Willa Cather takes the theme of the idea of the West to the prairies of Nebraska and the brave men and women who turned the limitless land into a way of life. Some came before the Civil War, but many were attracted by the "free land" available after the war. The Union Pacific Railroad was completed in 1869, and the Burlington Route entered southern Nebraska in the seventies, bringing thousands of settlers to the midlands prairie.

In her novels, Cather makes use of four landscapes. The first is the prairie and its farm; the second is the town, once removed from the land, where life becomes a bit more conventional; the third is a city like Lincoln, even further removed from the land, the seat of a midwestern university and a source of prairie culture; and the fourth is New York City and Cambridge, Massachusetts, the opposite of the land and the locations of a great eastern university that can educate the remnants of pioneer stock, transforming them culturally so that they can take their place in corporate America.

The development of modern America involves progression from land to city, but Cather insists that as a product of the land, prairie stock will be transformed in ways different and better than those who never knew the land. This is the main theme of *My Antonia* (1918), the story of the Shimerda family. Mr. Shimerda could never reconcile himself to this new world, and his loneliness and homesickness for Bohemia leads to his suicide. His daughter, Antonia, perseveres, sustains her husband in a way her mother could not sustain her father, and is the source of stability until a second generation is in place. The story is told from the point of view of Jim Burden, who, like Antonia, is a product of the land, even as he leaves Nebraska for a Harvard University law degree and eventually the corporate world of New York. The road has taken him in a circle, and though he has moved far beyond the realm of Antonia and the land, they share a beneficently determined past. As Jim tells us at the end: "I had a sense of coming home to myself. . . . For Antonia and for me, this had been the road of Destiny. . . . Whatever we had missed, we possessed together the precious, the incommunicable past."[10] But much of this is sheer nostalgia for a world now gone. Cather realized that the frontier experience was over, was now in the material hands of men like Wick Cutters, who had lost contact with the land and whose obsession for money was self-destructive.

Cather treats a variation of this theme in *A Lost Lady* (1922), a novel that had a tremendous influence on F. Scott Fitzgerald's *The Great Gatsby*. Captain Forrester, who came to the plains after the Civil War and was instrumental in building the railroad, embodies the theme of the frontier. His spirit is carried on by his young wife, Marian, who becomes for Niel Herbert, the moral presence in the novel, a force for good. Frank Ellinger and Ivy Peters, both of whom have lost contact with the land and in turn corrupt Mrs. Forrester, embody the force of evil. The novel ends on a note of loss: Niel "had seen the end of an era, the sunset of the pioneer. He had come upon it when already its glory was nearly spent . . . . This was the very end of the road-making West. . . . It was already gone, that age; nothing could ever bring it back."[11] But ideals die hard: Niel cannot forgive Mrs. Forrester for betraying the past, the spirit of the frontier, despite the fact that it is now an ideal (as in *The Great Gatsby*) that exists only in an imaginative reconstruction of an exhausted past.

Cather again offers a choice between an idealized past and a diminished present in *The Professor's House* (1925). The contrast here is drawn by setting the primitive Cliff City (modeled on Mesa Verde on the border between Colorado and New Mexico) against Washington, D.C. Dug out of rock cliffs, the lost city may have had a population of as many as seventy thousand. As it became more civilized, it became less militant and was probably destroyed by a less advanced tribe. Monuments of the land go unattended in Washington: Tom Outland, who found the city, is unable to get the federal government to declare it a national monument.

The professor's study of the Spanish conquest establishes a thematic contrast to the story of Cliff City, a story of military victory, not defeat. The professor has come to the end of a distinguished career and feels that he has little to live for. When his family is away, he almost dies when the wind—facilitating his self-destructive wish—blows out the stove pilot light. He is saved by Augusta, the devoted family servant, who is the Antonia figure in the novel—the spirit of willed life, of the cliff dwellers, the spirit of the pioneers, of the landed past.

The novel contrasts two states of mind: a modernist desire to control the land in pursuit of material goods, and a pioneer desire to live in harmony with the land. The latter ideal is embodied by Augusta and by the inhabitants of Cliff City; it also supplies a source of meaning to Tom and the professor, who can now better reconcile the contradictions between the present and the past, who can now commit himself anew to life. Cather ends this novel on a positive note, but the import of her total writing was not so sanguine, and Cather anticipates the theme of historical decline. She depicted in fictional terms what Frederick Jackson Turner documented in historical terms: the frontier was gone and with it the symbiosis between man and the land.

IX

A work that owed much of its historical assumptions to Spengler and T. S. Eliot's *The Waste Land* as well as to Cather's *A Lost Lady* was Scott Fitzgerald's *The Great Gatsby*. Gatsby invents a Romantic self that cannot stand the test of experience in the material world of Tom Buchanan. As we have seen, Spenglerian decline set in when a culture moves from a landed to urban society, when instinct gives way to reason, myth to science, and marketplace to abstract theories of money. Faustian man, with his desire for the infinite, gives way to the new Caesar, just as Gatsby gives way to Tom Buchanan, the frontier to the new city, radical individualism to new forms of power inseparable from money. Fitzgerald's novel is more than the story of the rise and fall of radical individualism; it is also a story of the rise and fall of Faustian culture, the limits that the new urbanism brought with it.

Consistent with the way Spengler's views apply to a reading of *The Great Gatsby*, Nick Carraway observes New York becoming less homogeneous and more diverse, less grounded in nature and more in artifice, more the product of manipulated money—factors that accommodate the move from Spengler's culture to civilization, initiating a process of cultural decline. The city harbingers great promise (the "wild promise of all the mystery and beauty in the world"), while another reality moves toward death (the death of Gatsby, Wilson, Myrtle, the death that roams the street: "a dead man passed us in a hearse"). Hope and disappointment, promise and despair, life and death merge in this novel.

Gatsby brings his sense of promise to the city in which he will die; the splendid buildings that make up the New York skyline find a contrast in the valley of ashes. Fitzgerald's city offers the promise of heaven, while delivering the reality of hell. The valley of ashes takes its being from the biblical Gehenna, the wasteland hell on the outskirts of Jerusalem, in the valley of Hinnom; men (demons) with pitchforks run about stirring the ashes as Nick Carraway's train passes through the modern embodiment of biblical hell. Fitzgerald's world appropriately turns on contrasts; Faustian expansiveness (the skyline) finds limits (the valley of ashes): Romantic history gives way to the entropic.

Gatsby's story inverts the East-West experience. Instead of moving from the East to the West and exploiting the wealth of the frontier, Gatsby moves from the West to East and exploits the wealth of the city. Instead of becoming an incarnation of the frontier experience like James J. Hill, he becomes the incarnation of urban anonymity. Nick Carraway also embodies such anonymity when he walks New York in the evening, a kind of displaced flaneur, watching and watched, alone in the crowd. If being a part of the land brings a sense of community, being alone in the urban crowd brings a haunting, but not an unwelcome sense of loneliness, if not serendipity. One is the opposite of the other: if the land offers roots and stability, the city offers new possibility, unknown opportunity, the effervescence of the unexpected, at least in Nick's mind, where so much of the reality of this story abides.

In an early draft of the novel, Fitzgerald concluded chapter 1 with the words: "so we beat on, boats against the current, borne back ceaselessly into the past." He moved those words from the end of chapter 1 to the end of the novel when he realized that the sentence summarized the meaning of his novel: that an idealized America—a lost innocence once located in the idea of the West—better existed in the past than present. At the end of the novel, Nick seeks this lost ideal and returns to the West. Nick's words to Gatsby—"you can't repeat the past"—become words that he fails to apply to himself as he heads west in search of a lost ideal. Fitzgerald thus ends his novel on a note of ambiguity: what Nick will find in his return to the West remains a matter of speculation. He will be rid of Tom with Tom's arrogant sense of privilege that goes with money, but he is unlikely to find a redeeming ideal in his father's hardware store.

Nick's return to the West is to an America that has been changed by time. It is a continued pursuit of an Enlightenment expectation that brought with it the belief that one could create oneself out of Romantic possibility and determination and remain true to that creation. Gatsby comes close to realizing that incarnation, but Tom is the serpent in this garden. Fitzgerald completes this historical picture in *Tender Is the Night* and *The Last Tycoon* when he demonstrates that the spirit of America is now more a product of Tom Buchanan's material values than Gatsby's idealized expectations.

In *Tender Is the Night* (1934), the Spenglerian element is even more pronounced. Here Fitzgerald made conscious use of the European setting. He depicted the breakup of the European aristocracy following World War I as they gave way to a new-money class embodied by the Warren (war end?) family. The Warrens ruled by virtue of their money; they were grand consumers: trains crisscrossed the county carrying goods to satisfy their desires. All of these elements have Spenglerian reference. As we have seen, Greek culture gave way to Roman civilization, the major movements turning on Pericles, Alexander, and Caesar. When history transformed modern Europe, the major events turned on Charlemagne, Napoleon, and the new Caesars (the product of Prussian military and industrial money). In each sequence, the turning point involved the passing of control from a landed aristocracy to an urban money-center (it is no accident that Dick Diver's final decline takes place in Rome, against a backdrop of decadence).

When Dick leaves Rome, he is a defeated man, which anticipates the appearance of Tommy Barban, the new "barbarian" who comes with the end of every civilization. As in Eliot's *The Waste Land*, Fitzgerald makes use of the "falling tower" theme when he superimposed one imperial period of time upon another, the modern upon the ancient. As the West (Europe and later America) lost its vitality, a new threat came from the East: the fall of Rome anticipated the fall (i.e., the decline) of London, Paris, and New York (each city was marked by decadence or brutality, such as the brutality of Abe North's death in New York).

The fate of both Abe North and Dick Diver embodied the fate of America after the Civil War. Fitzgerald believed that American cultural values divided with the advent of the Civil War, a Jeffersonian agrarianism giving way to a Hamiltonian industrial society. In an earlier draft of the novel, Abe North was named Abe Grant, suggesting his connection to both Lincoln and Grant and to both antebellum and postbellum America. Fitzgerald filled in the details with the help of Spengler's historical formula: Grant paralleled Napoleon; 1865 in America was the equivalent of 1815 in France. The new capitalism and technology transformed both landscapes; Paris and New York were now historically interchangeable.

In "My Lost City" (1932), Fitzgerald projected success and failure onto New York and created two cities: the city of his prep-school dreams of success and the city of his postwar experience working in advertising and living in a drab room in the Bronx. Once again Fitzgerald's world divided in two with the thrill of expectation giving way to the disappointment of reality. America embodied this division: "behind much of the entertainment that the city poured forth into the nation there were only a lot of rather lost and lonely people."[12] In this essay, Fitzgerald tells us that New York, with its Romantic potentiality and its realistic squalor, had limits. Where New York stopped, America began. One could never escape the larger destiny that contained the city itself. Beyond the Romantic city was provincial America, founded on a Puritan legacy that incorporated both God and money, a religious and secular state of mind.

In his early novels and short stories, Fitzgerald showed how difficult it was to create the Romantic self in the face of this Puritan legacy. *This Side of Paradise* (1920) turned on this theme. Princeton became the safe harbor that supplied a buffer against the outside world, softening the contradictions that were built into a money economy grounded on spiritual belief, anticipating the ideals that led to the disillusionment with a war that supposedly preserved such ideals. *The Beautiful and Damned* (1922) picked up where *This Side of Paradise* left off. Adam Patch was a product of the post–Civil War period when the agrarian values of Jefferson gave way to the industrial values of Hamilton. The result was a schizophrenic nation that could no longer accommodate what both Amory Blaine and Anthony Patch needed to fulfill a sense of identity.

Fitzgerald's last treatment of what might be called entropic history comes in *The Last Tycoon* (1941), which once more dealt with the man of Romantic aspiration caught in the materialistic culture that defeats him. Monroe Stahr, the last of the Faustians, is counterpointed against a former Hollywood czar, who commits suicide at "the shrine" of Andrew Jackson's Hermitage, a shrine because it was Jackson who championed the common man and who fought the rise of the national bank in the name of yeoman culture. Jackson's shrine embodies the meaning of the agrarian South; in contrast, Schwartzman came from New York and rose and fell as a Hollywood mogul in an urban, celluloid world. The novel demonstrated how far America had moved from the landed, frontier culture of its origins. A new order had come into being, the material demands of which accounted for the defeat of Stahr and the suicide of Schwartzman.

The entropic process was now so swift that it called into question the ability of the Romantic hero to exist in modern America. The attempt to create an idealized self became more difficult in the face of a Puritan legacy and a materialistic culture, a culture now controlled by power custodians (Spengler's new Caesars). The vitality that Gatsby displayed in holding together his Romantic sense of self was greatly diminished in *The Last Tycoon*. Gatsby, the idealist, eventually succumbs to Tom Buchanan, the materialist. But in *The Last Tycoon*, there is even less distance between the Romantic impulse and its materialistic fate. Fitzgerald's America was a far more hostile place when he was writing *The Last Tycoon* in 1940 than when he was writing *The Great Gatsby* in 1925. In fifteen years, the process of cultural entropy had speeded up, and the Romantic hero foundered more quickly on the shoals of institutional materialism.

X

Like Fitzgerald and Hemingway, Thomas Wolfe (1900–1938) was published by Scribner's and edited by the famous Maxwell Perkins. Wolfe was the author of four autobiographical novels, two of which were published after his death in 1938: *Look Homeward, Angel* (1929), *Of Time and the River* (1935), *The Web and the Rock* (1939), and *You Can't Go Home Again* (1940). The novels deal with the same biographical experiences and thus duplicate each other. The novels also make use of the same themes: the theme of art vs. life, the city vs. the small town, and the search for a spiritual father. All of these themes are encapsulated in Wolfe's theory of time as a contrast between the river (time as flow) and the rock (time as intractable).

Wolfe conflates two opposed traditions of literature. The first involves a Whitmanian search for meaning on the road—that is, the search for a meaning to life by experiencing it. The second is a Joycean realm of art as privileged meaning, art as providing a unique way of seeing, as a coda to the meaning of life. The Whitmanian emphasis involves the search, the Joycean involves a way of seeing; the Whitmanian mode involves horizontal time, the Joycean involves vertical or perpendicular time.

Wolfe believes that there is a confluence between the two forms of art: the search precedes the way of seeing. This takes us to what there is to be seen. For example, contrasts involve the difference between the city and the town, the North and the South, America and Europe. The young man in these novels becomes disillusioned with his natural father and rejects both the birth father and the provincial town. This moment of repudiation involves a journey to the city in search of a larger self. While the city is throbbing with life, the urban experience is a lonely one: people pass each other in the night; time is in flight; the Romantic essence to life (what Wolfe refers to as the "unfound door") remains beyond reach, even as the search takes the seeker to distant lands. Like Joyce's young artist, Wolfe looks for the moment of epiphany, for a moment of truth, the key experience that will unlock the found door.

The journey brings an encounter between two kinds of characters that make up what is essential in American life: the Babbitt figure vs. the hedonist. The Babbitt figure is the philistine who has reduced the meaning of life to material pursuits; the hedonist seeks pleasure as the end of life, wastes his time in debauched pursuits, and is morally rudderless. The Wolfean hero finds little basis to choose between the two. At times the hedonist gives way to the aesthete, the person who reduces the meaning of life to forms of art. Wolfe's protagonist is often attracted to such a personality before he dismisses him as too frivolous.

Wolfe most clearly defines these character types in *Of Time and the River*. Eugene Gant witnesses the Babbitt figure as he rides in the smoker of the train that is taking him from the provincial South to Harvard University and the urban East. Robert Weaver, whom he meets in Boston, embodies the hedonist. The two types offer extreme ways of experiencing life: one reducing it to an obsession with investment profit, the other to a mindless pursuit of pleasure, both to trivial ends. The aesthete, Francis Starwick, seems to offer more substantial possibilities. Eugene is attracted to him at first, but then he realizes that Starwick's pursuit of the beautiful is as empty as Babbitt's pursuit of money. Starwick wants to write the great American novel structured on the Mississippi River, a region where he lived as a child. But he has lost contact with that world; indeed, he has lost contact with the land. He goes to Europe, adopts Continental manners and values, and repudiates America.

Starwick's fate ironically parallels the fate of George Webber (the Gant figure renamed) in Wolfe's last novel, *You Can't Go Home Again*. Here Webber comes to realize what was a truism for F. Scott Fitzgerald—that you cannot buy back the past, cannot realize ideals located in the past. The past is not a stable, solid block of meaning to which one can return at will. Present reality transforms the past. Because the past is constantly being emptied of meaning, "you cannot go home again," cannot go back to family, lost loves, old friends, familiar places. Once time has moved on, as Proust knew, past meaning both alters the present and transforms itself. To seek meaning in the past is to seek it in a realm that will never come again. Perhaps Wolfe's most genuine contribution to American literature was his ability to see that the ideals of the past have been transformed by a materialistic (commercial/industrial) society and that an antebellum world was lost forever.

XI

In many ways, William Faulkner begins where Thomas Wolfe leaves off. Faulkner's world divides in two: events take on meaning depending on whether they take place before or after the Civil War. By 1865, the South was transformed; the old aristocracy was gone and so also their mansions along with the land that brought the mansions into being. All was in a process of decline. The burden of this transformed time fell on a new generation, thrice removed from the war but still living with the legends that were passed down and trying to make sense out of a new social reality infused with the commercial and industrial being that the North imposed on the South.

Faulkner's world is heroically diminished, tragic in its fall from high to lower estate. A sense of decline sits heavily on the remains of the old aristocracy, whether it is Sartoris, whose sense of remorse is turned outward toward a life of self-destructiveness, or Quentin Compson, whose remorse is turned inward toward suicide. The decline has a mutant quotient, spawning Benjy, the idiot child of the Compson family, and James Bond, the deranged end product of the Sutpen line.

Faulkner's world is basically naturalistic, a realm in which heredity and environment have extreme influence; but it has been transformed into a modernist realm through the universalizing use of myth and the internalizing of historical time. In *Absalom, Absalom!* (1936), the Absalom story becomes a parable of the Civil War, with Thomas Sutpen's children turning upon him and on each other, as the fratricide element of the novel finds its equivalent in the war itself, which in turn is universalized in the Cain and Abel story.

Faulkner's heroic world has been turned upside down, leaving us in the realm of modern gothic. Faulkner's story of Temple Drake is a modern version of *Clarissa* (1748) by Samuel Richardson (1689–1761). The sublimity of the romance has been inverted. We are in the dying if not dead world of the father; the estate is in gothic decline; the world of the children is one of incest and fratricide. Romantic principles like honor have been played out and are now abstract ideals, dead to the living. The wilderness has given way to the wasteland.

Behind Southern Agrarianism was the belief in property, at times breathtaking in its scale (Sutpen's "one hundred" refers to the one hundred square miles of land that he owned, along with its slaves, sharecroppers, and declining wilderness). Sutpen's decline has its counterpart in other cultures and repeats the stories of both Greek and biblical tragedy. The story of Sutpen is that of the aristocratic ideal emptied of meaning, leaving only its empty shell, rituals cut off from their origins, an ironic commentary on itself. The mind has been driven compulsively inward, looking for causal explanation (Quentin); women have become caricatures of southern maidens (Rosa Coldfield) or southern virtue (Temple Drake); property has replaced honor; money, time.

As Faulkner inverts the heroic quality of the romance, he inverts the Christ story in *Light in August*. Joe Christmas incarnates hate turned back on itself. The product of Doc Hines and later McEachern's racial hatred, he is beyond redemption, whether the redemptive motherly love of Mrs. McEachern or the redemptive sexual love of Bobbie Allen. The product of miscegenation, the black pants and white shirt he wears symbolize his divisive black and white nature, which the novel presumes but never verifies, making his story a state of mind. Joe Christmas incarnates the modern South, its history turned back upon itself, the self in pursuit of its own destruction.

In the center of Faulkner's Jefferson is the courthouse, on top of which is the town clock, ironically centered as is the jail beneath. Thus in the center of Faulkner's world is both the clock and the jail, time as prison. "All was is," Faulkner tells us. There is no escape from history, the past now infused with the present in a kind of Bergsonian bond that plays itself out as Spenglerian decline.

The events leading to the end of the wilderness are recounted in the collection of stories that make up *Go Down, Moses* (1942), including perhaps Faulkner's best novella, "The Bear." Sections 1 through 3 of "The Bear" involve the story of Ike McCaslin, who grows up in Mississippi after the Civil War. From the time he is ten he goes on a bear hunt with his cousin Cass Edmonds and the leading citizens. This part is an initiation story. When he is sixteen, Boon Haggenbeck and the mongrel dog Lion kill the bear. Chronologically, the next section of the story takes place in section 5, not 4. It is two years later; he is now eighteen: Ike has come back to the wilderness to find it no longer wilderness. The lodge is gone, hunters have disbanded, and the lumber company has moved in and is cutting what remains of the forest. In section 4, three years later, Ike is twenty-one: he has come into his inheritance at the same time that he discovers that his grandfather, Carothers McCaslin, has seduced one of his slaves and later had a child by the girl (his own daughter) who was born of that union. Ike repudiates his legacy, becomes a carpenter suggestive of the Christ story, and lives a hermetic existence. The novella closes with the train, now carrying its load of lumber, snaking its way through the diminished wilderness, symbolic of the serpent in the garden. The New Testament links the fall in the garden to original sin. Faulkner links the fall of the New World garden to miscegenation, often coupled with incest, his proxy for original sin. In one instance, the garden has given way to the imperfect world of humanity; in another instance, the garden has given way to the lumberyard.

Faulkner's is an agrarian world in the process of industrial transformation.

Much that is evil in Faulkner's world has come down the railroad tracks from Memphis, roughly fifty miles to the northwest, and tainted the town. The new South in great part was embodied by the Snopes family, who came mysteriously from the North, infiltrated the town through Frenchman's Bend, and is now in the process of claiming possession of the town in the name of greed. What takes place in Faulkner's world is seen mostly through the eyes of the town, and much of that involves a process of decline from the world of the old aristocracy. The story of the town with its transformation of the old aristocracy and the rise of the Snopes family is told in a trilogy made up of *The Hamlet* (1940), *The Town* (1957), and *The Mansion* (1958). The three novels compose a sustained story involving the loss of honor and chivalry. Yet such a loss was destined: the present perpetually prolongs the past.

As we move in Spenglerian terms from an agrarian to an urban realm, we move from harmony to disharmony, from one value system to another. We move through the heroic, the tragic, the Romantic to a fallen world in which the capacity for action is gone. We are left with Flem Snopes, whose world is now overlooked by Gavin Stevens, the man of paralyzed will. Change transformed Faulkner's postwar world, and yet the seeds of this change were planted long before, when the idea of property was extended to those who oversaw rather than those who actually worked the land—when the land became equated with money rather than with work. The prewar South prided itself on chivalry and honor, now overtaken by materialism and greed. The sins of the fathers have been passed down to the sons, one of the many biblical themes that universalize the meaning of Faulkner's world. Despite the differences, the worlds of Fitzgerald and Faulkner have shared elements, especially the Spenglerian belief that we are locked into a past, the ideals of which are long gone.

XII

After the Second World War, Theodor Adorno challenged Spengler's theory of history. Adorno appreciated the predictive aspect of Spengler's theory, especially the prediction that there would be another world conflagration after World War I: the people's rights, posited by the Constitution of 1848, would be abrogated, the individual replaced by the party. Spengler foresaw "the helplessness of liberal intellectuals in the shadow of rising totalitarian power." But in connecting history with the growth and decline of products of nature, "history becomes transformed into a second nature, as blind, closed, and fateful as any vegetable life, human freedom lost to the bondage of nature."[13] At a time when a sense of culture prevailed over the idea of nature, it is not surprising that Spengler lost intellectual relevance.

Adorno concludes his essay by dismissing Spengler, quoting from a critique by James Shotwell to make his final and fatal point, that inherent in Spengler's definition of civilization, based upon the corrupt intent of imperial motives, is the inevitability of decline: "From the savage raid and slavery down to the industrial problems of today, the recurring civilizations have been largely built upon false casuistry. The civilizations that have come and gone have been inherently lacking in equilibrium because they have built upon the injustice of exploitation. There is no reason to suppose that modern civilization must inevitably repeat this cataclysmic rhythm."[14] Spengler's theory of history, based upon a theory of the rise and fall of imperial civilizations, leaves no room for progressive change: "Spengler's universal structure reveals itself to be a false analogy drawn from a bad but unique occurrence."[15] Spengler has lost the authority that he had after World War I, and it demands a retrospective look to realize the influence he had on the modern imagination. His theory of Western decline found its complement in the ideas of Henry Adams, Pound, Eliot, Cather, Fitzgerald, Wolfe, and Faulkner and its parallel in the thought of Nathanael West and William Carlos Williams.

10 ❖ SPATIAL FORM

I

When Joseph Frank coined the term "spatial form,"[1] he was referring to narrative elements that avoid strict chronology, that are held in place by the mind of the reader. The work unfolds by narrative leaps that involve emotional rather than temporal connections and necessitates a second reading that allows the linking of textual elements in the reader's mind. It is thus the reader that makes spatial form possible—a reader who has read the text previously so that the leaps in narrative can be anticipated, the narrative gaps joined. The reader collapses meaning in the mind, filling in the ellipses of the text.

Both the novels of Proust and Joyce progress by spatial form. Spatial form was a radically new way to organize a narrative and a major departure from the narrative technique of the times. Although Marcel Proust (1871–1922) was born in the same year as Stephen Crane and Theodore Dreiser, he created a totally new form of fiction. Proust's *À la recherche du temps perdu* was translated by C. K. Scott-Moncrieff as *Remembrance of Things Past*, using a phrase from a Shakespearean sonnet. A better title, certainly more literal, might be "The Search for Lost Time," which catches the way the novel fuses past and present time. Proust's major novel was the work of a lifetime. The original French edition appeared in sixteen volumes between 1913 and 1927, the last volumes published five years after his death. *Swann's Way* was privately printed in 1913; *Within a Budding Grove* appeared in 1918, winning the Goncourt prize; and *The Guermantes Way* was published in 1920–21.

As previously noted, Proust early in his writing career worked on a novel, *Jean Santeuil*, found years after his death and published in 1952. Like Joyce's *Stephen Hero*, which was an early version of *A Portrait of the Artist*, Proust rewrote his novel into *À la recherche du temps perdu*, transforming a more representational novel into a time-obsessed work held together by consciousness and memory.

Before he could rewrite his novel, Proust had to develop a theory of art. During a visit to Venice, he discovered the work of John Ruskin (1819–1900) and translated *The Bible of Amiens* and *Sesame and Lilies* (1865). His actual theory had a number of components: Ruskin on aestheticism and the connection between the idea of beauty and Venice; Bergson's philosophy of time (Proust had attended Bergson's lectures at the Sorbonne); and the influence of the aesthetic novel *À rebours* (1884; translated as *Against the Grain*, 1922) by Joris-Karl Huysmans (1848–1907), dealing with an aristocratic hero who turned experience into sensation.

Huysmans modeled his character on the sickly Count Robert de Montesquiou, whom Proust used for his own Baron de Charlus. Like Mann before him, Proust connected the artistic impulse with forms of disease. He takes us back in the memory of Swann to the hypochondriac aunt, the love given to and from his mother, Swann's marriage and life in Paris. The novel depicts people both young and grown old. Beneath the transitions of time is a society less genuine than fraudulent that gives substance to the literary idea of decadence.

Malcolm Bradbury charts two avenues to the world in Proust's novel.[2] *Swann's Way* leads outward from Combray to Paris, to the Jewish bourgeois, to literary soirées, and to the life of art and culture. *The Guermantes Way*, which goes along the river and by the chateau of the Guermantes family, one of the noblest of France, also leads outward to Paris and the elegant Faubourg St. Germain. The first path leads toward the decadence of the salon; the second path leads toward the decline of the aristocracy. The two realms remain essentially separated from each other, only occasionally coming together, as when Robert de Saint Loup marries Gilberte Swann. Both belong to the end of an era: the aristocracy gives way to the bourgeoisie, and the belle époque ends with the war and the rise of a new literary audience.

Any discussion of literary modernism and memory must take us back once again to Henri Bergson's belief that the universe is inseparable from mind and that the self is created out of memory. While Bergson's ideas are not identical with Marcel Proust's narrative method, similarities nevertheless exist. Bergson creates two realms of reality, one accessed by intelligence, the other by intuition; Proust also discussed two orders of reality, one a product of habit, the other of the unconscious. The major difference between the two is that in Bergson, man is continuous with time and in Proust, discontinuous. Memory for Proust is an uncontrolled and uncontrollable series of images of the past—flat, colorless, and without life, governed by habit. But buried in the unconscious are other memories that are rich, vibrant, and authentic and that reveal themselves through accidental association. Sensation—especially the sensation of taste and smell—releases from memory deep and elusive secrets that we cannot evoke by intelligence or will. The madeleine dipped in tea involuntarily evokes Aunt Leonie at Combray. Loss in Proust is greater as an emotional than as a physical experience. When Marcel's grandmother dies, he does not feel the full impact until he bends down to take off his boots, something his grandmother used to do for him.

Past time is lost, mostly wasted and irretrievable, in the face of change. The past intact can never be regained, but it can be relived as a new experience involving the fusion of past and present, the present as a prism through which to interpret the past. Proust moves the novel away from physical reality to character subjectivity, with memory fusing time present and time past. The consciousness that one brings to the past creates the meaning of the past. Memory cannot work separately from mind-based reality. There was no longer any pretense to a direct source of the real as with Balzac and Zola. As Malcolm Bradbury has put it, "Proust broke open the French heritage of realism."[3] Proust did for the novel what Freud did for psychiatry, what Mendel did for biology, the Curies for physics, Picasso for art: he changed its very nature.

Proust is far more interested in the product of memory than in the process of memory. He is obsessed with lost time, not as a form of reality, but as a means of illuminating the present. Time regained is never the same as time lost; the essence of time regained is a revelation about time lost. Time regained is a creative process, a way of freezing time and unlocking meaning. While memories are as fleeting as physical time, they are the means by which we redeem physical time. As in Bergson, the connection between the past and the present in Proust is not a mechanical one. The connection between past and present creates a third order of meaning, each allowing insight into the other, and out of this interpenetration of meaning comes a sense of epiphany, the unfolding of concealed meaning, which is what the modernist believed was the ultimate function of art. As Georges Poulet has told us, "The Proustian novel is . . . a series of images that, from the depths where they have been buried, rise to the light of day. A struggle for life bursts out between them."[4]

The present and the past thus interpenetrate and are interconnected. The quality of mind that we bring to our memories affects the very nature of those memories. At one point in his narration, when he is on the train back from Combray to Paris, Marcel, the narrator, loses faith in his artistic capacity: "It was, I recall, when the train stopped in open country. The sun shone halfway down the trunks of the raw trees, which bordered the roadbed. 'Trees,' I thought, 'you have nothing more to tell me, my cold heart no longer hears you. Here I am in the midst of nature's beauty, yet it is with indifference, with boredom, that my eyes note the line that separate your luminous foliage from your shadowy trunk."[5] Memory heightened by resplendent emotion can transform physical reality. When the emotions change, so does memory, and so also the reality.

Such Proustian moments abound in modern narrative. One remembers the scene in *The Great Gatsby* when Gatsby finally reconciles himself to the fact that he has lost Daisy Fay. At this moment, his resplendent world becomes an ordinary place. In words that parallel Proust, we are told, "he must have felt that he had lost the old, warm world, paid a high price for living too long with a single dream. He must have looked up at an unfamiliar sky through frightening leaves and shivered as he found what a grotesque thing a rose is and how raw the sunlight was upon the scarcely created grass."[6] Gatsby's gorgeous world of memory is contingent upon the emotions that sustain it. When emotion changes, it alters memory, and reality also changes. A rose becomes grotesque; the sunlight is as "raw" on Gatsby's grass as it is on Marcel's trees.

If the Fitzgerald passage reaches to Proust in one direction, it reaches in another to Gertrude Stein's "a rose, is a rose, is a rose." Her statement contains within it two totally opposed meanings based on two different ways of seeing the same thing, as well as the difference between literal-mindedness and the working of memory. It was all a matter of perspective. From the perspective of the rose as a thing, a rose is a rose—that is, a reality that remains unchanged, the emphasis upon sameness. From the perspective of a viewer bringing different emotions to the rose, the rose is a rose is a rose—the emphasis is upon difference, the capacity of charged memories evoking different emotions to change the rose. Between these two opposed meanings, embedded within the same statement, is the history of literary modernism—the transition from a literature of realism to a literature of inward meaning and consciousness.

II

If Proust gives us one version of the inward vision, James Joyce offers us another version. Joyce worked his way through all of the narrative problems that faced the modernists. One could argue that Joyce was the paradigmatic modern who took us from the "slice of life" realism of the early *Dubliner* stories to the literature of memory as dream in *Finnegans Wake*. *Dubliners* is Joyce's exercise in his later repudiated realism. In this collection of stories, Joyce allowed a look into the meaning of Ireland that links him with the transitions taking place in Ibsen's Norway and Chekhov's Russia. In *A Portrait,* Joyce rewrote an earlier, realistic version of Stephen Dedalus's life into a highly subjective, impressionistic work. But it is *Ulysses* in which the major transformation in Joyce's work takes place. In *Ulysses,* a mythic and symbolic world replete with private memory is super-imposed upon the realistic setting of Dublin, bringing the flux of matter and the flux of mind into conjunction. In the "Proteus" chapter, Joyce treats the whole matter of being as flux. Stephen ponders if there is any way to arrest the flow of life and comes to an answer that is remarkably close to Bergson's. Matter, Stephen concludes, is moving toward forms that are built within it. As the acorn becomes the oak tree, the fetus becomes the child; language becomes various forms of style (a point developed at length in the "Oxen of the Sun" chapter).

In *Portrait,* Stephen claimed that the artist had insight into these unfold-ings ("entelechies," as Aristotle had termed them) in the form of epiphanies. An epiphany was a sudden revelation of physical meaning, in which the significance of, say, the beautiful (to which Stephen is about to commit himself) is brought forth by the splendor of the "bird woman" he sees on the beach. This takes Joyce very close to Proust's belief that the artistic imagination releases and then inter-prets memory. A similar scene occurs in *Ulysses.* In the "Ithaca" chapter, Bloom returns home with Stephen, surrogate father united with lost son, surrogate son with lost father, before father and son go their separate ways. After Stephen leaves, Bloom prepares for bed and takes off his boots (within which he has journeyed the last eighteen hours to the far reaches of Dublin). When he picks a piece of toenail, the odor suddenly releases a vault of memories in a scene that acknowledges a Proustian basis for memory (Proust's novel had been published in the previous year), albeit grounded in a Joycean earthiness, far removed from the more genteel Proust.

In *Ulysses,* the idea of epiphany and the Proustian sense of memory as stimu-lated association give way to an almost pure Bergsonian sense. In the "Circe" chapter, we have Leopold Bloom confronted, as in an expressionistic drama, by his most recent past. As if in a dream, characters rise up as symbols of guilt to confront him about his deeds and misdeeds, especially his past sexual activity. Later in the same chapter, Stephen is confronted by the ghost of his mother, who rebukes him for not praying at her deathbed and whom he again defiantly rejects, this time with a swing of his ashplant (cane) to the chandelier in Bella Cohen's brothel, accompanied by his shout of "nothung," an act of rejection that links him with Wagner's Siegfried. Throughout *Ulysses*, the past has impinged upon the present in the suggestion that Leopold Bloom is the modern incarnation of Homer's Ulysses, just as Stephen is connected to Telemachus, and Molly to Penelope. The re-presentations do not, of course, end there: Bloom is also connected to the Wandering Jew, to Elijah, to Moses. The connections are ironic, serving to contrast the heroic past with the diminished present. But they also suggest that modern narratives are simply past stories in a different mode—that Bloom is the modern Ulysses, that the historical past and the present interpenetrate the same way that Bergson believed that past and present memory interpenetrate.

One could argue that what was taking place on the personal level of memory in the modernistic text had a correspondence on the level of history. One such parallel, for example, involved (the old) historicism, the belief that a period of time (Burckhardt's Renaissance) or of space (Leopold von Ranke's Germany) had a geist, or spirit, a recoverable identity built into it. The idea that most determined the modernist idea of time was thus dependent upon the belief that forms were realizable through time, accessible both through the processes of memory and of history. And lastly, we know of the influence that Vico had on Joyce, and we can connect Viconian cycles with the cycles of Spengler and Toynbee and modernist history in general, which leads to the belief in the continuity of time that we find in Joyce from *Ulysses* to *Finnegans Wake*.

But the story does not end there. According to Israel Rosenfield, modern brain research has disproved the assumption that memory is localized in the brain. The argument here is that memories are generalizations of previous experiences, ways of organizing sensory stimuli that permit them to be related to past experiences. The brain does not sort information but determines what combinations of stimuli are useful to create categories by which we order the stimuli that supply information essential to knowing our environment. These categories depend upon many areas in the brain creating subcategories from which our perceptions are abstracted. Rosenfield summarizes it in this way: "there are no specific recollections in our brain . . . only means of reorganizing past impressions, for giving the incoherent dream-like world of memory a concrete reality. Memories are not fixed but constantly evolving generalizations—recreations [what I have been calling "re-presentations"] of the past, which give continuity, a sense of being with a past, a present, and a future. They are not discrete units that are linked up over time [as we find in Proust] but a dynamically evolving system."[7] What Rosenfield is describing—the brain constantly reorganizing, reinterpreting, and re-presenting the past—is exactly what we find in Joyce's *Ulysses.* Moreover, Rosenfield points out that Freud saw the connection between the grief we experience over the loss of a loved one and the state of mind of a melancholic depressive. This state of depressed mind that finds its equivalent in grieving involves, Rosenfield believes, the brain trying to reorganize the way it processes stimuli, trying to find new connections in order to reorganize memory so that we can cope with present pain.

Something like this happens in both the "Circe" and the "Penelope" chapters of *Ulysses*: Bloom's grieving over the loss of Molly to Blazes Boyle explains why he reassesses his manhood, attempts to justify his guilt as if he were in a court of law, and constantly reconfigures himself. While Bloom's memories of Molly may be in one sense stored up for recall, in another sense his whole way of remembering is similar to the obsessional neurotic who is trying to reorganize old memories, in effect laying down new channels in the brain that allow new avenues into the environment, allow us new ways of organizing the information of memory that open the future. Molly does something very similar in her monologue, in effect reconfiguring her own sexual past in which she eventually dismisses Blazes Boylan from thought. Homer's Ulysses wins over the suitors through heroic actions. Joyce's Ulysses wins over his rival through acts of memory, through the inward turn that gives new meaning—and continuity—to time. In this context, Bloom is a re-presented Ulysses.

The story retold from the depths of Molly's memory becomes a very different story from the one we have gleaned from Bloom's perspective. Recent events not only alter the depths of memory, they create an added reality that is neither pure past nor pure present but the elision between them. This elision supposedly produces simultaneity of events and is what Joseph Frank meant by spatial form. But, of course, no text written in words results in simultaneity of events, since words unfold on the page linearly and thus the events described unfold sequentially. When two narrative events take place at the same time, one has to precede the other in the language of the text. It is only after a text has been read at least once that we can read it spatially, because now a reader can hold in memory the narrative connections that make up spatial form. When the New Critics dismissed the role of the reader as an "affective fallacy," they failed to take into consideration how the reader "completes" the meaning of a modernist work. Spatiality (i.e., a presumed simultaneity) stems from reader participation: these texts, which take memory as their subject, are equally dependent upon the memory of a reader.

Memory and language meet in consciousness. Joyce realized that the unfold-

ing of consciousness could be the basis for a new kind of novel—a novel with
an aesthetic hero for whom sensibility was more important than sentiment, and
who was more interested in being defined in the context of the beautiful than in
the naturalistic context of biological necessity and a determining commercial/
industrial environment. In *A Sentimental Education,* Flaubert had shown Frederic
Moreau playing sentiment out to its final absurdity. Flaubert had also shown in
Salammbo and *The Temptation of Saint Anthony* how an aesthetic consciousness
could transform the novel.

But the greatest catalyst here was Walter Pater. In *The Renaissance,* Pater
had said, "What is important . . . is not that the critic should possess a correct
abstract definition of beauty for the intellect, but a certain kind of temperament,
the power of being deeply moved by the presence of beautiful objects."[8] Henry
James had given us such a novel—one that turned on a character who could
be moved by beautiful objects, a character like Hyacinth Robinson in *The Princess Casamassima* (1886), who, in the presence of St. Marks Square in Venice,
abandons his anarchistic plans because he has come to believe that it is more
important to create the beautiful than to destroy it. This kind of commitment to
aestheticism became one of the controlling ideas of literary modernism. Virginia
Woolf, Marcel Proust (whose early imagination was deeply influenced by Pater's
contemporary, John Ruskin), and Thomas Mann would turn this impulse into a
literary movement.

Joyce saw such an aestheticism as the basis for rewriting his bildungsroman,
A Portrait of the Artist as a Young Man, where the novel turns in the famous beach
scene on Stephen Dedalus's commitment to the beautiful to the exclusion of
other values. As Stephen walks through Dublin, he begins to see through aesthetic eyes, and objects take on impressionistic meaning:

> His morning walks across the city had begun; and he foreknew that as
> he passed the slablands of Fairview he would think of the cloistral silverveined prose of Newman; that as he walked along the North Strand .
> . . he would recall the dark humor of Guida Calvacanti and smile; that as
> he went by Baird's stone cutting works in Talbot Place the spirit of Ibsen
> would blow through him like a keen wind.[9]

As comparisons between *A Portrait* and *Stephen Hero* clearly show, Joyce moved
away from modern realism toward modern aestheticism—two different modes
of narrative reality. There was some carryover in this transition. Behind Herbert

Spencer's naturalism was the Romantic belief that nature was a mirror of truth, that symbols revealed the evolutionary nature of reality hieroglyphically. And even as he abandoned neorealism, Joyce clung to the belief that objects in nature unfold with meaning. Such unfolding was what he meant by epiphany—and such unfolding was inseparable from a theory of symbolism. But Joyce went beyond both literary naturalism and symbolism when he began to control such symbols in the context of myth. The beautiful bird-like girl who supplies the epiphany in chapter 4 of A Portrait takes on symbolic meaning because the novel is controlled by the Daedalus-Icarus myth—that is, by the myth of bird-like flight. Joyce had begun to develop this method in the story "Grace," where the major details of the narrative are controlled by a Dantean vision of hell. He brought the method to near perfection in "The Dead," where the feast of the Epiphany itself controls the meaning of the story, from the name given the key characters (e.g., Gabriel Conroy) to the possible date (6 January) on which the story takes place. There is little doubt that Gabriel d'Annunzio, whose assumed name becomes a commentary in itself on Joyce's story, influenced him in developing such a symbolic-mythic method.

In moving from aestheticism to mythic symbolism, Joyce moved from the early stages of modernism to what today is referred to as high modernism. In fact, it is the work of Joyce, Mann, and Proust among others that embodies our very definition of the modern. The novel that best reflects this process is Ulysses, where Joyce brings all of these narrative elements into play, where a realistic plane of reference is symbolically held in place once a mythic structure has been superimposed upon it. What we have here is the literary complement to what was going on in archaeology—the discovery of layered cities, the realization that different historical realms were superimposed upon each other. Jackson Cope and others have convincingly argued that Heinrich Schliemann's discoveries of Troy and Arthur Evans's discoveries in Crete (Mycenae) had a tremendous influence on such works as Il fuoco (1900) and La città morta by d'Annunzio (1863–1938)—works that in turn influenced Joyce as early as when he was completing the Dubliners stories. In fact, in George Moore's The Lake, the character Nora Glynn participates in such an archaeological dig. After Schliemann, we know of as many as nine cities superimposed on each other in Troy: Cities 7A and B were the city of Homer. The archaeological structures here found its literary equivalent in The Cantos, The Waste Land, and especially Ulysses.

Joyce's interest in the Mediterranean world may have been motivated by another source. As early as 1907 we know that he believed that there was a connection between Mediterranean and Irish culture. In a lecture he gave in Italian at the Università Popolare in Trieste in April 1907, he argued not only for a connection between Iberia and Ireland (long speculated) but also for a direct connection between Ireland and the early Phoenicians and later Egyptians based on a theory of sea trade and common elements of language. Joyce would eventually have been attracted to Victor Berard's theory that the Ulysses story was deeply influenced by Phoenician culture, hence making it a Jewish poem. Joyce's belief in the symmetry between ancient Phoenicia, Greece, Crete, Egypt, and Ireland played into his eventual acceptance of the Viconian theory of history.

While Joyce's interest in Vico has been generally connected with *Finnegans Wake*, we know from Richard Ellmann that Joyce was interested in Vico while he was working on *Ulysses*.[10] This is not surprising given Joyce's interest in Flaubert. *Bouvard et Pécuchet* indicted the supremacy of the rationalistic Enlightenment mind with its trust in factual accumulation. *Salammbo* revealed Flaubert's own use of Vico, in which one order of space and time (Carthage at the time of the Punic Wars) reflects another order of space and time (Paris in the Second Empire).

As we have seen, Vico believed that there were three cycles of time—an age of the gods, of heroes, and of men—and then a *ricorso*. There was thus always a historical foreground and a background, and the Viconian cycles lead inevitably to the parallax view, to use a term that, like "metempsychosis," comes to us from *Ulysses* itself. "Parallax, as explained by Sir Robert Ball, [whose work *The Story of the Heavens* Bloom thinks of as he looks up at the Ballast Office Clock] is the visual result produced when one holds up a finger in front of one's eyes and observes a far object: the finger appears to be doubled. Conversely, if one looks at the finger: the far object appears to be doubled. In the astronomical sense of parallax, distant heavenly bodies observed from different points on the planet appear to be in different positions even though their positions remain the same."[11]

This notion is clearly significant to Joyce's new way of thinking about narrative. The parallax view creates two realms of activity—a foreground and a background, one of which blurs when the other is focused upon, which is to say that the positioning between the two is subjective, held together by historical consciousness. As I have suggested, Joyce was already using something similar to this method in "Grace" and "The Dead" and *A Portrait*; but in *Ulysses* the method dominates by calling attention to itself.

We know that Joyce was thinking of adding a story entitled "Ulysses" to *Dubliners*—a story based on his own experience of being knocked unconscious in a fight and assisted by a Dublin Jew named Albert Hunter, who took him home.

But if the Ulysses myth was early in Joyce's mind, it compared with another myth that also obsessed him at this time—the myth of the Wandering Jew. The origins of this tale are complex, but the legend seems to involve a "man in Jerusalem who, when Christ was carrying his Cross to Calvary and paused to rest for a moment on this man's doorstep, drove him away (with or without physical contact, depending on the variants), crying aloud, 'Walk faster!' and Christ replied, 'I go, but you will walk until I come again!'"[12] The Wandering Jew is fated to walk the world and neither to die nor to find rest until the Second Coming. Earlier forms of the legend involved Enoch in the Old Testament who "walked with God." "Better known is the case of Elijah, who not only was carried up to heaven in a fiery chariot as a reward for his courageous and untiring efforts on behalf of Jehovah, but also became identified in Semitic mythology with Al-Khadir . . . who was a vegetation god and a healer of the sick."[13] The legend has many analogues, including the Sinbad the Sailor legend, which Joyce clearly had in mind while writing *Ulysses*.

One can see why Joyce would have been interested in the Wandering Jew legend. If one begins with Al-Khadir and moves through Enoch to Elijah to Leopold Bloom, one completes the Viconian cycle of time. Once Joyce became aware of Victor Berard's theory of the Phoenician (that is, Semitic) influence on the Ulysses legend, he collapsed the Wandering Jew story into the tale of Ulysses. Like Ovid's, Joyce's world turned on metamorphosis and changing identity.

Why Joyce abandoned the Wandering Jew legend for the Ulysses story is understandable: first, the Ulysses legend was better known to a general public; second, it existed in more coherent form and was thus more easily foregroundable; third, the Ulysses legend allowed him to carry the theme of the family and the idea of return (nostes) in a way the Wandering Jew legend did not; and fourth, once Joyce had become aware of Victor Berard's theory of the Phoenician—that is, the Semitic—influence on the Ulysses legend, he had, in effect, collapsed the Wandering Jew story into the story of Ulysses. So it was fitting that his modern Ulysses be Jewish, just as he had come to believe that the Mediterranean connection with Ireland justified making Dedalus into an Irishman.

The argument over the importance of the Ulysses legend to Joyce's novel has gone on since its publication; critics like T. S. Eliot and Richard Ellmann emphasize the mythic parallel, while those like Ezra Pound and Hugh Kenner minimize them. But if Joyce believed a parallax view stemmed from his use of Vico, then there need be no disagreement. The two planes of the novel, the foreground and background, the realistic and the symbolic, are both in play (as

Eliot and Ellmann claim), but they cannot be held in focus at the same time (as Pound and Kenner intuited). And while the Viconian connection seems there, one does not have to insist upon it, because what Joyce was doing here was simply adopting the elements of Romantic realism to the modern. In repositioning Romantic realism, Joyce had in effect created what we mean by modernism. Many critics have seen this in different terms: Edmund Wilson and Harry Levin, for example, by talking of Joyce's superimposition of symbolism onto naturalism, and Wyndham Lewis in his attack on Joyce for spatializing time—that is, for allowing the simultaneous to overpower the sequential.

What Joyce was doing in *Ulysses* was creating a great archetypal structure. And, as in every archetypal pattern, the emphasis was upon the repeat in history, to use Pound's phrase. What is essential to see in *Ulysses* is that Joyce's archetypes are organically positioned—that is, they reflect natural occurrences built into time. The emphasis in *Ulysses* is on flow: life involves various forms of flow. Life flows through the novel the way the river flows to the sea. The novel does not spare us the flow of bodily substance and fluids: Bloom in the jakes, Stephen and Bloom masturbating on the beach, Stephen and Bloom urinating in the garden, Molly and Gerty McDowell at the start of their periods. Besides flow as physical process, we live in a world of happenstance: flow at this level is the flow of time or what we mean by history.

As physical matter is transformed, so is historical matter; Al-Khadir gives way to Elijah, and Elijah to the Wandering Jew, all replicated in the person of Ulysses/Bloom. Just as the embodiment of Molly's life flows through her memory, the English language in the "Oxen of the Sun" flows through time, much as gestation is a matter of flow when it issues forth a newly born child. Joyce used all of the four great paradigms of the Western world—nature, history, consciousness, and language—sometimes all at once. But in *Ulysses* he never thought of life as inseparable from natural and historical process, from the organic processes that control flow. What he was doing was in harmony with what Virginia Woolf, William Butler Yeats, Ezra Pound, Thomas Mann, and William Faulkner were doing—and what is key to the idea of the modern.

Joyce had told us that he conceived of *Finnegans Wake* "as the dream of old Finn, lying in death beside the river Liffey and watching the history of Ireland and the world—past and future—flow through his mind like a flotsam on the river of life."[14] Locating the story in dream, Joyce was, of course, locating it in a kind of linguistic consciousness. John Bishop in *Joyce's Book of the Dark,* a reading of *Finnegans Wake,* has argued that Joyce believed in the "upward" direction of the Viconian cycles. Man builds himself by developing a full consciousness, which in turn more fully develops our use of language and the ability to establish civil institutions. Buried in our language are the secrets of our past and the hope of our future, particularly in the night language of dream, which reveals what the mind thinking in daylight cannot face. Once reality gives way to layered language, diachronic time gives way to synchronic or spatial time, and Joyce's sleeping hero embodies "all the historical forces that have produced him and the conflicting desires which structure his dreams."[15] The individual contains the universal; individual memory is global memory; here comes everybody.

If the starting point of *Ulysses* is the Wandering Jew/Ulysses story, the starting point for *Finnegans Wake* is the Osiris story, where the myth of the gods finds its prototype. Osiris murdered by his brother Seth, his body dismembered and the parts scattered, is brought back to life by his sister-wife, Isis, after she reassembles his body, at which time she conceives their son, Horus, who lives to revenge his father's murder (cf. the story of Tammuz, Adonis, Dionysius, and Christ). Rise and fall, fall and rise—such is the pattern of *Finnegans Wake*, where Finn McCool of Irish legend gives way to Humphrey Chipden Earwicker. If the Osiris legend is the prime myth of the gods, the prime myth at the level of heroes is the Tristan and Isolde story, where the old King Mark is replaced by his nephew Tristan, who steals the love of Mark's wife, Isolde, which in *Finnegans Wake* finds its equivalent in the struggle between the father and the brothers over the love of Iseult (sometimes called Issy with its suggestion of the Osiris legend), whose name carries the idea of the story, just as the setting of the novel in Chapelizod (Isolde's chapel) reinforces that connection.

We know that during the writing of *Finnegans Wake*, Joyce began to think of his characters in relational terms because he devised a series of signs, or sigla, for his major characters, and thought of many of the sigla as interchangeable. The meaning of all the main characters of the novel change in relation to themselves, depending upon what phase in the Viconian cycle we find them. Earwicker is seen, for example, as the dismembered god, as Oliver Cromwell, as a Norwegian ship captain, as a man named Buckley in the Russian Revolution, and as a Chapelizod pub keeper. His secret act in Phoenix Park partakes of Adam's original sin and as a sordid act in the modern city. The two brothers, Shem and Shaun, penman and postman, bohemian and bourgeoisie, one a wasteful gracehopper and the other a prudent ondt, one a member of the Gripes and the other of the Mookse, represent polarized space and time (Joyce vs. Wyndham Lewis, England vs. Ireland) before they eventually are reconciled on the level of universal consciousness. As the sigla change, so do the characters, until it is hard to know, as one commentator puts it, "who is who when everybody is somebody else."[16]

In a work organized structurally like *Finnegans Wake,* we lose our sense of foreground and are left with almost only background: Dublin and Ireland and the real-life people who make it up begin to disappear or become flatter and thinner to the point of invisibility. It becomes harder to identify with characters as characters; we lose a sense of the everyday and of a specific place, and what can be abstracted from the events becomes more important than the events themselves. This is the direction the novel has gone since *Finnegans Wake,* and we can see the influence that Joyce had, directly or indirectly, on such contemporary novelists as Samuel Beckett, John Barth, Donald Barthelme, William Gaddis, Thomas Pynchon, and Don DeLillo.

Second, once we enter a structural world, we enter a narrative realm that is relational rather than centered. If one talks about the Osiris legend or the Egyptian Book of the Dead as the center of *Finnegans Wake,* one can substitute the Oedipus legend, as Margot Norris has done, and show how it serves exactly the same function. Narratives become intertextual, taking their meaning from other narratives or from themselves, which is what they are really about. The sense of resulting play is almost endless, as the reader of *Finnegans Wake* soon finds. The letter the hen digs up in the chicken coop parodies the story of the Book of Kells, which was buried, dug up, reinterpreted, as well as parodying the Osiris myth and its cognates, and parodying finally modern literary criticism when the letter is subjected to both a Freudian and a Marxist interpretation. Such practices constantly disrupt the story, calling attention to it as a structural (constructed) event. The text multiplies signifiers in a way that challenges the signified, a process that is also at work on the level of language: Joyce made draft after draft more linguistically complex, taking us to what postmodernism means by differal, dispersal, and différance.

Lastly, we can see that the change came not from without by revolt, but from within his own system. The lesson here is historically clear: within every system of organization there is a principle of disorganization that disrupts the system from within. Within the Viconian organic theory of nature and history is a structural theory that emerges as Joyce began to think in universal time and monomorphic terms. The journey from "The Dead," through the "Proteus" and "Circe" chapters of *Ulysses* to *Finnegans Wake* was a matter of transformation, a paradigmatic shift within the system itself.

V
FROM ROMANCE TO NIHILISM

11 ❖ FROM ROMANCE TO REALISM

The narratives that make up the modernist canon cover an immense amount of ground, from mythic romance to noir realism. Realism has come to mean many different things. In its origins as practiced by Balzac and Zola, it was a form of "truth," allowing access to a shared reality that was empirically available to an objective observer and consistent with theories of history such as historicism, with its belief that there was one true meaning to historical unfolding. Under the influence of Nietzsche, Stevens, Stein, and the high moderns, realism gave way to a theory of "perspectivism," the assumption that reality was a product of the way it was perceived, a belief not inconsistent with dialectical history, each thesis in search of an antithesis that could accommodate a synthesis. As transformed by structuralism, each starting point was hypothetical, relative to an alternative and thus relational in meaning. And under the influence of postmodern authors such as Pynchon, DeLillo, and Umberto Eco, realism became a string of clues without a conclusion, an unfolding of suppositions that had no verification in outside reality, the historical equivalent of the uncertainty principle.

We have moved from the objectivity of Zola, to the ambiguity and moral ambivalence of Henry James, Edith Wharton, Ford Madox Ford, and Djuna Barnes, to the linguistic experimentation of Gertrude Stein, to the introspective variances of Gide, Kafka, and Beckett, toward the radical revisions of postmodernism, which in itself was subject to being transformed by theories of gender, race, and popular culture. As the novel evolved, the mythic element gave way to more dubious states of mind, character motives became more ambivalent, narrative meaning more ambiguous, and the meaning of plot more difficult to assess. Modernists like Ford Madox Ford and Djuna Barnes resorted to unreliable narrators. The burden of meaning in a story came more to depend on the reader as variations of interpretation increased.

As we move from modernism to postmodernism, we also drift toward nihilism. The novel is transformed as we move from the mysterious origins of Rider Haggard to the destructive elements of Joseph Conrad, from Conradian plausibility to the social transformations and psychological doubt we find in Ford Madox Ford and Djuna Barnes. We move beyond Thomas Mann when André Gide questions middle-class conundrums that preclude existential reality; and we move beyond Gide when Céline, Kafka, and Beckett reveal the power of the void. The romance, once infused with mythic meaning, now culminates in cosmic emptiness, harbinger of the apocalypse that we find in Pynchon and his contemporaries.

I

Northrop Frye tells us that we have three ways of organizing archetypal symbols in literature. First, there is myth, which makes use of both the apocalyptic and demonic. Second, we have the romance, in which mythical patterns are more closely connected with human experience. And third, there is realism, more directly connected to individual experience, which as it moves toward the ironic in Joyce, Kafka, and Cocteau takes us back to myth. Modernism in its evolution tended to move from romance to forms of realism. The transition from imperialism as a subject of romance (as we find it portrayed as adventure in Rider Haggard) and imperialism as a form of realism (as we find it portrayed as a destructive process in Conrad) involves two opposed views of historical process. In between the romance and the anti-romance was the thriller—the mystery, detective, or spy story. While these subgenres were distinct in narrative purpose, sometimes themes merged as when a Sherlock Holmes story depicted threats to the nation coming from the imperial frontier. When the emphasis was on character development, the narrative offered more introspection and less pure adventure. This distinction often defined the difference between high-brow and lowbrow material, and the difference between the two was clearly established. Graham Greene, for example, distinguished his highbrow work from his lowbrow "entertainments" (as he called them), and the novels of Raymond Chandler and Dashiell Hammett more directly appealed to suspense than did the novels of Hemingway and Fitzgerald. Chandler and Hammett, in fact, were on the way to the "tough guy" novel of Mickey Spillane, a subgenre clearly distinct from the neorealism of Hemingway and Fitzgerald. It was only after the demise of modernism as a literary movement that critics began collapsing highbrow modernism and lowbrow modernism into each other.

The popularity of Sherlock Holmes in late Victorian times was surpassed only by the popularity of Rider Haggard's novels. The novels of Doyle and Haggard play dialectically off each other. In the character of Sherlock Holmes, Conan Doyle depicts the supreme rationalist and looks to a progressive future. Whereas Conan Doyle believed causality could be rectified, Rider Haggard believed in the future as the continuation of the past. One is a mechanistic, the other a teleological view. One puts the emphasis upon causes realized in time; the other upon ends eventually fulfilled. One led to a materialistic naturalism, the other to Romantic idealism. In the characters of Ludwig Holly and Allan Quatermain, Rider Haggard depicts the scholar and white hunter whose interests are archaeological and anthropological and looks to a glorious past that contains universal truths. Holmes demystifies the past and challenges cult meaning; Haggard suggests that secrets buried in the primitive past can unlock historical meaning. Such secrets are usually connected with a lost, primitive society or a cult that has handed its mysteries down in hieroglyphic—that is, in encoded—ways.

Haggard's best-known novel, *She* (1887), has a narrative frame: it claims to be an edited manuscript sent to a publisher. Haggard was exploiting the late Victorian interest in archaeology and anthropology that would culminate three years later with Frazer's monumental *The Golden Bough*. The novel once again introduces us to the powers of the chthonic. The citizens of Kor create a magnificent city cut out of rocked land only to be destroyed by a pestilence from which they were unable to recover. Powers come from and are reclaimed by the earth. Morton Cohen conjectures that Haggard may have had in mind the remarkable ruins of Zimbabwe, "an inscrutable stone metropolis that has puzzled archaeologists since its discovery in the late nineteenth century."[1] Haggard uses his story to suggest the power of primitive cults confronting more primitive powers. Freud is believed to have been reading *She* while working on his theory of the uncanny. Certainly the novel treats the return of the repressed, the inevitable expression of the hidden. Haggard brought two popular themes into conjunction: a journey into the heart of Central Africa that unlocks a realm of mystery and intrigue, and a narrator who can interpret its significance.

Haggard's narrative devices were used by many of his contemporaries, often for different purposes: Bram Stoker used them to take us to the edge of empire, where we make contact with the "undead" (as in *She*). Less popular novelists more realistically handled these exaggerated experiences. Conrad deviated from the narrative devices of the romance when he took us into heart of the Congo, where primitive mysteries were revealed. He was not interested in the fire that illuminated Kor, or the mine city painfully carved out of pure rock in *King*

Solomon's Mines, or the engineering that made Milosis a monument to the Sun. His focus was on psychological rather than physical reality—on the destructive darkness that consumed Kurtz.

II

Marlow's experience is a journey back into time, back before civilization into the origins of existence.[2] There we find the primitive forces that civilization still employs but tries to conceal. Conrad tells us that there is little difference between civilization and savagery: he sees in the transformed Kurtz the rapaciousness that drives life, the force that equates the jungle and the city.

The city of Brussels has organized the chaos/horror of life. Marlow refers to it as "a whited sepulchre," a sepulchral city, suggesting both Baudelaire's and later T. S. Eliot's city of the walking dead. The city is a monument to power, but Marlow sees that it cannot be separated from the reality of death and the forces that pull us back to the primitive, back to the earth. Death and degeneration are laws of life, setting limits to the meaning of the city and to life itself. As an Enlightenment entity, the city tries to deny its limits, emblematizes its capacity to rule the world, but Marlow sees beneath this arrogant surface. Kurtz also sees at once the beginning and the end: the basis upon which civilization rests and the tenuousness of the human condition.

Marlow's lie to Kurtz's intended is necessary for civilization—indeed, for life—to go on: the ugly reach of the city into the jungle is concealed by sentiment, to maintain what Wallace Stevens would call a Supreme Fiction. If the intended is to keep her sentimental sense of love, she must not know of Kurtz's African mistress, or of the greed, the death, the degeneration; if the imperial mission is to continue, she must keep sending men out in the name of "progress." The uncanny nature of truth is concealed by civilized lies. As such, *Heart of Darkness* conveys a more putative secret than Rider Haggard's *She.*

Conrad, as Allan Hunter believes, "is putting the record right about a large number of what he identifies as popular fallacies"[3] Conrad thus takes us from Romantic expectation to doubt—to the destructive element that must become a way of life for the truly initiated. We end on a boat on the Thames River: the story has come full circle. The Thames, we are told, runs into the Congo, connecting imperial Africa to the Roman imperialism of England, creating moreover a seamless albeit uncanny reality that connects the modern city with the primitive jungle, the familiar with the strange. Like a Buddha, Marlow has perceived the mystery of existence.

Conrad may be working with one of the main ideas of Herbert Spencer: that the evolutionary movement is from the homogeneous to the heterogeneous, from the simple to the complex, from the undifferentiated in form and function to the differentiated. The difference between the jungle and the city is thus a matter of degree rather than of kind; as the city becomes more complex, so does its means of organization, but such organization is always being tested by the primitive urges that it tries to suppress. Conrad thus challenges Spencer within his own terms, denying a progress to history as Kurtz degenerates rather than evolves. A look at other Conradian novels supports this conclusion: the moral squalor of Verloc's London, the chaos after Jim's death in Patusan, and the tyranny in Razumov's Russia do not suggest progress. Built into nature are physical limits beyond which humanity cannot go, and the metropolis, as heterogeneous and complex as it may be, is subject to the same laws as is the jungle village.

Conrad, like Stoker, challenges Conan Doyle's Enlightenment trust in reason and Rider Haggard's awe of a mystical past. Bram Stoker depicted the power that cult worship still had in a civilized realm. But Conrad goes one step further and reveals the thin line between the claims of civilization and the forces of nature, suggesting how tenuous is a residual order when exposed to degenerative forces, and how vulnerable both from within and without is the sepulchral city.

Just as Conrad rewrote Haggard and Doyle, recent popular forms rewrote Conrad. Novels and films like *King Kong* and *Star Wars* keep elements in the Conradian vision alive. *King Kong* suggests an affinity between beauty and the beast when it takes a gorilla from its natural habitat in the jungle to the modern metropolis, which has to destroy it to preserve the distinction between primitive and civilized. *Star Wars* projects into space the white-hat, black-hat duality of the western. The heroic and enlightened mission of Luke Skywalker confronts the primitive or dark side embodied by his putative father, Darth Vader, as Marlow confronts Kurtz. The difference between Conrad and these later more popular forms is that Conrad brings the key themes back to the human perspective of Marlow and Kurtz, while the popular forms concentrate more directly on the effects of primitive force, often expressed as a natural violence beyond human restraint.

III

When Henry James visited America in 1904, he was greatly disappointed to see the extent to which it had been commercialized. He voiced his discontent in a travelogue, *The American Scene* (1904), and in the novel *The Ivory Tower*, which significantly he never finished. As he indicated in his book on Hawthorne, James admired the aristocratic institutions of Europe that he felt America lacked. An early expression of his ideas came in *The American* (1877). But as he lived on, James became more aware that the old aristocracy was crumbling, and the choice between a decadent Europe and a materialized America was becoming less viable.

Three themes dominate his fiction: the transplanted American—the Europe-America theme in which a character is in conflict with his or her culture; the wayward child—the child in conflict with the family; the role of the artist—the artist in conflict with mass culture, or the power of aestheticism, or the need to experience deeply. All three of these themes relate to one major theme: modern conflict has brought an end to innocence. James's early, middle, and late periods of writing make use of this composite theme. As for technique, in James's fiction choice has become more ambivalent: characters no longer choose between absolute dichotomies. Choice carries with it a moral dimension; moral decisions in turn have become more nuanced, more an arbitrary, deeply subjective matter that moves the narrative toward a new kind of agency.

In early works like *The American,* James depicts Christopher Newman, who gave up the seamy world of American business, tried to find himself among the dying French aristocracy, and became a victim of its corruption. Newman to his credit is unfixed and free, still exploring realms of new possibility. Valentine is also open-minded, and this constitutes the common ground between them. If Newman's character stems from a kind of philistinism, Valentine's honor rests on decadent conventions. But Valentine's honor is not totally without substance. While his duel is senseless, Valentine tries to redeem the honor of his mother and brother. *The American* is an attempt to structure in human terms the conflict between European and American values. The pawn in this process is Claire de Centre. Newman is interested in her as a woman and wants to save her from a degenerate society; his motives are both romantic and noble: his desire is to see her break out of her cultural confines. The Bellegardes are interested in her as property and want to preserve family heritage; they would prefer that she not marry outside of royalty so long as the marriage brings with it a comfortable endowment. James suggested that Newman triumphs morally when he burns the letter incriminating the Bellegardes, but they anticipated his restraint, and it was an empty triumph: Valentine is dead, and Claire in the convent.

This novel misled many nineteenth-century readers because it inverted the structure of the popular romance: one expected to see virtue triumph in the end. *The American* begins as a comedy of manners and ends as a tragedy of manners. There is a shift in tone in the novel as it moves toward melodrama. In comedy there is usually a conflict between fixed and free characters, and virtue triumphs in the end. In melodrama, forces over which they have no control thwart the free characters, and good gives way to evil. As in most of his fiction, James's characters are defined against a fallen world. America and Europe supply opposing values: the American is untutored, naïve, unsophisticated; the European is refined but degenerate, with past values remaining but not the means to preserve them, with the pride and honor of the aristocracy resting on pretense.

In his middle period James wrote *The Portrait of a Lady* (1881), a novel in which Isabel Archer duplicated Newman's plight. Like Newman, she wants to experience life, to be free. But James is telling us that one is vulnerable when freedom is devoid of experience and knowledge. The source of her vulnerability stems from the breakup of the Old World. European aristocracy is now made up of new men like Gilbert Osmond, an American expatriate and parasite on the old aristocracy. In order for Osmond to exist, he must have money. Once Isabel acquires a small fortune (60,000 pounds), she becomes his prey.

James sees the old aristocracy giving way to a new social order incarnated in the Touchettes. They are American expatriates who have made a fortune in banking. But they also are in decline, not because they lack money, but because they lack energy. The sickly Ralph Touchette embodies their condition. They could never make the money again that they now have. James other characters establish a spectrum of social types: Caspar Goodwood, the naive American, whose wealthy parents own textile mills; Lord Warburton, a viable member of the British nobility; Henrietta Stackpole, the liberated woman; Madame Merle, the expatriated American and the mother of Osmond's Pansy.

Like so many modern novels involving the upper class, the story is told against a realm of decadence. *The Portrait of a Lady* is a novel about the loss of innocence. Isabel refuses to marry both Lord Warburton and Caspar Goodwood because she wants to experience life more fully. Madame Merle takes advantage of Isabel's search for experience. Isabel ends up doing what Ralph Touchette wanted when she "chooses" her own destiny. But the outcome of the novel questions and contradicts the wisdom of her desire. James is suggesting that freedom demands responsibility. Moreover, the freedom that exists in a corrupt society is in turn corrupted: one is no freer than society allows.

Caught between going back to America and Caspar Goodwood, or returning to Italy and Gilbert Osmond, Isabel "chooses" Osmond, accepting her loveless marriage. James was caught between two worlds, the old aristocracy and the new capitalism. He could not, for different reasons, accept either totally. But

James was not willing to give up on the integrity of the individual in the face of this cultural dilemma: the need to exercise the will, no matter how constrained, became a dominant factor. Isabel tells us why she will return to Osmond: by returning, she accepts the responsibility of her initial decision, makes her fate a matter of choice, a matter of will. The need for freedom necessitates opportunity. Isabel's self-understanding distinguishes her from the mere passive victim. Her choice, no matter how misplaced, becomes an important expression of character in a world becoming more limited in possibility. By rejecting almost all of the deterministic assumptions of literary naturalism, James turns the modern novel in a totally new direction.

A representative novel of James's late period is *The Ambassadors* (1903) a tessellated novel that in a complex way treats many of the earlier themes. The central character, Lambert Strether, is the "ambassador," sent by the wealthy Newcombe family to Paris to bring home their son, Chad, who is deeply involved in a romance with a Parisian divorcée, Mme Vionnet. Strether embodies the passive character that we find in much genteel fiction, the character like John Marcher and Newland Archer who is empty, to whom nothing happens, who is afraid to act and to experience life. In his youth, Strether failed to seize the opportunity for love, and he brings this Puritan restraint to Paris. But once there he is surprised to see how much Chad has grown, and he realizes that he has misspent his own life and that time has passed him by.

"Misspent" is the appropriate word: metaphors involving time and money dominate the novel. At first Strether thinks of money as a kind of bank account, something to be accumulated. But as he sees how richly experienced Chad's life has become, he begins to think of money as something to be spent. The difference involves two states of mind: the first sets cautious limits to the way life is lived; the second encourages investment in life, remaining open to new experience. By the end of the novel, Strether has betrayed his trust as ambassador and encouraged Chad to remain in Paris, to marry Mme Vionnet, and to relinquish his American opportunities. But Chad chooses otherwise, and he returns to America and to his family fortune, leaving Paris and his new life behind him. The ending reworks the situation that James gave us in *The Portrait of a Lady*. Instead of Chad remaining in Europe like Isabel, he returns to America and to a life that reminds us of Caspar Goodwood. Strether, however, chooses to remain in Paris, but his choice in many ways is like the Jamesian choice of the earlier novels, vacuous and empty: Chad has gone back to America, Mme. Vionnet has been rudely rejected, and no one has gained or benefited from the experience, except perhaps Strether, who now better understands where his own life went astray.

The novel is a product of modernist technique. Each experience is a scene, a kind of picture or illustration that advances the novel in time. And the meaning of time is complex: Strether superimposes his own memory onto scenes that involve Chad's fate; sees a younger version of himself in Chad; realizes the mistakes he made in not accepting love when he was a young man in Boston; and encourages Chad not to make the same mistake. Each moment, in other words, is infused with personal meaning (memory). Whereas Proust allowed the present moment to color the meaning of the past, James allows the past to color the present moment. For both James and Proust, time is a multilayered reality. But in each case it moves toward no fulfilling ends: it simply moves as a state of mind. James empties his world of all meaning except for the mind imposing memory on time: objective reality gives way to an uncertain subjectivity. In expository works like *The American Scene*, James clearly tells us that he dislikes the way America is becoming more materialized. In his fiction, he also disdains such materialism, but the sense of decline in the novels has a different quality: James personalizes history, making time confrontational.

IV

Edith Wharton's *The Age of Innocence* (1921) is a study of the high rich in New York City around the year 1870. At the beginning of the nineteenth century, Boston, New York, Philadelphia, and Baltimore were equivalent cities in size and wealth. But in 1825, New York pushed through the Erie Canal, connecting it to the Great Lakes and creating a hinterland. Overnight New York doubled in size and became the prime city in America, the canal creating an avenue for the export and import of its goods to and from the Midwest. Edith Wharton's *The Age of Innocence* examines this world from the top down, concentrating on those who were the benefactors of this new prosperity. It is a world insulated by money, a homogeneous society that can exclude what it will not accept. The business world is controlled by men, but the domestic world is controlled by women, matriarchs like Mrs. Manson Mingott, who rely on a system of decorum to hold this world together. Despite the money and the moral structure, the solidity of this world is cracking. The men are getting weaker and the women more concerned with appearances than reality.

The novel's central character is Newland Archer, the product of two established families, the Newlands and the Archers. He is a lawyer, but he does not keep hours and lives off the fortune his father left him. He is engaged to May Welland but is in love with Ellen Olenska, who married unhappily into Polish nobility, has left her husband when he was unfaithful, refuses to go back to be his trophy wife, and has come to New York in anticipation of getting a divorce, despite the public disapproval this has engendered. Newland, trapped within the conventions of this world, is unable to move from passion to action, and he allows his life to be determined by his passivity. He is the man to whom nothing happens. As his name suggests, he walks in the footsteps of James's John Marcher and anticipates the vacillation of Eliot's Prufrock. All of these characters illustrate Freud's belief that modern man has become overcivilized, separated from instincts. Newland is his own worst enemy, manipulating events that save him from acting passionately: he talks Ellen out of getting a divorce, then tells her he would marry her if she was free. He sets the limits and then bewails his condition. Newland is locked into a realm of hypocrisy of his own creation.

The love story in *The Age of Innocence* is coupled with a business plot involving Beaufort, a scheming banker. He is greedy and lecherous and in pursuit of Ellen. This comes to an end when his bank fails because of his dubious investments. Such a person seldom gets into this circle because a person's wealth is ascertained beforehand, and there were few money adventurers. In a world that takes its being from money, he is the snake in the garden. The novel turns on the "kinds" of money one can display: invested money has a higher social value than money that comes from trade or speculation, despite the fact that all of these families made their money initially in trade (the Struthers, for example, are on the fringe of society because their money comes from shoe polish).

The "innocence" of the novel's title is a guise: the money that holds this world together has no innocence, and a character like May Welland will go beyond "innocence" when it is a matter of survival and then retreat back into it as a disguise. At the end of the novel, May Welland and Count Olenska are dead, and Newland and Ellen are now free to marry. Newland is in Paris, where Ellen is now living. But he refuses to call on her and waits in a park while his son goes up to her apartment. His dream of what life with Ellen could have been is more real than Ellen: passion has given way to imagination.

As the ending suggests, Wharton's novel treats a realm that is both insulated and isolated. The novel was written in 1920 but describes the year 1870. Historically this was a turbulent time involving post–Civil War expansion, the corruption of the Grant administration, immigration, the rise of a labor force, and the birth of the megalopolis. And yet there is no outside world in this novel: it is a sealed world, and there is nothing—Beaufort excepted—that violates it. What we see in macrocosm, we see in microcosm: at the end Newland walks away from Ellen insulated by a state of mind, just as this society walks away from outside political and social reality insulated by money. But such insulation could not last forever. As manufacturing eventually depended on a larger rather than a select clientele, Wharton's world was compromised by the assembly line and mass production. The most radical change occurred after World War I with the emancipation of women, the increase in divorce, the less rigid social and sexual customs. It was only a matter of time before Edith Wharton's world would give way to that of F. Scott Fitzgerald. Much still depended on the function of money as the difference in the finances of Tom Buchanan and Gatsby suggest, but money now works in a more demonstrative and less insulated way.

Wharton's other novels are variations on the theme of *The Age of Innocence*. *The House of Mirth* (1905) treats those who have been excluded from this society. Lily Bart becomes a social outcast. Selden and Rosedale are two versions of the outsider: Selden because he does not have enough money, Rosedale because he is Jewish. Selden and Rosedale embody two extremes: if Rosedale is coarse and aggressive, Selden is vacillating and ineffectual. Rosedale is aggressive because he desperately wants to become a part of this world; Selden is passive because he has rejected the life of high society and found nothing to take its place.

Lily could have blackmailed her way back into society, but she destroys the letters Bertha Dorset wrote Selden, with whom she is in love, and she chooses to reject the luxurious world of high society. Like Newland Archer, she creates the situation that then controls her fate. Once again, Wharton makes use of the microcosm-macrocosm relationship: the conflict within Lily Bart is the conflict within the society of her time. Two forces war within her: a desire for the elegant life and an honesty that sees the sham and hypocrisy of that life.

Wharton's world has a tendency to become melodramatic: good and evil become confrontational. Beaufort embodies evil in *The Age of Innocence*, Trenor in *The House of Mirth*. Trenor gets Lily in his debt and then demands "favors": he invites her to his house in the name of his wife who is out of town, and then tries to seduce her. The novel turns on such melodramatic scenes: this is a key scene because Selden sees Lily leaving Trenor's house late that night and begins to believe the gossip. Lily's death, perhaps by suicide, is more symbolically than realistically justified. Her action takes her to a state of behavior more extreme than the situation calls for, but it is nevertheless consistent with the dictates of the novel. Lily's sense of space becomes more restricted as the novel progresses: we move from the spacious grounds of Rhinebeck, to the restricted domain of Roslyn, to the small hotel suite, to a single room in boardinghouse. Lily has reached the dead end of choice because both Rosedale and Selden, in their opposite ways, have negated the possibility of positive choice and a viable existence. Her death by an overdose of chloral hydrate is symbolically consistent with her diminished sense of space and lost options, but nevertheless it is often read as an accidental overdose in pursuit of sleep. But no matter how Lily's death is interpreted, it harbingers the eventual end of this kind of high-society struggle. The next version of the Lily Bart character will be in the more open society of Dreiser's Carrie Meeber. The male version of the story awaited Fitzgerald's Jay Gatsby.

Another Wharton novel that treated the money society in a formulistic way is *The Custom of the Country* (1913). Again we have the aspiring character in the person of Undine Spragg, whose perspective is determined by the likes and dislikes of people in the social register. Undine told Mr. Dagonet, to the astonishment of his dinner guests, that Mabel Lipscomb would get a divorce because her husband "isn't in the right set." She embodied the ruthless spirit and drive of the new rich. Someone like Ralph Marvell, who lived by the old courtesies, was incapable of coping with the likes of Undine. As was her narrative penchant, Wharton again gave us the serpent in the garden in the person of Elmer Moffatt, who corrupted Ralph's genteel sense of morality and fair play. Moffatt is a product of the lower classes, a man with a mysterious past who marries Undine, both of whom are ruthlessly ambitious. The real victim of this societal change is Ralph Marvell: bereft of traditional meaning, Ralph commits suicide. Undine used Elmer and then Ralph in the climb to the top. Undine's climb works against the moral grain of the times: she is unable to break out of "the mysterious web of traditions, conventions, prohibitions that enclosed her in their impenetrable network."[4] Wharton gives us vivid portraits of men and women caught in a web of social conventions: they are destroyed by situations that are a combination of their own ambition and greed and the destructive social forces that they bring into play.

V

Under the influence of Henry James's sense of moral ambiguity and Freud's theory of the subconscious, or latent thought, modern reality became a freighted matter in which memories, feelings, and thoughts took on meaning independent of the thinker. Added to that was the fact that social institutions were undergoing radical change. The aristocracy was losing its privileged place, the estate was in a process of decline, and the man of leisure now brought dubious concerns to his credentials. All of these elements seem to be present in Ford Madox Ford's *The Good Soldier* (1915). Written simultaneously with the gathering war clouds of World War I, the novel catches the bewilderment, the veil that conceals events that characterize the era.

The novel involves two couples—Edward Ashburnham and his wife, Leonora, and John Dowell and his wife, Florence—and their meeting every year in Nauheim, Germany, a spa town to which they resort for their health. Edward, who has a heart condition, is among the last of the aristocrats; his fortune has dwindled under his debauched way of living and poor management, and Leonora has taken over control of the estate, at the same time tolerating Edward's infidelity. The Dowells are American expatriates, touring Europe mostly out of boredom. Florence falsely claims a heart ailment so as to avoid having sex with Dowell, enlisting him as a kind of resident nurse, at the same time carrying on sexual affairs with others, including Edward.

The novel really begins after Edward and Florence have died, and Dowell tries to make sense of the past. From the beginning to the end, he gets it all wrong. Dowell is impressed with Edward, a former British army officer, a man of great presence and attraction, especially attractive to women. Dowell believes his admiration of Edward is generally shared. But Dowell does not have the slightest suspicion that his wife is having an affair with Edward, and he has to rely on Leonora for much of the information he relates. Moreover, he sees Edward as the solid cornerstone of the British empire, despite the fact that Edward's own aristocratic claims are in serious doubt: he has recklessly led a debauched life, including having an affair with Nancy Rufford, his own ward.

Dowell's blindness allows the novel to go in opposite directions: it restores the lost values of Edward and the aristocracy at the same time as it exposes those values for the sham that they have become: it both preserves and questions the imperial past. Ford has skillfully perpetuated a physical world that is held in place by flawed perception and moral tolerance. Like so much that characterizes literary modernism, reality is a product of mind, held in place by perspective.

Not only does *The Good Soldier* suggest that British well-being depends on false perception, it also exposes a historical decline that is transforming the modern empire. This process of decline will become the subject of perhaps Ford's greatest achievement, his *Parade's End*. Originally a tetralogy made up of *Some Do Not* (1924), *No More Parades* (1925), *A Man Could Stand Up* (1926), and *The Last Post* (1928), *Parade's End* was published as a separate novel in 1950.

Christopher Tietjens is the last of an aristocratic line with all of the attributes that might be favorably connected to such a claim. He is a decent man, a man of honor, who lives by a code of noblesse oblige. Ironically, he is a man completely out of touch with his world, whether it be the domestic realm he shares with his wife, Sylvia; the world of the estate Groby that he shares with his brother Mark; the world of intrigue that he shares with Valentine Wannop, whom he desires as mistress; the realm of the military that he shares with his godfather, General Campion; or the world of the army that he shares with the men who serve under him.

All of his values are either misdirected or misunderstood in a world growing more self-indulgent and devoid of virtue. In fact, his charity and goodwill infuriate those closest to him, and he finds himself the object of scorn that he can neither understand nor deflect. His goodwill is tested most viciously by his wife, who is continually unfaithful to him, and who hates him all the more for his virtue, especially his tolerance of her behavior. He rejects the possibility of a divorce because it would publicly embarrass her.

He has stepped aside and refused to claim any part of his father's estate, provoked by his belief (later proved misguided) that his father had committed suicide, an act of which, like divorce, he disapproves. As a result, he has left the estate and its vast income to his oldest brother, Mark. Despite his wife's ill will, he does not protest when Mark offers to pass the estate on to Sylvia and their son, even though he believes the boy has been fathered by another man (again, an assumption that is probably wrong).

Despite his demonstrated abilities in government service, he is disliked on the job, even by Macmaster, his closest friend, who resents him because he has loaned him a large sum of money that the aggrieved Macmaster cannot repay. All those around him constantly test Christopher's goodwill, and he is more resented than admired. This is less true with the woman he wants to be his mistress, Valentine Wannop, but who always seems to be out of reach.

These personal events materialize into Christopher's undoing, as the political events move his world toward war. When war finally comes, it is as the logical conclusion to Christopher's fate. As he finds himself caught in one hostile situation after another, the nation finds itself caught in a worldwide conflagration. The war is Ford's symbol of the break that has fractured Christopher's society. None of his virtues have any relevance in a world that will not accommodate the outdated values of a true gentleman, just as the hostile nations will not diminish or relinquish their own competing claims to imperial largesse or war as the means of realizing those claims.

Christopher's experiences in the army are as misguided as his experience as a civilian. General Campion upbraids him for his generosity to his men, a violation of the distance the general feels that should be maintained between officers and men. Christopher tries to shield an incompetent senior officer, a quixotic act that goes unappreciated by the officer and disdained by the command. Christopher feels the war is going badly because of poor communication between parts of the army, an idea he then applies to life itself. His most substantial realization is that it is the war itself and not who is victorious at the end of the war that matters. The war is the true divide: the war itself has changed his world forever; nothing will be the same again. He has fallen out of one era and is unprepared for another; all he looks forward to is the privacy he hopes will come with postwar peace.

But before he can find peace, he finds the courage to dig himself and two of his men from a bomb crater and to carry one of them to safety, despite enemy fire. This act of heroism brings only disgrace when the general relieves him of his command. No longer able to make even absurd sense out of his situation, Christopher makes his separate peace: for him this marks the end of war and of his place in government service. He can no longer return to Groby, now rented to a vulgarly rich American, or to his brother who, like Christopher, has withdrawn from the new era. Like Mark, Christopher has left deceit, selfishness, and confusion behind him. Along with Valentine, he retreats to a cottage, where they prepare for the birth of their child—and for an unknown future. The novel closes on a symbolic note: the American woman who has rented Groby has cut down the Great Tree, an immense cedar that has stood as a symbol of aristocratic authority, hierarchy, and privilege for generations. Now that the tree is gone, the estate is a different place. Perhaps better, perhaps worse, it now shares an enigmatic state of being with the nation itself.

VI

Ford Madox Ford created a realism based on the reader not being able to connect the dots, stemming from the inability of the narrator to understand the story he is telling, and the inability of the last of the aristocrats to find meaning and understanding in a world that no longer shared their sense of values. Djuna Barnes takes this sense of misunderstanding one step further, and in *Nightwood* (1936) gives us realism based on the inability of the major characters to find reciprocity in others. Here Barnes took a limited number of characters and depicted them at spiritual odds with themselves and with each other. Her story unfolds like a rejoinder to Plato's belief that individuals are incomplete until they find the complement to their soul. But instead of finding the mate who completes them, Barnes's characters encounter the person who will most disrupt their lives.

The novel brings into being two worlds—one of day, the other of night. These realms have their analogue in historical time. The realm of night takes us back to the mysterious origins of humanity; the realm of day takes us through the transformations of civilization. This process, however, instead of securing historical stability, has led to historical dysfunction. We live in an evolutionary divide: human beings have lost their animal instinct but have not found a new source of emotional unity. The human species is thus out of sync with itself, and the individuals who make up the species have fragmented and mutated into radical forms of the self at the cost of not progressing toward a unified psyche.

The central character in Barnes's narrative is Robin Vote. At the beginning of the novel she has apparently fainted. "Born somnambular," she has fallen into a strange, comalike sleep. She lies on her bed seemingly arrested in the midstep of a dance. Her room, in the midst of the city, has taken on the vestiges of the jungle, complete with a variety of plants and singing birds. These details suggest her suspended state, both historical and personal. She seems caught between two evolutionary states, the jungle and the city, the primitive and the civilized; she is frozen in a physical moment of beauty, caught as if in a frieze.

Robin has married Felix Volkbein, who has coaxed her into having a child. But this has led to a crisis in her life: she lives aimlessly, wanders listlessly about the city, even as she converts to Catholicism. The nuns in whom she confides realize that she is living prehistorically: her mind is confined to an ancient realm that precedes the concept of sin and absolution; she is outside the boundaries of both modern history and religion, a mutant embodiment of a malfunctioned evolutionary process. She gives birth to a sickly son, takes to drink, resorts to more wandering, and becomes distracted beyond Felix's means of communicating with her. Finally, she abandons both her child and Felix and leaves Paris for America.

In America, she takes up with Nora Flood, historically rooted in an ancestral family, working now as an advance agent for the Denckman Circus. At the circus, the lions are strangely attracted to Robin, who once again seems caught between human and bestial worlds. With Nora, Robin leaves New York, finally settling once again in Paris, where she wanders the street and bars at all hours of the night, as her relationship with Nora begins to disintegrate. As with Felix, Robin cannot be confined to home or domestic routine, and Robin eventually leaves Nora for Jenny Petherbridge. Jenny and Robin, we are told, are the opposite halves of the human entity: both are caught between a bestial and human state— Robin is the beast as it turns human; Jenny is the human as it turns beast.

The last character that makes up the cast of Barnes's novel is Dr. Matthew O'Connor, a psychiatrist in communication with Robin and with Robin's lovers. He lacks the power to bring any of them together again; indeed, he has been partly responsible for their estrangement. Torn between a trust in medical science and a leaning toward Catholicism, he also reveals a divided self, lacks residual meaning, takes pleasure in his transvestite behavior, and longs to be a woman. The last four chapters of the novel find him at the center of activity as the principal characters ironically try to find meaning through him.

The novel concludes in upstate New York, where we find Robin, who has returned to Nora's ancestral house and taken up residence in the chapel. We last see her confronted there by Nora and the dog, the human and the animal, caught once again between two modes of living being, unable to relate to either: she embodies the prolapsed nature of modern humanity. The novel concludes with this emblem of human estrangement. Barnes's characters are neither fully animal nor totally human: they reside in an evolutionary halfway house, removed from a basic animality but not entirely human. Unable to bring the two ends of evolution into sync with each other, they are evolutionary misfits, mutant selves unable to find a reconciling principle in themselves or in others.

No other modern author transformed the human race so radically as did Barnes in *Nightwood:* her characters are divided souls, living in a state of isolation and decline, remote from the possibility of authenticity, at odds with their environment, lacking harmony between themselves and others. The novel has a modernist structure: the main characters are introduced in the opening chapters, their meaning recast in the closing chapters; each chapter is distinct in meaning, existing relationally rather than building on a cause-to-effect progression. Whatever narrative principle may be at work is not sustained. Intentionally difficult in the way it makes use of discontinuous symbolism and of references that the reader must hold together in order to affect a sense of the whole, especially in matters of chronological unfolding, *Nightwood* is a perfect example of what Joseph Frank meant by spatial form.

12 ✤ AUTHENTICITY IN A COUNTERFEIT CULTURE

I

While modernism as a literary movement cannot be reduced to one author or even to a group of authors, Thomas Mann, Marcel Proust, and James Joyce are often looked upon as the authors who, as a group, summarize the literary methods distinct to literary modernism. Their achievement was immense, but they could never have accomplished what they did if modernism as a state of mind had not preceded their efforts. Taken together, these three authors supply the means of thinking of movements like literary modernism as formulating a synoptic text that both precedes and anticipates the writing of individual works—a composite text that serves as a modernist ur-text.

With the breakdown of a homogeneous urban community, we are left with the problem of giving identity to mass man in a secular society, a question Thomas Mann (1875–1955) readily addressed. Mann believed, for example, that music was more vital when it was a part of religion. In the Renaissance, music was severed from its religious purposes and became a cultural force of its own. This secularism reached a high point with Beethoven and Wagner, where it was reduced to nineteenth-century religious liberalism.

Mann believed that individualism and liberalism were the basis for modernism, part of a cult that led to the degeneration of culture. Mann's characters seem initially satisfied with their middle-class status, but this satisfaction turns out to be blind complacency. They try unsuccessfully to penetrate beneath their social routine to regain a lost vitality. Mann positions an energized materialism giving way to a decadent aestheticism. Almost all of his major characters—Hanno, Tonio Kröger, Gustav Aschenbach, Felix Krull, and Adrian Leverkuhn—are caught in this downward drift, which takes them to or near to their death.

His *Buddenbrooks* (1900) treated the decline of a bourgeois family, the collapse of its material "calling," and the emergence of a powerless artistic temperament. In *Tonio Kröger* (1903) and *Death in Venice* (1912), Mann depicted the modern artist obsessed with decay and disorder, drawn to the dark underside of Romantic life. These are fundamentally modernist themes, brought into being by the conflict between the bourgeois and aesthetic worlds. The present has been spiritually and materially emptied by the rise of mass culture and the commercial city. Mann, who saw himself working in the tradition of Schopenhauer, Nietzsche, and Wagner, regretted the passing of an older Germany of philosophy and Kultur. The modern artist must confront a Nietzschean disorder as he becomes more superfluous in the face of bourgeois materialism, exiled to search for spiritual meaning on his own. The artist is a part of the degenerative, decadent process: aesthetic transfigurations accompany biological decline. Mann tried in *Tonio Kröger* to reconcile artistic and bourgeois values, but the artist—cut off from ordinary people and life—becomes an urban outcast. Mann believed that when an inner idea of self was weakened, personality was eaten away from within. His artist, like decadents generally, becomes weary and yearns for death.

Aschenbach is an older Tonio; transforming reality into an impossible ideal, he loses contact with life. *Death in Venice* is a story of repressed homosexuality, but it is also an allegory of the decay and dying of an Old World that has lost direction in the face of modernism. Venice, like Aschenbach, is also dying from within: both try to keep their illness a secret from the world. Mann pointed to the absence of vital myth as a fatal quality of modern existence. He pointed to the need of realizing our irrational nature within a rational society. He saw that beneath the assumed order of the modern city was a destructive disorder at work. *Death in Venice* is perhaps Mann's first use of the mythic method—to give shape to contemporary history by manipulating a parallel between the contemporaneous and antiquity. Many readings of this story emphasize Mann's use of the Dionysus myth. Some critics even go so far as to see a connection in names: Aschen (ashes) Bach (Bacchus), and Tadzio and Sabazios (another name for Dionysus). The stranger that Aschenbach sees in the cemetery is a Dionysian figure (he even disappears ghostlike into one of the Greek statues), and the cholera that infects Venice is a plague often connected with the appearance of Dionysus. Even the pomegranate juice that Aschenbach drinks with dinner has relevance, since pomegranates supposedly came from the blood of Dionysus. Aschenbach's dream is more directly connected with the Dionysus story, having in common wild music and dancing, shrill cries of the votaries, uniform dress of the maddened women, and the sacrificial animal whose raw flesh is eaten and warm blood drunk. The irresolvable tension at the heart of the Dionysus myth between reason and emotion, life and death, subliminally lures Aschenbach to cholera-ridden Venice. When Aschenbach's attraction to the beautiful involves the pursuit of Tadzio, he gives in to decadence. Just as the city displays a false order that belies decline, he fails to come to terms with the chaos within himself. Like Conrad, Mann knew that art, like civilization, hides a destructive process. The fate of the artist, like that of all great cities, involves an inescapable attraction toward death. The "falling tower" theme dominated the modern imagination, even before being initiated by Eliot. The darker, Dionysian forces of life overtake Aschenbach.

The other side of Mann's mythic coin is *Reflections of a Nonpolitical Man* (*Betrachtungen eines Unpolitischen,* 1914–18), which attacks the liberal belief in progress. Mann sees the greatness of Germany, but he is also aware of its evil potential. Mann made slightly different use of these themes in his later works. Hans Castorp in *The Magic Mountain* (1924) goes from North to South, order to disorder, health to disease, out of the normal time of the flatlands into the timelessness of the uplands. His three-week stay in the sanatorium extends to seven years, and he begins to see himself in a more detached way, his new reality tested once again in Mann by the meaning of death. In *The Magic Mountain*, the rational, Enlightenment position is given to Settembrini, an Italian humanist, who espouses modern, progressive liberalism. He is opposed by Naphta (modeled on the Hungarian-Marxist critic Georg Lukács), an Eastern European Jew, abandoned in a pogrom, adopted by the Jesuits, a crypto-Communist and proto-Nazi, capable of mixing Catholicism and terrorism.

Settembrini, like Mann's brother Heinrich, believed in material progress. Naphta, like Mann himself, distrusted bourgeois materialism and democratic liberty. The former partakes of the Apollonian principle, the latter of the Dionysian. One believes in while the other distrusts the nation-state. The dispute between Settembrini and Naphta—between belief in an old-line democracy and an emerging totalitarianism—canceled each other out, leaving an amorphous idea of mass man.

The novel ends with Settembrini and Naphta fighting a duel: Settembrini fires into the air; Naphta shoots himself in the head. This deadly ending anticipates the war clouds gathering beneath the mountain, a *Götterdämmerung* that gives the lie to mountain hopes, freeing Hans from its dictates. He and Settembrini descend the mountain to fight on different sides, their fate left unclear. Mann himself could not reconcile the differences between Settembrini and Naphta—

reason vs. the irrational, the individual vs. mass man, and the Apollonian vs. the Dionysian. Nietzsche had infected Mann's imagination: order and disorder were inseparable: reason cloaked mystery, order was subject to chaos, life gave way to death. At this point, Mann's narrative follows that of Conrad into the destructive element, that realm of dark gods that challenge Enlightenment promise.

Mann's stories take place between energized and decadent realms, but in one story the two realms come together. Mann's "Mario and the Magician" (1930) makes political use of the dichotomy between the individual and the crowd. The story takes place in Torre di Veneri, Italy, where a hypnotist has mesmerized a crowd. The hypnotist embodies the power of fascism, the misuse of subjugating control in both Italy and Germany. When Mario assassinates him, the masses are liberated, freed from a destructive power. The question then becomes, How is this freedom to be used? This problem dominates Mann's last major novel, *Dr. Faustus*.

In *Dr. Faustus* (1948), Mann brings this struggle to the dead end of contradiction, and the liberal agenda gives way to cultural madness. The story of Adrian Leverkuhn is told against the rise and fall of Nazism. He makes a pact with the Devil, willfully contracts syphilis, and finally goes insane. Mann drew heavily upon the life and thought of Nietzsche in his depiction of Leverkuhn. Nietzsche justified existence as an "aesthetic phenomenon," equating self with the freedom of art. Carried to an extreme, such freedom is an extension of the liberal ideology, and Leverkuhn embodies the destructive nature of radical individualism. His use of atonalism, or the twelve-tone musical system, moves him further away from any kind of grounding of the self in traditional art. As modern life became more rationalized, mechanized, and industrialized, art was driven underground—back to the primitive, mythical, and irrational. In his earlier work, Mann was sympathetic toward mythic explanations, relying heavily upon the myth of Dionysus and embracing Nietzsche's idea of eternal return—that history would continue to re-present itself (as Joseph is a re-presentation of Adonis-Tammuz-Jesus). But Leverkuhn takes primitivism to a radical extreme, and his belief that culture must be grounded on pagan cult aligns him with the mystical nationalism that Mann connected to the Nazis. His story is told by Serenus Zeitblom ("time bloom," suggesting inevitability), a product of the Enlightenment. But Leverkuhn's Romantic excesses puzzle him, and Zeitblom is both complicit and helpless in the face of Leverkuhn's runaway energy, a rather sorry end to Enlightenment ideology.

By its very nature, the Faustus myth is a celebration of destructive individualism. To the traditional story of Faustus (originating in 1587 with Johann Spiess in Germany and made famous by Christopher Marlowe and Goethe), Mann adds questions involving disease, art, and cultural disintegration. Leverkuhn embodies the impossibility of compromise between the forces of individual genius and the forces of totalitarianism. He embodies both the artist and the nation that wills its destruction. He takes us to the dead end of community, the impossibility of Augustine's *De civitate Dei*, the opposite of Mann's political hopes in *Reflections of a Nonpolitical Man*.

As Michael Harrington points out, "In Faustus, the world is so mad that madness is the only sensible reaction to it. The old definition of decadence as the triumph of society over community, of Gesellschaft over Gemeinschaft, returns in tragic form to define the situation."[1] Such a state of mind destroys the city from within. There is no longer a possibility of harmony in Leverkuhn's world of music. As Harrington rhetorically asks, "In a completely secular world, devoid of transcendence and filled with war and upheaval, what ground is there for harmony? Conventional beauty is a lie, the artist is faced with unrelieved chaos."[2] In *Faustus,* Mann took us to the inevitable end of Enlightenment and Romantic individualism, to the destructive end of both the community and the liberal agenda.

II

If there is a social/political consciousness and a personal consciousness, the two are not always in sync. André Gide was the modernist novelist who explored the chasm between the two and the resulting effect of being emotionally estranged from one's immediate surroundings. Gide anticipates the existential novel. He gives us characters who are socially decentered, peripheral to their environment. Their task is a multiple one: they must realize that they contain the potential to become many different selves, that they must choose how they want to define themselves, and that the human struggle involves creating what is unique in the self rather than accepting the stereotypical definition that society would otherwise impose upon them. Gide's concept of self is the diametrical opposite of the evolutionary process. Man is the sum of what he chooses to be, not the sum of his genetic makeup or his DNA or cellular unfolding.

Gide began his career as a symbolist under the influence of Malarmé, whose symbolic reality dominated his early career. But he moved beyond pure symbolism toward a new kind of realism in which a character's consciousness was engaged by an antithetical being, by the irreconcilable division between mind and reality. One of his first exercises in creating a new realism was *The Immoralist* (1902), which involves the story of Michel, a young, wealthy archaeologist, who marries Marceline and goes to Biskra on his honeymoon. There he becomes seriously ill at the same time that he realizes that he is homosexual, that working within is a hidden self that he is only beginning to understand. Marceline nurses him back to health, even as he becomes more distant, while she becomes gravely and eventually fatally ill.

Put this way, Gide's use of character sounds contrived. But what he is saying is more pervasive and more convincing. Gide suggests that the individual sense of self is more complex than its stereotypical social definition and that one must continually keep that sense of multibeing alive. He gives new meaning to the word "diversity," seeing it as characteristic of the individual self and not just a heterogeneous community. Gide anticipated Jean-Paul Sartre's idea of human nature as something that we create rather than accede to. As we are the potential speaker of many languages, we are the potential product of many selves, and we must determine which self we want to realize.

Gide brings two elements into play: Michel must reconcile consciousness with an understanding of self, and self with an understanding of the outer forces that determine consciousness. In other words, he must break the vicious circle within which he is trapped. His quest is for a freedom that he feels will release a submerged energy that has never been tapped. He feels separated from that energy, not only by immediate conventional restraints and morality, but also from the layers of civilization that seem aligned against him. The restraints of Christian morality have been reinforced by bourgeois society.

Gide believed that one should be true to an inner life rather than to the workings of society. In terms of the traditional novel, he turned away from the social dictates of Balzac and Dickens and substituted the psychological dictates of Nietzsche and Dostoyevsky, who explored an inner realm of meaning that was "illogical, inconsecutive, and contradictory." Gide's characters, as opposed to traditional characters, "are simultaneously impelled in opposite directions, and so achieve a richer anxiety than the neurotic whose two personalities alternately prevail."[3]

Gide once more makes use of this theme in *The Counterfeiters* (1925), his most celebrated novel and the one that best reveals his belief that consciousness, like the manifestation of art, pushes against an intractable reality. In his use of this theme, one can see that this is not a modern novel in the traditional sense of the word. First, many elements of plot are left unattended, unfinished, or uninformed (e.g., what does fate or the future hold for the majority of the principal characters: Vincent, George, Olivier, Bernard, and Passavant?). Life, like the novel, is open-ended; one's fate is never sealed so long as one has the capacity to act differently. Second, the principal characters' paths cross and recross, suggesting that they partake of the same social reality; but some are better able than others to alter the effects of that reality. Third, a novelist within the novel generates the discussion of the relationship between art and reality. Edouard's book involves a novelist caught "between what reality offers him and what he himself desires to make of it." Edouard's desire to write his novel involves his ability to mediate the control of his characters, to alter their ability to shape their own reality. Edouard's initial writer's block reveals his own inability to move beyond the static consciousness of his world, a condition at the end of the novel that he has presumably resolved.

Both art and life involve a search for identity that demands a consciousness that can create its own reality: Gide has given us the novel of the chameleon hero. As Edouard tells us, "I am never anything but what I think myself, and this varies so incessantly, that often, if I were not there to make them acquainted, my morning's self would not recognize my evening's." In Gide's world, the "I" of the novel has no permanent reality, no essential grounding, but absorbs its reality from its response to a preexisting reality.

The novel takes its meaning from narrative cross-purposes: there is a collective consciousness at work in the novel that entwines the major characters as they fight to remain independent of social forces and of the pull that each character has on the other. The novel is a study of how characters strive to remain independent of and outside a realm of conformity while each is caught in a "counterfeit" reality that works against such independence. Gide has created a social vortex from which each character resists or tries to escape. Undo that vortex or strengthen the characters' resolve to create their own identity and we have a transformed order of characters more free to choose themselves in a less restraining world. One can see why Jean-Paul Sartre thought of Gide as the father of a new kind of fiction. Like Wallace Stevens, Gide believes that imagination leads the way, altering reality by suggesting new possibilities. In anticipating the existential novel, Gide takes us a step beyond the existing modern novel.

III

With the breakdown of the Romantic self, the modernist idea of identity moved in two directions: toward totalitarianism and toward nihilism. Orwell depicted the former movement, Conrad the latter. Nihilism, of course, was a way of undoing the totalitarian solution, even as it emptied the life cycle of meaning. Thus, strangely, the modernists' search for the ideal took them to forms of nihilism. The transition from Haggard's romance to Conrad's darkness is only one of a number of manifestations of this ironic twist in the history of the modernist movement. We find a similar turn from the ideal to its opposite in Spengler, Heidegger, and the many American writers discussed in chapters 9 and 13. Another example of the drift toward nihilism can be found in the works of Louis-Ferdinand Céline (Louis-Ferdinand Destouches) (1894–1961). Céline's most noted works were *Journey to the End of the Night* (*Voyage au bout de la nuit*, 1932) and *Death on the Installment Plan* (*Mort à credit*, 1936), both of which were exercises in the search for authenticity in the face of the grotesque.

Life became a journey toward death. The imperial army, the city and its slums, the industrial revolution—these and other modern institutions have robbed life of ideal meaning. Like Heidegger, Céline saw modern technology as the root of the problem. Like Pound, Eliot, D. H. Lawrence, and others, he grounded his beliefs in racial prejudice, specifically a distrust of Jews. Céline found himself questioning the validity of democracy, moving toward sympathy with Nazi Germany, perhaps because he shared their anti-Semitism. After France was liberated in World War II, Céline was charged with being a collaborator, forcing him to flee to Germany and then Denmark, where he was imprisoned before being expatriated to the Baltic, there to remain until he was pardoned in 1951. But repatriation did not bring a change of heart: like so many of his contemporaries, Céline continued to believe that the imperial, military, industrial life had become a killing machine.

In *Voyage*, he addressed these and other manifestations of modern life, and he demonstrated how death was built into each condition. Céline takes us mechanically through each adventure, suggesting that we live in a Jansenist world, fallen without redeeming grace. Old age, physical illness, mental disorders fascinated him because they all anticipated death. Céline's sense of anguish is intense, going beyond even the existentialists like Sartre and Camus, taking him to the nihilism of Samuel Beckett: the task is to go on living in the face of life's emptiness. As a Beckett character put it, "I can't go on, I can't go on, I go on."

Voyage begins by suggesting that war—all war—is absurd: Bardamu, Céline's narrator, takes us to the Flanders front in World War I. There he realizes that the French officers rather than the Germans were more likely to get him killed, sending him out on needless missions, often capriciously motivated, seldom furthering any military goal. Bardamu sustains an incongruous perspective, employs grim humor, when he focuses his attention upon staying alive in contrast to the officers who are intent on military maneuvers. Two different states of mind contradictorily define a common situation, until both extremes become one when a shell explodes within the lines, killing his comrades, including the officers: death is the common denominator. Self-preservation mocks military heroism when cowards live and heroes die; war mocks love when the dead are thrown into each other arms. In the end, the logic of war is to avoid the ever-present reality of death:

> [The colonel had] been flung onto the embankment on his side and the explosion had thrown him into the arms of the dispatch bearer, who was dead also. They were in each other's arms and would continue the embrace for ever, but the cavalryman hadn't his head any more, only his neck open with blood bubbling in it like stew in a pot. The colonel's stomach was slit open and he was making an ugly face about that. It must have been painful when that happened. So much the worse for him. If he'd gone away when the firing began, he wouldn't have had it.[4]

The cumulative effect of war takes Bardamu, when he is wounded, to the cor-ollary of death, the military hospital. From there his next national mission is to the Congo, where in the footsteps of Conrad he becomes a witness to imperialism. Imperialism shares the absurdity of war: its practice negates its justification. Its practitioners become its victim as much as the natives who are held captive, only the practitioners go about their duty willingly, while the natives (to their credit) have to be coerced. Both war and imperialism depend upon coercion, a state of being that cannot be sustained forever and is thus subject to inevitable overthrow:

> And so, as I say, there were lot of Negroes and whites working away with me in the warehouses and on the plantation of the Porduriere Company of Little Togo when I was there—little clerks like me. The natives after all have to be bludgeoned into doing their job—they've still got that much self-respect. Whereas the whites carry on on their own; they've been well schooled by the State.[5]

The remainder of *Voyage* deals with Bardamu's journey to America and his work as a doctor in the slums of Paris. In both worlds he witnesses the loss of the humanity. In New York, one becomes lost in the crowd. In Detroit, the machine (automobile) usurps the human element. Back in France, Bardamu gives his full attention to his poverty-stricken patients, whose lack of social position reduces them to a subhuman status. Throughout *Voyage*, Céline has depicted the inability of modern man to sustain humanity in the face of growing capitalistic-industrial system that elevates production and profit beyond humanity.

Within the extremes of totalitarianism and nihilism were more variations of the self. As the mind moved inward, the physical world became a subjective reality. Joyce's Dublin took the meaning projected on it by Stephen Dedalus and Leopold Bloom, or the extended quality of a dream that characterizes *Finnegans Wake*. Reworked by Samuel Beckett, Joycean reality gave way to phantasmagoria and the spectral, shriveled to the compass of an isolated room or barren ruin. We move, that is, toward the extremes of mass culture or toward the isolated self, toward totalitarianism or toward esthetic solipsism that then collapses into nihilism. Wells and Orwell take us to the totalitarian self, Conrad, Céline, and Beckett toward the nihilistic self. All of them in their different ways were responses to Enlightenment optimism.

IV

As we have seen, one response to the Enlightenment stemmed from the rational realms of science and technology, from the assumption that by understanding the laws of nature one could control nature and turn that control into forms of wealth. The end desire of this process was power. Another response involved the kind of self that Wordsworth created out of memory that led to an aesthetics of self as defined in one context by Oscar Wilde and in another by Joyce. Wilde's aestheticism created the dandy, the self as an art object. Joyce through Stephen Dedalus, whether taken literally or ironically, established a realm in which artistic meaning unfolded as an epiphany and reality was transformed by the imagination. The end desire of this process was the beautiful. Later, intensified through the philosophy of Bergson, this form of aestheticism led to Proust, the subject of Beckett's first book.

Samuel Beckett's fiction begins with epistemological doubt. Like Descartes, he wants to split mind from body and then mind from its surroundings. But unlike Descartes, Beckett believes the mind and reality are too infused to separate subject from object. Whereas Descartes conceived of creation as a hierarchy of creatures moving toward a final cause and the ultimate form of God, Beckett stressed the tenuous connection between mind and body and between mind and anything like final form. Trapped between a desire to die and a fear of death, Beckett's characters live in a halfway house, driven on by a life force, a Schopenhauer-like cosmic will. His characters are caught in a process of discontinuous time, separated from a past that offers no traditional way of meaning and a future that has already been emptied.

Both aspects of the Enlightenment have been discounted: Beckett's characters can find no meaning in Enlightenment power or Romantic beauty. They lack the means to create a personal identity through memory and past experience; they fail to find beauty in their own being, or the natural world, or the creative process of the imagination. The modernist seeker quests to find a way out of this radical nihilism. Nietzsche believed that consciousness freed from rationality could come to terms with reality. Jean-Paul Sartre tried to fill the vacuum with existential will power. Michel Foucault went one step further than Nietzsche, located meaning as a form of consciousness inseparable from the discourse of culture and held in place by social institutions (power). Beckett found all of these ways of coping with the self too exaggerated, too heroically under the control of consciousness, too much a product of inflated will, or too embellished with institutionalized power.

More than any other modernist, Beckett's onslaught on post-Enlightenment man was total. He limited rationality and the imagination; he questioned the human will; he robbed time of linearity and cyclicality; he took from nature any process by which it could complete itself; and he recognized (long before Derrida) the tenuousness of language, which he saw as subject to competing claims on the mind. Beckett emptied the modern self of residual meaning and then discounted the means of reinstating what he had subverted. Under such an onslaught, there was no self, no community, and no history. As we turn inward to a shell of self and to a consciousness that negated outward reality, we come to the Beckett who went beyond Conrad, even beyond Céline, in the journey toward nihilism.

V

The grotesque picks up where decadence leaves off. As we saw, decadence involves a degenerative activity that is part of an aesthetic process as when Huysmans's Des Essenties prefers the artifice of the city to the rhythms of nature. The grotesque involves an inversion of natural process, as when the wheat fields in The Great Gatsby bring forth ashes instead of wheat; the grotesque can also emerge from the inversion of the social process, as when authority betrays its protective function and becomes destructive, as in Orwell's 1984. The final effect of the grotesque involves the familiar becoming strange. A class reunion has this quality, when friends from the past go unrecognized until reintroduced. A friend can change personality and become grotesque under the influence of alcohol or a mental breakdown. In literary terms, we find forms of the grotesque in Nikolai Gogol, Sherwood Anderson, Nathanael West, and especially Franz Kafka, although the grotesque can stem from different contexts depending on the author.

In Gogol's "The Overcoat" and "The Nose," both the coat and the nose take on grotesque meaning, embodying items that change one's status in a society where appearance determines reality. In these stories, the ordinary gives way to extraordinary, the common turns fantastic, and the familiar becomes foreign. Sherwood Anderson and Nathanael West also made use of grotesque realism. Both felt that modern man was sexually repressed and that this repression expressed itself grotesquely. The result was behavior taken to extremes, often opposite extremes. West, for example, contrasts the inhibitions of Homer Simpson with the uncontrolled sexuality of Miguel. West's world is both strange and unpredictable: hands jump and dangle like fish gasping for air; an encephalitic dwarf appears out of rags and old blankets discarded in a dark apartment corridor. Architecture appears to result from an explosion in a time machine; houses clot the hills, some seemingly hanging in the air. Meat and fruit look unnatural in the neon-lighted bins of a thirties supermarket. Tod's frustrated lust leads to a pent-up violence, in his case expressed as thought. But when the Hollywood seekers become frustrated, they express it in physical violence. In Anderson, sexually starved men fear the sexuality they crave. In both Anderson and West there is the return of the repressed—a subterranean realm waiting to erupt in violence both on the individual and communal level, attesting to the fact that reality is constantly charged and the familiar conceals the abhorrent.

The writer who best depicted the grotesque as inseparable from the human situation was Franz Kafka (1883–1924). Born in Prague, then belonging to Austria, Kafka had a sense of the grotesque that stemmed from the anxiety that accompanied human alienation in a world growing more unintelligent and hostile. *The Trial* (1925) deals with a man put to death for unspecified crimes governed by an inscrutable system of laws. Kafka's novel is a pure example of "open" symbolism. He gives us a plot, the frame of which can carry symbolic meaning in different directions. Kafka's K. is accused of an unstated crime. He is then ordered to appear for a "trial" at a warehouse in a shabby section of town, where a washerwoman admits him to a fifth-floor occupied by elderly men (jurors) with straggly beards. When the washerwoman is attacked, K. flees the building. When he returns a week later, the washerwoman once again greets him, although this time the court is not in session. She tells him that the trial at this level means little, even if he is acquitted of his unspecified crime, because

a higher court can charge him again. The woman's husband leads him to the
law offices of the court, where he enters a room filled with petitioners. All of
the petitioners have been waiting, some for many years, for a response to their
defense to an unnamed crime. Their petitions are all either unread or simply
misplaced and lost. Upon the advice of his uncle, K. hires an Advocate, a defense
lawyer, an old man who stays in bed most of the time. The room housing the
Advocates—shabby and untidy, dangerous with a hole in the floor—is in the
attic above the petitioners' room. Realizing that the Advocate is redundant to
the system, K. dismisses him and decides to defend himself. Titorelli, the court
painter, informs him that there is no hope for complete acquittal, an opinion
restated by the court chaplain. A year later at nine o'clock, on the evening before
K's thirty-first birthday, two men in frock coats and top hats accost him. They
secure his hands, walk him to a quarry, and while one holds his throat, the other
stabs him in the heart, turning the knife twice.

Kafka takes us beyond Gogol; in his insistence on the grotesque as inevitable
to the human condition, he writes an open-ended allegory that can mean almost
what any reader wants it to mean, so long as it remains a story in which runaway
authority (natural, religious, political, or social) controls individual fate. The
novel can be read as an allegory of the human predicament: a story of human
fragility, of human vulnerability in the face of submission to a larger, unpredictable, unknown force, the workings of God or nature. Kafka's K. is dealing with a
power as irrational as the destructive forces of nature—wildfires, floods, earth-
quakes, tsunamis, hurricanes, tornadoes, volcanoes—forces that strike innocent
victims at random, offer no basis for petition, and kill without explanation. Or
K.'s condition could be the product of Original Sin, which has put him in conflict
with divine authority, cast guilt upon him, and demands his death (sacrifice)
as a source of redemption. Or K.'s story can offer a parallel to those dying of
terminal diseases like cancer, a malady that strikes innocent and guilty alike, is
not fully understood, offers no rational explanation of its behavior, renders the
petitioner's plea futile, and takes its victim to the realm of death. Or K.'s story
could be that of a citizen in a totalitarian country, in which civil rights have been
suspended, petitions are of no use, authority knows no limit, and the customary
penalty for even a minor offense is death. Or K., like Kafka himself, could simply
be the exiled Jew, living in a hostile environment (the Hapsburg empire), subject
to a foreign system of laws with no sense of self-realization, identity, or avenue
of escape. Kafka gives us the setting, characters, and plot of his novel, but it is
the reader who must supply the meaning. And in supplying the narrative mean-

ing, the reader participates in its symbolic meaning—a sustained allegory of the human condition.

The other Kafka (unfinished) novel that gives us a symbolic paradigm of the human condition is *The Castle* (1926), which depicts the futile effort of a citizen to make contact with the mysterious authorities that rule his village from the castle above. (In Kafka's Prague, a castle on the hill dominated the city below. One could argue that Kafka's novel had its origins in a realistic realm before it was symbolically transformed.) We are once again in the world of a character simply called K., who arrives one winter night in a town dominated by the castle of Count West-west. He has been summoned to the town by the count to be the new land surveyor. The next morning he leaves the inn to report at the castle, but as he approaches the castle, it recedes before him. He sees two men leave the castle, but they refuse to stop, and K. returns to the inn. There he finds the two men he had seen coming from the castle. He asks them to have a sled ready in the morning to take him to the castle, but they refuse; a telephone call instructs him not to come to the castle; a messenger named Barnabas soon follows with a letter from someone at the castle named Klamm instructing him to report to the superintendent of the town. Barnabas takes K. to his home, where he meets his two sisters, Olga and Amalia; he later comes upon Frieda, the barmaid at the local tavern, who was the mistress of Klamm and who K. hopes can deliver him to the castle. In the meantime, the superintendent tells him that a surveyor was needed several years before, but no one knows who has requested K.'s presence in the town. Nevertheless, K. stays on, working as janitor at the town's school. He learns from Olga that her family is now an outcast group because her sister has refused to be the mistress of some authority from the castle. His meeting with Olga, however, generates the jealousy of Frieda. K. is informed that an important official from the castle wants to see him. At the inn, K. finds the official asleep; there he also sees Frieda and tries to explain that his relationship with Olga was innocent, but she believes otherwise and leaves him. At this point, the novel breaks off, although on Kafka's word, K. would continue his efforts to reach the castle; on his deathbed, he would receive a call from the castle.

The Castle is a bit more difficult to assess than *The Trial* because it is not complete. But the general meaning seems in keeping with the meaning of *The Trial*. Once more we have a symbol of gratuitous authority working its absolute will on powerless subjects. As with the workings of the trial, the castle is an authority unto itself, despite the fact that it has cut off communication with the town below. Given information from Kafka that K. will receive word from the castle on his deathbed, one interpretation of the story could be religious: the mysteries of life and death will be revealed at the moment of death. A more plausible interpretation might suggest a symbolic relationship between the castle and the town in which we have an equivalent of the human condition: what issues from the castle, like the forces of nature or political mandate, is in the realm of dictated authority, while the relationship between the human beings in the realm below (e.g., K.'s relationship with Frieda and Olga) is unpredictable and tenuous.

In *The Castle*, Kafka has given us a symbolic successor to *The Trial* that once more goes to the essence of the human situation, defines the human predicament, and demands reader participation to complete. (Kafka's novels fit the paradigm of symbolic motives that we found in Kenneth Burke: the stories begin with forms of authority or hierarchy in control, taking advantage of an innate sense of guilt and demanding sacrifice or "victimage" as the means of redemption.) Again Kafka has demonstrated that the human predicament reduced to its essential meaning is grotesque.

But the best example of Kafka's use of the grotesque is "The Metamorphosis" (1915), the story of a salesman who wakes one morning to find himself transformed into a repulsive insect. Kafka's story may have its origins in his own family: he was in fear of his father and in love with his sister; both feelings created a source of guilt and self-loathing that made him feel less than human. This self-loathing was transformed—as in surrealism or dream—into symbols that have no cognitive basis—that is, where there is no logical connection between the subject of the dream and what the subject is transformed into. Such "open" symbolism seems to be in the air in the early part of the twentieth century: Kafka and Freud—one in Vienna, the other in Prague, both a part of the Hapsburg empire—had much in common.

A major influence on Kafka at this time was the machine: he appreciated the Charlie Chaplin films that depicted modern man becoming more and more mechanical, another example of transformation at work. As a lawyer, working by day for an insurance firm, Kafka was continuously exposed to the unpredictable nature of modern existence: the accidental was literally a part of his life. Kafka's story is an extreme example of the familiar becoming strange to the point of horror, of physical reality revealing symbolically a state of mind involving anxiety and self-hatred—a fear of what humanity can become. This state of mind was dissected further in *In the Penal Colony* (1919), an examination of a torture system that symbolically objectified an inner sense of guilt and retribution appropriate to an era of global war.

13 ✤ NEOREALISM AND BEYOND

I

In "The Ideology of Modernism" (1957), Georg Lukács attacked modernism for repudiating the past. He faulted the modernists for working in a historical vacuum, for suggesting that human beings could be separated from their material conditions, from the confines of history. He championed historical realism and disparaged Joycean stasis and Brecht's belief that the function of art was to change, not reflect, society. Lukács believed that consciousness stemmed from class distinctions: each class had a different consciousness based on social institutions and the need for decorum. He argued that the proletariat came the closest to the consciousness imbued in communism. With equal insistence, he questioned the modernist tendency to reduce reality to language, arguing that language can be treated separately from consciousness.

Lukács's concerns were not isolated. One of the major concerns of the moderns was explaining the connection between consciousness and social reality. William James (1842–1910) challenged the agency and coherence of self. In his youth, James suffered from bouts of anxiety that stemmed from a sense of being powerless, that he was too weak to struggle against a hostile world. He overcame this effect when he came to see that he had more control over his life than he had presumed. Pragmatism was a product of the will, connected to the belief that life was a struggle between "ego" and "world." James was a voluntarist: he believed that the will was the key to human behavior.

But James qualified what he meant by will. In his psychology classes at Harvard (1878 to 1890) and in his *Principles of Psychology* (1890), James moved away from Descartes' rationalism, which presumed some sort of unified ego or soul, insisting that the idea of self needed to be grounded in experience and not in intangible and abstract concepts. In limiting thought to the range of actual experience, James relegated what was not experienced to the realm of conjecture. He was concerned with the self as Known and Knower. The Knower Self took us close to Descartes' rationalism. But the Known Self was multifaceted, composed of a material self, social self, and spiritual self. This movement from a unified to fragmented sense of self was axiomatic to modernistic thinking.

As a pragmatist, James was an antirealist; he did not believe in reality as representation, as something outside the mind that we could all share as "true." He argued that belief was a matter of fulfilling our needs, that what we sought involved what best accommodated our living requirements. The whole process involved an intelligent organism struggling in its enclosed environment, in an ideological bubble. Theories acquire meaning, become "true" when they prove successful. Here James seems close to Darwin's theory of natural selection, the belief that ongoing life is a matter of adaptation.

James's pragmatism works in terms of stated propositions and their consequences. Philosophical disputes collapse into insignificance when subject to a test of their concrete consequences. If one proposition does not offer a better course of action over another, then there is no basis for choice, and both propositions are useless. James's emphasis upon the consequence of a proposition took him to a liminal religious awareness when he insisted that matters of faith are legitimate forms of belief when they create an order of mind that satisfies spiritual needs. Prayer, for example, can lead to a sanguine state of mind that reinforces religious hope and encourages self-fulfilling possibilities.

Ernest Hemingway did not share James's religious inclinations, but he did share the other half of James's thinking—the connection between belief and experience. In *The Sun Also Rises* (1926), Jake Barnes is more interested in addressing practical rather than metaphysical questions. He tells us, "I did not care what it was all about. All I wanted to know was how to live in it. Maybe if you found out how to live in it you learned from that what it was all about."[1] His foil, Robert Cohn, lives the unexamined, derivative life in search of intangible ideals, getting his ideas and values from Romantic books. In *A Farewell to Arms* (1929), Lt. Henry's experience at the front, especially his absurd wounding, tempers his earlier anticipation of the glory of war, and leads to his "separate peace," his break with Romantic reality and quixotic ideals never tested against his own sense of experience and concrete reality. Abstract words, he tells us, offended him: "Abstract words such as glory, honor, courage, or hallow were obscene beside the concrete names of villages, the number of roads, the names of rivers, the numbers of regiments and the dates."[2] One may need to go beyond a physical sense of place to experience the complexity of life, but Hemingway's more skeptical characters are wary of metaphysical pronouncements. Hemingway's fiction is an exercise in empiricism, of experience and observation, of transforming the abstract into the concrete and of enduring life's travail.

As we have seen, William James once suffered from anxiety attacks based on a sense that life was overpowering. Hemingway's fiction often involves the person who goes on in the face of psychological impediments or physical loss, whether the loss is the result of war (Jake Barnes, Lt. Henry, Robert Jordan), or the result of being victimized by social parasites (Harry Morgan), or the result of various forms of combat (Pedro Romero), or the deep-sea hunt (Santiago). The source of hostility in Hemingway's fiction can range from world conflagration to domestic imbalance, as Francis Macomber learns. There is, of course, a major contradiction between Hemingway's appeal to a neostoicism and his own death by suicide. But if his characters survive their ordeal, they do so with a Jamesian will, with a sense that they are stronger than life's impediments and that we go on.

Walt Whitman and William James take us to a divide in the flow of historical events: Whitman takes us to Romantic Oneness and to transcendental reality; James to literary realism, out of which came literary naturalism. The Romantic view proved inadequate as a basis for discussing the new, urban-industrial America. Stephen Crane, Norris, Dreiser—all presented historical obstacles Whitman could not romantically reconcile. What emerges is another America that Whitman began to see too late. Whitman's optimistic poetry takes its being from Romantic myths involving the land, the frontier, the hope of a new political vision, a world of new possibility. This vision begins to compete with that of an America subject to political graft and special interests.

Just as Whitman's eleven other poems speak to "Song of Myself," so do other works in the American canon. Whitman embodied the process of disillusionment that accompanied the unfolding of American literature in general. Willa Cather was still able to celebrate the Whitman-Emersonian sense of possibility, especially in *My Antonia,* Steinbeck less so in *The Grapes of Wrath,* Nathanael West not at all in *The Day of the Locust.* Fitzgerald turned the whole problem into a major theme in *The Great Gatsby* by portraying the destructive fate of an idealist who located the ideal in an exhausted past and pursued what had become a dead dream. A major theme of the new realism involved an end to innocence. Modernist literature often involved an idealist in conflict with a hostile reality, a reality that became more hostile as the agrarian/industrial divide widened, as the end product of commercial materialism became less meaningful as a way of life.

Neorealism moved us away from aesthetic privilege. It transformed the romance, moved it toward a more examined sense of modern reality as well as toward the cosmic emptiness of Pynchon and DeLillo. The romance had accommodated the possibility of fantasy, the use of magical or supernatural events, and was a product of the imagination; realism demanded plausibility, an empirical and time-bound frame of reference, and was the product of experience. Rider Haggard's novels of Africa were infused with fantasy; Conrad's journey up the Congo River made use of actual experience. Kipling's stories of India were pure romance, while Forster's *Passage to India* and Orwell's Burma essays came out of their understanding of the culture, as Hemingway's account of war in *A Farewell to Arms* came out of his direct wartime experience.

II

Another important influence on the transformation of modern reality was Gertrude Stein (1874–1946). Born in Allegheny, Pennsylvania (now a part of Pittsburgh), her childhood years were spent with her parents in Europe—mostly Austria, France, and England. Back in America, she went to Radcliffe, where she studied with William James, and then went on to medical school at Johns Hopkins, where she dropped out when she lost interest. Following her brother Leo to Europe, she lived in London before settling in Paris, where she became friends with the major artists, especially Picasso, and where she encouraged such American expatriates as Ernest Hemingway. From her famous salon at 27 Rue de Fleurus, she collected the major painters of her era (Renoir, Matisse, Cézanne, Braque, Picasso). There she wrote experimental novels (*The Making of Americans: a history of her family*) and autobiography (*The Autobiography of Alice B. Toklas: an account of her Paris years through the eyes of her companion*).

Through these works she formulated innovative principles of narrative and language. Her writing was deeply embedded in theories of ontology and epistemology, and she was a firm believer in "perspectivism"—that reality stems from the way it is perceived. She once said, "nothing changes in people from one generation to another except the way of seeing and being seen."[3] Flaubert influenced her early work: *Three Lives* (1909) is her version of *Trois contes*. She then tried to apply cubist techniques to her prose in *The Making of Americans* (written between 1906 and 1911, but published in 1925) and *Tender Buttons* (1914). It was Hemingway who persuaded Ford Madox Ford to publish *The Making of Americans* serially (nine installments, April to December 1924) in the *Transatlantic Review* (the book was published in whole the next year by Robert McAlmon). Both

Hemingway and Fitzgerald were impressed with the early writing in *The Making of Americans*, but they also agreed that the writing declined after the beginning. Each worked unsuccessfully to get it published, Fitzgerald recommending it to Maxwell Perkins at Scribner's.

Much of her writing during this period was intentionally obscure, involving experimentation that led to a new prose style, culminating in the more accessible writing of *The Autobiography of Alice B. Toklas* (1933). But the writing in *Toklas* still showed traces of the early experimentation, especially in its use of inverted chronology, its run-on sentences, its refusal to capitalize proper nouns, and its cumulative detail that located emotional effect in the paragraph. Once called the Mama of Dada, Stein's career encouraged forms of experiment, from her long-term curiosity with automatic writing to her interest in the avant-garde. She created a feud within modernism when she attempted to use language in a way that spoke to human subjectivity, to the emotional as well as rational side of our being. Stein's work played into the theories of Dada and surrealism and of automatic writing.

Her theories of language in particular owe much to her interest in painting. She was particularly indebted to Picasso's cubism and, as previously mentioned, attempted to apply some of his techniques involving the pictorial arts to literature. Cézanne is the link between Picasso and Stein. As Stein has said: "Everything I have done has been influenced by Flaubert and Cézanne, and this gave me a new feeling about composition."[4] Until Cézanne, painting had a central figure and background. But Cézanne's paintings have no center. Stein saw Picasso doing something similar in his cubist painting and believed this principle could apply to writing: as foreground, middle ground, background disappeared in painting, so beginning, middle, and end disappeared in narrative. In each case, fragmentation eliminated a center and led to a multiplicity of viewpoints from which the parts had to be reproduced into a recreated ("re-presented") whole.

Modernist painters worked two kinds of cubism: abstract (sometime called analytic) and synthetic. In the abstract, the fragmentation has its source in the object itself; in the synthetic, the fragmentation has its source in the artist. In both, the cubist broke surfaces into planes seen simultaneously from different angles, robbing a subject of realistic representation in the hope of decentering reality and capturing a fourth dimension. Stein's *Making of Americans* owes much to Picasso's and Braque's experimentation (1909–13) with cubism. She once said, "Pablo is doing abstract portraits in painting. I am trying to do abstract portraits in my medium, words."[5] In simulation of Picasso, Stein invented the prose portrait and captured Picasso in words as he had captured her in paint. Stein also gave us portraits of Braque, Gris, and Sherwood Anderson. Both Picasso and Stein believed that art had priority over life. When someone commented to Picasso that his portrait did not look like Stein, he replied, "it will."

What was happening in Picasso's painting and Stein's prose was inseparable from the intellectual revolt of the moderns, who were no longer satisfied with historicism or the old science, with reducing understanding to the logic of pure reason or to the idea that cause-and-effect explanations captured the essence of truth. Stein attributed "the making of cubism" to "the belief in the reality of science, commenced to diminish." Donald Sutherland put it more directly: "the nineteenth century was still interested in causes and purposes and explanations. It was dominated, if not by Evolution, under which everything, even if incomprehensibly, served some future purpose or other, combined in some way to some far-off divine event toward which the whole creation moves, at least by a sense of direction in History, whether Hegelian or Marxist or what not."[6]

But Stein may have been misguided in her belief that the techniques of painting and writing were interchangeable. Painting and literature are two different expressive mediums, and their properties are not the same. Nevertheless, Stein felt she could accommodate the tenets of cubism in a work like *The Making of Americans.* She would do this by destroying chronological order, by fragmenting the portraits of her story, and by writing in a repetitive, associative style. She felt these devices would allow her to approximate in prose what Picasso was doing in painting.

This involved a new way of seeing, turning "being" into "becoming." Like Proust, she wanted a "sustained present." Repetition was the key to both life and language: life was extended repetition, so was language. Wallace Stevens believed an object changed when seen from a different perspective. Stein believed an object changed when described a second or third time: repetition involved a different perspective. Each experience involved a new reality, and the second way of seeing the same thing actually involved a new way of seeing. Stein was working a new mode of modernism. While Mann worked the meaning of decadence and aestheticism, Proust the meaning of memory and emotion on time, and Joyce the universality of time through myth, Stein worked a fragmented narrative held together by repetition and variation.

But, as suggested above, there is a discrepancy between cubist painting and Stein's prose. In a painting, the fragments are seen simultaneously. In writing, the fragments come in sequence and have a cumulative rather than simultaneous effect. Stein was mistaken in thinking that the same principles applied to the pictorial that applied to writing. But while she may have failed to find prose techniques that are the equivalent of cubism, her effort to do so created the means of depicting a new state of mind, complete with evolving consciousness. Stein may have been a bit inaccurate in believing that she had in a one-to-one way transformed cubist painting into prose technique, but her attempt in that direction was not without benefit: she did create a new narrative reality. This would become even more evident when her technique, as adapted by Ernest Hemingway, led to a uniquely powerful new kind of prose.

Stein's *Tender Buttons* (1914) was another exercise in cubism. Here she depicted (she might say "painted in prose") everyday/household objects in an attempt to catch their essence. Not only does she work, as in *The Making of Americans*, with fragments, she now uses words that are off-key (i.e., indirect and poetic in their meaning), placing them in ways that disrupt the logic of syntax. For example, she describes rain as "Water astonishing and difficult altogether makes a meadow and a stroke." As Harry Garvin has explained, restated in a more direct way, she is saying: "A sudden ('astonishing') hard ('difficult') rain with lightning ('stroke') and thunder reveals ('makes') a meadow."[7] In describing rain in this transformed way, she "defamiliarizes" her world; the familiar becomes strange (or uncanny): we now think of rain in a new way, as something unique and different from our common experience. But this exercise depends heavily on using words that are imprecise in meaning and taxing her reader's understanding and patience. Some believe the tradeoff was worth it: she had brought a new technique to modernist writing and added another dimension to its meaning.

In Stein's experimental work, the everyday took on new import when it was informed with a new order of modern consciousness. Under the influence of William James and pragmatist thinking, belief became a matter of tested experience, which led to a new way of thinking about literary reality. She in turn influenced such major writers as Sherwood Anderson, Ernest Hemingway, and Thornton Wilder (Stein's *The Making of Americans* [1925] influenced Wilder's *Our Town* [1938]). What Whitman claimed to see as simultaneous and whole, Stein saw as discontinuous and in parts.

III

Under the influence of Stein and others, literary naturalism was eclipsed. As naturalistic ideology thinned, its literary aspects changed as well. Some naturalistic novels—for example, James M. Cain's *The Postman Always Rings Twice* (1934)—moved away from the theory, presenting a naturalistic story without the racial or hereditary background—without, that is, the documentation that previously made it naturalistic. Cain's transformation of the naturalist novel made it suitable for the philosophical uses to which Albert Camus put it. In writing *L'étranger*, Camus needed an "elemental" character, someone that lived on the level of his senses, but not naturalistic reality. Camus found such a character in Cain's Frank Chambers. Camus worked other similarities: the climax of each novel is a murder, followed by a court hearing; the novels conclude in a murder cell with the principal characters waiting to be executed, talking or writing to a priest. The most obvious parallel between the two novels is that both Frank Chambers and Meursault are misfits, passive heroes who respond to immediate stimuli. Described in terms of their external behavior, they react rather than act, qualities of behavior they share with naturalistic characters.

Even earlier, other novelists such as Ernest Hemingway kept their characters in contact with nature. They did this not to demonstrate theories of evolution or degeneration, but to test them against natural events such as the big-game hunt, deep-sea fishing, or the bullfight. Hemingway created a natural aristocracy outside of society, which allowed more individual will and self-determination than one would find in naturalistic fiction. Hemingway's narrative aim was to get the protagonist outside of modern history, especially outside a mechanical urban order, on a boat or on an island, where a code of primitive values ruled. Such a narrative maneuver allowed Hemingway to contrast elemental and civilized man. Another device involved locating a story in a moment of transition, like that of the Spanish civil war, in which two ways of life—primitive and modern—were in conflict. And lastly, Hemingway set up geographical opposites, as he did in *The Sun Also Rises*, when he contrasted Jake Barnes in Paris and Jake in Burguete. Hemingway struggled to locate his pre-urban vision in idealized action and rituals that partake of the land and the sea, until finally he displaced urban reality with the extended arena.

Hemingway not only contrasted the primitive and civilized, but he depicted this world impressionistically. Impressionism accompanied the move from naturalism to modernism, from an objective to a subjective reality. The distinction between descriptive detail (in which the detail controls the mind) and impressionistic detail (in which the mind controls the detail) is objectivity on the way to becoming subjectivity. Pater first came to terms with this process,[8] a lesson learned by Conrad, who influenced Stephen Crane, who in turn influenced Hemingway. Hemingway's is a naturalistic world seen through a Paterian prism, the emphasis upon a recording consciousness rather than biology, heredity, or environment.

Literature noir owes much to Hemingway. In the traditional novel, good and evil are demarcated with the protagonist on the side of "good," the antagonist on the side of "evil." In noir fiction, these terms are reversed: the noir character, whose perspective dominates what and how we see, works outside the realm of good—that is, the noir character is most often the antihero, like Hemingway's Harry Morgan; instead of embodying the values of society, he lives outside the law, on the edge of community. The women in noir literature and film are femme fatales, like Margo Macomber: they have no desire to settle down or raise a family. Their presence is destructive: when not out to destroy a man, they demand the dominant role. At the center of a noir plot is the assumption that everyone is degraded: nobody is innocent; good and evil blur as moral choices; redemption and betrayal are one and the same. The noir novel with its antihero takes us to the edge of a democratic society, to marginal men and women living by their wits. Once they are further socially removed, they will become the drifters in the novels of James M. Cain, the seekers in Kerouac, the homeless derelicts in Nelson Algren and William Kennedy, and the family outcasts in Joyce Carol Oates.[9]

Hemingway supplied the model; popular culture did the rest. Popular culture transformed Hemingway and not vice versa. Once we have a novel like *To Have and Have Not*, we have the basis for the "tough guy" novel of Raymond Chandler and Dashiell Hammett. Hemingway also bridged the connection between the cowboy and the detective, the transition between Gary Cooper and Humphrey Bogart. His code hero owes much to the western, the subgenre whose values Hemingway brought to his depiction of Africa and the Spanish civil war.

IV

What Africa and Spain were for Hemingway, Hollywood was for Fitzgerald. In Fitzgerald's world, an energy system is depleted and decadence becomes an aesthetic process. In Hemingway's world, a natural aristocracy outside of society is tested against the trials of nature and the arena. Fitzgerald, influenced by Spengler, concentrated on the end product of history. Hemingway was less concerned with a sense of an ending than with the meaning of our origins and how the primitive rituals involving life and death could be preserved in an ever-increasing technological society. Hemingway moved us away from historical decline; Fitzgerald rushed us into it.

The center from which they moved to their respective extremes was Europe itself. Fitzgerald joined Spengler in believing that the power of Europe was passing to a new-moneyed class that had come out of the industrialized West. They in turn would be opposed by a new breed of exploiters, the product of Arabian oil money, which threatened the dominance of the West. Third World threats prevailed: it had happened before with the fall of Rome and more recently with the decline of London. Would New York be next? This concern became Fitzgerald's equivalent to T. S. Eliot's "falling tower" theme. *Tender Is the Night* reveals the sterility that undermines modern life: Baby Warren testifies to the growing decadence of London, and Abe North's brutal death in New York suggests a submerged violence, an urban savagery, at work. Like Eliot's work, Fitzgerald's fiction is deeply rooted in cultural tradition and unfolds symbolically. Like the writing of William James and Gertrude Stein, Hemingway's fiction depends more upon immediate experience and unfolds imagistically. Between them, Fitzgerald and Hemingway worked two different aspects of American neorealism.

When we get to John Dos Passos's trilogy, *USA* (1930–36), we find characters moving in a vortex of activity toward forms of defeat and failure, more the victims of social forces than biological necessity. While the end result in Dos Passos's fiction may be similar to that of naturalistic fiction, the process by which his characters meet their fate is far different. Dos Passos depicts the pervasive power of capitalism: his characters are like flies in the spider's web. Although naturalism has been transformed, we can still find a sense of decline and degeneration in a number of modernistic texts: Mann's Buddenbrooks family, Faulkner's Compson family, the fate of Fitzgerald's Anthony Patch and Dick Diver. But the naturalistic explanation of their decline is now omitted. The sense of a scientific observer is gone, the ironic point of view is modified, and the emphasis is more upon a state of individual consciousness than naturalistic reality.

V

Modernist literature moved inward toward mythic consciousness and then toward forms of skepticism and doubt. Balzac had moved the novel toward the realms of realism, Zola toward naturalism, while Joyce and Woolf reversed that process, moving the novel inward toward forms of consciousness, a method that was adapted to the newer realism of Hemingway and Dos Passos in which we confront a reality with the emphasis on an interpretive mind and a realism devoid of naturalistic documentation. The postmodern novel would move one step beyond this configuration, collapsing the mind into the (language of the) text itself or into the dictates of culture.

Most influential in this transformation was Roland Barthes. Barthes not only questioned the priority of realism over other modes of fiction; he contended that mass man was no longer the beneficiary of literary Enlightenment: literature lost its therapeutic function as Georg Lukács's nineteenth-century sense of hope gave way to postmodernist doubt. The transition from realism/naturalism to modernism to postmodernism thus involved a radical change in the way key ideas were conceptualized. As we have seen, Barthes's theory of narrative turned on the ways it could be read, and the ways it could be read depended upon a series of literary codes or conventions. The process not only changed what we meant by realism, but it also changed the way we read a realistic text. The text was now self-referential, based on a theory of homologies that worked like the grammar of a language system rather than a mimetic system with its need for physical or historical representation. Barthes had supplied the means for the novel to go beyond the neorealism of Hemingway and Dos Passos, not by changing the novel, but by changing the way it was to be read.

VI
POSTMODERNISM AND
MASS CULTURE

14 ⊹ GENDER AND RACE

Changes in the sources of consciousness led to an understanding of the radical difference between modernism and what followed. These changes were amplified by concerns with gender and feminist matters along with that of race. We have reached a point in the critical record where the distinction between modernism and postmodernism is generally accepted. But what is not sufficiently recognized is that we have also gone beyond postmodernism. In the last generation, we have moved from the defining concern of structuralism to the concerns of two movements that entered the discussion in the sixties and seventies and have moved into a position of dominance today: the rise of gender and feminist theory and the relevance of the Harlem Renaissance. Along with theories of mass and popular culture, these movements became the basis for new concerns, for a new way of looking at literary modernism.

I

One difference between modernism, postmodernism, and what followed postmodernism is the difference between the idea of form and the idea of the text. Form involves the interpretation or the meaning given to an individual literary work based on the relationship of its parts to the whole. Text involves the combined or accreted readings connected to that work. One source of meaning stems from the writing of the work; another source of meaning stems from the reading of the work. The first creates an "originary" meaning, the second a supplemental meaning. Each has a validity of its own, although the two taken together may be in opposition (as Nabokov's *Lolita* inverts Stevens's *Ideas of Order*). Each generation creates a text—that is, reinterprets a work of art, especially a classical work of art—in order to open it up to new interpretation, to go beyond what might seem to be exhausted possibilities of interpretation.

The critical task is to keep the modes of literary reality separate, not to conflate them. The T. S. Eliot who went to the mythology of the Cambridge anthropologists is radically distinct from the Eliot who has been connected with Harlem jazz. As the cultural preoccupations of each generation change, the critical context for making sense of the literary text will also change correspondingly. Every generation brings to a literary movement a vanguard interpretation, and such radical revisions of a literary movement then justify rearguard correction. The process involves knowledge of where we have been as well as where we are going. As suggested above, the most recent change in the modernist contour involves connecting the movement with gender and feminist theory, with the Harlem Renaissance, and with popular culture.

Gender theory stems from the rise of feminist activity, although in subject matter gender theory is larger than feminist activity. The feminist movement was greatly influenced by the black protest movement of the sixties. Similarly, out of racial protest came an awareness of the inequality between the sexes and the need to liberate women from their cultural stereotypes. Feminist black spokespersons like bell hooks in *Feminist Theory: From Margin to Center* have seen the patriarchal society as the root cause involving the suppression of both blacks and women.

As the protest movement challenged the status quo, so did the feminist movement with its theory of gender. One of the principal assumptions of gender theory is that reality is a product of culture, not nature. Feminists would argue that culture transformed nature, creating its own reality. Behind the distinction between nature and culture is the assumption that the dictates of culture are human constructions; thus natural laws are a product of negotiation subject to revision and change and not written inextricably into the physical universe. One could argue, for example, that the system of traffic lights stems from the fact that red and green are on opposite ends of the color spectrum with yellow in the middle; thus traffic signals have their origins in nature—that is, in the physical spectrum of color. The feminist response would resist this conclusion on the grounds that traffic colors are arbitrary and have meaning only because we agree to give them the meaning they have. When all reality is constructed reality, there can be no physical laws governing sexuality or other aspects of natural or human activity, despite Darwinian and genetic claims to the contrary. When all reality is constructed, it is provisional and subject to revision.

One of the primary subjects of feminist concern involved the nature of consciousness. In its early application, gender theory depicted the feminist mind as sharing common cause, but over time this idea was radically revised as feminists became aware of the divergence of activity within the feminist agenda. While modernism as a literary movement evolved from an emphasis upon individual consciousness to a preoccupation with mass consciousness (as embodied, for example, in the theory of the crowd), feminist and gender thought moved from the idea of a common cause to the concern with individual applications of that cause.

In recent gender theory, there is a reluctance to see gender as a fixed principle of identity. Consistent with a general distrust of master narratives and universal assumptions, gender identity is more often seen as fluid and variable, constantly changing, depending upon time and context. Women are separated by class, race, and other differences—and not seen as part of a homogeneous group. There is no single feminism, no political party. Recent feminist critics have rejected Freud's biological determinism, which divides the species into men and women, each desiring the opposite sex. With such distinctions in mind, feminists see the opposition between men and women as socially constructed rather than as physically given. Mass culture with its ideological dichotomies has extended the culture wars. Built into feminist assumptions is a distrust of mass culture and a call for the freedom of mind and body that motivated modernist writers like Virginia Woolf. The most powerful voice in this discussion is that of Judith Butler in books like *Gender Trouble: Feminism and the Subversion of Identity* (1990).

Feminist theory evolved from empathy with to antipathy for mass culture, moving from generic concepts to focus on the individual. In retrospect this led to revisionary attitudes toward women at the height of the modernist period, seeing them as more central to the movement than previously depicted. We have already discussed Virginia Woolf, Gertrude Stein, and Djuna Barnes in this context. Edith Wharton, Willa Cather, and Charlotte Perkins Gilman could be added to the list. Three more women who have become the focus of recent feminist interest are Mina Loy, Jean Rhys, and Hilda Doolittle (H. D.). These women might be considered modernists after the fact; they were less directly associated with high modernism in its dominant stage than they are retroactively connected with it today.

Mina Loy (1882–1966) was an artist and poet who participated in various calls to new forms of art throughout the Western world. She was a friend of Gertrude Stein in Paris and through her met Apollinaire and Picasso. She admired Marinetti in Italy and was for a time caught up in the futurist movement. In America she lived in Greenwich Village, where she was associated with Mabel Dodge, Carl Van Vechten, and Hutchins Hapgood. There she caught the attention of Walter Arensberg, a major patron of modernist arts, and encouraged him to finance a new journal, *Others* (launched in 1915), where she published her best-known poetry, including *Love Songs*, which contained intimate descriptions of lovemaking. Through this magazine she came to know and support such major modernist figures as William Carlos Williams, Marianne Moore, and Man Ray.

Another woman who has recently been read into the modernist movement is Jean Rhys (1890–1979). Born in Dominica, West Indies, her father was a Welsh doctor, her mother a third-generation white Creole. Rhys spent her formative years traveling between the West Indies and Europe. She was in Paris during its height as a cultural matrix and there had an affair with Ford Madox Ford, which he described in his *When the Wicked Man* (1931). Her sense of being sexually used led to her fascination with the theme of dominance and dependence, especially the aspect of what motivated relationships between dominant men and powerless women. This became the theme of her best novel, *Wide Sargasso Sea* (1966), in which she retells the story of Bertha Mason, Edward Rochester's mad wife, recasting from a feminist point of view Charlotte Brontë's *Jane Eyre*. Bertha is one of her prototypical characters, the product of a paternal world in which a helpless woman is victimized by both a dominant man and self-serving women. Here we have an excellent example of how present meaning recasts the past. Published in 1966, Rhys's novel is a product of postmodern feminist thought and could not have been written by either Brontë or the high modernists. Indeed, T. S. Eliot's relationship to his first wife, Vivien Haigh-Wood, has its own resemblance to the Rochester-Bertha situation.

Hilda Doolittle (1886–1961) was in retrospect more important to the modernist movement than she was given credit for at the time. Like Mina Loy, she was connected with important figures and played a significant part in developing various ideas about poetry, especially imagism. She was close to Pound and Marianne Moore and was married in 1913 to Richard Aldington, a marriage that competed with her love for Bryher (Winifred Ellerman), her lesbian lover. Bryher was the daughter of a wealthy industrialist, who married her to Robert McAlmon to create the illusion of respectability. McAlmon used the money that he received from his father-in-law to start a publishing house in Paris, in which he published Hemingway, Stein, Pound, Nathanael West, and Djuna Barnes. Bryher encouraged H. D. to become the patient of Sigmund Freud, and this led to her writing several long essays about Freud that in retrospect move him toward the center of modern ideology.

II

If women were claiming their rightful place at the forefront of literary modernism, so were ethnic groups like the blacks, who were finding their own voice in America. Between the wars there was a tidal wave of mobility in America, especially among the black population that began to move en masse from the South to the North, from rural America to cities like Chicago, Detroit, and to Harlem in New York. It has been estimated that the movement involved as many as 2 million people, drawn as part of a mass movement by the lure of industrial jobs. The exodus created its own momentum and drew upon itself for spokes-men and leaders such as W. E. B. Du Bois and Marcus Garvey, who were part of an educated black elite necessary to lead a liberation movement. The movement lasted from about 1920 to 1935 and brought an outburst of creativity to the arts in these cities, especially New York, where the movement came to be known as the Harlem Renaissance.

The artistic intent behind this movement was to bring an understanding of black culture to the population at large—to depict black aspirations, black hopes and fears, and to allow the black man and woman to go beyond what Ralph Ellison called "invisibility" to become in their own right a recognizable cultural presence in America. The movement, in other words, worked to undo the current of mass culture by emphasizing the injustice that came with generic thinking, especially when that concerned racial stereotyping.

The movement gave rise to a number of influential periodicals, such as Du Bois's the *Crisis*, which he edited from 1910 to 1934. Alain Locke in *The New Negro* (1925), an anthology, actually named those he felt would make a difference in the call for a new racial agenda: Langston Hughes, Claude McKay, Countee Cullen, Nella Larsen, among others. But the Harlem Renaissance was not a coherent movement; it brought together many men and women with dif-ferent views on racial and other matters. Moreover, the Harlem Renaissance is more connected to high modernism today than it was during its historical zenith. In the twenties and thirties, the Renaissance and high modernism were two separate cultural movements, on separate tracks, with different agendas. In the last generation or so, the two movements have been conflated, and they are now seen as one. Two writers from the Harlem Renaissance whose works have been brought into the modernist canon are Jean Toomer and Zora Neale Hurston. Their work has been dubiously confused with high modernism, but in retrospect Toomer and Hurston had little to do with the mainline movement known as modernism. On the other hand, they were both part of the beginning of the Harlem movement and its decline, and they partook of the sweep of the movement with all its ideological differences.

Jean Toomer (1894–1967), despite his efforts, was never able to reconcile himself to his black identity, perhaps because each of his maternal grandparents was born of Caucasian fathers. Despite his interest in African American history, he desired at one point in his career to do away with racial classifications, arguing that a sense of self was larger than racial identity, that the individual was larger than the crowd. This idea was central to his best-known novel, *Cane* (1923), a study contrasting rural life in the South with urban life in Washington, D.C., ultimately claiming the synthesis between the two was to be found in the processes of art.

He voiced most of his early racial beliefs in the *New York Call* between 1919 and 1920, catching the attention of Waldo Frank, who was part of the *Seven Arts* crowd, which included Sherwood Anderson, Kenneth Burke, Hart Crane, Lewis Mumford, Alfred Stieglitz, Georgia O'Keeffe, and others. The *Seven Arts* magazine promoted an indigenous American literature and opposed writers like James, Pound, and Eliot, who forsook America for Europe. Toomer's connection with this group was short-lived and stopped short of shared concerns. In 1925, he moved in a different direction when he met Orage, Ezra Pound's mentor, who introduced him to the philosophy of George Ivanovitch Gurdjieff. Gurdjieff taught that ancient mysteries were available to modern recapture, subject to release through disciplined living. This led to Toomer's lifetime search for some kind of spiritual harmony through experimental living that brought him to the study of many disciplines (such as the architecture of Frank Lloyd Wright, whose wife, Olga, was a student of Gurdjieff) before finally becoming a Quaker, and to stretches of experimental living in places like Portage, Wisconsin; Taos, New Mexico; and Paris. Toomer's life and writing career are testimony to the difficulty inherent in a racial search for identity, torn as he was between his white and black lineage, between rural and urban America, and between various forms of spiritual philosophy and experimental living. He could find resolution neither in his own person nor in a racial identity, neither in the dictates of self nor in those of the crowd.

Toomer's failure to reconcile inner yearnings with an outer reality is the subject of another novel that was the product of the Harlem Renaissance, *Their Eyes Were Watching God* (1937) by Zora Neale Hurston (1891–1960). Hurston was born in Alabama, but she grew up in Eatonville, Florida, the first incorporated all-black town in America, where her father was a Baptist minister and three-time mayor. She completed high school in Baltimore, attended Howard University in Washington, D.C., and went on to do graduate work at Barnard, where she studied with Franz Boas, perhaps the best-known anthropologist at the time. *Their Eyes Were Watching God* owes more than a little to Boas's teaching, especially his belief that race is a cultural matter, the product of the way a community expresses itself, and that happiness stems from forms of self realization, an inner sense of fulfillment and not riches or prosperity. Each culture expresses its own distinct, inner meaning, a truth she learned from her anthropological research on Haiti. The god of the novel is a force that sets limits to human progression, not a traditional deity.

These are the truths that Janie Crawford learns in the course of living the story that constitutes Hurston's novel. She is married three times. Her first husband is a rural farmer, many years older than she, who treats her as an extension of his property. Her second husband is also demanding, a successful businessman who owns the community store from the porch of which he oversees the town; elected mayor, he is more self-reliant than her first husband, but equally unwilling to allow her the freedom she wants, a truth she voices at his deathbed. Her third husband, a much younger man, is more relaxed in spirit and less dominating in attitude. They find a love that is not always in conformity with what the townspeople approve as love. They move from Eatonville to the Everglades and fall victim to a hurricane, where her husband, in saving her from drowning, is bitten by a rabid dog. Now, mentally unstable, he thinks she is unfaithful to him, and he begins shooting at her with a pistol, at which time she shoots back with a rifle, killing him. In the trial that follows, she is acquitted of murder, absolved by the white community, which sees her as the product of a black man's abuse, while she is harangued by the black community for allowing the white community to feel morally superior.

The novel is a study in cultural limits: Janie learns that she cannot go beyond her environment, that her life is circumscribed by dominant men, by the threat and then the reality of catastrophe, and by the unexpected, as when her husband becomes delusional. Despite the loss of the man she loves, she is content with what life has brought her and willing to go on in the face of its limits.

The initial response to Hurston's novel was not favorable. Hurston was writing at a time when a black novel was supposed to stem from political protest, and Hurston's novel lacked social dimension. Both Richard Wright and Ralph Ellison disliked it, mainly because it depicted an isolated black world cut off from the larger America. Hurston's career suffered from this prescribed view of realism; her reputation went into serious decline; and she died alone and in poverty in 1960. It was only through the efforts of Alice Walker that her novel was rediscovered and that her reputation as a major novelist was restored.

Once again we see how historical events can transform reality: Hurston's new standing is the result of the feminist call for a more introspective love novel (Hurston's novel has many of the qualities of Kate Chopin's *The Awakening*) and equally the result of a new interest in the black experience that goes beyond social clichés to a concern with an inner reality. The novels of both Toomer and Hurston are the products of social forces, literary achievement that was transformed by racial dictates. But like other works that stemmed from the Harlem Renaissance, their connection to modernism was more a retrospective phenomenon than an "originary" event, and they are the products of a critical conflation that has rewritten the historical record.[1]

15 ❖ MASS CULTURE

I

One way of looking at mass culture involves incremental history, the belief that it evolved over a period of time encouraged by new forms of technology and an expanding audience that could take advantage of those new forms of communication. This would put Johannes Gutenberg at center stage in world history, since in 1450 he revolutionized printed communication when he gave us the moveable type printing press, which extended the spread of the word, advanced further in the early 1600s with the rise of newspapers, and sustained in the mid-1600s with the inception of the Enlightenment, which encouraged the natural sciences and technology, superceded in its material progress only by the industrial revolution, which advanced world communication with inventions like the telegraph.

One could argue that Charles Dickens and Mark Twain were the products of mass culture: hundreds of people lined up on the docks of New York to meet the boats that held advanced installments of the novel that contained Little Nell's fate; Twain's own writing spoke to a generation of readers, and his company's publication of Ulysses S. Grant's autobiography was a national event. One could also point to popular works (the product of both print and film) that had an immense sale: *Gone with the Wind,* for example, sold 3.5 million copies in 1936–37.

But while these events changed the publishing world, they do not qualify as forms of mass culture. Just as there could be no science of microbiology until there was the microscope, there could be no mass culture until there was television. And this phenomenon has been extended by the Internet and the Web. Culture is limited to the technology that sustains it. Mass culture did not exist until two elements co-joined—electricity and TV, supplemented by previous means of mass communication like radio and film in which a message could reach far distances and be communicated to an immense audience. Suddenly millions of people witnessed a visitation of the pope, a soccer match, a military or environmental protest, or a concert by the Beatles or a rock band. Each crowd took on its own special meaning.

We can find Victorian commentators who were concerned with the early effects of mass culture like Matthew Arnold in *Culture and Anarchy* (1869). But the more up-to-date and systematic treatment of this development has understandably been left to such recent commentators as Theodor Adorno in *The Culture Industry: Selected Essays on Mass Culture* (1991) and Leo Lowenthal in *Literature and Mass Culture* (1984); it is also the subject of such well-known modern writers as Raymond Williams in *Culture and Society* (1958) and Michael Kammen's *American Culture, American Tastes: Social Change and the Twentieth Century* (1999). Walter Benjamin has studied the transformation of art in the face of mass culture in his "The Work of Art in the Age of Mechanical Reproduction" in *Illuminations* (1986).[1]

A new urban audience arose simultaneously with the rise of a television technology. Millions of people who would have protested other violations of their privacy allowed this invasive force into their homes. The inception of TV marks a before and after in the realm of mass communication. T. S. Eliot saw the danger of mass culture in its tendency to level all cultural forms. The end result involved a process (or at least a sense) of decline and a belief that a golden moment had inhabited the past. Eliot called for the emergence of elites to enlighten society, but elites were too isolated from each other to lead, and society became subject to a leveling effect, the product of the downward pull of the masses. Eliot came to believe that a national culture was stronger than the elements that made it up. He defined culture as:

> the way of life of particular people living together in one place. That culture is made visible in their arts, in their social system, in the habits and customs, in their religion. . . . These things all act upon each other, and fully to understand one you have to understand all. . . . The culture of an artist or a philosopher is distinct from that of a mine worker or field labourer . . . but in a healthy society these are all part of the same culture; and the artist, the poet, the philosopher, the politician, and the labourer will have a culture in common, which they do not share with other people of the same occupation in other countries.[2]

Eliot's definition raises a number of questions. He assumes that poets in dif-

ferent countries have less in common with each other than the poet and the
mine worker in the same country, and that religion can transform the commercial. He believes that culture is a homogeneous, unifying matter rather than a
stratified phenomenon that differs in accordance with class, profession, and way
of life. He diminishes the possibility that diverse cultural elements might be at
work in the same society.

Eliot may at one time have been correct in his belief that, in Western culture,
religion could distinguish itself from commercial activity. But with the rise of
public media like television, religion became a commodity, a product of televan-
gelism. Eliot's cultural dichotomy was challenged: as religion became a business,
its commercial aspect transformed the spiritual, and we had the rise of religious
structures that would seat thirty thousand or more and a television audience in
the millions.

Culture adapted to technology, not vice versa. One can catalog the modern
technological advances that have changed social reality starting with the automobile, moving to television, and ending with the computer and the World
Wide Web. Individual consciousness was inseparable from the communication
system itself: individual thinking became the product of a systemic, constructed
consciousness; the system now thought us rather than vice versa.

Michael Kammen's work offers insights into various forms of cultural change
that constitute mass culture. He insists that such a culture must be nonregional,
standardized, and commercial. He also sees the need to distinguish between
cultural realms. Kammen suggests that modernism witnessed three major
cultural transformations. He sees the years from 1885 to 1930 as involving a
commercial transformation; from 1930 to 1965 as involving the rise of popular
culture (or what he also calls "proto-mass culture"); and from 1965 to the present as involving the rule of mass culture. The first realm saw the rise of such
phenomena as Buffalo Bill's Wild West Show as well as burlesque and vaudeville;
the second period saw the rise of magazines like the *Saturday Evening Post* and
such commercial plans as the Book-of-the-Month Club; the third period saw the
era of television, with 14 million TV sets in America alone after World War II,
anticipating such worldwide events as the televising of the Super Bowl game or
soccer matches with tens of millions observers.

II

Mass culture transformed all that preceded it through its phenomenal commercial reach, illustrated by best sellers like Ian Fleming's James Bond novels and

J. K. Rowling's Harry Potter adventures. As of the summer of 2007, there were 121 million copies of the Harry Potter novels sold in the United States and 325 million copies in print worldwide. The seventh and final volume, *Harry Potter and the Deathly Hallows,* had an initial printing of 12 million copies in the United States alone, and 8.3 million copies were sold within an initial twenty-four-hour run, each copy earning a five-dollar royalty. After that, the U.S. sales totaled 5,000 copies every minute.[3] Rowling has made over $1 billion in royalties, becoming the highest-paid author in the history of commercial writing.

The Potter books were originally marketed for a pre-adolescent female audience between the ages of nine and eleven, but to the amazement of the publishers they had appeal to a much larger, even adult audience of both sexes. The achievement of books like this is not in their vision or their craft, but in their sales record, which in turn is the product of mass culture, the ability of a commercial publisher to control an extended commercial market. But the sales success of the Potter books does not completely overshadow some subsidiary reasons for its popularity. The conjectured success of these books stems in part from their plot, from their reassuring attitude toward life, their narrative promise of delivery from disaster, the promise of some ultimate security. (There was never any possibility that Harry might die in the seventh and last volume.)

The Potter books established a parallel universe to our own in which magic and other means were available to the young hero, who must confront the evil embodied in the fallen wizard, Lord Voldemort (world death). Voldemort desires to conquer the wizardry world; he has killed Potter's parents but suffered bodily annihilation himself when he tried to kill Harry, who was protected by his wizard's power. Voldemort has divided his dormant soul into seven parts and stored six of them in horcruxes. In order to eliminate Voldemort and rid the world of his evil, all six horcruxes must be destroyed. That goal becomes Harry's task.

The Potter books make use of classical myth and fantasy elements but in a cartoonish way in this realm of suspended physicality, where reality takes on the quality of Baudrillard's simulacra (signs pointing to other signs rather than a reality). Voldemort, like the Christian Devil, is a kind of fallen angel; Harry's quest for the horcruxes parallels the search for the Holy Grail. Like a stereotypical Orestes, Harry is sworn to revenge the death of a parent. Rowling has employed the quintessential elements of myth: hierarchy, guilt, redemption (through sacrifice), and victimage. And lastly, she has both displayed human vulnerability and rescued it from archetypal threat. Just as contemporary politicians create a strange symbiosis between the threat of terror and the promise to protect the masses from such a threat, the Potter novels create a hero whose power of magic allows him to cope with destructive threats. Both the political and the Potter narratives exist in the realm of unexamined fantasy, but they comfort the masses by promising reassuring ways of coping with lethal situations. Each reassurance pays off: the first in political power, the second in authorial royalties.

Modernism was being transformed by its concern with the anxieties of mass culture. Not only was the nature of the audience changing, the content of the artistic product was also being radically revised into what we now know as postmodernism. Postmodern qualities included a flattened use of character in an exotic situation, a threat to world security or a plot imbued with world events (like terrorism and before that the Cold War), and a protagonist who follows a string of unresolved clues. Instead of dealing with the interiority of (what E. M. Forster would describe as) "rounded" character, these works deal with far-fetched situations endowed with larger-than-life characters. These narratives are totally formulistic, creating even before the Twin Towers disaster of 9/11 a confrontational evil (e.g., Lex Luthor in the Superman saga, the Joker in the Batman sequence), that moved these works toward a new form of romance infused with emerging comic-book antirealism, including the Potter novels with their reliance upon magic and feats of wizardry. The triumph over forms of evil offered a narrative comfort that mass readers found reassuring.

While the Superman story goes back to 1938, it supplies strange parallels to the more recent use of fantasy that has become the model for the postmodern romance. A long and informed essay by Umberto Eco connects the Superman story and the structure of postmodern romance.[4] In fact, all of these works—Superman, Potter, Bond—rely on a hero who has distinguished himself from the rest of humanity: Superman because of his strength and supernatural powers; Potter because of his wizardry magic; Bond because of his extreme qualities of character, including his dedication to the Crown, his intelligence and cunning, his endurance and technological resources, his belief in the special destiny of the Western world, his good looks and physical conditioning, and his bon vivant code of living (which is why in the film versions a sequence of actors was needed to preserve Bond's youthful vigor and handsome appearance). While these protagonists are heroically superior in various ways, that superiority is often tested by degenerate forces or by their own physical limits. Even Superman is vulnerable to the effects of Kryptonite. As Umberto Eco demonstrates, the element that these works have in common is their iterative nature: they all take place in a perpetual present, and each novel or sequence starts at the beginning and repeats a version of the same plot. Each story is sealed in its own sphere of time, cut off from events that would consume the hero by subjecting him to the limits of chronology.

Much that is true of Superman carries over to the indomitable James Bond. Thirteen of Fleming's novels totaled sales of more than 45 million copies by the spring of 1966, and the movie versions (twenty-two in number, among them *Doctor No, From Russia with Love, Goldfinger, Thunderball*) had brought in some 100 million viewers.[5] As in the Potter books, the Bond novels supply the means of eradicating threats to a newly energized United Kingdom. Bond's supreme antagonist is a stereotypical villain—a vile enemy who plots an international conspiracy organized by SMERSH or SPECTRE. The founder and chair of this network is Ernst Stavro Blofeld, whose headquarters move from Paris, to Leningrad, to Moscow, to Switzerland as the center of world peril moves from city to city. He embodies the international threat to the empire that must be challenged by Bond in the tradition of imperial spy novels like Kipling's *Kim*, John Buchan's *The Thirty-nine Steps*, and Somerset Maugham's *Ashenden*. Early in the story Bond will confront the villain; at this time he will also encounter a voluptuous young woman who is in the employ of the villain but who is attracted to Bond. At some point in a totally iterative plot, the villain captures Bond and threatens his life; Bond escapes, implements a counterplot, and eradicates the threat of evil; he is then rewarded with the sexual favors of the young woman, now his ally.

Fleming's Bond is in the providential tradition of Doyle's Sherlock Holmes. Like Holmes, Bond brings an old-fashioned, upper-class loyalty to his task as spy, never questions the political policies of the nation, and protects the welfare of the state from outside threats. He is less empirical than Holmes (who isn't?), often triumphing by employing the tough-guy techniques of the American private eye (the double "0" in 007 indicates that he has killed at least two enemies of the state). He makes use of spy gadgetry while demonstrating his savoir-faire: he insists that his tournedos béarnaise be served rare; his three-part-gin, one-part-vodka martinis be splashed with the French aperitif Lillet and shaken over ice; and his Bollinger champagne be served with Russian caviar. From his Swiss watches to his Savile Row and Brioni suits to his British sport cars, he demonstrates an elegance of manner that is consistent with postmodern concern with commodification and that gives new meaning to the idea of conspicuous consumption, an idea consistent with the fact that his name is derived from Bond Street in St. James Square London.[6]

Despite the background use of the imperial theme, the Bond stories move beyond the elements of literary modernism in their use of intentionally flattened and stereotypical characters functioning in cartoon-like situations. Whereas the Bond novels look back to the generic nature of fantasies like the Superman story, they also look forward to adaptations that we find in a recent Pynchon novel. Pynchon's *Against the Day* (2006) has a sci-fi quality and a sense of wackiness that suggests it was inspired by Ian Fleming and written by a silly H. G. Wells.

Pynchon's novel takes us beyond the modernism of T. S. Eliot, even with its Eliotic suggestion that Western civilization never recovered from the effects of World War I. Like Eliot, Pynchon reduces the process of war to degeneration, and degeneration to a series of historical episodes. Kit Traverse, a mathematical genius, is pursued by the henchmen of the evil capitalist Scarsdale Vibe in a chase that takes him through Europe to Siberia, allowing Pynchon to comment on the episodes that led up to World War I. But Pynchon's use of history is so exaggerated that it takes him beyond Eliotic history to the far-fetched, anti-historical quality of the Bond stories. Indeed, Pynchon's novel can be read as caricature—a parodic version of Fleming's plot. Both Fleming's and Pynchon's characters are ultimately the products of imperial capitalism, both threatened (Fleming by the Cold War, Pynchon by paranoid fantasies) by the workings of capitalism, each consistent with Fredric Jameson's critique of how capitalism moved from modernism to postmodernism, transformed as it passed through forms of consumerism, imperialism, and globalization.

III

As cultural changes multiply, so does the idea of self. Forms of culture presumed a "meme," a unit of cultural information transmitted from one generation to another, the cultural equivalent of the human gene; such genetic information evolved via a process similar to Darwin's natural selection: certain ideas survived while others did not; the surviving ideas then mutated and spread.

Low culture involved the province of genres such as detective stories, westerns, and sitcoms, or a combination of popular genres, as when the white-hat, black-hat plot of the western is adapted to the fight between good and evil in outer space. But pop culture forms can be heightened, as when Conrad limits the use of the supernatural elements we find in Haggard and deepens Marlow's historical and moral consciousness. The main distinctions between high and low cultures are that the latter resorts to fantasy, creates a larger realm of hypothetical reality, appeals to a larger audience, and is less introspective.

When the transformation was an inner, self-mutated process, it produced a bifurcated self, as in Robert Louis Stevenson's *Jekyll and Hyde* (1886). The division of self between a social and hidden realm found expression in other theory, such as Freud's distinction between ego and id and the postmodern distinction between nature and culture. The historical transformations of the times brought into question the autonomous self. The individual was dwarfed by radical change. World population, for example, was increasing at an exponential rate; government was becoming more intrusive; bureaucracy more invasive; and politics in general more leveling. Moreover, the realms of knowledge and information were increasing at a rate beyond the capacity of the individual to master them. Once the idea of mass culture was in place, the concept of self would be radically revised. Such change stemmed from a number of sources, such as the idea of the crowd as defined by Le Bon, Freud, Elias Canetti, or the totalitarian state as depicted in dystopia. Whatever the source, the individual was diminished. Descartes' subject disappeared. These transformations prepared the ground for the transition from modernism to postmodernism. As depicted by cultural critics such as Georg Lukács, the Frankfurt school, and Fredric Jameson, consciousness became an extension of mass culture and modern capitalism (or, inversely, capitalism became reified consciousness).

In the last two centuries, we have moved from one kind of industrial society to another. The eighteenth century was the product of a primarily commercial society; the institution on which that society turned was property. The nineteenth century was an era of heavy industry; its society revolved on the factory. The late twentieth and early twenty-first centuries were an era of postindustrial society; its social axle is the corporation. We have moved from a society in which priority was given to property (capitalism) to power (industrialism) to authority (postindustrialism), from trade to factory goods and from factory goods to information and services. This has involved changes in government structure: the move from a federalized state, to a nation-state, to a global economy; from craft to mass production; from an emphasis upon domestic goods to an emphasis on military weapons.

Central to this discussion is Theodor Adorno's treatise on the *Dialectics of Enlightenment*. Adorno is concerned with new forms of technology and the Enlightenment satisfaction with man's control over nature and over others. Such control is the source of both power and wealth and can express itself obsessively, at which time rational progress becomes irrational regress. This loss of perspective becomes the basis for Marx's idea of use value: a product has use value when it satisfies human needs. The thought here of an abstract need in

be redeemed. T. S. Eliot's questing knight travels across the urban landscape to find redemption in the Chapel Perilous. Like Pound and Joyce, Eliot used myth to convey major beliefs. That use of myth was one of the hallmark elements of literary modernism. Recently, however, the use of myth has been challenged by a new generation of critics. David Chinitz, for example, reads Eliot's poetry as a part of pop culture, questions the validity of mythic readings. He takes Eliot's use of vaudeville elements in an early draft of *The Waste Land* as proof of Eliot's approval of low comedy, when the purpose of such use was to show the unpredictability of taste and the loosening of moral restraints. The high modernists made use of pop culture to disdain it (Joyce reduces it literally to toilet paper). The major modernist figures—Joyce, Pound, Eliot, Stein, and Stevens—created more distinctive characters who disdained rather than embraced more popular forms.

Authority works in all cultures through institutions, and this is even more so in a mass culture, where so much opinion is in free play. The impetus for academic/literary change comes from the forces at work in the most prestigious universities. In the past, Yale led the way in the name of New Criticism; then came French deconstruction under the influence of Derrida, Hillis Miller, Geoffrey Hartman, and Harold Bloom, who only recently has distanced himself from his earlier pronouncements. Once instituted as a movement, or even as a revisionary call, the work of these institutions can bring about radical transformations in the profession.

Each generation of literary critics breaks the hold on past criticism, opens up the field to new authority, and guards that authority like the knight at the Chapel Perilous until a new system of interpretation is introduced. Harold Bloom's "anxiety of influence" describes this phenomenon in different terms. Turning to Freud's theory of the Oedipus complex, Bloom believes each generation has a need to remove the authority of the father, a process analogous to the sacrificial death of the father/king that supposedly restores the fertility of the land.

The desire for power—the authority to create and control reality—is a fundamental human urge at work in both primitive and modern society. As much authority is at work in academic literary criticism as in the fashions that control the design of clothes or sport cars. Rear-guard criticism thus has a place in the critical process, assessing the authority of the new as it eclipses the past, keeping an audience aware of what has been transformed when current authority gives interpretive status to new literary readings.

Cultural values were of immense concern to the high moderns, were the means to social redemption. Eliot felt such redemption would come through religion; Pound through economics; Joyce through aestheticism; Stevens through new uses of imagination; Stein through new language and forms of consciousness. Pynchon reversed this state of mind when he combined high and low culture, turned historical expectation with its worldwide sense of catastrophe into spoof. Pynchon's questing heroine (as in this case Oedipa Maas in *The Crying of Lot 49*) can no longer cut through the confusion of multiplied cultural clues to even claim a basis for redemption.

V

The difference between popular culture and mass culture is in part quantifiable: the Book-of-the-Month Club attracted thousands of patrons; the Ian Fleming and Rowling novels and their movie versions attracted millions of readers and viewers. Almost every work that qualifies as a mass culture product is larger than life with a cast of characters with whom a large segment of the reading and viewing audience can identify. When stretched into a series of books, or films, or TV episodes, they create a sense of suspense from installment to installment, generating an interest that often goes beyond the complexity of the work itself. To add substance to the work, it is often infused with archetypal themes taken from world classics; almost every one of these works, for example, involves forms of goodness in conflict with forces of evil.

As with the Harry Potter and James Bond novels, *Star Wars* created a popular form for mass-culture consumption. Space travel involved going where no one had gone before, confronting unknown species, even as the moral situation remained the same with an earthly democracy engaging an evil empire. *Star Wars* was a political morality play in which good once again confronted evil; it was *Wagon Train* in space, a thematic residue of the western adapted to the anxieties of the Cold War. *Star Wars*, the product of George Lucas, was rich in its use of Greek and Christian mythology, making use of such archetypal themes as the confrontation between father and son, the compelling attraction of power, the universal workings of empire, and the precarious nature of democracy when faced with totalitarian options. But while *Star Wars* engaged classical themes, it did not bring the meaning of universal concerns back to an informed consciousness, although one could argue that was the (failed?) function of Luke Skywalker. Moreover, Lucas's sustained optimism reversed the high modernists' sense of historical decline, changing the modernist "aura" or its authenticity.

In the realm of art, Andy Warhol drained traditional art of its aura. In the realm of music, Elvis Presley gave us a parallel experience. He drained the music genres of blues, gospel, and country of their individual aura as he turned the more standard forms into rock 'n' roll, taking it beyond the traditional offerings of Joe Turner, Ray Charles, and Chuck Berry, generating millions of fans in the process. Luciano Pavarotti changed the aura of classical opera when he brought it to the masses. Pop culture could not have existed without mass culture to sustain and support it, and both needed to be taken into account when they challenged aura in the literary realms of high modernism. This phenomenon has been well studied by Walter Benjamin in his essay on art and mechanical reproduction and by Theodor Adorno and the Frankfurt school.

VI

As we have seen, a divisive way of looking at pre- and post mass culture involved the difference between what Ferdinand Tönnies in 1887 called *Gemeinschaft* (in which an organic community takes its being from human relationships) and *Gesellschaft* (in which a more impersonal society adheres to a calculating process involving commodity production under capitalism). Walter Benjamin was concerned with the historical shift from such a personal community to the mechanical order. The difference between the two kinds of societies was again differentiated in the German distinction between culture (*Kultur*) and civilization (*Zivilisation*): culture involved an aesthetic, organic relationship to the world; civilization embodied a commercial, artificial orientation stemming from the decadence of capitalism. Benjamin's work on Baudelaire, who lived on the cusp, took its meaning from the transformation from one order to the other. As Richard Wolin has succinctly put it:

> The fact that [Baudelaire] incorporated the often grotesque images of mid-nineteenth-century city life into his poetry qualifies him as the first "modernist," the first true poet of urbanism. Because he stood so to speak on the cusp between two historical eras, witnessing the extirpation by modern industrial capitalism of the last vestiges of traditional life, Baudelaire is ideally situated to chronicle this important process of transition. In this connection, Benjamin seeks to show how the philosophy of history penetrates the very heart of the purportedly autonomous activity of the heart.[9]

Benjamin's work on Baudelaire gave him an understanding of how cultural meaning was changing within the transition from an agrarian to a commercial/industrial society—especially how the meaning of art was being changed under the influence of mechanical reproduction. Just as the individual was being transformed, mass culture changed the very nature of artwork. Whether it was Homer's *Iliad* (myth) or medieval Christian painting (religion), the artwork originally existed in a realm of its own with a ritual or cultic function attached to it. Benjamin argued that, in the Renaissance, painting's ritualistic basis began to lose favor to a secular cult of beauty. This trend was suspended for a moment by Romanticism and the influence of aestheticism, especially the new religious sense that was a by-product of "l'art pour l'art," which helped bring about a reaction to the commodification of art. But, Benjamin continued, the process of mechanical production eventually transformed the artwork. When produced en masse, the originality and individuality of the work was lost. From the photograph, to the phonograph record, to film—each work was no longer unique, no longer commanded respect as a religious or cult object. The work lost what Benjamin called its "aura," its authority as art. Its status as an aesthetic object was replaced by its function as an instrument of communication: its "cult value" became "exhibition value." Technical forces now controlled "aesthetic distribution." Just as the individual was diminished by the rise of masses, so art was diminished in an era of mechanical reproduction.[10] Standards of excellence are no longer agreed upon; at this point the ability to discern between works of art is lost. We enter the John Keats vs. Bob Dylan dilemma in which we lack the means to determine preference.

Benjamin's point is reinforced by the work of Andy Warhol, especially his painting of Campbell soup cans with their thirty-two kinds of soup, and his portraits of such celebrities as Marilyn Monroe, Elizabeth Taylor, and Jacqueline Kennedy in which the same portrait is displayed serially often against a different color background or transformed slightly when a part of the screen becomes clogged with paint. In each of these paintings, we have the same image with a slight variation, just like cars off the assembly line in Detroit. Warhol has mass-produced what should be unique, robbing the portraits of their individual aura, creating a multiple self, as indeed the self is multiplied when it becomes part of the crowd.

When the artwork lost its aura, we lost the ability to distinguish between high and low culture, between the works of T. S. Eliot and the vaudeville or jazz performance. And the situation did not stop with the production of art. In a postmodern culture, a sense of the unique gave way to multiple reproductions. The Henry Ford assembly-line mentality created a new reality. In 1949, William J. Levitt bought a 1,500-acre potato farm on Long Island on which he built 17,500 identical, prefabricated, four-room houses, the project known as Levittown. To access this "community," the Long Island Expressway was needed, and to the horrors of mass housing we must add the additional horrors of mass transportation. We are now in the world of Robert Moses, whose Cross Bronx Expressway displaced thousands of middle-class inhabitants, erased the community of East Tremont, and divided what had been a vibrant working community into dead space, just as the Southeast Expressway had divided downtown Boston into dead space. The aura of a community was gone, transformed in Marshall Berman's eloquent words into "monoliths of steel and cement, devoid of vision or nuance or play, sealed off from the surrounding city by great moats of stark emptiness, stamped on the landscape with a ferocious contempt for all natural and human life."[11] The high modernists tried to define human life as a state of living (i.e., a unique form of) consciousness. Postmodernism transformed that condition into states of consumer desire, soon transformed again into political movements and cultural fashions, activity that robbed modernism of what Benjamin called its aura.

VII

The Institute for Social Research at the University of Frankfurt, the academic center for a group of cultural critics known as the Frankfurt school, came into being in 1923. It was based on the Marx-Engels Institute of Moscow and was established to study a range of disciplines from philosophy to such cultural matters as music, film, and mass entertainment. Official members of the Frankfurt school were Theodor Adorno, Max Horkheimer, Herbert Marcuse, Leo Lowenthal, and Erich Fromm (with Georg Lukács and Walter Benjamin sometimes serving in an advisory capacity: their ideas, even when rejected, were instrumental to the platform).[12]

The Frankfurt school was a postmodern phenomenon in its insistence that culture had preempted nature. These critics no longer were interested in the aesthetic dimensions of art. They thought of art as simply a mode of production, an idea fundamental to Marxist assumptions that moved them toward cultural criticism. Art became inseparable from the workings of a commercial society and mass culture. Whether it was the work of T. S. Eliot or Andy Warhol, it was all a form of commercial production. Warhol made this point himself when he turned to commercial objects (Campbell soup cans) and mass-produced images (Marilyn Monroe or a dollar bill) for his subject matter.

Someone like Fredric Jameson begins right here. He sees postmodernism as inseparable from Ernest Mandel's idea of late capitalism: international finance, multinational corporations, a maze of interlocking deals that express themselves as pastiche or structures like John Portman's Bonaventure Hotel, which fills space without ordering it, where the mazelike structure becomes the figural embodiment of late capitalism itself.

Jean Baudrillard turns this argument around. Instead of seeing postmodernism as a kind of centrifugal (efferent) experience, he sees it as a centripetal (afferent) experience, as a center so overloaded with data and other forms of information and sensory clotting (what he calls "hyperspace" or what Don DeLillo refers to as "white noise") that it leads to an implosion within the system.

Jameson and Baudrillard are not as far apart as they maintain, and some might find it reassuring to discover two postmodern theorists in combat over what is a mimetic principle. While the postmodernist insists that there is no meaning built into time, they nevertheless claim that it unfolds in figural ways. This is because every system has to be made representational if it is to have a critical use that one can apply to literature, or art, or architecture.

The Frankfurt school was most adamant in distinguishing high culture from popular culture, and yet no group of critical thinkers was more advanced in defining the way mass culture accommodated the spread of popular culture. The school was especially influential in defining the place of the individual within the realms of mass culture. They combined Freudian and Marxist thinking, bringing psychoanalytic and political criticism into common focus. Paramount to their philosophy was the belief that (1) consciousness followed social change; (2) monopoly capitalism (imperialism) was the basis for the fascist society; and (3) the rise of new technologies led to the desire to control nature. The import of these ideas was that the new technology and the totalitarian state had led to a contracted ego. As the state with its bureaucracy and technology was extended, the individual was diminished and lost status.

A study that was central to the discussion of mass culture was Leo Lowenthal's *Literature and Mass Culture* (1984), a composite of essays, some written as early as the thirties. Although badly out of date, Lowenthal's book is still useful in its consideration of how mass culture became a legitimate object of academic study, supplying relevant cultural categories and terms. Lowenthal points out that the history of Western literature contains writers who wrote for an audience beyond their class. Shakespeare is an obvious example, as are Montaigne and Pascal in France. The origins of the novel—the narratives of Defoe, Fielding, Richardson, Smollett, and Sterne—spoke broadly to the new middle class in England, as did the work of Goethe in Germany.

But mass culture is a modern phenomenon. Lowenthal documents this observation in his critique of David Riesman's *The Lonely Crowd* (1950). Riesman believed that a fundamental change had altered American society: pioneer individualism and the communal solidarity of those living on the land had given way to the atomized anonymity of a mass culture. Every paradigm is subject to revision (note, for example, the retrospective challenge to Frederick Jackson Turner's frontier thesis), and Riesman's thesis has been called into question, albeit devoid of an alternate explanation of its argument. Riesman and his coauthors (Nathan Glazer and Reuel Denney) discuss two personality types that make up the urban/industrial community: the inner-directed and outer-directed man. The former, in the tradition of Emerson, looks inward toward aesthetic activity; the latter, in the empirical tradition of the philosopher Wilhelm Dilthey and the sociologist Georg Simmel along with the pragmatic philosophy of William James and John Dewey, looks outward to the activity of a commodity culture. The first gives rise to forms of self-reliance, the second to prevailing social institutions and their mandates. Riesman's division of human types in an industrial culture has a remote parallel to H. G. Wells's division of humanity into the Eloi, who have become overly refined, and the Morlocks, who have become grossly degenerate. Thomas Mann saw humanity heading in a similar direction in *Buddenbrooks*, with an overly refined personality unable to compete in a material culture. Whatever the explanation, social critics for nearly a century believed that human nature had been transformed by the changes incurred through mass culture. This assumption tended to run parallel to literary modernism rather than intersecting with it.

Along with Lowenthal, the Frankfurt school's interest in mass culture owed much to Theodor Adorno. Adorno went to Freud to find the reason that the individual forsakes reason to join with the masses in a way that is opposed to the individual's interest. The reason that the individual surrenders the self to a mob, Freud concluded, involved the transfer of the libido. There is, in other words, a manifest sexual basis to this phenomenon, whether it involves German fascism, or the esprit de corps of an army, or the solidarity of the Church through the mystical body of Christ. Hitler held the state together by a code of authority, but behind that was a love for Germany and a sense that the masses were a part of its destiny. An army appeals to the same order of patriotic meaning. The Church promises the means to redeem the sinner, which is why it must perpetuate the notion that evil is a physical reality and that a personified evil walks among us. Not only must the crowd be bonded by libido and directed by an inner purpose, it must also be organized by its hatred of a common enemy, whether it is the

Jews in Nazi Germany, the foe of the army, or the secular humanist or apostate who is outside the Church.

VIII

A discussion of modernism and what followed it would not be complete without a brief consideration of the effect of such mass movements as the baby boom and the rise of a hippie generation. The hippie movement had its origins primarily as an antiwar response to the Vietnam War. But a subtext and a larger concern involved a response to a culture that took its being from capitalism, thus consenting to material priorities, the authority of the corporation with its cadre of lobbyists controlling political decisions, and the equally nefarious influence of the military-industrial complex sustaining the need for new weapons and thus perpetuating the desire for war. The hippie movement was specific on what it considered the enemy and clamored for a new vision based on a liberated mass culture, free to realize an idealized inner self that they connected with LSD and lovemaking. In its Lawrentian desires, we came full circle.

Two major spokesmen for this major countercultural movement were Jack Kerouac and Allen Ginsberg. Kerouac took his literary bearings from Thomas Wolfe and Henry Miller. His writing is autobiographical in the Wolfean sense: there is the desire to find meaning in movement, the meaning of the road. And his writing is also hedonistic in Miller's sense: the pursuit is for pleasure, for mind-blowing experience that comes with experimenting with drugs and sex. If his own work leans more toward Wolfe, the work of his friend William Burroughs leans more toward Miller. Like F. Scott Fitzgerald in *This Side of Paradise* and J. D. Salinger in *The Catcher in the Rye*, Kerouac wrote for a new generation of readers who were ready to break out of the conformity that held life in the fifties in place.

On the Road (1957) was essentially a rewriting of *The Town and the City* (1950): both were based on the same experiences, but in the later work Kerouac was more forthcoming and presented a less cosmetic version of events. He was also using a device he referred to as "sketching": the object focused upon was intensified by the impressions it called to mind. Kerouac felt that there was a connection here between what he was doing with prose and what a musician like Lee Konitz (who carried on the tradition of Charlie Parker) was doing in "riffing"—that is, moving beyond the score and improvising as he went along. Kerouac once said that Konitz "inspired me to write the way he plays."[13]

Despite the experimentation with style, *On the Road* is a traditional novel in the travelogue mode. Divided into four parts, each part involves a road trip that

Kerouac took with Neal Cassady between 1946 and 1950. There is a formulistic progression: we start with the desire to escape a realm of depression; an initial cautiousness gives way to frenetic activity and then to recklessness; this culminates in a misfortune that terminates the trip; the return is to an initial state of boredom.

The desire to find meaning on the road comes to nothing. When the Kerouac figure travels from one coast to the other, the trip starts with a sense of expectation and ends on a note of emptiness. "There was no way to go but back," concludes the narrator. The road is endless, running in loops that mock destination. If there is a purpose to such activity, it must inhere in the traveler, not the road. Man is the source of meaning: a purpose to life is self-generated, not found in random experience, despite adolescent expectation to the contrary. (The appeal of both Wolfe and Kerouac to adolescent readers perhaps stems from this aspect of their work.) In an essay, "After Me, the Deluge," Kerouac indicts the whole beat generation as being aimless and world-weary, expecting life and not themselves to supply a sense of purpose.

At some point in the writing process, Kerouac had a change of heart, out of which came *Visions of Cody* (published posthumously in 1972). This involved going back and rewriting the events that made up both *The Town and the City* and *On the Road*. The difference would be that in the previous works Kerouac had put the emphasis on himself through the use of an alter-ego (Sal Paradise), allowing introspection to carry the meaning of the novel. In *Visions of Cody,* he put the emphasis directly upon Cassady (Dean Moriarty), allowing character depiction to carry the meaning of the novel. As opposed to *On the Road*, which ends at night in the East, *Visions of Cody* ends in the West with a new day dawning.

But the hopeful ending turns out to be more rhetoric than narrative possibility: Kerouac's ability to move from despair to hope as a conclusion suggests an arbitrariness of narrative meaning. The movement back and forth between an intractable reality and a drug-induced euphoria was an emotional limbo, taking him nowhere. The last novel that Kerouac wrote, *Big Sur* (1962), was the story of his mental breakdown. The destruction of self seems intricately connected to the cultural degeneration that had been Kerouac's previous emphasis. While more hopeful, *Visions of Cody* proved to be an interlude in his final sequence of novels.

Kerouac began and ended his writing career emphasizing the connection between historical and personal decline. He eventually realized that time in motion does not do justice to static time, time as duration. He thus tried to combine the two by making use of stories that unfolded on the road, but he interrupted the flow with blocks of contemplated thought that suspended the moment.

Like Thomas Wolfe, Kerouac tried to capture two realms of time: horizontal, or progressive, time and perpendicular, or static, time: the first is time in motion; the second is time contemplated. But time contemplated is constantly shifting as the past is transformed by the present, so that ideals once outlived and absorbed into the past are gone forever.

IX

The other major voice of the hippie movement was that of Allen Ginsberg. Despite their ongoing rivalry that took them to the edge of hostility, Kerouac and Ginsberg were close friends. Like Kerouac, Ginsberg found life one continued experiment—an experiment with drugs, with sex, with poetry itself. Between the two—and along with William Burroughs and Ken Kesey—they embodied the counterculture of the sixties and took over where the hippies left off. They turned to other cultures—especially the religion of Hinduism and Zen Buddhism—for opposing states of consciousness. Their writing was deeply personal, so personal that it was not always intelligible even to an informed reader; they achieved recognition by defying tradition and authority and encouraging protest. Ginsberg was a genius at working the public relations of a mass audience, and he managed to get the more important news media to cover the group's activities. Their lives and their writings were perfectly in tune with the demands and expectations of a mass culture: they defied conformity, led the way to the edge, and became the physical or vicarious model for others that made their activity important. They became famous by insisting they were famous.

In *Howl* (1959), Ginsberg was rewriting Pound's "Hugh Selwyn Mauberly." Pound told us that the best in his generation was gone, lost to a corrupt civilization, a bitch gone in the teeth. Ginsberg tells us that the best in his generation is also gone, lost in mental hospitals. The poem begins, "I saw the best minds of my generation destroyed by madness." The poem is dedicated to Carl Solomon, who Ginsberg met in Rockland Psychiatric Hospital, but it is made up of a number of friends who had mental breakdowns and Ginsberg's relationship to them. It is not their chosen, far-out existence that has brought them to the edge or over the edge of sanity. As Ginsberg would have it, they are all the victims of an industrial society that has created the hostile environment that has provoked the search for an anodyne: the need for alcohol, for experimental drugs, for new forms of both homosexual and heterosexual experience.

Two generations removed, we can better come to terms with the hippie and counterculture movements. While Kerouac and Ginsberg pursued a course of self-destruction, others turned the freedom of the movement into true improvisation. Out of the residue of these movements came technological advances, primarily the work of persons like Steve Wozniak and Steve Jobs that led to computer technology, and with it the World Wide Web and avenues of communication outside the control of established authority. In a real way, these advances embodied one of the hopes of the counterculture movement by opening up a privileged society and creating new cultural opportunities. But it was only a matter of time before such technology became inseparable from corporate America—listed on the stock exchange, the product of investment capitalism, subject to the workings of the market and to political authority and legal maneuvering.

Like so much that inspired modernism as a literary movement, the desire for an ideal was often frustrated, when it did not lead to its opposite. The worst aspect of the movement resulted in the pursuit of mind-blowing addiction, the psychic destruction that Kerouac describes in *On the Road* and Ginsberg depicts in *Howl*. If the movement can be thought of as a conclusion to modernism, then modernism began with a search for the beautiful and inner meaning and ended with psychedelic frenzy and psychosis. In between, it offered other experimental ways of confronting reality.

16 ✤ ALONE IN THE CROWD

[Television] is a medium of entertainment which permits millions of people to
listen to the same joke at the same time, and yet remain lonesome.

—T. S. ELIOT

In his *Post-Historic Man,* Roderick Seidenberg distinguishes between the individual and the community. His premise is that with the transformations brought
on by capitalism we lost a sense of community to the rise of individualism and
forms of narcissism. His thesis was consistent with the theories of the most
respected sociologists at the turn of the twentieth century. Ferdinand Tönnies
makes the same argument in his distinction between *Gemeinschaft* (community,
beyond self-interest, common beliefs, family, division of labor, and organic) and
Gesellschaft (society at large, individual self-interest, mechanistic, motivated
by money rather than cooperation, and marked by class/social conflict). Georg
Simmel theorizes that money stabilizes a system of relative values and allows a
holistic view of the self in the otherwise destabilized flux of a capitalistic society.
Émile Durkheim argues that a sense of individual helplessness led to the rise of
suicides. Max Weber insisted that a Protestant individualism encouraged the rise
of capitalism. And Thorstein Veblen held that behind capitalism were forms of
individual display that involved conspicuous consumption.

Seidenberg's thesis was also consistent with the assumptions of both literary
naturalism and modernism. A novel like Frank Norris's *The Octopus* depicts the
breakdown of the community spirit as the railroad inflates its rates and prevents
wheat farmers from selling their product at a reasonable profit. If the railroad
and the farmers could have functioned as a community, they both would have
profited. In acting only in terms of self-interest and looking only for the largest
profit, the railroad violated a sense of community and fragmented the farmers as

a group, encouraging them to act individually, often in reckless ways. Among the moderns, T. S. Eliot bemoaned the rise of individualism at the expense of community. In a lecture in Virginia in 1933 that became the basis for *After Strange Gods*, Eliot tells his more-or-less homogeneous audience that they have the makings of a community, an organization of like selves, at the same time disdaining New York with its diversified population, which made community impossible. The Southern Agrarians anticipated Eliot's assumptions when they argued for the homogenous nature of the South as opposed to the heterogeneous nature of the North. Moving in the opposite direction, writers like Ayn Rand sponsored the cult of radical individualism and, with her followers, challenged the validity of altruism as a state of mind or principle of behavior.

The movement toward individuality was transformed in the middle of the twentieth century when the atomized individual became absorbed into the crowd, the new masses that rose coincidental with the rise of new technology such as television and later, of course, the Internet. These movements had their effect on the literary imagination—from the rise of the individual hero (often a social outsider or anti-hero) to the perpetuation of a mass audience and the claim to herd mentality that characterizes such phenomena as the best seller, the rise of polling information, and the pervasiveness of fashion in the realm of commodity consumption. The move from the breakdown of community, to the rise of individualism, to the absorption of self by the crowd involved radical social transformations that eventually led to redefining all of these elements in keeping with a changing sense of self.

I

The crowd can stand for all kinds of related meaning[1]—for the city, for mass culture, for human possibility, for human opacity. Whitman's metaphor for the city was the crowd, but the crowd individualized: out of it stepped Poe, Lincoln, Daniel Webster, and Henry Clay. It combined all of humanity as well as the great men who were the instruments of history. The particular was realized in the universal, the One in the Many: as he learned from Emerson's "Self-Reliance," the great man in the crowd keeps "the independence of solitude." The American burden was to reconcile the individual with the masses. The poet extrapolates from the crowd to the nation. The crowd was inseparable from America's destiny as the nation moved toward urbanism (between 1810 and 1860, the population of the United States grew six times faster than the world average, reaching 30 million by the Civil War, the proportion of Americans living in cities growing from 6 percent to 20 percent of that total). Whitman never separated himself from this urban transformation: his poetry takes its power from the Emersonian vision transformed into street speech.

In the tradition of Whitman, Walter Benjamin connects the artist with the crowd: such an embodiment resides with Baudelaire's flaneur, who goes to the crowded arcade to be alone, to be within and yet separate from the throng, to be both observer and observed. We can find this prototypical figure in much modern literature: the Tiresias figure in Eliot's London, Nick Carraway in Fitzgerald's New York, Tod Hackett in West's Los Angeles.

Denis Donoghue has illuminated the metonymic quality of the crowd in his critique of Poe's "The Man of the Crowd." Poe's story involves a narrator who is looking out of the bow window of a London coffeehouse, reading the crowd by speculating on the lives of those who make it up. Suddenly he sees an old man, decrepit and wild looking, amidst the crowd, and on impulse he follows him through the streets of London—walking all night, through the next day, into the dusk of the next evening. At this point, the narrator approaches the mysterious figure, looks into his face, and sees him as incarnate of the crowd. He comes to the conclusion that this anonymous figure is the doer of an evil deed ("the genius of deep crime") and believes that further pursuit will reveal no more about this mysterious person. (If Poe's crowd embodies a generic form of mankind, the old man's "crime" may be a form of original sin—that is, a flaw deeply engrained in the human species.) The story ends with these words in German: "er lasst sich nicht lessen" (he does not permit himself to be read).

Prototypical characters—the man in the crowd and the mysterious stranger that we find in Poe and Twain along with participants in the carnival and masquerade—are analogues of the Dionysus myth: the mysterious person who comes out of the wilderness and whose secrets disrupt the community. This incarnation of the mysterious stranger speaks to an unpredictable, often runaway (sexual) energy. Donoghue takes the mysterious stranger in a different direction. He sees Poe's man in the crowd as an emblem of man in the modern city, mass man no longer intelligible to the common observer. As Donoghue puts it, "Many nineteenth-century writers felt that the crowd, the masses, huddled or crushed or driven to the degree of anonymity, marked the forces in modern life that could not be comprehended."[2] The incremental forces of modernism have turned the crowd into a thing, and the narrator now "feels the crowd only as the mechanical consequence of force: it has already become a thing."[3]

Another way of seeing Donoghue's point is to see the crowd as a product of national surveys or polls that supposedly reveals the meaning of the masses. In Alan J. Pakula's 1974 film *The Parallax View,* the sinister Parallax Corporation uses a general questionnaire to recruit sociopaths whose moral characteristics suggest they may have the necessary attributes to be potential assassins. While there may not be any organization with the intent of the Parallax Corporation, the National Opinion Research Center at the University of Chicago sponsors the General Social Survey, which has been exploring the American psyche since 1972. After the United States Census, the survey is the most frequently analyzed data source in the social sciences. Every other year, three thousand adults are interviewed in person for about ninety minutes. Since 1972, there have been twenty-six surveys covering a vast array of concerns on subjects political, religious, and sexual in nature, leading to data that supposedly reveal behavioral attitudes.

Such polls offer a constructed rather than a physical reality. Such information is both interesting and useful as hypothesis. But like Poe's man in the crowd, the process turns the masses into a "thing," a statistical record, perhaps more the product of social stereotyping than of human understanding and physical finding. While polls often reveal a general state of mind, they cannot reveal the subconscious motives that infuse that mind, and many elements can be drawn into the poll's orbit, creating a reality of their own. There is no positive way of knowing if the constructed and physical realities are in sync. Despite their predictive value, polls can get it all wrong. As Harry Truman learned, if it was up to the polls, Thomas Dewey would be president.

In Poe's crowd, the city and mass culture have come together. The crowd is there, challenging to be read in all of its ambiguity, creating a panoply of modernist insight. Eliot saw the crowd as the walking dead; Pound, more circumspect, saw a ghost-like quality (apparitional) in the faces of the Metro. The crowd embodies Fitzgerald's world infused with a Romantic readiness that may never come again. Nick Carraway finds both opportunity and loneliness in the crowd. After the initial excitement infused with new possibility, Nick detects in the crowd a feeling of loneliness:

> I began to like New York, the racy, adventurous feel of it at night and the satisfaction that the constant flicker of men and women and machines gives to the restless eye. I liked to walk up Fifth Avenue and pick out romantic women from the crowd and imagine that in a few minutes I was going to enter into their lives, and no one would even know or disapprove. . . . At the enchanted metropolitan twilight, I felt a haunting

loneliness sometimes, and felt it in others, poor young clerks who loitered
in front of windows waiting until it was time for a solitary restaurant
dinner, young clerks in the dusk, wasting the most poignant moments of
night and life.[4]

Poe's crowd takes us to a critical impasse; Fitzgerald's to romantic albeit lonely
possibility. As Donoghue's critique of Poe's story suggests, the need to "ground"
the idea of mass culture has led to constant speculation regarding the meaning
of the crowd. Benjamin, Le Bon, Freud, Canetti all have a theory of the crowd.
Not all of these theorists see the crowd as hostile and unread. The idea of the
crowd does well in revealing empirical data, but less well as the source of more
abstract matters, as confirmed by a recent experiment. Intrade, a political Web
site with general access to the public, proved eerily accurate in predicting the
presidential winner in each of the fifty states in the 2004 election. Equally surprising, Intrade proved strangely accurate in guessing the weight of an ox based
on the average estimate in a bunch of guesses. The collective judgment of many
people was proven more accurate than the judgment of an individual expert.

But when it came to determining political policy, the crowd often did not
recognize what was best in its own self-interest, according to Bryan Caplan in
The Myth of the Rational Voter: Why Democracies Choose Bad Policies. Part of the
reason is that the crowd is often uninformed about complex political issues and
may be misled by special interests. But Caplan goes a step further and argues that
voters as a group are irrational in ways worse than ignorant. They are prone to
vote against self-interest when it comes to taxation, especially taxes that would
help the environment; will vote against interaction with foreigners, even when
it would lead to more open trade; vote against productivity if it involves downsizing; vote in ways that suggest a tendency to exaggerate economic problems.
One might question if all the problems characterized here are really matters
that work against the self-interest of the group: a vote against downsizing, for
example, could be a vote imbued with self-interest. Contrary to Caplan's thesis,
one could argue that the postmodernist crowd is really a product of mass culture
with all the biases of that culture. But whatever might be its collective source,
the point still remains that the crowd takes on individual characteristics based
on abstracting human qualities from the group.

A theory of crowds is thus an exercise in diversity. We find a gentle crowd in
Benjamin's arcade, intent on shopping or seeing and being seen. Dreiser's Carrie
Meeber witnesses such a crowd when she looks out the parlor window of her

hotel and joins it when she walks down Broadway. We find the hostile crowd at the angry protest of Zola's coal miners in *Germinal,* the inflamed crowd among the zealots who make up Dreiser's lynch mob or his striking streetcar workers, and the violent crowd in the frustrated seekers who bring disappointed dreams to Hollywood in Nathanael West's *The Day of the Locust.* The modernist crowd can move in various Freudian directions, can both express and repress emotion. Henry James, Edith Wharton, T. S. Eliot give us morally paralyzed characters who have lost contact with their sexual feelings and who make up the passive crowd we find in *The Waste Land* ("A crowd flowed over London Bridge, so many, / I had not thought death had undone so many") as opposed to Nathanael West, who gives us the volatile crowd that expresses its repressed feelings as acts of violence.

II

A way to cope with mass culture involved affirming primitive values, especially undoing the connection between human elements and technology. William Carlos Williams (1883–1963) took this task as his poetic subject. Williams's was not the symbolic vision: nature was not divinely infused with meaning; the poet's function was not to read the symbolic meaning of nature but to create that meaning; symbolic reality was not in objects or in the mind but in the fusion of the two. The past did not build incrementally upon itself: history was like the seasons of the year with each spring a new beginning. A look to the city (Paterson, New Jersey) disclosed an indisputable truth: the past had been contaminated. In the name of commerce and industry, the land had been betrayed, the river polluted: the city awaited the redeeming poet, awaited a new beginning. The imagination was a "force," not a "focus"; it made its way by compass and followed no path. Like Emerson and Whitman, Williams fell back on Romantic assumptions. In *Kora in Hell* (1920), he celebrated the earth as the source of all life. Life, like Kora (Persephone), emerged each year from the barren ground, a theme he treated again in *Spring and All* (1923), which connected the renewed-life process with the Dionysus myth. Giants lie buried in the earth: their release is connected to earthly myth, the dark, unknown region of our consciousness. In *In the American Grain* (1925), influenced by D. H. Lawrence's *Studies in Classic American Literature* (1923), Williams attacked the influence of the Puritans and called for a renewed idea of America, as he did in *A Voyage to Pagany* (1928), his answer to Henry James's vision of Europe. Only a new beginning could erase the destructive nature of the past, undo the loss of mythic consciousness that had been swallowed by the crowd.

Hart Crane (1899–1932) also inherited Whitman's vision: the hope and the doubt, the order and the chaos. Crane tried to bring Whitman's observations up to date. "Crossing Brooklyn's Ferry" (1856) anticipated *The Bridge* (1930), since it was the ferry that connected Manhattan and Brooklyn before the building of the bridge. As a suspension bridge, it holds itself up by displacing stress, similar to the arch, by the dispersion of its own weight, internal forces absorbing external pressure. The bridge is Crane's symbol for cosmic unity: the connection of the finite and infinite, past and present, East and West, agrarian and industrial. Crane wanted to heal the "iron-dealt cleavage," the disharmony between man and machine, between primitive and mass culture. He believed there could be an organic unity between an industrial culture and nature, and he tried to create a poetic vision that would reveal such harmony. But his attempt exposed the impossibility of the Romantic vision to come to terms with industrial reality and mass culture. As he worked on the poem, he began reading Spengler, and as with Whitman, doubt clouded hope: the poem's optimism gave way to pessimism.

Crane made use of the major modernist themes. *The Bridge* moves from the city to the frontier, to the West, and then back to the city in what has become an archetypal American journey. The city and the frontier, the city and the land, interpenetrate: one reinforces the other. The section of the poem entitled "Cape Hatteras" is Crane's hymn to Walt Whitman, his attempt to update Whitman's history of America. But the view is hardly sanguine: America has become more materialistic than even "Democratic Vistas" predicted, more diffuse than his theory of the crowd anticipated. The plea is to some kind of unity that will emerge out of the chaos. The underlying hope is for a New Atlantis, a renewed connection between what has been torn asunder and what awaits recombination. When the poet returns to New York from the West, he once again encounters the crowd, this time in the subway where he meets Poe, whose Dionysian presence challenges the optimistic vision of Whitman.

The circle is now complete: we leave the city of divided consciousness and emerge into the open air of Atlantis. Crane wrote this part of the poem first and was never able to find the historical elements that would justify such a conclusion. He was relying on material—the myth of the land, the power of Dionysus, the theme of the West, the hope for a New Atlantis—that took its meaning more from a tradition of mythic belief rather than from the convictions of his poetic argument. Crane tried to steer a course between T. S. Eliot's sense of cultural exhaustion and William Carlos Williams's belief in new beginnings, but he could not go beyond history, could not find the historical elements that would lift Eliot's vision or justify Williams's. Like Whitman before him and Williams after, his sense of hope foundered when it had no tangible basis, when it became lost in the crowd.

III

In its most extreme form, the crowd can be thought of as a personification of the human species. The atavistic bridges the species and the individual. In this context, we must postulate the Darwinian belief that humanity has within it an animal residue, a bestial element that is supposedly countered by the institutions of civilization. The struggle is thus between the individual capable of cruelty and debasement, and civilization, whose institutions try to restrain a potential savagery in the individual. The problem of mass culture is thus a battle between what is worst in the species and what is best in civilization, a struggle that many commentators like Mark Twain see tipping the balance toward the corruptibility of the individual, supporting the assumption of the degeneration inherent in the species. We can find such an assumption at work in the philosophy of Nordau, in Zola's depiction of Nana, in Norris's portrayal of Vandover, and in the inertia that controls the fate of Dreiser's Hurstwood.

The problem as stated here in inverse terms was embodied by the transformations of ideas experienced by H. G. Wells. In *The Time Machine* (1895), Wells portrays the journey into time as revealing two forms of life that have moved further and further away from each other: the Eloi have become so refined that they are near extinction, and the Morlocks have become so coarse that they have sunk beneath the animals. In *The Island of Dr. Moreau,* Wells recasts this plot: Dr. Moreau has surgically transformed the island animals, giving them rudiments of humanity such as the ability to think and to use language. But the transformation from animal to human is tenuous. Some of the animals slip back to their basic nature, revolt against Moreau, and kill him and his assistant. Wells distinguished between the transformations that stem from evolution (organic or living change) and those that stem from technology (mechanical or artificial change).

Wells promulgated these ideas for almost forty years, but he radically revised them in *Mind at the End of Its Tether* (1944), a book written two years before his death. Wells not only repudiated the efficacy of a racial mind, he predicted the end of the universe, as we know it. Wells never came to terms with the way totalitarian power could be abused, and his idea of an advancing racial mind had no basis in historical fact. Thus, while his agenda ended at the dead end of doubt, it carried with it the repudiation of two powerful constructs within which he had been working: the Enlightenment construct, which he had repudiated, and the Darwinian construct, which he had radically revised. Once faith in these traditions was gone, he had nothing left. The debate that went on within Wells himself went on within the modern movement itself. The high modernists put their trust in the corrective power of the individual; the more utopian modernists put their trust in the fate of the masses. The duality here, in its many manifestations, would be at the core of any discussion of mass culture.

One of the earliest visions of the connection between mass man and the totalitarian state was *We* (1924) by Yevgeny Ivanovich Zamyatin (1884–1937). Zamyatin's dystopian novel is set in the twenty-sixth century in a state made "perfect" by science and technology. A dictatorial bureaucracy rules the Single State. The citizens live in glass houses, watched by the political police; they all wear the same uniform, which is numbered, live on synthetic food, and march in fours to the anthem of the state. The state works on the assumption that freedom is the source of evil: in the Garden of Eden, man was happy until he sought freedom. But freedom is not so easily repressed and returns in the desire for love, outlawed by the state, and in other "primitive" urges.

Zamyatin, inspired by H. G. Wells, wrote his anti-utopian novel at the time of Lenin's death; the object of satire thus appears to be the industrial state more than Stalin's regime or the Soviet Union. The Well-Doer is modeled, at least in part, on Frederick Winslow Taylor, the father of scientific industrialism. In his *Principles of Scientific Management* (1911), Taylor formulates the strict division of labor that subsumes the individual to the machine. While the effects of technology may be his main theme, Zamyatin nevertheless anticipates the evil of Stalinism: he depicts the fate of would-be individualists in a highly organized conformist society, a theme treated earlier by Dostoyevsky in "The Legend of the Grand Inquisitor" and later by Huxley and Orwell. There is, in fact, a direct line of connection from the Grand Inquisitor, to the Well-Doer, to Mustapha Mond in Huxley's *Brave New World* and O'Brien in Orwell's *1984*. In all of these works, the individual is sacrificed to higher authority. In order to guarantee conformity, the state must eliminate the autonomous self.

IV

This brings us back to the crowd. As a physical presence, the crowd is a potent political weapon. The political leader can use it for advocacy purposes when he or she assembles literally thousands of people together in the name of a cause, whether that cause is to protest or justify war, to favor or oppose forms of immigration, or to legalize or criminalize abortion. The crowd becomes a form of testimony, a symbolic statement. And each cause engenders its own crowd. The individual is empowered by absorbing the power of the crowd. The individual collectively creates the power of the crowd and then acts in the name of the power it creates. From its capacity to share consciousness, no matter how shallow, to its capacity to act in moral unison, no matter how dubious its claim to moral authority, the crowd takes on the meaning of and metaphorically embodies mass culture.

The individual can try to rise above what is destructive in the species or give consent to its pull. But the pull of the crowd ultimately overpowers any sense of individual right and wrong. The ironic aftermath often involves individual guilt. This predicament has long been with us: Hester Prynne wears her sin like a badge, but more often the sin is kept hidden; we can see it in the way members of the town hide their secret lives from one another—a major theme in novels by Sherwood Anderson, in Edgar Lee Masters's *Spoon River Anthology* (1915), or in a novel like Grace Metalious's *Peyton Place* (1956), the source of the modern soap opera, a dramatic mode that manufactures a special reality everyday for millions of viewers, mostly women. So much that passes as sinful is really built into humanity if, as the naturalists would have it, we are still under the influence of our animal nature. In an era of mass culture, the individual can never completely step out of the crowd, can never completely shed the workings of the species with its built-in temptations: a shared motive system based on mass values holds a larger realm in place.

V

Mass culture has become an idea of contemporary concern, central to a process of revision experienced by both modernism and postmodernism. A number of books addressed the prospective and retrospective influence of mass culture and its emergence out of crowd theory.[5] Arguments vary: some contend that the rise of mass culture provoked the idea of art for art's sake, a way of distancing art from a commercial society, the idea of art as a realm unto itself separate from the new consumerism. Thus mass culture helped spawn the dandy, the desire to turn oneself into an art object separate from the vulgarity of the crowd. As Wylie Sypher has pointed out, the dandy is "a substitute for the aristocrat who had lost caste. The dandy is a middle-class aristocrat, a figure who could make his entrance only in the cities that were becoming the milieu for the bourgeoisie."[6] The dandy is a product of a consumer society, which he then feels superior to because of his privileged self-fashioning. The dandy distances himself from the bourgeois values that brought him and his culture into being.

More in the center of discussion today is the connection between mass culture and new forms of ideology, including the connection to gender theory, racial movement, and the influence of popular culture. Another set of books connects mass culture and decadence with the rise of fascism. Fascism rests heavily on the belief that the future of a nation-state is controlled by destiny, that with national discipline and strong leadership the state will realize its predetermined purpose. The common denominator in all these studies involves social control. As a topic, the idea of mass culture has gone beyond literary and cultural concern to become a prime concern of the social sciences.[7]

From the eighteenth to the twentieth century, the search was for the political ideal, whether it involved democracy, fascism, or communism. What all of these systems had in common was the need for power. Power supposedly rested with the institutions of each form of government, but those who controlled the institutions executed power. The institutions were stable while the individuals behind them were replaceable. Power was a constant, its exercise a variable. Thus, while the institutions of government were impersonal, the use of those institutions was personal and subject to human limitations. Each form of government to various degrees rose and fell on the misguided behavior of those who exercised power through political institutions, whether the power was in the hands of a Hitler, a Stalin, or a Nixon.[8]

The more sinister meaning of the crowd is determined by its historical context. Relevant here is the discussion of Hannah Arendt involving Adolf Eichmann, executed in Jerusalem for his participation in the mass murder of Jews during World War II. In a famous phrase, she speaks of the "banality of evil," the ability of the Eichmanns to kill as if such genocide were part of a bureaucratic function, like a clerk disposing of cases in a large insurance firm.

Thomas Mann anticipated the individual loss of identity in the realm of mass culture in his story "Mario and the Magician" (1930), in which a crowd is mesmerized by a hypnotist who symbolizes the totalizing use of fascistic power. The spell can only be broken by the death of the hypnotist, so strong is his power over the crowd. The individual lacks the strength, the citizenry the political means (the control of institutions) to overthrow power. Thus, as the central authority becomes stronger, the citizenry becomes weaker. Just as the revolutionary individual finds himself in conflict with history, the idealized citizen finds himself in conflict with institutionalized power. The move of modernism toward postmodernism has involved the loss of individualism in the face of mass culture.

Forms of government follow forms of power. As the society becomes more complex, the popular way of thinking about it becomes more simplistic and the means of regulating it become more extreme. Soon the threat is as much from authority as it is from lawlessness. If the aim of terrorism is to disrupt ordinary life, the authorities insisting on the need for surveillance begin to do the job of the terrorists—that is, they disrupt normal life in the name of national safety, security, and social order. Civil rights become a casualty of the process. Soon the difference between the forces of order and that of disorder are blurred, and power has become the common denominator. Governments go by different names in an era of mass culture, but eventually they begin to resemble each other as individual rights give way to the capriciousness of institutional demands. This has been a shared literary assumption, a legacy of mass culture, and one of the main concerns of the postmodern agenda.

To be sure, the nineteenth-century crowd as defined by Le Bon has lost much of its force. This occurred with the passing of the military draft, the weakening of labor unions, the diffusing of the civil rights movement, the sense of futility based on the fate of crowd-politics in the sixties. New forms of the crowd have taken the less palpable form of online masses connected by fiber optics. As Schnapp and Tiews have put it:

[T]he millions worldwide who marched against the war in Iraq, the hundreds of thousands who continue to bring down regime after regime in the former Soviet bloc, the oceanic multitudes who participate in mass acts of mourning like the funeral ceremonies of Pope John Paul II, the legion of fans who regularly fill athletic stadiums, [all] argue against any rush to declare the crowd at its end.[9]

The individual defined within terms of the crowd, along with the motif of the maze, are key metaphors for the postmodern experience. The maze destroys any sense of a center; the crowd compromises the idea of an independent, individuated, liberal self. As the sense of community becomes more pervasive, the ability to see it clearly becomes more opaque. Reason becomes more elemental, reduced to its lowest level, avoiding complexity. Advertising works by reducing a product to a jingle, to bumper-sticker mentality, to a phrase that is then repeated over and over. The process does not stop with the hype that goes into consumer goods; matters as complex as going to war are reduced to the same level of simplicity and then repeated in a context that plays up national pride and support of the military. The crowd as an agent of transformation supports a theory of mass culture that leaves modernism behind and gives us a new literary reality, along with a physical reality that we must now confront.

17 ✦ POSTMODERNISM

I

In "Preface to Lyrical Ballads," Wordsworth maintained that "poetry is the spontaneous overflow of powerful feelings: it takes its origin from emotion recollected in tranquility."[1] The emotions recollected re-create the original experience before they fade away and leave the poet with access to the past out of which poetry will come. The poet is able to build upon these emotional blocks, moving eventually to forms of thought and ultimately to a moral sense. A number of critics have made the connection between David Hartley's theory of association and Wordsworth's belief that poetry is remembered experience. Wordsworth read Hartley's *Observation on Man, His Frame, His Duty, and His Expectations* (1749; 1791), and "Tintern Abbey" was influenced directly by Hartley's *The Pleasure and Pains of the Imagination*.

In one context, Hartley's theory takes us toward behaviorism: memory is localized and imprinted in the brain to be restimulated by new sensations that set off a chain of remembered association. Such a theory of memory and how the brain works has been long discredited, but it created an impressive legacy of aesthetic and psychological thought. A good deal of Romantic theory came out of this notion, from Shelley's theory of genius to Keats's idea of negative capability. And while Coleridge and the German Romantics came to think of the imagination as an aesthetic faculty that recapitulates God's creation in artistic form, the imagination once was thought of as the storehouse for remembered images, thus making art the end product of memory. At one time, theories of the brain seemed to confirm the connection between emotions and memory: the assumption was that memory was located in the limbic area of the brain, the area most directly connected with emotion.

Going in an opposite direction, the idea of recollected emotions moves to the belief that memory can collapse the past and the present into a kind of "time spot" in which the past and the present become one. This creates in effect a new reality and offers insight into the very notion of time and being, involving a theory of memory, as we have seen, that complements the time theories of Henri Bergson and Marcel Proust's aesthetics of lost time. Closely related is the phenomenology of Martin Heidegger and his quest for "Being" (as opposed to "being"), plus his obsession with Hölderlin, the German poet who most closely employed the theory of Wordsworth.

Embedded in Wordsworth's theory of memory, in other words, are the two extremes that will dominate ideas of modern reality: one moves toward behaviorist theory, is alert to the way environment works, and emphasizes sensation as the source of a conditioned response—attributes that will become the basis of literary naturalism. The other moves toward literary modernism with its emphasis upon memory as a way that the past is collapsed into the present as a new form of Being. Postmodernism moves one step beyond this and believes that consciousness is inseparable from the culture itself.

II

There is a radical transformation of meaning between modernism and postmodernism. Postmodernism opposes all forms of foundationalism (the belief that one system of meaning rests upon another), essentialism (including transcendentalism), and realism (the belief that there is a correspondence between an abstract notion of "truth" and a reality that never deviates from that truth). Metanarratives are especially suspect, as are methods of discovering historical truth such as dialectical materialism or forms of evolution that presuppose teleology or origins, mandated ends or beginnings. The postmodern vision decenters man and radically diversifies his powers. Consciousness becomes the product of mass culture, and highbrow and lowbrow activities are collapsed into each other; the mixture of aesthetic modes creates an intellectual pastiche, a hybrid style. Memory in any form—Bergsonian intuition, Darwinian evolution, Proustian spots of time, Joycean epiphanies—all become irrelevant. The workings of nature, especially the belief that meaning is built into nature or into time, are seriously questioned. One of the major assumptions of postmodernism is that meaning is a human construct, the result of paradigmatic thinking, and the product of the mediated questions we chose to answer.

III

Thomas Pynchon clearly dismantles the major assumptions of modernism. In *V* (1963), the question of mythic truth is examined. Herbert Stencil goes in pursuit of V, who embodies both his lost mother and Henry Adams's idea of the Virgin. The Virgin was the mythic/symbolic source of medieval unity, a symbol the modern era had transformed into the dynamo, the source of both decadence and multiplicity that Adams attached to the machine. Decadence, Pynchon would have it, is a falling away from what is human, a process we witness with V. Pynchon's conclusion evokes once again a Spenglerian truism: we foist off our lost humanity on inanimate objects and abstract theories.

Stencil discovers that history is stencilized, what he brings to it is what he finds. Once again, consistent with the time theories of Henry Adams, modern history is seen running down entropically like an unwound clock, the subject of the Benny Profane plot. Pynchon's double plot comes together like a V. All of his themes—the working of entropy, myth and history as empty pursuits, the human transformed into the mechanical—are embodied in his treatment of the lost realm of Vheissu, a frozen city whose heat loss summarizes the major events of the novel. Pynchon's heat loss robs Eliot's city of a redeeming mythical energy, transforming it into a process of decline—the diminished realm that postmodernism equates with mass culture.

Mass culture takes us to the postmodern, which in turn takes us to the maze, that realm without a center, where the mind is electronically overloaded, where the inability to read the signs is conveyed by Roland Barthes, whose newly arrived Parisian is bewildered by the need to "read" Tokyo. Indeed, mass culture in all its complexity is the equivalent of a voyager from one culture trying to understand the meaning of a foreign culture. In Thomas Pynchon's *The Crying of Lot 49*, we are in the world of Oedipa Maas. Oedipa's task is to come to terms with the legacy of Pierce Inverarity, who has developed San Narcisus, a kind of ersatz Los Angeles, whose name suggests the inability of contemporary man to go beyond the obsession of self. Inverarity's influence stretches across America, if not the postindustrial world. Oedipa Maas discovers that she does not have the perspective to come to terms with such a legacy because she is part of it, inseparable from the system she is trying to understand. Pynchon clearly has in mind Heisenberg's belief that the subjects of a scientific experiment cannot separate themselves from the experiment itself: a residual subjectivity will always be a part of the experiment, and so with the attempt to recapitulate history.

Pierce's empire, she suspects, has affinity with the Tristero system, an underground network that feeds off the establishment. The Tristero came into being simultaneously with the rise of capitalism, and then, like capitalism, moved across two continents, attacking the establishment in its most vital area, its communication system. Thus the Tristero made raids on the Pony Express and established an underground mail delivery system in the modern city, which is to say that the Tristero took its being from what the establishment entropically jettisoned. While clues clot her path, every clue leads not to the Tristero but to another clue. Every testimony is undetermined. She visits Mr. Thoth, whose name refers us to the Egyptian *Book of the Dead* and the longest reach of memory. Thoth is ninety-one years old, the grandson of a Pony Express rider who died when he was ninety-one; Oedipa believes Thoth may be able to illuminate the mystery of the Tristero. But old Mr. Thoth's memory is so impure that he cannot separate the stories his grandfather has told him about the Pony Express from the cartoons that he is watching on TV. Through the media, consciousness infuses culture and adds an extrinsic dimension to memory. Typical of postmodernism, neither Thoth nor Oedipa can separate their consciousness from the culture of which they are a part. Where the culture ends and the self begins is no longer a viable question.

Gravity's Rainbow (1973) takes us beyond the mechanistic and the heuristic and questions the meaning of the Enlightenment itself. Rocketry is a by-product of Enlightenment thinking, the belief that man can control the forces of nature and turn that control into forms of wealth and power. Embedded in the Enlightenment quest is the threat of death, an unconscious desire for self-destruction. This sense of self-destruction is enforced by "Them," the secret force that seems to be the source of paranoia in most Pynchon novels. The victim of this historical state of mind is Tyrone Slothrop, whose exposure to Imipolex G has transformed his body into the equivalent of the rocket. (Anything close to realism is quickly turned into fantasy in the giddy workings of Pynchon's imagination.) Slothrop goes in search of an explanation of his condition that takes him into the Zone, the mechanistic realm where reason is transformed by science and technology. Here history is reduced to film, and the end of both (history and film) is suggested by the end of the novel, at which time the rocket falls from the sky onto the theater. That the novel begins in Europe and ends in Los Angeles parallels the Enlightenment arc (with its move from Europe across the continent of America to the Pacific shore).

The whole novel has a James Bond–like quality, a global reach and a realm of insidious power, behind which is the villainous conspiracy that Slothrop must engage. But Pynchon adds another dimension to Ian Fleming, and his Bond story takes on the historical fantasy of a Rider Haggard adventure and the scientific fantasy of an H. G. Wells novel. In this extended dimension, Pynchon's novel takes us beyond modernism. With its episodic plot, its discontinuous chronology, its flattened characters emptied of consciousness (with the exception of paranoia) and conditioned by mass culture (that is, by the dictates of social mandates from which they cannot free themselves), Pynchon's novel is vastly different from a novel like Joyce's *Ulysses*. In Joyce, myth, history, self, and consciousness are all in play; Joyce's is a monomorphic structure; parts are organically related to a vibrant whole; time moves in continuous ways. Pynchon has deliberately negated each of these systems, emptied Joyce's novel of its universality, created a polymorphic reality, a perverse order programmed to self-destruct, a world on a collision path with history as runaway technology. Joyce's world is redeemable; Pynchon's is not.

IV

Descartes believed that cognition centered human meaning: thought separated us from the surrounding world and centered reality. The key to that reality was the subject, humanity in the process of thought. In the nineteenth century, the shift in emphasis from a commercial to industrial society led to a radical transformation in the idea of society. Marx, for example, believed people were organized according to their material investment in the means of production. In an information age, Marx's concern with the nature of production has given way to the nature of communication. Postmodernism has seriously contested Descartes' and Marx's assumptions. There is no longer a subject to give reality centered meaning, and the industrial process is no longer all-defining. Meaning now stems from a variety of sources: consciousness stems from forms of structure (Saussure), discourse (Foucault), paradigms (Kuhn), systems (Bertalanffy), or grammar and rhetoric (Derrida, de Man).

One of the more recent cognitive theories is that of Ludwig von Bertalanffy, who believes that we process many forms of thought from many different sources: from nature and our genetic makeup, from our environment, from a vast social web of interconnected information that works as loops of inquiry. These loops take us to points of agreement and disagreement with others; they are diverse and complex in their makeup, refuting the idea that we self-generate consciousness and share physical reality as a source of truth. Rather, our consciousness is pre-given and links with other forms of meaning in ways similar to the linkage of circles within circles of information that we find on the Internet. Meaning unfolds randomly and in related links rather than in logical and causal units.

A major postmodern novelist who makes use of these ideas and who takes us beyond the narrative meaning of Joyce and Eliot to the relational realms of Bertalanffy is Don DeLillo. As a study in Bertalanffy's theory of loops and the postmodern problem of uncertainty and indeterminacy, DeLillo's *White Noise* picks up where Pynchon's *The Crying of Lot 49* left off. DeLillo takes us to a world where industrial production has given way to information theory and communication systems. The novel divides into three sections. The first deals with Jack Gladney and his family, his job as the head of Hitler Studies at the College-on-the-Hill; the second deals with a toxic chemical spill that releases a deadly cloud into the air and forces the town to evacuate; the third deals with Jack's growing awareness that his wife has a serious anxiety problem over a fear of dying, has become an object of experiment conducted by one Willie Mink, who has seduced her, and that Mink is in a motel on the outskirts of the old industrial section of the town, where Jack goes to kill him.

DeLillo has given us a narrative reality that sharply deviates from that of high modernism and has come to embody what we mean by postmodern. He has substituted a structural system for a symbolic system, has questioned historical origins, and has emptied the autonomous self of meaning. We no longer have the belief that consciousness is the final authority, that the mind is distinct from body and from environment. Instead, the mind is inseparable from the world it is trying to organize, and inseparable from the language by which it thinks through what it organizes. Meaning is no longer built into historical time: time is now devoid of teleological unfolding as we discount progress, destiny, and cyclical meaning. One may still think of time in this way, but the contours are the product of our own thought and are not built into time, nature, or history.

We create rather than discover meaning, and in so doing we substitute culture for nature. We generate meaning through paradigms of thought, and we are inside the paradigms subjected to our own questions and limited to our own answers. There is no mandated hierarchy: we have lost any authority to which we can refer our questions. This change results in a loss of cultural status as well as informational authority. Popular culture competes with high culture. There is now no basis for claiming that a Shakespearean sonnet is better than a friend's postcard, or why we should prize a Rembrandt painting over one by Andy Warhol.

TV is now closer to being a final authority than are the courts, the legislature, the church, or the university. TV gives meaning to life as it supplies news and puts information and daily data in a manufactured perspective. TV certifies reality: an event is not "real" until it is worthy of TV. And TV creates reality: the toxic spill takes on different meaning as it climbs a linguistic hierarchy, moving from "plume," to "dark cloud," to "airborne toxic event." The toxic spill is both real and constructed. As with an earthquake with its constructed reality (an epicenter, a number on the Richter scale, and the predictability of aftershocks), we cannot come to terms with the toxic spill as a reality until it is reconstructed by TV or some other paradigmatic source.

The novel addresses many of these cognitive matters through Murray Jay Siskind, the resident semiotician, who brings to the novel a structuralist's viewpoint—the belief that all meaning is constructed, that we manufacture reality, and that that reality is determined by the way it is seen whether as a photograph of the most photographed barn, auto crashes in films, or the meaning of crowds.

Once a thing has been defined, it is difficult to see it in a different way. This idea becomes a metaphor for the novel as a whole and is embodied in the idea of the supermarket, which reassures us that life is meaningful by being well-lighted, ordered, knowable, and well-stocked with commodities that can relieve anxiety so long as we can continue to function in a predictable way. The disorder we encounter in life is the "white noise" to which DeLillo refers in the title of his novel. This is the static in the system, and it anticipates the breakdown of the system itself, the black noise we know as death.

We do not know if the impressive sunsets at the end of the novel are the result of the toxic chemical or the antibodies that ate up the chemical, but the sunsets are obviously connected with the inevitability of death, and not knowing their origin is in keeping with the mystery of death that is a major source of anxiety in the novel. The human being is the only animal that both fears and anticipates death, and man is the only creature that thinks in language and preserves experience in the form of memory, which gives shape to time, meaning to repetition. Willie Mink has connected human anxiety over death with the language and memory centers of the brain, and he hopes to blunt those centers with the experimental drug dylmar, thus eliminating such anxiety at its source.

The Willie Mink plot moves the novel from one plane of far-fetched realism to another. Willie Mink shares a crepuscular quality with Clare Quilty. And while the novel makes use of caricature (of academic pretense, unjustified university authority, risks of medical research, inept response to national disaster), the ending moves closer to the surrealism that one finds at the end of Nabokov's *Lolita* or Ellison's *Invisible Man*. The ending is far-fetched, has all the qualities of a cartoon, and intentionally breaks the narrative continuity of the novel in Pynchon-like ways. In its use of mixed narrative modes, the novel turns on itself and takes on the pastiche quality that is characteristic of the postmodern novel.

The elements of plot that DeLillo uses here, he also uses in his other fiction. Within every system of organization there is a principle of white noise or disorganization, and DeLillo is sensitive to how such a principle works. In the postmodern novel, time spots of memory give way to interconnecting loops that bring the disorganization of our experience into mutual play. We see this in a novel like Don DeLillo's *Libra* (1988). The memories of Lee Harvey Oswald connect him divergently with the poverty of his boyhood, his trip to Russia and marriage to Marina, his contact with the Castro people in the United States and in Cuba, and his contact with the radical right and former agents of the FBI. Memory, now as complex as the postindustrial culture of which we are a part, is no longer a Proustian aesthetic experience. Or if it has Proustian elements, they are now so embedded with other perceptions of reality that they no longer screen reality but stand relationally to it.

DeLillo negates prevalent theories of modern history. He discounts, for example, the Enlightenment trust in linear history, driven by a belief in progress; the Romantic idea of history, driven in turn by notions of destiny; and he discredits historicism itself, the position in the novel held by Nicholas Branch, who believes that if he can master the data connected with the assassination of John F. Kennedy that "truth" will reveal itself.

Opposed to all these ideas of history is a narrative supposition that controls historical unfolding in *Libra* (as well as his earlier novels)—namely, that history is made up of interpenetrating systems or circles of events that overlap each other and defy logic. In *Libra*, the life of Kennedy, Oswald, and Castro, pro- and anti-Castro forces, and two groups of CIA and FBI agents crisscross and connect in absurd ways. Such historical configuration works against telling the story in traditional ways. If there is to be an explanation, it must come from an arresting construct—that is, a hypothesis that holds in place historical process long enough for us to grasp events otherwise in flux.

The desire (say of Oswald) to create an identity (to grasp in either a personal or public way a sense of who he is) is to play into what is illusionary in history. In *Libra*, DeLillo wants us to reconsider both the traditional explanations of the Kennedy assassination, to question the meaning of personal identity, and to consider the impossibility of an "idea" of America. Influenced by Bertalanffy's systems theory of an interconnected reality, DeLillo takes us to realms of the disconnected and progression through arbitrary mental links to the closest that we will come to potential meaning.

V

In Umberto Eco's *Foucault's Pendulum* (1989), we can see memory transformed along relational lines. In Eco's novel, three editors from an occult publishing house feed into a computer information from the history of the Knights of the

Templar, a medieval organization that seems to be involved in a plan that will allow them to tap an interstellar force and hence control the world. What begins as comic-book play turns deadly when the modern inheritors of the Knights become aware of their activity and believe that they know of the missing link that will allow them to complete the Plan. The reality they create as fiction becomes real when the Templars believe they can act upon it in a novel that seems to owe much, at least in narrative idea, to Eco's interest in the myth of Superman and to Pynchon's *Lot 49*. As in the Superman story, we have a world threat; and just as Oedipa sees everything connected to the Tristero, the editors begin to believe everything is connected to the Plan. As in Heisenberg's uncertainty theory, they only find what they are looking for: "At every bookstall we stopped and rummaged; we sniffed newsstands, stole abundantly from the manuscript of our Diabolicals [their authors], rushed triumphantly into the office, slamming the latest find on a desk."[2]

The central character is named Causabon (after George Eliot's character who is looking for the key to all learning). He tells us: "whatever the rhythm was, luck rewarded us, because wanting connections, we found connections— always everywhere, and between everything. The world exploded into a whirling network of kinship, where everything pointed to everything else, everything explained everything else" (384). In this realm of interconnectedness, the mind organizes the world in pragmatic fashion according to its needs. What is needed to complete the Plan is found, even if the connections have to be rethought, the loops of explanation reconfigured.

The tenuousness of this process drives one of the editors, Belbo, back to the memories of his boyhood in a town in the Piedmont area of Italy, where in 1943 the resistance fighters liberated his town from the fascists. The remembrance of this childhood event marks the most heroic activity of his whole life, and Belbo keeps returning to these memories, which he describes as "sweet" (272). Causabon understands what Belbo is saying: those memories give a sense of permanence to his life in a world that is otherwise flux. They break the residual iterative pattern of his existence that Eco believes links comic-book reality and postmodernism. They can be read simply and clearly in contrast to the complexity of signs and counter-signs, representations and re-presentations, which make up his present life. Belbo, we are told, remembered those days "as a time of clarity: a bullet was a bullet, you ducked or got it, and the two opposing sides were distinguished, marked by their colors, red or black, without ambiguities—or at least it had seemed that way to him" (272). Causabon is a bit more dubious about

the unadulterated nature of these memories, but he stops short of deconstruction. "Why," he asks, "should I deprive Belbo of his Combray? The memories
were sweet because they spoke to him of the one truth he had known" (273). Not
only is the Plan a construct, but we learn that Belbo's memories, which seem to
give permanence to his flux of thought, are a construct also. We construct reality
and then find the means in living events and related details to make that reality
tangible.

VI

Once a writer has reached a point of eminence, a kind of taxonomy sets in. This
happened with John Barth, and the critical response to his work reflects both its
change of character and preferred ways of reading. In the fifties, he was considered an American existentialist; in the sixties, a black humorist; in the eighties,
a postmodernist—a term he helped to institutionalize through two influential
essays: the first, "The Literature of Exhaustion," in which he helped delineate the
way high modernism was playing itself out; and the second, "The Literature of
Replenishment," in which he made the case for a postmodern fiction.

Postmodernism takes us beyond the varied states of modern consciousness to
the question of what would happen if we postulate a universe that is intelligible
only in terms of the postmodern way we choose to talk about it, whether in terms
of discourse, or of structure, or of episteme, or of systems theory. Consciousness
becomes part of a system that we bring into play rather than something separate,
out front, and all-subsuming. As a result, we lose the elements that constitute
modernism: we no longer have a sense of history filtered through a centered and
all-powerful subjectivity; we no longer have the Romantic sense of art versus life
with art the product of individual genius; the more stark aspects of life are no longer transformed by aesthetic concerns such as the pursuit of the beautiful; myths
are inseparable from history rather than, as T. S. Eliot would have it, a way of
ordering history. The old stories are transformed: the Homeric epic, the story of
Don Quixote, and the tales of Scheherazade are seen through contemporary eyes.

In his essays, Barth gives credit to Borges, Calvino, and Gabriel García
Márquez for pointing us toward this new narrative mode, but his generosity
slights his own influence, for it is impossible to think of the novel in traditional
terms after reading Barth. In *The Sot-Weed Factor*, he rewrites comic realism, and
in *Letters*, the epistolary novel. In *Lost in the Funhouse*, he questions whether we
can continue to sustain the mythic self and a historical center. In *Chimera*, Scheherazade, Perseus, and Bellerophon become contemporary men and women,

who Barth then takes into the labyrinth, that postmodern realm with no center, where lack of repetition forecloses memory, and where the maze becomes one with consciousness.

VII

The German critic Franz Roh first used the term "magic realism" in 1925 to describe a group of postexpressionist painters. But by 1949, the term referred to a narrative quality found in Latin American fiction. Such fiction did not distinguish between realistic and nonrealistic events. In these works the supernatural, the mythic, and the fantastic existed side by side with an everyday realism, each sharing a narrative or character's consciousness. The term took on weight in the sixties under the influence of fiction by Gabriel García Márquez, Jorge Luis Borges, and Carlos Fuentes. Borges has connected the movement to Kafka's "The Metamorphosis." After a fantasy beginning with Gregor Samsa awakening as an insect, realism takes over. This intervention between fantasy and reality creates a realism that works on a plane above reality, like surrealism or Freudian dream. Such fiction takes its meaning from a "constructed" reality—that is, a reality that has its origins in the imagination before that imaginative realm takes on its own reality.

In Borges's "Funes the Memorious," memory works in relation to such a fantasy construct. Like Eco, Borges contends that we select the memories that we need to cope with reality. An accident has altered Funes's mind to the point that he can forget nothing. As a result, "Funes remembered not only every leaf of every tree of every wood, but also every one of the times he had perceived or imagined it."[3] He could reconstruct every minute of every day that he lived, although it took a day to reconstruct a day. As a result, Funes becomes dysfunctional. He could not think generically: the word "dog" flooded his memory with the details of every dog that he had ever seen to the extent that he could not grasp the idea of dog. He could learn languages instantaneously, but he could not think in any of them. "To think," Borges concludes, "is to forget differences, generalize, make abstractions. In the teeming world of Funes, there were only details, always immediate in their presence" (66).

What both Borges and Eco are saying is central to the idea of structuralism. Theoretically, memory functions like language, and we cut into memory the way that we cut into language. Potentially, every person has the capacity to speak every language known to mankind. But individually we speak one or maybe two or three languages. Like language, time exists synchronically as well as diachronically: synchronically all history exists simultaneously, "always already," so to participate in one moment is to participate potentially in all time.

As we have seen, language as the model for history is problematic. To model history on language is to bring into relationship two different orders of experience. Language to function must be whole and complete from the start, which is exactly what human history is not. Moreover, the synchronic does not distinguish between memory and history: memory is the past recoverable to an individual; history is the past recoverable from all time. No individual can contain historical time. And even if something like war did exist synchronically from Homer to, say, Vietnam, once we have experienced nuclear war, the meaning of war changes so drastically that we are no longer talking about the same order of experience. Moreover, memory and language are two different kinds of process: language has to function sequentially; words unfold linearly, one after another, and it is impossible for narrative to make use of a synchronic moment. Memory, as electric energy, can overlay images of the past, but such a process, as both Eco and Borges have shown, involves selective rather than full memory.

VIII

Both postmodern fiction and magic realism owe more to the workings of memory than to theories of structural language. Such memory must work selectively, functioning like a construct; so forgetting is as important as remembering, as we see in Salman Rushdie's *Midnight's Children*. Here the main character, Saleem Sinai, is born at the stroke of midnight on 15 August 1947, the moment of India's independence in a novel that tries to come to terms with the rise of India as a nation-state. The novel retrospectively depicts fifty years before independence from the point of view of Saleem's grandfather; it then portrays the recent past from the point of view of his parents; finally it engages more contemporary matters from Saleem's point of view. In a novel that borrows from Latin American magic realism, Saleem discovers that his telepathic powers connect with one thousand other midnight children. These powers give simultaneity to Indian history, including the rise of Pakistan. But for Pakistan to exist it must forget its connection to India, must engage in a kind of national amnesia: forgetting, the novel concludes, gives meaning to reality.

IX

In *One Hundred Years of Solitude*, Gabriel García Márquez treats many of the same themes. The novel involves the story of Macondo, a fictional village, based on Marquez's hometown of Aracataca in Colombia. Time in the novel is meant to function synchronically—the past, present, future supposedly fused with myth, history, the supernatural, and the real. But the novel ends by telling four separate stories (the history of the Buendia family; the coming of the United Fruit Company to Macondo; the Deluge or the Great Flood, which brought four years of rain; and the decline of the family). These stories unfold sequentially: García Márquez is thus no more successful than anyone else in reconciling simultaneity with the linear unfolding of language.

The family divides into two groups—the Aurelianos and the Arcadios: the Aurelianos are solitary dreamers, small in stature, who pursue illusionary quests; the Arcadios are large and strong and pursue adventures that never affect the world in which they live. García Márquez tells us that both pursuits are destructive. Ursula Buendia is the great matriarch of the family, the primary source of its strength: she lives through one hundred years of the novel as the family meets crisis after crisis. Before she dies, she holds in her memory the reason why the family has declined. Each cycle of time in Colombia sees men going off to war or off to illusionary pursuits before they retreat more and more into the solitude of defeat and disillusionment, while the women hold this world together. But just when such memory might have application, Ursula dies—and the redemptive power of memory is cut off. History itself seems no more stable: the history of the family has been told on a parchment in code by Melquiades, who grasps the meaning of the story in its entirety. But as Aureliano reads Melquiades's manuscript, a whirlwind sweeps down and blows the parchment away. History is tenuous, based on memories that will eventually die or on forms of transmission that are also vulnerable to loss.

X

If forgetting is redemptive in *Midnight's Children,* forgetting is destructive in *One Hundred Years of Solitude.* In *The Unbearable Lightness of Being* (1991), Milan Kundera brings great insight into the responsibilities of remembering and forgetting. The lightness of being involves the linearity of time, living life in its randomness, its trivialities, with little or no sense of responsibility. The heaviness of being takes us to Nietzsche's eternal return and involves the circularity of time, repetition, and the responsibility for one's actions. Tomas and Teresa, despite their attempts to break the repetitiousness of their lives, finally accept the cycles of their life, building memory upon memory. Sabina and Franz, on the other hand, are in flight from themselves: one moves from Prague, to Paris, to New York, to

California; the other from Paris to Cambodia, where he dies in a publicity stunt. The stories of these lives are told against the occupation of Prague and the need for the inhabitants to take responsibility for the evil that they passively engender (a comparison is made to Oedipus). It turns out that the novel repudiates the unbearable lightness of being in the name of the bearable heaviness of being. Not to accept Nietzschean heaviness is to give in to what Kundera modishly calls "kitsch"—aesthetically inferior sentiment, commercially sidetracking, ignoring what offends us. Some memories are too important to erase: we forget, Kundera says, at great risk.

XI

A history of the novel involves five narrative modes: comic realism, romantic realism, naturalism, modernism, and postmodernism. Each narrative mode creates its own reality. Out of the modes come different versions of history, and thus different ways of coming to terms with a historical era. Out of the modes come different versions of society, and thus different versions of social justice. And out of the modes come different versions of memory, and thus different ways of recovering and coming to terms with the past and the idea of self.

Naturalism reduced memory to a behaviorist phenomenon. Modernism reduced memory to forms of Bergsonian durée: the mind became a container of memories awakened by the association of new experience so that present and the past were continuously interpenetrating. Less transparent, postmodernism, including forms of magic realism, reduced memory to cultural consciousness: memories were reinforced or canceled by what the culture accepted or rejected. Remembering and forgetting became part of an overall power element that held a culture together. We remember what benefits those in power; we forget what is deemed hostile or irrelevant. Social institutions—the law, the library, the media, the educational system, literature, and pop culture—hold memories in place or work to erase them. Hitler would not let his people forget Versailles; Stalin would not let his people remember peasant relocation. Thus in postmodern terms, memory (both remembering and forgetting) helps create reality, and reality is held in place by institutional force, which in turn is held in place by forms of established power.

What is remembered becomes a construct for what is "real"; complete memory is canceled on the grounds that the past cannot be fully retrieved and that we remember—or embellish what we remember—so long as it is to our advantage. Postmodern memory is thus another form of constructed reality:

reality is mediated, a product of what we remember and what we forget. While the problems that befall us are sometimes beyond our powers, the way we try to solve those problems depends upon how we interpret or define them, or, as Kenneth Burke would say, the way we "symbolize" them—that is, the way we create reality. While all literary modes involve a prism through which to interpret reality, postmodernism puts more emphasis upon the prism than the reality—or, rather, the construct (the prism) becomes the reality. As a result, postmodernism—with parallel movements like magic realism—is the most highly antimimetic of all the modes.

But we have now gone beyond postmodernism to a realm that has transformed modernism once again by redefining it around the idea of gender, race, and forms of institutional power, including popular culture. We have thus moved in this study from transformations involving realism to modernism to postmodernism to a realm beyond postmodernism—from a representational (physical) reality to a subjective (state of mind) reality to a constructed (prismatic) reality to an even newer reality recuperated along the lines of manufactured history and popular (mass) culture. Each transformation has given rise to a different literary meaning with a corresponding difference of text. This is an age of constructed meaning: we shape reality in ways that allow us to cope.

CODA

Even if all the constitutive features of postmodernism were identical with and cotermi-
nous to those of an older modernism—a position I feel to be demonstrably erroneous but
which only an even lengthier analysis of modernism could dispel—the two phenomena
would still remain utterly distinct in their meaning and social function.

— FREDRIC JAMESON, *Postmodernism, or, The Cultural Logic of Late Capitalism*

I

To think of modernism as a literary movement involves thinking of it as a period
of time. Initially the postmodern critics rejected the idea of periodization. As
Hillis Miller has argued, literary ideologies are too heterogeneous to be thought
of as literary movements. Recent concerns have overshadowed the originary
elements, and we have been left with several versions of literary modernism.
But a movement can contain contradictions as well as shared and unshared
convictions. Moreover, to discuss the break from, say, Zola's naturalism to Joyce's
aestheticism involves seeing a "rupture" in that transition, what Fredric Jameson
refers to as a "coupure," the rupture itself marking the beginning of distinct literary difference, validating periodicity.

Literary criticism supplies the means of talking about the history of literature
as a series of periods. The problem becomes more complex in charting the transformations, the changes, within the periods. As we have seen, modernism as a
literary movement involved a theory of aestheticism; replaced by concerns with
myth, symbol, and form; followed by a shift to structuralism and poststructuralism. The deconstructionists among the postmodernists condemned theories of
master narratives; they questioned the generic meaning that came from the use
of periodization and literary movements. But their attempt to repudiate metanarratives and periodization became a contested matter, primarily because of the

oppositional thought of critics like Fredric Jameson, who saw a symmetrical relationship between forms of capitalism (industrial or commercial capitalism, imperial or colonial capitalism, late or monopoly capitalism, and multinational or global capitalism) and the rise of modernism and its transformations as forms of postmodernism. Jameson's insights into the connection between postmodernism and late capitalism—a paradigmatic way of looking at history—helped bring about the present-day obsession with fashion, consumerism, and mass culture: topics that took modernism in new directions to the workings of the avant-garde; to black dialectic, the Harlem Renaissance, and jazz; to gender theory; and to forms of popular culture and mass markets.

In its origins, modernism was in reaction to Zola-like realism. It repudiated mechanistic assumptions for the organic reality of a lost Romanticism. In its earliest stages, modernism owed its being to forms of aestheticism, to an impressionism that helped the mind center reality, and to a theory of symbolic reality and a Paterian quest for beauty. The emphasis was upon cyclical time and universal meaning, even as each turn of the cycle suggested decline rather than progress. Modernism was ripe with contradictions: it went in search of the ideal and found its opposite; a neorealism moved toward matters of doubt and forms of nihilism. A second stage of modernism saw it transformed by theories of structuralism, literary "form" giving way to literary "text," the autotelic work transformed by a paradigmatic or constructed reality. A third phase of modernism transformed it once again to a consciousness that was now inseparable from culture and a text now imbued with elements of jazz, black dialectic, and popular culture. As an aspect of popular culture, modernism had turned itself toward the mass market and the postmodernism of Fredric Jameson's late capitalism.

We have thus come a long way from Virginia Woolf's impressionism to Thomas Pynchon's and Ian Fleming's comic-book reality. We can talk about different versions of modernism by contrasting Joyce's *Stephen Hero* with his *Portrait*, *Portrait* with *Ulysses* and *Finnegans Wake*, *Ulysses* with *Gravity's Rainbow*, and (coming full circle from forms of realism to forms of romance) *Gravity's Rainbow* with Ian Fleming's *Casino Royale*, in which we are back in a world devoid of subject and subjectivity, inhabited by flattened and stereotypical characters. At various points in this cycle, we have moved from one kind of "reality" to another, from an elitist modernism to a pop-culture modernism.

Along with modernism involving different modes of literary realism, we have a modernism that created different kinds of reality by shifting critical interest from one realm of being to another among the three realms. The first involves the reality of nature: we live in the realm of physical forces such as gravity and entropy and are the product of evolutionary adaptation and natural selection (these physical processes are not dependent upon human thought and are not the product of paradigmatic assumptions); the second is the reality of culture: we construct meaning that determines our social reality; and the third involves the reality of language: we engage a verbal system that creates its own reality distinct from the other two.

In the transition from realism/naturalism to postmodernism, there has been a radical shift in ideological emphasis. We have moved from the belief that there is direct access to objective truth to a belief in perspective, that there is no singular truth: reality is a matter of the way it is perceived. We have given new interest to such phenomena as the crowd, seeing in this social reality a state of mind analogous to that of the city. Lastly, the last several decades have made inroads in questioning the realist/naturalist–modernist split. Neuroscience, evolutionary psychology, sociobiology, and cultural anthropology have added a revised dimension to the behaviorism that modernism rejected in moving beyond realism/naturalism. Attention has shifted once again from inward to outward, from the individual to wider forces such as the effect on behavior of DNA and genetic makeup, brain chemistry and serotonin (a chemical derived from the amino acid tryptophan, a neurotransmitter that can affect emotional states); these newly considered physical factors are once again central to an understanding of human behavior. While such factors will not newly authorize the old realism/naturalism, they do make the break between them and literary modernism less stark and suggest the need for a new definition of human nature that takes us beyond both premodern and postmodern stereotyping.

II

The attempt in this book has been to describe in detail a historical process, the evolution of literary elements that constitute the rise and fall of modernism as a product of intellectual tipping points, a study in the accretive cultural elements that constitute what we mean by "text" as well as the making of a literary movement. It is primarily a retrospective process, a summary look at literary modernism, a critique of the major texts that make up this movement, along with the extrinsic elements that informed those texts. This extended scope takes us to the intellectual and cultural matters that both preceded and followed this literary movement. It is not a call to dismiss the new in the name of the old, but to see the transformations as generational shifts in literary interest involving a radical revision of textual meaning. The critical need thus involves recognizing changes in the movement while preserving a sense of historical origins.

Perhaps because there was a confluence of so many different elements, the age of modernism was an era of contradictions. The modernists went in search of hope and found despair; in search of a regenerating ideal and found the void. Whether it was Pound's obsession with the quattrocento, or Eliot's with a lost sensibility, or Fitzgerald's with a pre-industrial frontier, or Dos Passos's with the Jeffersonian vision, or Hemingway's with a pastoral Spain, they often located the ideal in the past and then found the ideal was inaccessible or had changed, and the past was beyond employ. They went in search of the primitive and found transforming powers of technology: the machine was transforming nature in a radical, sometimes monstrous, way, leading to the modernist emphasis upon the grotesque (nature inverted) and the uncanny (the familiar as strange). They never fully worked out the tangle between mechanistic and organic form (often confusing organic form—a living process—with the artificial); equally entangled were matters of myth, symbol, and structural forms of reality. In brief, they went in search of homogeneity and found heterogeneity.

The modernists put the emphasis upon individual subjectivity, the connection between individual and universal time as expressed through the use of mythic symbolism; the result put reliance on cyclical time, juxtaposing present and past time, connecting modern civilization and the workings of the primitive with history as the story of both cultural rise and fall. The movement away from high modernism involved language transformed from a window onto reality into reality itself, myth and symbol transformed by theories of structure, and structure as the product of paradigm. Less evident but equally transforming changes involved the loss of causality, and with it linear history and periodicity. The end of modernism also brought the loss of the philosophical subject, the transformation of the liberal self, the impact of new views of consciousness and identity, the effects of mass culture, and the attempt of the literary imagination to give meaning to the convergence of these matters. This literature took on extended meaning when seen in a social and political context, and so did the prevailing literary criticism when read in the same context.

High modernism is distinct from versions of the avant-garde, itself a contradictory product of Dadaism and futurism. It was the end product of a different culture from the activity of the Harlem Renaissance and of different cultural problems from feminist and gender theory. At best, we can find reference to these movements in high modernism, but they do not create a critical mass of their own. So much that now passes under the rubric of modernism is really a product of postmodern thinking, with its mass-culture assumptions, which gives us a totally different sense of modern reality. What often gets overlooked is that these changes did not just lead to a new way of talking about the literary text; they led to a new kind of text, a new way of conceptualizing the text altogether, a new literary reality, a new literary ontology or "being." Such transformations, engaging and engaged, produced new critical assessments. But they ignored the meaning of what got left out, what the changes did to the original way of looking at the text, to the view of reality that brought this literature into being in the first place. We will never be able to return to the original vision in any pristine way; we must now see it in terms of the way it was transformed. This book attempts to restore a semblance of that originary meaning, even if that meaning is filtered though the critical transformations of three generation of readers.

Modernism involved a search for identity, the meaning of "self" as we move toward mass culture. Such a study acknowledges that we have moved beyond the Romantic vision, beyond realism and naturalism as well, to a new literary reality that gave preference to a new subjectivity. Such subjectivity brought with it a belief in the myth of the land, the meaning of the frontier, the constraints of the town, and the search for self on the road. Embedded in modernism was a new realism, a naturalism without the documentation and theory, a sense of the grotesque that tried to capture the inner essences of a world becoming more mechanical, more manufactured and artificial. All of this was transposed onto a background of the rise of mass culture that was absorbing the individual as it gave rise to an institutional leader. This entailed seeing the vanishing subject, consciousness collapsed into culture, and the loss of a center. If the flaneur (the artist alone in the crowd) suggested the modernist situation, the maze (with its absence of linearity, repetition, predictability) embodied the postmodern predicament.

An assumption behind this book is that literary reality takes its meaning from historical reality; that there is a world beyond the text; that literary movements like modernism cannot be separated from the intellectual, cultural, social, and political concerns of their times. I have attempted to demonstrate this idea in an extended way by showing, in other books, the connection between literature and the city, realism/naturalism and the rise of an industrial/urban society, and, in this study, modernism as an attempt to save a residual individualism against the forces of mass culture.[1]

Modernism as a movement evolved: not all its markers were in place at one time. But in its emphasis on subjective reality, in its use of myth and symbolic form, in its progression to a structuralism that transgressed taxonomic borders in ways that denied causality and periodization, in its fascination with the intersection of the primitive and the civilized, in its use of cyclical history and belief in the monomorphic or the universality or oneness of time, in its obsession with forms of decline, in its adding structuralist dimension to (Marxist, Freudian, anthropological, historicist) thought, in its analysis of mass culture into which it collapsed consciousness—in all of these matters and in its attempt to connect the present moment with the workings of the past through a pronounced use of memory as the source of human identity, modernism became a distinct literary movement that influenced the intellectual scene for roughly seventy-five years, especially the era between the world wars. The importance of these matters justifies a retrospective update. While remnants remain, modernism nevertheless marked an era that, despite the opinion of diehards to the contrary, in its totality will never come again. But through an understanding of its transformations, we can reconstruct a history of modernism as a series of incarnations. This will allow us to better see where we have been even as we debate where we are going.

1

A CHRONOLOGY OF LITERARY MODERNISM

1853–74	*Der Ring des Nibelungen*, by Richard Wagner
1857	*Les fleurs du mal*, by Charles Pierre Baudelaire
	Madame Bovary, by Gustave Flaubert
1862	*Salammbo*, by Gustave Flaubert
1869	*A Sentimental Education*, by Gustave Flaubert
1870–71	France declares war on Prussia on 19 July. On 2 September, France is defeated at Sedan, ending the Second Empire. The Third Republic is proclaimed on 4 September.
1871	The Paris Commune (21–28 May)
	The Descent of Man, by Charles Darwin
1871–93	*Rougan-Macquart* novels, by Émile Zola
1872	*Erewhon*, by Samuel Butler
1873	*The Renaissance*, by Walter Pater
1874	First impressionist exhibition in Paris. Impressionists exhibited their work outside official salons: Monet (1840–1926), Renoir (1841–1919), and Pissarro (1830–1903) worked outdoors, often painting urban settings. Manet (1832–1883), Degas (1834–1917), and Cézanne (1839–1906) joined the group.
	The Temptation of Saint Anthony, by Gustave Flaubert
1877	*The American*, by Henry James
1878	*Life and Habit*, by Samuel Butler
1879	"Daisy Miller," by Henry James
	Evolution, Old and New, by Samuel Butler
1880	*Le roman expérimental*, by Émile Zola

1881	*Bouvard et Pécuchet,* by Charles Flaubert

The Portrait of a Lady, by Henry James

1884	*À rebours,* by Joris-Karl Huysmans

Thus Spake Zarathustra, by Friedrich Nietzsche

1885	Leopold II, king of Belgium, takes possession of the Congo

Marius the Epicurean, by Walter Pater

1886	Van Gogh (1853–1890) and Gauguin (1848–1903) settle in France,
	marking the rise of expressionism

The Bostonians and *The Princess Casamassima,* by Henry James

Dr. Jekyll and Mr. Hyde, by Robert Louis Stevenson, introduces the
	theme of the double

She, by Rider Haggard

1890	*The Golden Bough,* by Sir James George Frazer

Principles of Psychology, by William, James

The Tragic Muse, by Henry James

1891	*The Picture of Dorian Gray,* by Oscar Wilde

1892	"The Yellow Wallpaper," by Charlotte Perkins Gilman

1893	*Degeneration,* by Max Nordau

1894	Dreyfus affair divides France

1895	*The Time Machine,* by H. G. Wells

1896	*The Crowd: A Study of the Popular Mind,* by Gustave Le Bon

The Island of Dr. Moreau, by H. G. Wells

Matter and Memory, by Henri Bergson

1898	*The Nigger of the Narcissus,* by Joseph Conrad

1899	*The Awakening,* by Kate Chopin

The Symbolist Movement in Literature, by Arthur Symons

Theory of the Leisure Class, by Thorstein Veblen

When the Sleeper Wakes, by H. G. Wells.

Youth and *Heart of Darkness,* by Joseph Conrad, are published
	together as a single volume by Blackwells

1900	*Buddenbrooks,* by Thomas Mann

Lord Jim, by Joseph Conrad

Sister Carrie, by Theodore Dreiser

1902	*Heart of Darkness,* by Joseph Conrad, appears as a single volume

The Immoralists, by André Gide

The Varieties of Religious Experience, by William James

1903	*The Ambassadors,* by Henry James

Tonio Kröger, by Thomas Mann

The Way of All Flesh, by Samuel Butler

1904 *Nostromo,* by Joseph Conrad

1905 *The House of Mirth,* by Edith Wharton

A Modern Utopia, by H. G. Wells

1906–11 *The Making of Americans,* by Gertrude Stein

1907 *Creative Evolution,* by Henri Bergson

The Education of Henry Adams, by Henry Adams

Pragmatism, by William James

The Secret Agent, by Joseph Conrad

1907–11 *Cours de linguistique générale,* by Ferdinand de Saussure

1907–19 *À la recherche du temps perdu,* by Marcel Proust

1908 Picasso experiments with cubism

1909 *Three Lives,* by Gertrude Stein

1911 Exhibition of postimpressionist paintings

Under Western Eyes, by Joseph Conrad

1912 *Chance,* by Joseph Conrad

Death in Venice, by Thomas Mann

1913 *The Custom of the Country,* by Edith Wharton

O Pioneers! by Willa Cather

St Petersburg, by Andrei Bely

1914 Assassination of Archduke Francis Ferdinand on 24 June, leading to the outbreak of World War I. On 3 August, the Battle of the Marne. Four years of trench warfare follow.

Tender Buttons, by Gertrude Stein

1914–18 *Reflections of a Nonpolitical Man,* by Thomas Mann

1915 *The Good Soldier,* by Ford Madox Ford

"The Metamorphosis," by Franz Kafka

The Rainbow, by D. H. Lawrence

"Sunday Morning," by Wallace Stevens

Victory, by Joseph Conrad

1916 *The Portrait of the Artist as a Young Man,* by James Joyce

1917 America enters World War I on 2 April. In October, Lenin gets control of industrial and military soviets, an event followed by three years of civil war.

1918 *Dada Manifesto,* by Tristan Tzara

My Antonia, by Willa Cather

1918–22   *The Decline of the West*, by Oswald Spengler
1919   Treaty of Versailles ends World War I
              Winesburg, Ohio, by Sherwood Anderson
1920   *Main Street*, by Sinclair Lewis
              The Rescue, by Joseph Conrad
              This Side of Paradise, by F. Scott Fitzgerald
              Women in Love, by D. H. Lawrence
1921   *The Age of Innocence*, by Edith Wharton
1922   *A Lost Lady*, by Willa Cather
              Ulysses, by James Joyce
              The Waste Land, by T. S. Eliot
1923   *Cane*, by Jean Toomer
              Spring and All, by William Carlos Williams
              Studies in Classic American Literature, by D. H. Lawrence
1924   *The Magic Mountain*, by Thomas Mann
              The Principles of Literary Criticism, by I. A. Richards
              We, by Yevgeny Ivanovich Zamyatin
1924–28   *Parade's End*, by Ford Madox Ford
1925   *An American Tragedy*, by Theodore Dreiser
              The Counterfeiters, by André Gide
              Mrs. Dalloway, by Virginia Woolf
              Dark Laughter, by Sherwood Anderson
              The Great Gatsby, by F. Scott Fitzgerald
              In the American Grain, by William Carlos Williams
              The Trial, by Franz Kafka
1926   *The Art of Being Ruled*, by Wyndham Lewis
              The Castle, by Franz Kafka
              The Sun Also Rises, by Ernest Hemingway
1927   *To the Lighthouse*, by Virginia Woolf
              Time and Western Man, by Wyndham Lewis
1928   *Lady Chatterley's Lover*, by D. H. Lawrence
              Orlando, by Virginia Woolf
              A Voyage to Pagany, by William Carlos Williams
1929   *A Farewell to Arms*, by Ernest Hemingway
              Look Homeward, Angel, by Thomas Wolfe
              The Sound and the Fury, by William Faulkner
1930   *The Apes of God*, by Wyndham Lewis

The Bridge, by Hart Crane

Civilization and Its Discontents, by Sigmund Freud

I'll Take My Stand: The South and the Agrarian Tradition

1930–36 *USA*, by John Dos Passos

1931 *Counter-Statement*, by Kenneth Burke

The Waves, by Virginia Woolf

1932 *Journey to the End of Night*, by Louis-Ferdinand Céline.

1933 President von Hindenburg installs Hitler as chancellor
on 30 January

The Autobiography of Alice B. Toklas, by Gertrude Stein

La condition humaine, by André Malraux

1934 *The Postman Always Rings Twice*, by James M. Cain

Tender Is the Night, by F. Scott Fitzgerald

1935 *To Have and Have Not*, by Ernest Hemingway

Permanence and Change, by Kenneth Burke

1936 *Death on the Installment Plan*, by Louis-Ferdinand Céline

Nightwood, by Djuna Barnes

1936–39 Spanish civil war

1937 *L'espoir*, by André Malraux

Their Eyes Were Watching God, by Zora Neale Hurston

The Years, by Virginia Woolf

1939 Outbreak of World War II when Hitler invades Poland on 1 September

The Day of the Locust, by Nathanael West

Finnegans Wake, by James Joyce

The Grapes of Wrath, by John Steinbeck

1940 Paris invaded by Germans in June, leading to the Vichy collabora-
tion

Darkness at Noon, by Arthur Koestler

1941 *Between the Acts*, by Virginia Woolf

1942 *Go Down, Moses*, by William Faulkner

"The Man Who Lived Underground," by Richard Wright

1944 Allies land in Normandy in June

The Mind at the End of Its Tether, by H. G. Wells

1945 Paris liberated; German surrender signed at Rheims on 7 May

1948 *Dr. Faustus*, by Thomas Mann

1949 *1984*, by George Orwell

1957   *Lolita*, by Vladimir Nabokov

            On the Road, by Jack Kerouac

1959   *Howl*, by Allen Ginsberg

1962   *Pale Fire*, by Vladimir Nabokov

1966   *The Crying of Lot 49*, by Thomas Pynchon

            "Structure, Sign, and Play in the Discourse of the Human Sci-
                ences," by Jacques Derrida

            Wide Sargasso Sea, by Jean Rhys

1976   *Of Grammatology*, by Jacques Derrida

1978   *Writing and Difference*, by Jacque Derrida

1988   *Libra*, by Don DeLillo

1989   *Foucault's Pendulum*, by Umberto Eco

2

FROM EMPIRE TO WAR:
A RETROSPECTIVE OF LITERARY MODERNISM

I

Much of the modernist agenda took shape in the context of imperial reach and the world wars that were the product of that policy. The struggle for imperial control dominated the international political scene after the Franco-Prussian War of 1870–71, and modernism and imperialism became contiguous matters. The major players in this deadly game were England, France, Germany, Belgium, and Portugal. Italy participated on the African fringe. The locus of their interests was Africa, India, the East Indies, and China. America had an open frontier, which allowed expansion and access to raw material; but with the closing of the frontier near the end of the nineteenth century, America manifested an expansionist urge, taking land away from Spain in the Caribbean and in the Philippines and annexing Hawaii in 1898.

Imperial inclination came with the closing of European frontiers. There was a need for new land, both as a source of raw materials and as a market for consumption. In Africa, the European slave trade declined during the first two decades of the nineteenth century. Forms of commercial activity, especially in West Africa, replaced this practice. The British had taken control of lower Niger and annexed Lagos as a Crown colony in 1861. The French conquered Algiers in 1830; expressed interest in Morocco, Tunis, and Egypt; and later laid claim to the Senegal valley with its rich gum trade. They also eyed the Sudan and Sahara. In South Africa, a large number of Boer farmers, unhappy with British rule, established their own independent republic, the Orange Free State and Transvaal, which led to the Boer War. England and France contested imperial rights to Egypt in 1882. The scramble for Africa was perpetuated when Leopold II of Belgium financed Henry Morton Stanley's exploration of the Congo. Germany entered the fray in 1884–85, laying claim to Southwest Africa and the East African coast between Mozambique and what would become Kenya, and to Togo and Cameroon in West Africa.

The claim to new land allowed the European industrial nations to justify investment of surplus capital. Whereas the largest amount of capital was being invested in Canada, Australia, and Latin America in the 1880s and 1890s, Africa was considered worthy of risk. In 1884–85, a conference on West Africa was called for by Portugal and supported by Bismarck of Germany. Its rulings, formalized by the Berlin Act of 1885, legitimized Leopold's claim to the Congo, declared the basins of both the Congo and Niger rivers free trade areas, and outlawed slave trade. Most importantly, the provision mandated that claim to foreign land depended upon demonstrating that it was being effectively occupied. Thus imperial claim demanded physical involvement. As a result, the French extended their activity in West Africa; the British in Zanzibar, Uganda, and Kenya; and the Germans in Tanganyika, including Rwanda and Burundi.

As the imperial countries created territories far from their capitals, they weakened their centers. They now needed armies to control the increasingly hostile natives and a police force to keep civic order; they had to set up and finance colonial administrations; they were forced to build roads, bridges, railroads, and harbors if raw materials were to be transported; they were required to survey their borders if their claims were to have international validity. Such infrastructure cost money, raised in part by taxing the natives (paid for by cash crops or by forced labor), which only led to more hostile feelings on the part of the natives.

Moreover, the imperial invader was more often prisoner of his situation than he was jailer. George Orwell documented this point brilliantly in his essay "Shooting an Elephant." In his youth, as a sub-division police officer in Moulmein, in lower Burma, he was called to control an elephant that had gone berserk. By the time he arrived on the scene, the elephant, which had trampled a native to death, was now calmly grazing. Orwell realized that he should simply watch over the elephant until his keeper arrived; the elephant after all had the value of a large piece of machinery and was now seemingly peaceful. But behind Orwell was a crowd of two thousand people who expected him to shoot the rogue elephant. Instead of the policeman controlling the crowd, the crowd controlled the policeman. He was obliged to act in an authoritative way. Orwell concludes: "I perceived at this moment that when the white man turns tyrant it is his own freedom he destroys. . . . For it is the condition of his rule that he shall spend his life in trying to impress the natives, and so in every crisis he has got to do what the natives expect of him. He wears a mask, and his face grows to fit it. I had got to shoot the elephant"—and so he did.[1]

In another essay, "A Hanging," Orwell observed the execution of a Burmese native. What caught his attention was how annoyed the head jailer became when the prisoners did not fully cooperate with the occasion: they walked too slowly toward the gallows or howled out their prayers or, in previous cases, the drop did not work properly or a prisoner hung onto the bars and necessitated the effort of six guards to separate him from his cage. The head jailer tried to reason with the uncooperative prisoner: "'My dear fellow,' we said, 'think of all the pain and trouble you are causing to us!'"[2] Once again the imperial experience reverses human priorities: the executioner becomes the victim, the hanged man becomes the instigator, his protest strangely reduced to an inconvenience that challenges the order of things in this deadly exercise of imperial authority.

Imperialism not only created a lethal state of mind for an occupying country; it also created a hostile state of mind between imperialistic countries. When one realizes that imperialism created the context for the forthcoming world wars, one can see just how expensive and destructive a proposition it was: embedded in imperialism were the seeds of its own destruction. It was thus not surprising that the great imperial countries would eventually abandon their colonies, and the modern world would witness imperialism giving way to a new nationalism. Ireland, for example, won dominion status in 1922 and independence from Britain in 1949.

But the transformation from colony to nation was often fraught with turmoil, as the situation in the Congo illustrated. When Belgium granted the Congo independence on 30 June 1960, it led to two factions claiming authority. This brought the Right (embodied by Mobutu and the military) and the Left (embodied by Lumumba and his Communist sympathizers) into conflict, with the military eventually triumphing—perhaps because it had the sympathy, if not the support, of the West.

Matters were equally unsettled on other continents. As early as August 1917, the secretary of state for India called for the "gradual development of self-governing institutions." But Indian independence from Britain was slow coming. With the outbreak of the Second World War, the Indian National Congress withheld military support. As a result, their leaders were jailed until the end of the war. At that time the situation was extreme, and the British were willing to accommodate Indian independence. While the myth of the land was strong in India, its call for national unity was not as strong as racial and religious difference. This resulted in partition: Pakistan was created, which accommodated the

Muslim population; and India was given independence, which accommodated the Hindu population. The problem of Bangladesh with its heavy Muslim population remained. A solution of sorts involved Bangladesh becoming East Pakistan, separated from its sister state by the physical presence of India but politically united to Pakistan over one thousand miles away.

In what is now Indonesia, the Dutch possessed the third-largest colonial empire, most of it concentrated in the East Indies, where 65 million people of different religious and ethnic background lived. Despite the mixed population, the Dutch preserved compliance. This harmony was broken when a Dutch-sponsored nationalist society (the Budi Utomo) confronted a republican group, the Indonesian Nationalist Party (PNI), led by Sukarno. Japanese forces invaded the archipelago in January 1942, the Dutch capitulating in March. When Japan surrendered in 1945, the PNI proclaimed Indonesia's independence. The Dutch resisted and fighting broke out in eastern Java. When attempts to reconcile the two factions failed, the Dutch launched a police action so brutal that they lost public sympathy. In August 1959, Indonesia became a unitary state, its center in Java, with Sukarno as president. Clashes between Indonesian Communists and the army led General Soeharto to claim the presidency on 12 March, 1967. Once again the military confronted and curtailed a Communist threat with the sympathy, if not the support, of the West.

II

The major event in the modernist period was World War I. The war had its origins in the imperial struggles that followed the Franco-Prussian War. At that time, Chancellor Otto von Bismarck of Germany aligned his nation with Austria and Russia in a triple alliance known as the Three Emperors' League. When German and Austria moved politically closer, Kaiser Wilhelm dropped Russia from the league in 1888. Russia and France then formed their own alliance and were later joined by England. The major nations of Europe were now divided into two hostile camps—a situation made more dangerous by the instability of the dual monarchy of the Austro-Hungarian Empire, ruled over by the House of Hapsburg. The fatal spark came with the assassination of Archduke Francis Ferdinand and his wife on 28 June 1914. Austria held Serbia responsible for this terrorist act and declared war on 28 July; Russia came to the defense of Serbia; and on 31 October, Germany declared war on Russia, which brought France and later England into combat, and World War I was under way.

The human cost of the war went beyond imagination. The Allies—Britain,

France, Russia, and Italy—mobilized almost 35 million men, 21 million of whom became casualties. The Central Powers—mainly Germany and Austria—mobilized 23 million men, 15 million of whom became casualties. America stayed out of the war until 2 April 1917, at which time President Woodrow Wilson went before Congress to ask for a declaration of war against the Central Powers. America mobilized 4,335,000 men for the war, 364,000 of whom died in battle. On November 11, 1918—on the eleventh hour of the eleventh day of the eleventh month—the armistice ending World War I went into effect.

Although the war defined a whole generation, it did little more than plant the seeds for another world war. F. Scott Fitzgerald suggested as much in his first novel, *This Side of Paradise* (1920), a study in modern disillusionment. Especially disillusioning was the claim that war was the means to universal democracy and the belief that this would be the war to end all wars. Ernest Hemingway gave us his version of wartime disillusionment in his second novel, *A Farewell to Arms* (1929).

As Fitzgerald and Hemingway had shown, the political failure that followed the Treaty of Versailles (1919) was predictable. The treaty was primarily the work of four men: Georges Clemenceau of France, David Lloyd George of England, Vittorio Orlando of Italy, and Woodrow Wilson of the United States. Feelings were still raw, and the demands of the French and the British proved in the long run unrealistic. Germany was to disarm and return Alsace and Lorraine (lost in 1871) to France, and to return land to Belgium and Poland, even though this split East Prussia from the rest of Germany; the Rhineland was to be occupied by the Allies for fifteen years; Germany was to pay for the occupation, plus pay exorbitant reparations despite its depleted economic situation. The League of Nations, which was to oversee future political turmoil, failed when the U.S. Congress (led by isolationists like Henry Cabot Lodge) refused to ratify its existence. The Holy Roman Empire came to an end with the decline of Austro-Hungary after the war. In its place, two new states—Czechoslovakia and Yugoslavia—came into being, despite the fact that each territory was composed of rival factions (tribes) hostile to any idea of unification.

The second major event in the modernist period involved World War II. Hitler was able to gain political control in Germany by rejecting the heavy demands of the Versailles Treaty and by creating social discord, playing especially upon anti-Semitism and his dislike for Communists. The rise of mass culture also worked in Hitler's favor, given his ability as a mob orator and his implementation of a propaganda machine. His National Socialist (Nazi) Party won 107 seats in the Reichstag in 1930 and 230 seats in 1932, making it the largest party.

President von Hindenburg installed Hitler as chancellor on 30 January 1933; following new elections, Hitler suspended the constitution and ruled by decree. Trade unions were eliminated; the propaganda machine evoked a mythical if not mystical German past; by 1935, a drive for "racial purity" was in place; and by 1938, Hitler had brought into being a new army with an elite SS corps and a secret police, or Gestapo.

Hitler's activity in foreign affairs was equally bold. Taking advantage of an exhausted West, Hitler withdrew from the League of Nations and, in violation of the Versailles Treaty, rearmed. In 1936, he occupied the demilitarized Rhineland; in 1938, he seized Austria; he then reclaimed the Sudetenland and called for the elimination of Czechoslovakia, which took place on 29 September 1938, when England's prime minister, Neville Chamberlain, capitulated to Hitler's threats. The world was astonished when, on 23 August 1939, Stalin signed a nonaggression treaty with Hitler. Bolstered now by little or no resistance on the eastern front, Hitler invaded Poland on 1 September 1939, an act that finally brought the European Allies into combat.

The side effects of the wars transformed Europe as much as the wars themselves. World War I, for example, indirectly led to the overthrow of the czars in Russia. In 1916, Russian Commander Aleksei Brusilov launched a failed counteroffensive that weakened the state and anticipated the collapse of the czars. The war paved the way for the Bolshevik takeover by unseating the provisional government of Aleksandr Kerensky. By October 1917, Lenin had control of the industrial and military soviets (as the elected representative bodies were called), but it took a three-year civil war to subdue the remaining political elements, especially the peasants.

Lenin deviated from strict Marxism in his belief that Russia could move directly from the realm of the czars to communism without going through the historical stages of capitalism. Instead of the state "withering away," the bureaucracy was expanded and nationalism enforced in the Ukraine. Moreover, communism as a world movement was fading. But theoretical doubts ended when Stalin took power after the death of Lenin in January 1924, putting Russia on a straight path to socialism despite whatever resistance it faced from the outside world. His main intent was to industrialize, which necessitated creating a surplus of goods. Stalin documented his extreme resolve with a disastrous "collectivization plan" for agriculture in 1928–29. Millions of peasants were forced onto collective farms; those who resisted were killed, anticipating the Great Purges of 1934–38 that killed millions more.

The Communist victory in the Russian Revolution stemmed from the combined efforts of Lenin and Stalin—the political genius of the one, the political ruthlessness of the other. The rise of Hitler and the threat from Germany helped Stalin unify the country around the truly heroic activity of the Russians on the eastern front, and the onset of the Cold War once again allowed the Russians to look outward rather than inward for political wrongs. When Nikita Khrushchev took power upon Stalin's death in 1953, he denounced Stalin, but the deed had been done: Stalin's nearly thirty-year reign had put the Soviet Union on an expansionist path it would follow until the early nineties.

Farther east, political life was equally unstable. China, losing its trading base during the war, was in shambles after the First World War. Sun Yat-sen worked to create a new order held in place by military power. With the help of Russia, he established a political party in 1923, the Kuomintang, with headquarters outside Canton. Here, under the command of Chiang Kai-shek, a military regime was put in place.

When Sun died in 1924, power flowed to Chiang, who broke with Russia and took advantage of political unrest to establish the Kuomintang as a national force. Chiang allied himself with the conservative element within the party, crushed the Communist-led factions including labor unions, and gradually moved north, taking control of the nation as he went, capturing Peking in June 1928. Some of these events André Malraux depicted in *La condition humaine* (*Man's Fate*, 1933). At this time, Chiang's government was granted diplomatic recognition by the major foreign powers, including the United States. Chiang then purged the Communists from the party, driving many from the cities to the countryside, where they gained influence. But when a "Soviet Republic" was formed at Kiangsi province in 1931, Chiang moved against them, forcing the Communists on the 6,000-mile Long March to the northwest; only thirty thousand of the original ninety thousand reached their destination. Out of this march emerged a new leader—Mao Tse-tung—who would be Chiang's prime foe.

By the early thirties, the political forces that would determine the future of China were in place. But in July 1937, before Chiang could complete his plan to eliminate the Communists, he found himself engaged in an eight-year war with Japan, which left the Kuomintang considerably weaker and the Communists considerably stronger, especially in the rural areas of China. By the end of the Second World War, the Red Army grew from about 90,000 to almost 900,000, and the Communist Party increased from about 40,000 to 1.2 million. It was only a matter of time before China would pass into Communist control.

The dispute between the Right and the Left would dominate world politics between the world wars and especially after. The Spanish civil war (1936–39) established the ideological contours. The war began as a revolt of army commanders in Spanish Morocco, led by Francisco Franco, unsympathetic to the socialist and anticlerical measures of the republican government of Azana. Cadiz, Saragossa, Seville, and Burgos supported the insurgent nationalists; Madrid, Barcelona, Bilbao, and Valencia favored the republicans. The insurgents were aided by Germany, which sent bomber planes and pilots, and by Italy, which sent fifty thousand volunteers. The republicans were aided by Russia, which sent advisers and technicians assisted by International Brigades and left-wing sympathizers from other countries. Many of the events here were described by Arthur Koestler, André Malraux, and Ernest Hemingway, among others.

The major antagonistic forces that would dominate the Second World War were thus in place. For three years the fighting continued; the "turn" came in 1938 when a six-month nationalist thrust to the sea severed republican lines in August and led to the collapse of the Catalan front in December. Two events—internal disputes among the republicans and the end of Soviet support—brought a conclusion to the war. Barcelona fell on 26 January 1939, Valencia and Madrid on 28 March. Fighting ceased three days later. Official Spanish estimates have placed the total number killed as high as 1 million.

The aftermath of World War II was a time of major turmoil, stemming from the rise of Soviet puppet governments and the withdrawal of the major imperial countries from their colonies. For example, Britain withdrew from South Africa and India; France from Vietnam and later Algeria; Belgium from the Congo; and the Dutch from Indonesia. As each imperial country abandoned its colony or colonies, it left a vacuum in its place, often filled by the military and opposed by radical forces. Civil wars raged throughout the postwar world, encouraging superpowers like the United States to tip the balance toward the more politically loyal, albeit domestically unpopular, factions.

With the rise in the East and the West of two hostile economic and political blocs came the Cold War, which would engage the world for almost a half century, from 1945 to 1990. The West had felt it had responded too late to the threats from Hitler, which encouraged a more precipitant response to the aggressions of Soviet communism and the seeming aggressions of world communism, despite the fact that such militancy involved national disputes raised by the vacuum created as the major imperial nations withdrew from colonial land, especially in Asia. The West was clearly more willing to support political strongmen (often empowered by the military) who were sympathetic to capitalism than to allow communism to expand, a situation that led to political disasters like American involvement in the Vietnam War. It was against this range of events that the modernist movement had to ideologically define itself.

NOTES

1. George Orwell, "Shooting an Elephant," in *Shooting an Elephant and Other Essays* (New York: Harcourt, Brace and World, 1950), 8.

2. George Orwell, "A Hanging," in *Shooting an Elephant and Other Essays*, 18.

3

BIBLIOGRAPHICAL ESSAY

I

Modernism as a literary movement has been the subject of concern by a variety of commentators involving many works that go back three generations or more and are often outdated when reconsidered in response to more recent events. The attempt to write a history of literary modernism stems from a belief that one can find a principle of organization generic enough to subsume essential elements. Early attempts at coming to terms with American literature involved seeing it in a social and political context. V. L. Parrington, Van Wyck Brooks, Floyd Dell, Randolph Bourne—all felt that literature took its being from a material culture and a historical reality. Parrington was a typical representative of this approach, bringing to literature an ideology of liberal faith in progressive history. His belief in a liberal system was redefined by Lionel Trilling, who in *The Liberal Imagination* (1950) divided the literary scene into "idea and reality" and rejected reality (embodied by Dreiser) in favor of mind (embodied by Henry James). This transformation of literary reputation coincided with the repudiation of naturalism and the inception of modernism. Those opposed to Parrington shared a deep distrust of progress. They dominated the discussion from about 1950 to 1965 and included such well-known historians as Daniel Boorstin, Richard Hofstadter, Perry Miller, and Henry Nash Smith.

One of the more important topics in the study of modernism involved the fate of innocence, often pursued in American literature as the search for an American Adam, connected in turn with the myth of the land or the frontier. This theme has generated such landmark studies as R. W. B. Lewis's *The American Adam* (1955), Henry Nash Smith's *Virgin Land* (1950), Leo Marx's *The Machine in the Garden* (1964), and (to a lesser extent) Roy Harvey Pearce's *The Continuity of American Poetry* (1965). Also relevant here is Philip Rahv's distinction between redface and paleface literature, which worked the difference between the vision of writers like Walt Whitman and Henry James. Leslie Fiedler treated the theme of a lost innocence in *The End to Innocence* and *Waiting for the End*.

The Adamic books often worked a subtheme, locating the essence of American literature in cultural topics like the pastoral (Leo Marx's *Machine in the Garden*), the romance (Richard Chase's *The American Novel and Its Tradition*), and the quest for identity (R. W. B. Lewis's *The American Adam*). These books upheld a dialectic or binary system of meaning—such as innocence vs. experience, technology vs. the pastoral, the romance vs. the novel, utopia vs. dystopia—and then affirmed one side of the binary opposition over the other, using it to define the American canon. It was only a matter of time before someone reversed the process—that is, affirmed the opposite term in the dialectic, as was the case with Harry Levin's *The Power of Blackness* as a thematic answer to R. W. B. Lewis's *The American Adam* (1955); Marius Bewley's *The Eccentric Design* (1963) as a refutation of Chase's *The American Novel and Its Tradition* (1957); Annette Kolodny's *The Lay of the Land* (1975) as a response to Smith's *The Virgin Land* (1950); and Marshall McLuhan's *Mechanical Bride* as an anticipation of Marx's *The Machine in the Garden* (1964). One binary opposite was never inclusive enough to account for what deviated from it, and these books were at best half the picture— interesting and important, but reductive—valiant but incomplete attempts to reach the whole through a part.

Another set of books were based on the benefits of expatriate experience as opposed to the belief that authentic writing depended on working indigenous concerns. Malcolm Cowley's *Exile's Return* (1934) addressed the expatriate adventure, while Waldo Frank's *Our America* spoke to the need of writers to put down American roots, a belief that was taken up by the *Seven Arts* magazine and became a key theme in the poetry of Hart Crane and William Carlos Williams.

Another avenue pursued by literary historians involved defining the modernist movement in terms of special techniques, especially the use of symbolism. One of the first studies to define modernism as a system of symbolism was Edmund Wilson's *Axel's Castle* (1930). Wilson eventually came to believe that modernism was a form of literary naturalism transformed by symbolism.

Other studies that saw an American symbolism culminating in the modernist movement included F. O. Matthiessen's *American Renaissance* (1941) and Charles Feidelson's *Symbolism and American Literature* (1954). Both Matthiessen and Feidelson believed that literary reality came to us through language. Matthiessen, however, believed that literature first conveyed the social reality of democracy before it conveyed the existential reality of the authorial self. Feidelson believed more directly in the self-reflexive quality of literary symbolism, that it created its own reality separate from the meaning of nature or material culture. In creating its own verbal reality, the symbolic work created its own unity (e.g., Melville's white whale symbolically suggested a realm of opposites) and did away with binary meaning.

Feidelson's argument was picked up by Richard Poirier, who, in the tradition of Emerson, argued in *A World Elsewhere* (1966) that symbolic reality involved another realm of being, a self-enclosed system that was a world unto itself, separate from physical reality. An end point in this progression toward self-enclosed textuality takes us to John Irwin, whose *American Hieroglyphics* (1980) is infused with a Derridean subtext that rejects the idea of origins in the name of repressed (double) meaning that robbed symbolism of is immediacy. True to its agenda, postmodernism negated both the modernist's use of myth and symbolism.

Going in the opposite direction, we have critics who approached modernism as a purely linguistic (literary) phenomenon. These critics—such as R. P. Blackmur and Cleanth Brooks—were products of the New Criticism. Blackmur's collection of essays *The Lion and the Honeycomb* (1956) presumed that there was a tradition of literature that went back to the Greeks (the lion) but was kept alive by modernist forms of rhetoric (the honeycomb). And Brooks gave us *The Well Wrought Urn* (1947)and *Modern Poetry and the Tradition* (1939)—the latter a study of the way earlier poetic techniques, especially symbolism, culminated in the modernist movement. As with the symbolist critics, both Brooks and Blackmur changed the critical terms by insisting that the literary work was self-reflexive, that its meaning referred back to itself and not to some extrinsic order of physical representation.

From the mid-thirties to the late sixties, Cleanth Brooks was perhaps the most authoritative critical voice in America, certainly the most articulate spokesman for the New Criticism. His critical pronouncements prevailed for a generation, including such claims that T. S. Eliot's *The Waste Land* depicted forms of death in life to be countered in a Dionysian (Christ-like) way by fertility rituals garnered from Jessie Weston. But Brooks's reading of the poem, dominant for nearly forty years, began to wane in the late sixties and early seventies. How did a critical truism that sustained its validity for so long suddenly lose its privileged capacity? The poem did not change. Brooks's reading did not change. Why then did Brooks lose his favored place in the critical record?

The reason, of course, was that Brooks lost critical authority. His reading of *The Waste Land* was consistent with his belief that major works of literature were the product of irony, the Romantic assumption of German theorists like Friedrich Schlegel that the world is paradoxical and that contradictory belief is necessary to capture its ambivalent meaning. Brooks found such contradictory belief in Eliot's poem when he highlighted Eliot's notion of salvific process, such as the belief that redemptive life stems from (Christ's) death. Brooks saw this irony—life stems from death, especially as this idea was reinforced by Christian dogma—as contributing to the poem's power, while someone like Jacques Derrida, who embodied the new authority, saw such contradictory meaning as consistent with the problematics of language. What sustained poetic meaning for Brooks disrupted it for Derrida. Brooks's neoconservative method gave way to generational change in the more radical sixties.

Brooks lost his critical authority when a new, stronger, more iconoclastic authority challenged it. (Ironically, Eliot's use of the grail myth, with its culmination at the Chapel Perilous, is an analogue of this idea: the guardian knight reigns until a stronger challenger overthrows him.) Derrida's deconstruction benefited from the general transformation of postmodern culture when a new generation of critics bridged the gap between traditional texts and newly legitimized cultural movements such as jazz and vaudeville. The influence of jazz and of black dialect helped reinforce the authority of Derrida and other new ways of reading Eliot's poetry. The past succumbed to the new: what had been critically privileged for forty years no longer prevailed.

Another formulation of the belief that literary technique validated literature was that of Mark Schorer in his influential essay "Technique as Discovery" (1948). The essay read like a manifesto from the New Criticism. His argument turned on the assumption that it was technique that transformed the content of a literary work. As Schorer put it, "the difference between content, or experience, and achieved content, or art, is technique." And technique involved "the means of exploring and defining values in an area of experience."[1] Schorer supplied examples of works that had been tested by technique as opposed to those that had not, among them Joyce's *Portrait* as opposed to H. G. Wells's *Tono-Bungay*. Joyce's language (technique), Schorer argued, validated the narrative experience, while Wells's did not. Clearly Schorer preferred a novel based on the use of "inner" over "outer" reality without ever documenting why one form of reality was superior to, rather than simply different from, the other.

The onslaught of books and essays connecting themes and techniques with the modernist movement was the basis for the revival of at least two major modern novelists—F. Scott Fitzgerald and William Faulkner. Fitzgerald's rebirth stemmed in great part from the interest generated by Arthur Mizener's biography *The Far Side of Paradise* (1951), and Faulkner's revival has been connected with the new attention generated by Malcolm Cowley's edition of the *Viking Portable Faulkner*. That the works of Fitzgerald and Faulkner lent themselves so well to New Critical dictates did nothing to hurt their revised place in the new canon.

The impetus for change took place both within and outside the established realms of existing criticism, each drastically revising the idea of modernism. A book that illustrates this premise and that complements the assumptions of my own study is Leslie Fiedler's *What Was Literature? Class Culture and Mass Society* (1982), a personal account of his experience in academe as modernism was being transformed by challenges to the status quo and radical diversions in the canon. Fiedler entered graduate school at the University of Wisconsin in the late thirties, a time when modern literature was not part of the curriculum and American literature was taught in chosen ways, usually featuring the New England fireside poets (Longfellow, Lowell, and Holmes) with Henry James at the edge of the canon eclipsing Poe and Whitman. Fiedler's doctoral dissertation involved a study of the medieval background of John Donne's poetry, a standardized topic for the times and one totally removed from his later interests.

Once in the profession, Fiedler led the way toward a radically new kind of thinking about literature that involved conflating elite and popular literature and looking for the way an unconscious meaning might emerge from a text (an idea that anticipates Fredric Jameson's theory of the political unconscious), the stereotypical concealing the archetypal. His famous (some would say infamous) discussion of the way Huck Finn and Jim bonded on the raft was a preliminary look at the same kind of situation in Melville and Cooper. He argued that primitive forces were primarily masculine and were expressed as love, while civilizing forces were primarily feminine and were expressed as domestic authority. In Cooper's novels, for example, time runs backward as Natty Bumppo moves from forms of civilization to virgin wilderness, from the domesticated to the uncivilized, just as Huck Finn moves beyond the authority of Aunt Sally when he cuts out for the Territory (frontier) ahead.

In his major book, *Love and Death in the American Novel* (1960), Fiedler delves into the working assumptions of American fiction by pursuing Freud's contention that the two dominant forces in human life are love (eros) and death (thanatos). In expanding this thesis, he examined with special critical care popular works that had hitherto lacked serious attention—works such as Stowe's

Uncle Tom's Cabin, Thomas Dixon's *The Clansman,* Margaret Mitchell's *Gone with the Wind,* and later Alex Haley's *Roots,* concentrating on how one novel became a response to another.

In revising the canon to give serious critical attention to what previously were considered inferior texts, Fiedler was going in the face of established literary authority. Critics and historians such as Martin Turnell had established a European list, F. R. Leavis an English literary tradition, and D. H. Lawrence and F. O. Matthiessen an American canon. What Fiedler was doing was challenging that tradition by changing the criteria by which literature was defined, substituting social and existential matters for aesthetic and belle époque concerns. In so doing, Fiedler widened the scope of literary study, adding archly that the curriculum had been subject to change "the moment people like me were allowed to join the profession."[2]

He went on to suggest that this new interest in popular literature encouraged reaching out to more popular forms in an attempt to satisfy the demands of a mass culture: "Once mass production of literature had become possible . . . all books, ranging from the art novels of Henry James or Marcel Proust, Thomas Mann or James Joyce, to best sellers by Jacqueline Susann or John D. MacDonald, Conan Doyle or Bram Stoker, are distinguishable from one another only after the fact. . . . [W]e absorb them, respond to them in quite the same fashion [as we do the more respected texts]."[3]

Fiedler was not only willing to revise the idea of modernism by considering the effect of popular forms on the canon, he was also sympathetic to the way new movements like feminist and ethnic studies tipped traditional ideas in different directions. Generational transformations of literature can come from many sources: change in the critical system that leads to new ways of reading a text; social events or concerns such as race and gender or consumer and mass activity that eclipse one historical agenda in the name of another; and an expanding and contracting canon that leads to different configurations of modernism and thus different ways that the literary movement can be defined. Leslie Fiedler's commentary on literary modernism made use of all three modes of literary transformations.

II

By the mid-sixties, the New Criticism was in decline and thematic criticism played out as other critics and new critical methodologies were being introduced that took us toward postmodernism. Perhaps the most influential critic to redefine modernism in the context of the postmodern is Fredric Jameson. Jameson began his career with a book on Sartre (1961), but instead of following Sartre's existential thinking, he was attracted to Sartre's work on Marxism. This led to *Marxism and Form* (1971), a study of major Western Marxists from Georg Lukács to the Frankfurt school. Jameson became especially interested in Marxist use of dialectic, which he believed was central to the cognitive process, overriding both cyclical and evolutionary thought as well as more empirical methods.

These pursuits led to *The Prison-House of Language* (1972), a study of Russian formalism as it was transformed by Saussure's theory of language; this combination marked the beginning of structuralism, which Jameson viewed ambiguously. He was attracted to the paradigmatic aspect of structuralism, which accommodated his interest in dialectic, but he lamented its antihistorical bias.

These concerns led to a more systematic analysis of the relationship between dialectic and history. In *The Political Unconscious: Narrative as a Socially Symbolic Act* (1981), Jameson considered the narrative contradictions that emerged from the dynamics of layered reality (economic, political, and social) in three novelists (Balzac, Gissing, and Conrad). As with theorists of transformational grammar, Jameson postulated that history has a deep and a surface structure with workings that transform the meaning of one into the other. In this study, Jameson moved away from the modernist aesthetic context to the political contradictions that inhere in literary realism. The goal in critical reading now involved "the construction of the bourgeois subject in emergent capitalism and its schizophrenic disintegration in our own time."[4]

Relying heavily on Georg Lukács's theory of reification, Jameson's most daring conclusion involved connecting the transformations of capitalism with the transformations of culture in general, especially as such change was revealed in literary movements. He created symmetrical categories between capitalism and cultural history: realism, for example, took its being from market capitalism, modernism from monopoly capitalism, and postmodernism from multinational capitalism.

In *Postmodernism, or, The Cultural Logic of Late Capitalism* (1991), Jameson focused on the cultural break, or "coupure" as he called it, that separated modernism from what followed. He was primarily concerned with the rupture in the late fifties or early sixties that signaled the end of what we have been calling high modernism. In his introduction to *Postmodernism*, he makes it clear that modernism needs to be reexamined in the light of a putative postmodernism:

If there is no pure postmodernism as such, then the residual traces of modernism must be seen in another light, less as anachronisms than as necessary failures that inscribe the particular postmodern project back into context, while at the same time reopening the question of the modern itself for reexamination.[5]

Jameson is primarily concerned with the workings of postmodernism on literary modernism, but such concern justifies a reverse attention—with the way the meaning of an originary modernism was transformed. The modern and the postmodern are not asymmetrical; there is an ideological break between the two that necessitates a reassessment of both modernism and postmodernism, a reassessment of the modern aspects that supposedly make up postmodernism and of the postmodern elements that have been read back into modernism.

This radical break was an ideological separation that came with the rise of abstract expressionism in painting, existentialism in philosophy, the end of representational fiction, and the passing of the aesthetic-based poetry of Wallace Stevens. These events came simultaneously with the rise of Andy Warhol in popular art, John Cage in music, and Jean-Luc Godard in film. But the biggest break was in architecture with the decline of Frank Lloyd Wright's harmonic use of nature and the rise of Corbusier's and Mies's retrograde use of space, to buildings that overwhelm the land. Organic theories of space gave way to such contrived ideas as those of Robert Venturi's *Learning from Las Vegas,* where layered glitz won out over Wright's attempt to reconcile building with its physical setting.

This was a time of ideological confrontation, with critics like F. R. Leavis, the American New Critics, and Theodor Adorno holding the line against the rise of popular (mass) culture as well as against social critics like Daniel Bell, whose theory of a "postindustrial society," and Ernest Mandel, whose theory of "late capitalism," anticipated a new consumer culture. Their use of a "genealogy" of history or lines of descent did away with linear or horizontal history; disciplines were layered onto each other: architecture, for example, was inseparable from modern economics, with its commissions and land values, and the novel looked to mass appeal based on comic-book reality (Pynchon's *Against the Day*), playful content, and sensationalist context.

Jameson was at the forefront in seeing postmodernism as a radical break with high modernism in which an elitist era gave way to the popular values of mass culture. He called attention to the elements that characterize postmodernism: its "depthlessness," its use of pastiche (mixture of random styles), its nostalgia, and its schizophrenic fragmentation of reality leading to the loss of the bourgeois subject.

Jameson worked the problematics of historical time in *A Singular Modernity* (2002), where he distinguished between modernism and modernity. Modernism involved a break in chronology: anything this side of the break is in the realm of the modern. Modernity was a category rather than a concept: it was a sum assessment of what the modern meant. Jameson insisted that periodization was a necessary by-product of historicism: every break in time was the basis for a period. Postmodernism undid the unfolding of time by conflating past and present into a perpetual present, cutting off the future and the possibility of Utopia, a situation that Jameson believed was correctable by reverting to the distinction between modernism and modernity.

III

While Jameson and his Continental counterparts like Louis Althusser were most important in describing the transition from modernism to postmodernism, there were other critics, mostly American, who were also aware of the radical break in literary tradition. Their books primarily studied the connection between modernism and culture, including mass culture. Among the best are Marshall Berman's *All That Is Solid Melts into Air* (1982), Andreas Huyssen's *After the Great Divide* (1986, but made up of earlier essays), and Matei Călinescu's *Five Faces of Modernity* (1977, republished in 1987). While the discussion has gone beyond these books, conceptually they chart a transformation between modernism and postmodernism that still has validity today.

Berman distinguished among such terms as "modernization" (the process of social change), "modernity" (the way such change is experienced), and "modernism" (the cultural representation of these changes). Berman, dealing with the subject as an extended idea, divided modernism into three historical phases with some overlapping of time: the commercial phase belongs to the sixteenth through to the nineteenth century; the revolutionary phase begins in 1790 and goes to the twentieth century, and the global, or world, phase dominates the twentieth century. Modernism involved ideological encounter, the most central struggle featuring the opposition between Goethe and Marx, between Faustian desire and historical play. The modern embodiment of the Faustian figure was Robert Moses, the city planner, whose urban agenda demolished the Bronx. The play in history is between the primitive and the civilized, the pristine and the transformed, in which neither state of mind is able to sustain a stable reality. Modernity brings forth radical change, a state of permanent becoming in a perpetual present. As a result, modernism completes Marx's truth: "all that is solid melts into air."

Andreas Huyssen's *After the Great Divide* (1986) is made up of ten essays previously published between 1975 and 1985 in *New German Critique*. Huyssen deals with three cultural movements: the avant-garde, modernism, and postmodernism. The avant-garde allowed modernism to stay ahead of itself, but when the avant-garde was co-opted by mass culture, modernism gave way to postmodernism. The "great divide" refers to the gap between high and mass culture. As the borders between the two became indistinct, Huyssen accepted the lost boundaries as a challenge. Despite his admiration for critics like Clement Greenberg and Theodor Adorno, who vilified mass culture, Huyssen saw it as having a momentum of its own that had obliterated the old dichotomies (e.g., tradition vs. innovation, conservatism vs. renewal), and he celebrated the lost distinctions as a call for a new critical context to accommodate this major change. Books like Huyssen's were instrumental in transforming modernism into what by the nineties became postmodernism.

Another book instrumental in distinguishing between modern and postmodern culture is Matei Călinescu's *Five Faces of Modernity* (1977, republished in 1987), which attempts to come to terms with the modernist situation. His second edition adds a chapter written in 1986 on postmodernism, hence we move from four to five faces, or phases, of modernism: modernism, the avant-garde, decadence, kitsch, and postmodernism. Călinescu's argument is that mass culture, kitsch, and the avant-garde worked against the aestheticism of an old Romanticism, bringing it and the modernism that emerged from it to a close. He argues that with the rise of industrial urbanism in the nineteenth century, a new class subject to bourgeois values came into being. This new order was a threat to the age-old humanistic and Enlightenment values that had emerged from the Renaissance and Enlightenment. A countercultural force to the new industrialism was Romanticism, which anticipated decadence with its exhausted quest for the beautiful as well as other forms of literary modernism.

Modernism, with its elitist/highbrow state of mind, fought to keep itself distinct from forms of popular expression, the product in part of the new technology that Călinescu believed was encouraged by the avant-garde and that he claims was a "deliberate parody" of modernity. Out of this leveling impulse came mass culture with its homogenized product that promoted an ersatz but satisfying middle-class art that Călinescu connects with kitsch. In painting, for example, *Les demoiselles d'Avignon* revolutionized art before painting sacrificed the figure to abstract painting. In music, atonality preceded the noise of rock 'n' roll. In summary, modernism was an attempt to hold onto the beautiful (of

Romantic aestheticism); it was an escape into the idyll of history, even as that sense of history gave rise to the decadence and decline that came with the industrial revolution and perpetual war. Under the assault of mass culture and with the support of the avant-garde, modernism lost its "aura" and became a form of kitsch. By writing a new and last chapter on postmodernism, Călinescu charts the end of modernism and brings this historical process to a close.

Much of the discussion summarized above, especially as it applied to the Călinescu book, took its being from the thinking of Clement Greenberg, who distinguished between low and high culture. Greenberg, who introduced and gave meaning to the word "kitsch," argued that T. S. Eliot and Tin Pan Alley may share the same culture because they are products of the same society, but the poetry of T. S. Eliot and Edward Guest share nothing because they function on two different levels of poetic expression, revealing two different aesthetic standards at work.

Modernism was not so much a product of an aesthetic movement as it was an aesthetic standard protecting high art from what was aesthetically inferior, which, as just noted, Greenberg referred to as kitsch. Kitsch was the product of the industrial revolution that urbanized the masses of Western Europe and America. It was composed of commercial art (magazine covers, illustrations, ads), pulp fiction, comics, B movies, and other low-art forms. Kitsch took its being from what was ersatz in culture, from vicarious experience, faked sensation, counterfeit reality, bogus emotion, and spurious thought. Greenberg believed modernism emerged in the middle of the nineteenth century in France under the influence of Baudelaire, Manet, and Flaubert. Originally it was part of the avant-garde until it became concerned with preserving the integrity of art in a growingly materialistic (kitsch) culture.

Greenberg's thinking shares much with Walter Benjamin's essay on art as mechanical reproduction. Kitsch becomes a product of a postmodernism separated by artistic standards from a modernism that worked to keep the boundaries distinct. Greenberg thus sees modernism and postmodernism as two distinct ways of relating to forms of art. One was not so much the completion of the other as its opposite: modernism sustained itself until it exhausted its forms, at which point the movement was taken over by avant-garde forms and by varied expressions of kitsch. Clement Greenberg anticipated the contour of the modernist/kitsch debate as early as his breakthrough essay "Avant-Garde and Kitsch" (*Partisan Review*, 1939). Greenberg's key essays, some of them radically revised, were reprinted in *Art and Culture* (1961).

Along with the groundbreaking work of Greenberg, edited books containing miscellaneous essays on literary modernism include Michael Levenson's *The Cambridge Companion to Modernism* (1999) and Walter Kalaidjian's *The Cambridge Companion to American Modernism* (2005). An earlier book, still richly important, is the collection of essays by Malcolm Bradbury and James McFarlane, *Modernism: A Guide to European Literature 1890–1930* (1976).

IV

The interest in major literary movements like modernism seems to come and go in cycles. The thirties, the sixties, and the nineties mark the high points in critical turnout with the extraordinary number of eleven books written in the span of one year alone—1990–91. In that extended year, we had Leo Bersani, *The Culture of Redemption* (1990); George Bornstein, ed., *Representing Modernist Texts: Editing as Interpretation* (1991); Marianne DeKoven, *Rich and Strange: Gender, History, Modernism* (1991); Denis Donoghue, *Being Modern Together* (1991); Astradur Eysteinsson, *The Concept of Modernism* (1990); Michael Levenson, *Modernism and the Fate of Individuality* (1991); Tom Lutz, *American Nervousness, 1903: An Anecdotal History* (1991); Judith Ryan, *The Vanishing Subject: Early Psychology and Literary Modernism* (1991); Herbert Schneidau, *Waking Giants: The Presence of the Past in Modernism* (1991); Susan Rubin Suleiman, *Subversive Intent: Gender Politics and the Avant-Garde* (1900); and Henry Sussman, *Afterimages of Modernity* (1990). Every twenty to thirty years a new look at a major literary movement is necessary simply to bring it ideologically up to date. The cascade of books in 1990–91 revealed a need for a reassessment of literary modernism as a major intellectual, cultural, and historical movement.

V

More recent books have shifted emphasis once again, and a host of new critics see modernism as more diffuse than earlier assessments, subject to the workings of pop culture, the product of being a constructed abstract rather than a literary reality.

Chris Baldick in *The Modernist Movement, 1910–1940* (2004) argues that the early modernists were not a coherent group with a coherent literary agenda. They barely knew each other, and when they did, they more often disparaged than celebrated each other's work: Woolf resisted the work of Joyce and Lawrence, Lawrence the work of Joyce and Woolf. Baldick believes that Joyce, Pound, and Woolf had little initially in common and that linking them together in a movement called modernism is a fabricated process.

While it is true that modernists like D. H. Lawrence and T. S. Eliot appeal to a radically different reality, it is also true that the modernists shared a number of intellectual and literary concerns: they built upon the assumptions of late Romanticism. Whereas Balzac and Zola were intent in depicting an outer reality, modernism was intent on capturing an inner reality. They placed humanity, especially human consciousness, at the center of life's workings and saw it as the foundation upon which nature and philosophy, religion and science rested. Initially, the intent was to depict forms of the beautiful, often using the imagination to restore a semblance of order to a sense of residual chaos; later they claimed access to a universal sense of time through the uses of myth and symbol and the application of cyclical history. The modernist empowered the past, often locating lost ideals in that realm.

Most of these modernist elements were radically revised when modernism was transformed by structuralism and poststructuralism. The search for the ideal often led to realms of contradiction when it did not take them to forms of nihilism. Sympathetic to literary experiment, they nevertheless favored an elitist society. They disdained the values of mass society, even as the workings of such movements would transform their own ideas.

The claim that the modernists are a coherent group, members of an intellectual elite different from the general culture, is asserted as much as it is contested. Lawrence Rainey in *Institutions of Modernism* (1998) argues that in creating a system of benefactors the modernists allowed a few wealthy supporters to take the place of a mass audience. Rainey is very good in recounting the connection between the major modernists and the money system that supported them, correcting the long-standing belief that the modernists were badly compensated for their work. It is well known that Eliot's *The Waste Land*, brokered by Pound, was published simultaneously in 1922 by the *Dial* in America and the *Criterion* in England; but it is not generally known that what transpired behind the scenes led to an extraordinary sum for the rights to publish Eliot's poem. The *Dial* had offered Eliot $150 for publishing rights, which Eliot declared was insultingly low. Despite the fact that neither editor of the *Dial*—Scofield Thayer nor James Sibley Watson Jr.—had read Eliot's poem, they offered to supplement their purchasing price by giving Eliot the Dial Award for that year with its $2,000 prize. As Rainey puts it, "Literary history records few spectacles so curious . . . as two editors of a major review offering a figure nearly three times the national income per capita—in 1986 terms, the payment would exceed $40,000—for a poem neither of them had seen or read."[6]

While extremely good on putting in context the finances behind modernist writing, Rainey overstates the situation when he contends that the high modernists were as much a part of the literary marketplace as the more popular writers, and that writers like Joyce drank from the well of popular culture. While admittedly Joyce was aware of a wide range of fiction, he clearly disapproved of much of it, and almost everything in this part of Rainey's argument needs to be qualified. It is true that Joyce cites *Turko the Terrible,* that Molly enjoys reading Paul de Cock, and that Bloom reads *Tid Bits* in the jake. But Joyce uses these references for satirical purposes, and one must remember that Bloom uses his reading material for toilet paper.

Moreover, despite Rainey's attempt to connect high modernism with forms of popular culture, he believes that because modernist work lacked popular appeal, modernists directed their energies toward wealthy benefactors like John Quinn, Harriet Shaw Weaver, and Scofield Thayer, who bankrolled them. Rainey's argument tries to split the difference between two opposing views of modernism and popular culture: he claims that the modernist work invited its "commodification," but did so in ways "temporarily exempted" from the consumption of the marketplace, and instead was integrated "into a different economic circuit of patronage, collecting, speculation, and investment," activities that were encroaching upon the larger economy (2–3). Joyce had his benefactor, so did Eliot, and Pound was exceptional in enlisting the support of the little magazines to carry on the modernist agenda. But a benefactor is not identical to the mass-culture marketplace, and Rainey's thesis has been rightly contested.

Astradur Eysteinsson in *The Concept of Modernism* (1992) maintains that modernism is an after-the-fact critical construct that exists as an abstraction and not as a reality. Eysteinsson's is an attempt to ground modernism in its own literary theory. For example, he treats Edmund Wilson on symbolism and Joseph Frank on spatial form. He sees a paradigmatic shift beginning in the mid- and late nineteenth century against the prevailing literary traditions, and with this shift the beginning of modernism. For Eysteinsson, modernism is a constructed reality, but the source of the constructed is the critic-poet and not the poet-critic: modernism becomes the product of critical rather than creative theory. All of these views—the belief that modernism was an inchoate, popular movement, the product of belated critical construction—must be qualified.

A book that reverses Eysteinsson's direction was Michael Levenson's *A Genealogy of Modernism* (1984), a study of key documents from 1908 to 1922 that depict modernism as successive phases of ideas and techniques (such as impressionism, imagism, vorticism) that attempt to establish a new aestheticism.

Other books that led to new ways of thinking about modernism as a literary movement would include Peter Nicholls's *Modernisms: A Literary Guide* (1995). Nicholls examined modernism as a series of literary movements beginning with Baudelaire and moving toward the avant-garde organized around discussions of French symbolism, forms of futurism and expressionism, and discussions of Dada and surrealism. The difficulty here is similar to the problem we encounter with many of the newer books on literary modernism: they are not wrong in their assumptions but often reductive in overemphasizing one aspect of modernism at the expense of other attributes. Nicholls's study, for example, involves modernism as a series of experimental movements that canceled themselves out, a series of passing fads that never amounted to a set of concrete beliefs or a coherent movement. He treats Joyce, but it is the fumbling, experimental Joyce rather than the mature, more doctrinaire Joyce. His study makes modernism mostly a French affair with the emphasis on marginal matters. His discussion of futurism, for example, attacks feminine sentimentality and eliminates the war between the sexes on the grounds that the future would offer a new vision of humanity: a "nonhuman type" constructed along mechanical lines, naturally aggressive, cruel, and all-knowing. Nicholls tells us that he will treat the "tension between the social and the aesthetic," but his book is more a study of experiments in the grotesque than a study of the traditional elements that constitute high modernism.

Peter Childs's fast-paced *Modernism* (2000) is a consideration of the philosophical foundations of modernism as derived from Darwin, Freud, Marx, Nietzsche, Saussure, and Einstein, along with a consideration of modernism as a composite of different mediums (such as film), literary genres, and textual strategies. Childs offers one of the most extended considerations of modernism, perhaps too extended and overdetermined, involving matters that seem to repudiate the idea of consistency: we are left with modernism as an incoherent literary movement with no shared ideology.

Another primarily negative view of modernism was Peter Burger's *The Decline of Modernism* (1992), a collection of essays Burger wrote between 1977 and 1991. Burger examined the intellectual friction between art and society, especially the confrontation that resulted with the rise of an eighteenth-century bourgeois society when it confronted a literary modernism that reduced life's imperatives to aesthetic matters. Burger was especially attentive to the countermovement of avant-gardism, which rejected the aesthetic foundation of life and hence the efficacy of literary modernism. A more traditional reading is John Carey's *The Intellectuals and the Masses* (1992), which argues that modernism was invented to shut out the common reader. Carey believes, as do I, that the modernist disdain for mass culture provoked an elitist stance. Others believe that modernism was a hybrid cultural affair. David Chinitz in *T. S. Eliot and the Cultural Divide* (2003), for example, argues that Eliot—attentive to jazz, vaudeville, Tin Pan Alley, and detective fiction—bridged high art and popular culture.

Michael North in his *Dialect of Modernism: Race, Language, and Twentieth-Century Literature* (1994) offers an important peripheral view on this matter. North's is a revisionist study that puts in place two modernist uses of language: the traditional voices of high modernists like Pound and Eliot and the retrograde voices of such Harlem Renaissance writers as Claude McKay and Jean Toomer. Each voice had come into its own by 1922, and one must be understood in relation to the other, perpetuating a racial divide bridged by Eliot's Shakespearean Rag, the narrative voice of Zora Neale Hurston, and the mixed voices that can be found in such writers as Charles Olson and Robert Creeley. According to North, "writers as far from Harlem as T. S. Eliot and Gertrude Stein re-imagined themselves as black, spoke in a black voice, and used that voice to transform the literature of their time."[7] North relies on the accident of common occurrence to carry the proof of such claims. Events that happen within the same year reflect literary commonality rather than the conjunction of separate interests: suddenly Eliot's *The Waste Land* is keeping company with Sampson Raphaelson's "The Day of Atonement" and *The Jazz Singer* simply because they were all published in 1922. Later Claude McKay's *Harlem Shadows* is added to this list for the same reason. Such links become increasingly tenuous. We are told, for example, that both Gertrude Stein and Picasso resented Matisse's claim that modernism began when he showed them a painted mask he found in a secondhand shop. This painted mask, with its connection to Africa, stands in for the painted mask Picasso placed over his naturalistic portrait of Stein. Picasso's painted mask then becomes the linguistic mask that Stein brings to "Melanctha": three separate and disconnected events now become one. North's desire to connect high modernism with black dialect rested more on coincidences than on reciprocity. His work is the product of great originality. But his final conclusion—"the effort toward an indigenous American cultural renewal coincided with a similar movement in Harlem" (128)—is stated rather than proved, even as it becomes the basis for connecting Claude McKay, Jean Toomer, and Zora Neale Hurston with the modernist movement. While such conclusions must be taken on faith, they became, as we have seen, the basis for a radical revision of modernism by a new generation of critics. Both North and Chinitz could illustrate their thesis, but not to the degree that they claimed, and the belief that modernism absorbed black culture as a defining component, while aligned with present-day ideology, was subject to reconsideration. Nevertheless, despite such lapses in argument, North's theory of black dialectic has become the basis for the transformation of modernism from one intellectual mode to another, and North has become a major spokesman in this debate. Another study that connected modernism to the Harlem Renaissance was Houston Baker's *Modernism and the Harlem Renaissance* (1987). Baker believes that literary form is a kind of mask and that the Harlem Renaissance writers created a disguised literature with modern affinities.

Chinitz's argument—along with that of Baldick—was anticipated in Christopher Butler's *Early Modernism* (1994). Butler saw modernism as a more interactive phenomenon than Baldick and less derivative of popular culture than Chinitz, leading to a distinctly avant-garde movement separate from popular culture, laying the foundation for new forms of consciousness, primitivism, and revised conceptions of personal identity.

A study involving modernism and the marketplace is Richard Ohmann's *Selling Culture* (1996), in which he contends that mass culture stems from the rise of high-circulation magazines at the turn of the nineteenth century. Another book dealing with mass culture is Ohmann's *The Making and Selling Culture* (1996), an edited series of interviews with corporate executives dealing with the way commodity goods such as Coca-Cola are marketed with contemporary culture in mind.

Books related to the connection between modernism and the avant-garde would include Peter Burger's *Theory of the Avant-garde* (1985), which argues that modernism looked to aestheticism while avant-garde literature challenged the autonomy of art. Peter Osborne's *The Politics of Time: Modernity and the Avant-garde* (1995) positions modernism as a form of historical time that valorizes the new at the expense of tradition. Modernism becomes a circular process in which the new undermines the previous unfolding of history. As a result, forms of permanence (Eliot's claims of myth, the New Critics belief in a "concrete universal") are repudiated.

Other studies of modernism and the avant-garde are Marjorie Perloff's *The Futurist Movement: Avant-Garde, Avant Guerre, and the Language of Rupture* (1986), which begins with the 20 February 1909, manifesto of F. T. Marinetti on the front page of *Le Figaro*, in which he called for an art based on the new technology of the modern city that was also the basis for his repudiating classical art. Perloff continues her study of the avant-garde in *Twenty-first-Century Modernism* (2002), in which she argues that the modern period is not over. She believes that both Eliot and Stein are modernists but that it took another generation before Stein could be recognized as such. Eliot's "Prufrock" (1915) was a celebrated work in the twenties, but it took a work like Stein's *Tender Buttons* (1914) another generation before it moved from "coterie" to "celebrated" work. Seeing Marcel Duchamp as the link between T. S. Eliot and Gertrude Stein, Perloff contends that by the mid-twenties Stein had picked up where Eliot had left off, and in matters of experimental language and poetics, contrary to prevailing thought, Eliot and Stein are "two sides of the same [modernist] coin."

Perloff sees early modernism as representational as opposed to a later poetry of free play and indeterminacy. Along this line of rupture she locates the symbolist mode of Eliot as opposed to the indeterminacy of John Ashbery. Despite her own ability to distinguish an earlier modernism from a later modernism, Perloff refuses to accept the distinction between modernism and postmodernism. She asks, "How long, after all, can a discourse—in this case, poetry—continue to be considered post- with its implication of belatedness, diminution, and entropy?"[8] But as Jameson has amply demonstrated, a claim for a postmodern literature separate from modernism depends on a context much larger than poetry. Perloff wants a post–World War II literature to stand on its own, but even within her own claims, her depiction of such poetry is an outgrowth of avant-garde elements that were disrupted by the Great War. To these elements she "re-presents" (her word is "rereads") modernist figures like Eliot, but now co-opted into a different poetic mode. We are then left with the puzzling conclusion that Eliot's symbolist mode is not that different from Stein's cubist mode, but both are different from Ashbery's indeterminacy along with a poetry of "rupture," even as she claims that there was no break between modernism and postmodernism. Despite what appears to be real confusion, Perloff's work is highly respected and has laid the basis for radically new ways of thinking about modernism.

NOTES

1. Schorer, "Technique as Discovery," 101–14.
2. Fiedler, *What Was Literature?* 112.
3. Ibid., 121.
4. Jameson, *The Political Unconscious*, 9.
5. Jameson, *Postmodernism*, xvi.
6. Rainey, *Institutions of Modernism*, 88; hereafter cited in the text.
7. North, *Dialect of Modernism,* iii; hereafter cited in the text.
8. Perloff, *Twenty-first-Century Modernism*, 2.

NOTES

1. MODERNISM AND ITS TRANSFORMATIONS

1. Lehan, *Realism and Naturalism: The Novel in an Age of Transition*; Lehan, *The City in Literature: An Intellectual and Cultural History*.

2. Hauser, *The Social History of Art*, 158–59, 165–66.

3. Ibid., 172.

4. For a discussion of women who made up the expatriate movement in Paris, see Shari Benstock, *Women of the Left Bank: Paris, 1900–1940* (Austin: University of Texas Press, 1986). For a discussion of the appeal of the expatriate movement among black writers, see Michel Fabre, *From Harlem to Paris: Black Writers in France, 1840–1980* (Urbana: University of Illinois Press, 1991).

5. Karl Popper, *The Open Society and Its Enemies* (Princeton: Princeton University Press, 1950). Popper does not believe that there is any meaning built into history; in fact, he believes a sense of destiny has led to many of the atrocities that characterize modern history. His views of history ran counter to those of many of the modernists, who believed in cyclical history or who pondered the mystery of unfolding time.

2. "PERSPECTIVISM"

1. Marjorie Perloff, "The Avant-garde Phase of American Modernism," in Kalaidjian, ed., *The Cambridge Companion to American Modernism*, 195–217. The degree of conformity between the avant-garde and the high modernist is a contested question. I argue for a discrepancy between the two, but the disconnection is not airtight: Stein's interests carried her to Dada and Pound's to futurism, despite obvious contradictions in such alignments. Pound, for example, despite acknowledging Marinetti and connecting futurism and the vortex, disputed his own argument when he grounded culture in an agrarian base. Along with Perloff in *The Futurist Movement*, Astradur Eysteinsson in *The Concept of Modernism* argues for a more coherent relationship between the avant-garde and high modernism.

2. Tim Armstrong's *Modernism, Technology, and the Body: A Cultural Study* (1998) is a study of the modernist writers' intervention in such physical procedure as bodily electrification, poetry and recorded sound, and cinema as an influence on mind. His *Modernism: A Cultural History* (2005) takes up commercial concerns, treating modernism as a form of market culture, engaging again such new modes of technology as the cinema.

3. Karl, *Modern and Modernism: The Sovereignty of the Artist, 1885–1925*, 401–2; Bradbury and McFarlane, eds., *Modernism: 1890–1930*, 14.

4. A senior White House adviser to George W. Bush was quoted as saying: "We're an empire now, and when we act, we create our own reality" (see Ron Suskind, "Without a Doubt: Faith, Certainty and the Presidency of George W. Bush," *New York Times Magazine*, 17 October 2004).

5. For a discussion of mass culture, see Thomas Strychacz, *Modernism, Mass Culture, and Professionalism*. For a more recent discussion of mass culture and crowds, see Schnapp and Tiews, eds., *Crowds*.

6. Despite the claim for an indigenous literature, the examples cited often reveal an international influence. Gide's *The Counterfeiters* offered a symbolic reality that Feidelson compared with Melville's *Pierre*. Kenneth Burke compared Mann and Gide as symbolic authors. The Feidelson essay on Gide and Melville appeared in his *Symbolism and American Literature*, 186–207. The Burke essay on Mann and Gide appeared in his *Counter-Statement*, 116–35.

7. Stanley Fish argues that a literary work is devoid of text until an informed reader or interpretive community derives a strategy for reading it. But Fish fails to consider that an author enlists such a strategy in writing the work. If an interpretive community can read Milton's "Lycidas" as a pastoral poem, Milton could have written it as a pastoral poem. Once "Lycidas" is considered as a pastoral poem, the poem has a text that precedes its reading.

3. THE MODERNIST EXPERIENCE

1. For a general discussion of French anti-Semitism, see McCarthy, *Céline*, 140.

2. John Harrison, *The Reactionaries: A Study of Anti-Democratic Intelligentsia* (New York: Schocken, 1966), 157.

3. Lewis, *Time and Western Man*, 211.

4. Ibid., 103.

5. Wyndham Lewis, *The Lion and the Fox: The Role of the Hero in the Plays of Shakespeare* (London: Richards, 1927), 67.

6. Arthur Koestler, *Arrow in the Blue, An Autobiography* (New York: Macmillan, 1952), 107.

7. Arthur Koestler, *The Invisible Writing: The Second Volume of an Autobiography, 1932–40* (New York: Macmillan, 1954), 389.

8. Ibid., 427.

9. Malraux discussed the history of the West in Spenglerian terms in a book with a Spenglerian title: *The Temptation of the Occident*. For a more detailed discussion of the connection between Malraux and the ideas of Spengler, see Armand Hoog, "Malraux, Möllberg, and Frobenius," in *Malraux: A Collection of Critical Essays*, ed. R. W. B. Lewis (Englewood Cliffs: Prentice-Hall, 1964), 91.

4. THE INWARD TURN

1. Henri Bergson, *Creative Evolution*, trans. A. Mitchell (New York: Holt, 1911), 102; hereafter cited in the text.

2. Samuel Butler, *Life and Habit* (London: Fifield, 1910), 261; hereafter cited in the text.

3. Samuel Butler, *Evolution, Old and New* (New York: Dutton, 1911), 346.

4. Samuel Butler, *The Way of All Flesh* (1903; New York: Penguin, 1966), 211; hereafter cited in the text.

5. Samuel Butler, *Erewhon* (1872; New York: Random House, Modern Library, 1927), 246; hereafter cited in the text.

6. D. H. Lawrence, *The Rainbow* (New York: Modern Library, 1915), 94; hereafter cited in the text.

7. D. H. Lawrence, *Women in Love* (1920; New York: Penguin, 1970), 191; hereafter cited in the text.

8. D. H. Lawrence, *Lady Chatterley's Lover* (1928; New York: Modern Library, 1983), 117; hereafter cited in the text.

9. For a broader discussion of Bergson's literary influence, see Douglass, *Bergson, Eliot, and American Literature*. See also Burwick and Douglass, eds., *The Crisis in Modernism: Bergson and the Vitalist Controversy*.

10. Karin Stephen, *The Misuse of Mind: A Study of Bergson's Attack on Intellectualism,* with a prefatory letter by Henri Bergson (New York: Harcourt Brace; London: Paul, Trench, Trubner, 1922, 1924).

5. DECADENCE/AESTHETICISM

1. Jouve, *Baudelaire: A Fire to Conquer Darkness,* 39.

2. Hauser, *The Social History of Art*, 158–59.

3. Ibid., 165–66.

4. Holbrook Jackson, *The Eighteen Nineties: A Review of Art and Ideas at the Close of the Nineteenth Century* (1913; London: Pelican, 1939), 104.

5. For a discussion of Stevens and aestheticism, especially his interest in Walter Pater, see Bates, *Wallace Stevens: A Mythology of Self,* 29–35.

6. Wallace Stevens, *Letters of Wallace Stevens,* ed. Holly Stevens (New York: Knopf, 1966), 426–27.

7. Wallace Stevens, *The Collected Poems of Wallace Stevens* (New York: Knopf, 1955), 66–70.

8. Bates, *Wallace Stevens: A Mythology of Self,* 94–95.

9. Ibid., 92.

10. Stevens, *Collected Poems,* 165–84.

11. Filreis, *Modernism from Right to Left: Wallace Stevens, the Thirties, and Literary Radicalism,* 154.

12. Bloom, *Wallace Stevens: The Poems of Our Climate,* 118.

13. Stevens, *Notes toward a Supreme Fiction,* in Stevens, *Collected Poems.*

14. Stevens, *Esthétique du mal,* in Stevens, *Collected Poems.*

6. MYTH

1. Frye, *Anatomy of Criticism,* 42. For an example of the realistic giving way to the mythic, see Frank Norris's description of the train slaughtering the sheep in *The Octopus.* The train symbolizes the power of the machine and by extension the railroad company, and the sheep symbolize the farmers and ranchers who have been displaced by the railroad company. In the course of describing the slaughtered sheep, Norris infuses mythic elements (e.g., reference to the Colossus, the Leviathan, the Cyclops) within the realistic detail, giving mythic status to the machine and suggesting the effect of its power over men and nature. Naturalism makes equal use of animal symbolism (cf. Zola's bête humaine) to suggest the atavistic basis of human life. The transformations that take us from nature to the machine often take on mythic meaning.

2. For a discussion of the possible connections between gothic fiction, romance, and realism/naturalism, see Elizabeth MacAndrew, *The Gothic Tradition in Fiction* (New York: Columbia University Press, 1979); David Punter, *The Literature of Terror: A History of Gothic Fiction from 1765 to the Present Day* (London: Longman, 1980); and William Patrick Day, *In the Circles of Fear and Desire: A Study of Gothic Fantasy* (Chicago: University of Chicago Press, 1985). For an attempt to treat the

romance as an early expression of modernism, see Nicholas Daly, *Modernism, Romance, and the Fin de Siècle: Popular Fiction and British Culture, 1880–1914* (Cambridge: Cambridge University Press, 1999). The argument here is that the romance opens up a primitive world analogous to that which we find in the modernist novel; but it is a world of elemental consciousness, better linking it with literary naturalism than with the more heightened consciousness of modernism. Another difference between the romance and modernism is that the modern novel makes more deliberate use of myth than does the romance.

3. Cope, *Joyce's Cities: Archaeologists of the Soul*.

4. Freud, *Civilization and Its Discontents*, 34.

5. Murray, *Five Stages of Greek Religion*, vi.

6. Ibid., vii.

7. Weston, *From Ritual to Romance*, 37–38.

8. T. S. Eliot, *Selected Prose*, ed. Frank Kermode (New York: Harcourt, Brace, Jovanovich, 1975). From Eliot's review of Joyce's *Ulysses*.

7. SYMBOL

1. Arthur Symons, *The Symbolist Movement in Literature*, with an introduction by Richard Ellmann (New York: Dutton, 1958), xv.

2. Ibid., x.

3. Schorer, "Technique as Discovery," 101–14.

4. Burke, *Permanence and Change*, 163.

5. Burke, *A Grammar of Motives*, 317. See also Burke, *A Rhetoric of Motives*, 285.

6. Burke, *A Grammar of Motives*, 318.

7. Burke, *Counter-Statement*, 157.

8. STRUCTURE

1. Derrida, *Writing and Difference*, 58. Derrida's essay "Structure, Sign, and Play in the Discourse of the Human Sciences" also appears in this collection (278–93).

2. One of the more accessible studies of Derrida is Christopher Norris, *Derrida* (Cambridge: Harvard University Press, 1987).

3. The following passage from Derrida's *Of Grammatology* offers an example of his verbal density: "Between the overture and the philosophical accomplishment of phonologism (or logocentrism), the motif of presence was decisively articulated. It underwent an internal modification whose most conspicuous index was the moment or certitude in the Cartesian cogito. Before that, the identity of presence offered to the mastery of repetition was constituted under the 'objective' form of the ideality of the eidos or the substantiality of ousia" (97).

4. Critical systems come and go, changing the way we read a text and then becoming subject to change themselves. With the help of Foucault, traditional literary history took on qualities of structuralist literary history. The result was the New Historicism, primarily the work of Stephen Greenblatt. Despite the name, the New Historicism was not really a historicism, rejecting the belief that each period of time (e.g., the Renaissance) or of national culture (e.g., the German Reich)

is described by a system of laws and had a geist, or intellectual identity, that unified it. The New Historicism was not a product of linear history, did not concentrate on historical periods or literary movements, and did not look for causal connections between events. Instead, the New Historicism worked with self-constituted tropes (e.g., self-fashioning, the gold standard, the metaphor of circulation or the machine) that were then considered both descriptive and yet independent of time. The attempt was not to reveal how history influenced the literary imagination, but how the literary imagination processed history: the text became a prism through which to view history and its related disciplines. In its search for homologies, its predication of a timeless history, its repudiation of causal connections, its emphasis on cultural events held together by institutional forms of power (as proclaimed by Foucault), the New Historicism shared many assumptions with structuralist thinking. As for the transformations within modernism, self-contained meaning gave way to relational (homologous) meaning.

5. Realism/naturalism was transformed by New Critical assumptions. For works that substituted New Historicist tropes for historical reality, see Amy Kaplan's *The Social Construction of American Realism* (Chicago: University of Chicago Press, 1988); Walter Benn Michaels's *The Gold Standard and the Logic of Naturalism* (Berkeley and Los Angeles: University of California Press, 1987); and Mark Seltzer's *Bodies and Machines* (New York: Routledge, 1992). For books that substitute structural assumptions for a conventional idea of history, see Daniel H. Borus's *Writing Realism: Howells, James, and Norris in the Mass Market* (Chapel Hill: University of North Carolina Press, 1989); and Phillip Barrish's *American Literary Realism: Critical Theory, and Intellectual Prestige, 1880–1995* (Cambridge: Cambridge University Press, 2001). For books that "re-present" naturalistic assumptions, see June Howard's *Form and History in American Literary Naturalism* (Chapel Hill: University of North Carolina Press, 1985), which, in its repressed use of history, reveals the influence of Fredric Jameson's theory of the political unconscious; see also David Baguley's *Naturalistic Fiction: An Entropic Vision* (Cambridge: Cambridge University Press, 1990); and Yves Chevrel's *Le naturalisme* (Paris: Presses universitaires de France, 1982). For a more complete analysis of the way structural and poststructural thought transformed realism and naturalism, see Lehan, *Realism and Naturalism: The Novel in an Age of Transition*, 235–50.

6. See Jameson, *Marxism and Form*; and Jameson, *The Prison-House of Language*.

7. Jameson, *The Political Unconscious*, 49.

8. For a discussion of the way that Jameson believes Marxism and structuralism (history and language) reinforce each other, see *The Political Unconscious*, 100.

9. Ibid., 9.

9. TIME/HISTORY

1. Burke, *Permanence and Change*, 89–90.

2. William Butler Yeats, *A Vision* (London: Macmillan, 1937), 261.

3. Yeats, for example, tells us in *A Vision* that the period from 1005 to 1180 "corresponds to the Homeric period some two thousand years before [in its] creation of the Arthurian Tales and the Romanesque architecture" (287). The period from 1250 to 1300 corresponds to phase 8 "because in or near that period, chivalry and Christendom have proved insufficient, the King mastered the one, the Church the other, reversing the achievement of Constantine" (288). The period from 1300

to 1380 belongs to the fourth gyre, phases 9, 10, and 11, "which finds its character in painting from Giotto to Fra Angelico, in the *Chronicles of Froissart* and in the elaborate canopy upon the stained glass of windows" (289). The period 1450 to 1550 resides in phase 15, the Italian Renaissance, and extends to phase 22, in which the "breaking of Christian 'synthesis' parallels the breaking of Greek traditional faith." (291). The period from 1875 to 1927, "like that from 1250 to 1300 a period of abstraction (phase 8)," anticipates "the first weariness" of modernism and is in sync with Spengler's (and Henry Adams's) prediction that the West was in a process of decline (299–300).

4. Ezra Pound, Canto 38, in *Cantos 1–117* (New York: New Directions, 1972).

5. Ezra Pound, "America, Roosevelt, and the Causes of the Present War" (1944), in *Money Pamphlets* (London: P. Russell, 1951).

6. Ezra Pound, trans., *Dialogues of Fontenelle,* in *Egoist* (1917): 370–71; see Clark M. Emery, *Ideas into Action: A Study of Pound's Cantos* (Coral Gables: University of Miami Press, 1958), 22.

7. For a discussion of the connection between Pound and Spengler, see Ronald Bush, "Pound and Spengler: Another Look," *Paideuma* (Orono, Me.: Ezra Pound Society, 1972), 63–65.

8. T. S. Eliot, *Collected Poems, 1909–1962* (New York: Harcourt, Brace, and World, 1963), 100–101.

9. A. Conan Doyle, "The Adventures of Five Orange Pips," in *The Adventures of Sherlock Holmes,* by Doyle (London: George Newnes, 1892), 108; quoted in Crawford, *The Savage and the City in the Work of T. S. Eliot,* 11.

10. Willa Cather, *My Antonia* (1918; New York: Vintage, 1994), 272.

11. Willa Cather, *A Lost Lady* (New York: Knopf, 1922), 168–69.

12. F. Scott Fitzgerald, "My Lost City," published in *The Crack-up,* by Fitzgerald (New York: New Directions, 1945), 28.

13. Adorno, "Spengler after the Decline," 51–72.

14. Ibid.

15. Ibid.

10. SPATIAL FORM

1. Joseph Frank's essay, entitled "Spatial Form in Modern Literature," first appeared in the *Sewanee Review* (1945) and was later collected in Frank's *The Widening Gyre* (New Brunswick: Rutgers University Press, 1963).

2. Malcolm Bradbury, in Bradbury and McFarlane, eds., *Modernism: A Guide to European Literature 1890–1930,* 401–4.

3. Ibid.

4. Poulet, *Proustian Space,* 94.

5. Marcel Proust, *Remembrance of Things Past (À la recherche du temps perdu),* trans. C. K. Scott Moncrieff and Terrence Kilmartin (London: Chatto and Windus, 1981), 133.

6. F. Scott Fitzgerald, *The Great Gatsby* (New York: Scribner's, 1925; reprinted by Macmillan, 1992), 162.

7. Israel Rosenfield, *The Invention of Memory: A New View of the Brain* (New York: Basic Books, 1988), 23–24.

8. Pater, preface and conclusion to *The Renaissance,* ed. Bate, 508–12.

9. James Joyce, *A Portrait of the Artist as a Young Man* (1916; New York: Modern Library, 1944), 204.

10. Ellmann, *James Joyce*, 340.

11. Bowen, in Bowen and Carens, eds., *A Companion to Joyce Studies*, 469.

12. As Chester Anderson has pointed out, the Wandering Jew is sometimes connected with Enoch, Elijah, and Ad-Khadir, who in Semitic mythology were vegetarian gods (see Anderson, *James Joyce and His World*, 11).

13. Ibid.

14. Bowen, in Bowen and Carens, eds., *A Companion to Joyce Studies*, 563.

15. Bishop, *Joyce's Book of the Dark*, 211.

16. Adaline Glasheen, quoted in Bowen and Carens, eds., *A Companion to Joyce Studies*, 595.

11. FROM ROMANCE TO REALISM

1. Morton Cohen, *Rider Haggard: His Life and Works* (London: Hutchinson, 1960), 108.

2. Joseph Conrad, *Heart of Darkness*, 1902; ed. Robert Kimbrough (New York: Norton, 1988), 10.

3. Joseph Conrad, *Notes on Life and Letters*, quoted in Alan Hunter, *Joseph Conrad and the Ethics of Darwinism* (London: Croom Helms, 1983), 11.

4. Edith Wharton, *The Custom of the Country* (New York: Knopf, 1994), 516.

12. AUTHENTICITY IN A COUNTERFEIT CULTURE

1. Michael Harrington, *The Accidental Century* (New York: Macmillan, 1965), 64.

2. Ibid., 65.

3. Guerard, *André Gide*, 96.

4. Louis-Ferdinand Céline, *Journey to the End of the Night*, trans. John H. P. Marks (New York: Avon, 1934), 16–17.

5. Ibid., 128.

13. NEOREALISM AND BEYOND

1. Ernest Hemingway, *The Sun Also Rises* (New York: Scribner's, 1926), 152. There may be a connection between the name of Hemingway's narrator, Jake Barnes, and Djuna Barnes, whom Hemingway knew when she was in Paris, living on Rue Jacob.

2. Ernest Hemingway, *A Farewell to Arms* (New York: Scribner's, 1929), 185.

3. Quoted in Frederick J. Hoffman, *Gertrude Stein* (Minneapolis: University of Minnesota Press, 1961), 11.

4. Stein in "A Transatlantic Interview 1946," 15; quoted in Dubnick, *The Structure of Obscurity: Gertrude Stein, Language, and Cubism*, 18.

5. Mellow, *Charmed Circle: Gertrude Stein and Company*, 164.

6. Gertrude Stein, *Picasso* (London: Scribner's, 1939), 12; Donald Sutherland, "Gertrude Stein and the Twentieth Century," in *A Primer for the Gradual Understanding of Gertrude Stein*, ed. Robert Bartlett Haas (Los Angeles: Black Sparrow Press, 1971), 151.

7. Harry Garvin, "How to Read Gertrude Stein," paper presented at the Modern Language Association conference, New York, 1974; quoted in Dubnick, 114.

8. Pater, preface and conclusion to *The Renaissance*.

9. For a detailed discussion of noir, see Copjec, ed., *Shades of Noir*, especially David Reed and Jayne L. Walker's "Strange Pursuit: Cornell Woolrich and the Abandoned City" (57–96), and Dean MacCannell's "Democracy's Turn: On the Homeless Noir" (279–97).

14. GENDER AND RACE

1. There have been a number of attempts to connect the Harlem Renaissance or its purposes and intent with mainline modernism. Three typical examples are Baker, *Modernism and the Harlem Renaissance* (1987); James De Jongh, *Vicious Modernism: Black Harlem and the Literary Imagination* (Cambridge: Cambridge University Press, 1990); and North, *The Dialect of Modernism: Race, Language, and Twentieth-Century Literature* (1994).

15. MASS CULTURE

1. A discussion of mass culture can be found in Matthew Arnold's *Culture and Anarchy* (1869). More recent considerations are Theodor Adorno's *The Culture Industry: Selected Essays on Mass Culture* (1991) and *The Authoritarian Personality* (1950), and Leo Lowenthal's *Literature and Mass Culture* (1984). It is also the subject of Raymond Williams's *Culture and Society* (London: Chatto and Windus, 1958) and Michael Kammen's *American Culture, American Tastes: Social Change and the Twentieth Century* (New York: Knopf, 1999). For the transformation of art in the face of mass culture, see Benjamin, "The Work of Art in the Age of Mechanical Reproduction."

2. T. S. Eliot, *Notes toward a Definition of Culture* (London: Faber and Faber, 1948), 120.

3. Source: Albert Greco, Institute for Publishing Research Inc.

4. Umberto Eco, "The Myth of Superman," from *The Role of the Reader* (1972), was translated by Natalie Chilton and first published in English in *Diacritics* in 1972 and republished in *The Critical Tradition*, ed. David H. Richter, 929–41 (New York: St. Martin's Press, 1989).

5. Kammen, *American Culture, American Tastes*, 21–22. The reference to Ian Fleming is taken from Mordecai Richler, "James Bond Unmasked," in *Mass Culture Revisited*, ed. Bernard Rosenberg and David Manning White (New York: Van Nostrand Reinhold, 1971), 341.

6. Mordecai Richler discusses the plot elements of a Bond novel in Rosenberg and White, *Mass Culture Revisited*, 342. Joan Rockwell discusses the evolution of the spy novel in "Normative Attitudes of Spies in Fiction," in Rosenberg and White, *Mass Culture Revisited*, 325–40.

7. Jared Diamond, "What's Your Consumption Factor?" *New York Times*, 2 January 2008.

8. The statistics here are drawn from Daniel Bell's *The Coming of Post-Industrial Society: A Venture in Social Forecasting* (New York: Basic Books, 1973), 132, 174.

9. Wolin, *Walter Benjamin*, 227.

10. Walter Benjamin, *Illuminations*, trans. Harry Zohn, ed. Hannah Arendt (New York: Schocken, 1969), 223.

11. Berman, *All That Is Solid Melts into Air*, 308.

12. For further reference to Georg Lukács and the Frankfurt school, see Lichtheim, *George Lukacs*, 108; Rodney Livingstone, ed., *Essays on Realism: Georg Lukács*, trans. David Fernbach (Cambridge: MIT Press, 1980), 4; Georg Lukács, "Marxist Aesthetics and Literary Realism," 203–17. For

a detailed discussion of the Lukács-Brecht debate, see Lunn, *Marxism and Modernism: An Historical Study of Lukács, Brecht, Benjamin, and Adorno.*

13. Jack Kerouac, "The Last Word," *Escapade* (December 1960): 104; quoted in Clark, *Jack Kerouac,* 102. Clark's is the most complete biography of Kerouac, but see also Miles, *Ginsberg: A Biography.* Two useful critical commentaries on Kerouac are Warren French, *Jack Kerouac* (Boston: Twayne, 1986); and Tim Hunt, *Kerouac's Crooked Road: Development of a Fiction* (Hamden, Conn.: Archon, 1981).

16. ALONE IN THE CROWD

1. An impressive recent study is Jeffrey Schnapp and Matthew Tiews's edited volume *Crowds* (2006). This book is a collaborative affair, organized by the Stanford Humanities Lab, involving a range of essays that look at the crowd as theater audience, sports crowd, religious pilgrims, and financial investors. The study suggests ways the crowd has been perceived spatially, depicted in film and classical art, concentrating on the individual as part of the crowd as opposed to the individual as distinct from the crowd. The study further considers the makeup of historical crowds such as those that composed the French Revolution, José Ortega y Gasset's *Revolt of the Masses,* to the crowds of the fifties as depicted in David Riesman's *The Lonely Crowd* and William Whyte's *The Organization Man.* The diffuse range of this book is in itself a statement of how the crowd has taken on a variety of meanings. Despite its breadth of concerns, the book could be stronger in seeing is the crowd as a state of mind, and also on seeing the connection between the crowd and mass culture.

2. Donoghue, *The Old Moderns,* 12

3. Ibid., 28.

4. F. Scott Fitzgerald, *The Great Gatsby* (New York: Scribner's, 1925; reprinted by Macmillan, 1992), 61–62.

5. The crowd has been frequently treated as a historical subject. Besides the previously discussed crowds of Le Bon, Freud, Canetti, and more recently of Schnapp and Tiews, we have such masterwork studies as those by George Lefebvre, George Rude (*Crowd in the French Revolution*), Eric Hobsbawm, and E. P. Thompson. These have been supplemented by Neil Smelser's *Theory of Collective Behavior* (1962); Sam Wright's *Crowds and Riots: A Study in Social Organization* (1978); Robert Nye's *The Origins of Crowd Psychology* (1975); Serge Moscovici's *The Age of the Crowd: A Historical Treatise on Mass Psychology* (Cambridge: Cambridge University Press, 1985); Susanna Barrow's *Distorting Mirrors: Visions of the Crowd in Late Nineteenth-Century France* (1981); and Jaap van Ginneken's *Crowds, Psychology, and Politics* (Cambridge: Cambridge University Press, 1992). Discussions more directly connected to the matter of mass culture include Strychacz, *Modernism, Mass Culture, and Professionalism* (1993); Nelson, *Repression and Recovery* (1989); Wald, *Revolutionary Imagination;* Călinescu, *The Faces of Modernity* (1977; revised as *Five Faces of Modernity,* 1987); Huyssen, *After the Great Divide: Modernism, Mass Culture, Postmodernism;* Burger, *Theory of the Avant-garde* (1984); Hewitt, *Fascist Modernism: Aesthetics, Politics, and the Avant-garde* (1993).

6. Sypher, *Loss of Self in Modern Literature,* 36.

7. For works by social scientists that address the meaning of mass culture, see C. Wright Mills, David Riesman, Alvin Goulder, and George Gerbner.

8. Whatever his misdeeds, Nixon's transgressions are not of the same magnitude as Hitler's

and Stalin's, and it is perhaps remiss to link him with them. But the point is not that all political rulers are ruthless to the same degree, only that the ability to exercise power often brings its misuse. Besides Nixon's obsession with the Vietnam War and the folly of Watergate, we could mention Eisenhower's U-2 incident, Kennedy's Bay of Pigs debacle, Reagan's Iran-Contra affair, and Bush's inept invasion of Iraq. Once power is available, diplomacy loses out to extralegal machinations or to military response, a truth seldom heeded by contemporary leaders who have learned to manipulate a mass culture politically and to exercise power regardless of consequence.

9. Schnapp and Tiews, *Crowds*, xvi.

17. POSTMODERNISM

1. Walter Jackson Bate, *Criticism: The Major Texts* (New York: Harcourt, Brace and World, 1952), 344.

2. Umberto Eco, *Foucault's Pendulum*, trans. William Weaver (San Diego: Harcourt Brace Jovanovich, 1989), 384; hereafter cited in the text.

3. Jorge Luis Borges, "Funes the Memorius," trans. James E. Irby, in *Labyrinths* (New York: New Directions, 1962), 65; hereafter cited in the text.

CODA

1. For a more detailed discussion of how critical change transforms the literary text and its meaning, see Richard Lehan, "Naturalism and the Realms of the Text: The Problem Restated," *Studies in American Naturalism*, 1, no. 1–2 (summer/winter 2006): 15–29.

SELECTED BIBLIOGRAPHY

The books listed here are the ones I have deemed most relevant to the idea of literary modernism and its extended vision or most appropriate to the arguments I have brought to this book.

Abrams, M. H. *Natural Supernaturalism: Tradition and Revolution in Romantic Literature.* New York: Norton, 1971.

Ackerman, Robert. *Myth and Ritual School: J. G. Frazer and the Cambridge Ritualists.* New York: Garland, 1991.

Adorno, Theodor. *The Authoritarian Personality.* New York: Harper, 1950.

———. *The Culture Industry: Selected Essays on Mass Culture.* London: Routledge, 1991.

———. "Spengler after the Decline." In *Prisms,* by Adorno, translated by Samuel Weber and Shierry Weber, 51–72. Cambridge: MIT Press, 1981.

Anderson, Chester. *James Joyce and His World.* New York: Viking, 1968.

Arato, Andrew, and Eike Gebhardt, eds. *The Essential Frankfurt School Reader.* New York: Continuum, 1982.

Armstrong, Tim. *Modernism: A Cultural History.* London: Polity, 2005.

———. *Modernism, Technology, and the Body: A Cultural Study.* Cambridge: Cambridge University Press, 1998.

Baker, Houston. *Modernism and the Harlem Renaissance.* Chicago: Chicago University Press, 1987.

Baldick, Chris. *The Modernist Movement, 1910–1940.* Oxford: Oxford University Press, 2004.

Bates, Milton J. *Wallace Stevens: A Mythology of Self.* Berkeley and Los Angeles: University of California Press, 1985.

Beckson, Karl. *London in the 1890s: A Cultural History.* New York: Norton, 1961.

Benamou, Michel. *Wallace Stevens and the Symbolist Imagination.* Princeton, N.J.: Princeton University Press, 1972.

Benjamin, Walter. *Charles Baudelaire: A Lyric Poet in the Era of High Capitalism*. Translated by Harry Zohn. London: New Left Books, 1973.

———. "The Work of Art in the Age of Mechanical Reproduction." In *Illuminations*, by Benjamin, translated by Harry Zohn; edited by Hannah Arendt. New York: Schocken, 1969.

Bentley, Eric. *The Cult of the Superman: A Study of the Idea of Heroism in Carlyle and Nietzsche*. Gloucester, Mass.: Peter Smith, 1969.

Berman, Marshall. *All That Is Solid Melts into Air: The Experience of Modernity*. New York: Simon and Schuster, 1982.

Bertalanffy, Ludwig von. *General Systems Theory: Foundations, Development, Applications*. New York: Braziller, 1968.

Bishop, John. *Joyce's Book of the Dark*. Madison: University of Wisconsin Press, 1986.

Blackmur, R. P. *The Lion and the Honeycomb: Essays in Solicitude and Critique*. London: Methuen, 1956.

Bloom, Harold. *Wallace Stevens: The Poems of Our Climate*. Ithaca, N.Y.: Cornell University Press, 1977.

Bornstein, George. *Material Modernism: The Politics of the Page*. Cambridge: Cambridge University Press, 2001.

Bowen, Zack R., and James F. Carens. *Ulysses: A Companion to Joyce Studies*. Westport, Conn.: Greenwood Press, 1984.

Bradbury, Malcolm, and James McFarlane, eds. *Modernism: 1890–1930*. London: Penguin, 1976.

Burger, Peter. *The Decline of Modernism*. Cambridge, UK: Polity, 1992.

———. *Theory of the Avant-garde*. Minneapolis: University of Minnesota Press, 1985.

Burke, Kenneth. *Counter-Statement*. Los Altos, Calif.: Hermes, 1931.

———. *A Grammar of Motives*. New York: Prentice-Hall, 1954.

———. *Permanence and Change*. 1935. New York: Bobbs-Merrill, 1965.

———. *A Rhetoric of Motives*. New York: Prentice-Hall, 1953.

Burwick, Frederick, and Paul Douglass, eds. *The Crisis in Modernism: Bergson and the Vitalist Controversy*. Cambridge: Cambridge University Press, 1992.

Butler, Christopher. *Early Modernism: Literature, Music, and Painting in Europe 1900–1916*. Oxford: Oxford University Press, 1994.

Călinescu, Matei. *Faces of Modernity*. Bloomington: Indiana University Press, 1977. Revised as *Five Faces of Modernity: Modernism, Avant-garde, Decadence, Kitsch, Postmodernism*. Durham, N.C.: Duke University Press, 1987.

Carey, John. *Intellectuals and the Masses, 1880–1939*. London: Faber and Faber, 1992.

Chace, William. *The Political Identities of Ezra Pound and T. S. Eliot*. Palo Alto, Calif.: Stanford University Press, 1973.

Chamberlin, Edward J., and Sander L. Gilman, eds. *Degeneration: The Dark Side of Progress*. New York: Columbia University Press, 1985.

Childs, Peter. *Modernism*. London and New York: Routledge, 2000.

Chinitz, David. *T. S. Eliot and the Cultural Divide*. Chicago: University of Chicago Press, 2003.

Clark, Tom. *Jack Kerouac*. New York: Harcourt, Brace, Jovanovich, 1984.

Cope, Jackson. *Joyce's Cities: Archaeologists of the Soul*. Baltimore: John Hopkins University Press, 1981.

Copjec, Joan, ed. *Shades of Noir: A Reader*. New York: Verso, 1993.

Crawford, Robert. *The Savage and the City in the Work of T. S. Eliot*. Oxford: Clarendon Press, 1987.

Davison, Peter, Rolf Meyersohn, and Edward Shils, eds. *Culture and Mass Culture*. Teaneck, N.J.: Somerset House, 1978.

Derrida, Jacques. *Of Grammatology*. Translated by Gayatri Chakravorty Spivak. Baltimore: Johns Hopkins University Press, 1976.

———. "ULYSSES GRAMOPHONE: Hear say yes in Joyce." In *James Joyce: The Augmented Ninth*, edited by Bernard Benstock. Syracuse: Syracuse University Press, 1988.

———. *Writing and Difference*. Translated by Alan Bass. Chicago: University of Chicago Press, 1978.

Donoghue, Denis. *The Old Moderns*. New York: Knopf, 1993.

———. *Walter Pater: Lover of Strange Souls*. New York: Knopf, 1995.

Douglass, Paul. *Bergson, Eliot, and American Literature*. Lexington: University Press of Kentucky, 1986.

Dowling. William C. *Jameson, Althusser, Marx: An Introduction to the Political Unconscious*. Ithaca, N.Y.: Cornell University Press, 1984.

Dubnick, Randa. *The Structure of Obscurity: Gertrude Stein, Language, and Cubism*. Urbana: University of Illinois Press, 1984.

Ellmann, Richard, ed. *Edwardians and Late Victorians*. New York: Columbia University Press, 1960.

———. *James Joyce*. New York: Oxford University Press, 1959.

Emerson, William. *Seven Types of Ambiguity*. New York: New Directions, 1966.

Eysteinsson, Astradur. *The Concept of Modernism*. Ithaca, N.Y.: Cornell University Press, 1992.

Fairhall, James. *James Joyce and the Question of History*. Cambridge: Cambridge University Press, 1993.

Feidelson, Charles. *Symbolism and American Literature*. Chicago: University of Chicago Press, 1953.

Ferral, Charles. *Modernist Writing and Reactionary Politics*. Cambridge: Cambridge University Press, 2001.

Fiedler, Leslie. *What Was Literature? Class Culture and Mass Society*. New York: Simon and Schuster, 1982.

Filreis, Alan. *Modernism from Right to Left: Wallace Stevens, the Thirties, and Literary Radicalism*. Cambridge: Cambridge University Press, 1994.

Ford, Sara. *Gertrude Stein and Wallace Stevens: The Performance of Modern Consciousness.* New York: Routledge, 2002.

Foster, John Burt. *Heirs to Dionysus: A Nietzschean Current in Literary Modernism.* Princeton, N.J.: Princeton University Press, 1981.

Freud, Sigmund. *Civilization and Its Discontents.* Translated and edited by James Strachey. 1930. New York: Norton, 1961.

Frisby, David. *Fragments of Modernity: Theories of Modernity in the Work of Simmel, Kracauer, and Benjamin.* Cambridge: MIT Press, 1986.

Frye, Northrop. *Anatomy of Criticism.* Princeton, N.J.: Princeton University Press, 1957.

Gogröf-Voorhees, Andrea. *Defining Modernism: Baudelaire and Nietzsche on Romanticism, Modernity, Decadence, and Wagner.* New York: Lang, 1999.

Goodman, Jane. *Modernism, 1910–1945.* Basingstoke: Palgrave, 2004.

Greenberg, Clement. *Art and Culture.* Boston: Beacon Press, 1961.

Guerard, Albert J. *André Gide.* Cambridge: Harvard University Press, 1969.

Hauser, Arnold. *The Social History of Art.* London: Routledge and Paul, 1951.

Hewitt, Andrew. *Fascist Modernism: Aesthetics, Politics, and the Avant-garde.* Palo Alto, Calif.: Stanford University Press, 1993.

Holbrook, Jackson. *The Eighteen-Nineties: A Review of Art and Ideas at the Close of the Nineteenth Century.* London, 1913. Reprint, Pelican, 1939.

Holderness, Graham, Bryan Loughrey, and Nahem Yousaf, eds. *George Orwell.* London: Macmillan, 1998.

hooks, bell. *Feminist Theory: From Margin to Center.* Boston: South End Press, 1984.

Howe, Irving, ed. *The Idea of the Modern in Literature and the Arts.* New York: Horizon Press, 1967.

Huyssen, Andreas. *After the Great Divide: Modernism, Mass Culture, Postmodernism.* Bloomington: Indiana University Press, 1986.

Jameson, Fredric. *Fables of Aggression: Wyndham Lewis, the Modernist as Fascist.* Berkeley and Los Angeles: University of California Press, 1979.

———. *Marxism and Form.* Princeton, N.J.: Princeton University Press, 1971.

———. *The Political Unconscious: Narrative as a Socially Symbolic Act.* Ithaca, N.Y.: Cornell University Press, 1981.

———. *Postmodernism, or, The Cultural Logic of Late Capitalism.* Durham, N.C.: Duke University Press, 1991.

———. *The Prison-House of Language.* Princeton, N.J.: Princeton University Press, 1972.

———. *A Singular Modernity: Essays on the Ontology of the Present.* London: Verso, 2002.

Jouve, Nicole Ward. *Baudelaire: A Fire to Conquer Darkness.* London: Macmillan, 1980.

Kalaidjian, Walter, ed. *The Cambridge Companion to American Modernism.* Cambridge: Cambridge University Press, 2005.

Karl, Frederick R. *Modern and Modernism: The Sovereignty of the Artist 1885–1925.* New York: Atheneum, 1988.

Kenner, Hugh. *The Pound Era*. Berkeley and Los Angeles: University of California Press, 1971.

Lehan, Richard. *The City in Literature: An Intellectual and Cultural History*. Berkeley and Los Angeles: University of California Press, 1998.

———. *Realism and Naturalism: The Novel in an Age of Transition*. Madison: University of Wisconsin Press, 2005.

Lernout, Geert. *The French Joyce*. Ann Arbor: University of Michigan Press, 1990.

Levenson, Michael, ed. *The Cambridge Companion to Modernism*. Cambridge: Cambridge University Press, 1999.

———. *A Genealogy of Modernism*. Cambridge: Cambridge University Press, 1984.

———. *Modernism and the Fate of Individuality*. Cambridge: Cambridge University Press, 1991.

Lewis, Wyndham. *Time and Western Man*. New York: Harcourt, Brace, 1928.

Lichtheim, George. *George Lukacs*. New York: Viking, 1970.

Lowenthal, Leo. *Literature and Mass Culture*. New Brunswick, N.J.: Transaction, 1984.

Lukács, Georg. *Essays on Realism*. Edited by Rodney Livingston. Translated by David Fernbach. Cambridge: MIT Press, 1980.

———. "Marxist Aesthetics and Literary Realism: Studies in European Realism." Reprinted in *Essentials of the Theory of Fiction*, edited by Michael Hoffman and Patrick Murphy. Durham, N.C.: Duke University Press, 1988.

Lunn, Eugene. *Marxism and Modernism: An Historical Study of Lukács, Brecht, Benjamin and Adorno*. Berkeley and Los Angeles: University of California Press, 1982.

Manganaro, Marc. *Myth, Rhetoric, and the Voice of Authority: A Critique of Frazer, Eliot, Frye, and Campbell*. New Haven, Conn.: Yale University Press, 1992.

Martin, Timothy. *Joyce and Wagner: A Study of Influence*. Cambridge: Cambridge University Press, 1991.

McCarthy, Patrick. *Céline*. New York: Viking, 1975.

Mellow, James R. *Charmed Circle: Gertrude Stein and Company*. New York: Praeger, 1974.

Miles, Barrry. *Ginsberg: A Biography*. New York: Simon and Schuster, 1989.

Miller, J. Hillis. *Poets of Reality*. Cambridge: Harvard University Press, 1965.

Murray, Gilbert. *Five Stages of Greek Religion*. 1912. New York: Doubleday, 1951.

Naremore, James, and Patrick Brantlinger, eds. *Modernity and Mass Culture*. Bloomington: Indiana University Press, 1991.

Nelson, Cary. *Repression and Recovery*. Madison: University of Wisconsin Press, 1989.

Nicholls, Peter. *Cambridge History of Twentieth-Century English Literature*. Cambridge: Cambridge University Press, 2004.

———. *Modernisms: A Literary Guide*. Berkeley and Los Angeles: University of California Press, 1995.

North, Michael. *The Dialect of Modernism: Race, Language, and Twentieth-Century Literature*. New York: Oxford University Press, 1994.

Ohmann, Richard. *Selling Culture: Magazines, Markets, and Class at the Turn of the Century.* London: Verso, 1996.

Osborne, Peter. *The Politics of Time: Modernity and the Avant-garde.* London: Verso, 1995.

Pater, Walter. Preface and conclusion to *The Renaissance,* by Pater. In *Criticism: the Major Texts,* edited by W. J. Bate, 508–12. New York: Harcourt, Brace, 1952.

Peck, Daniel. *Faces of Degeneration: A European Disorder, 1848–1919.* Cambridge: Cambridge University Press, 1989.

Perloff, Marjorie. *The Futurist Movement: Avant-garde, Avant Guerre, and the Language of Rupture.* Chicago: University of Chicago Press, 1986.

———. *Twenty-first-Century Modernism: The New Poetics.* Malden, Mass.: Blackwell, 2002.

Poggioli, Renato. *The Theory of the Avant-garde.* Cambridge: Harvard University Press, 1981.

Poplawski, Paul, ed. *Encyclopedia of Literary Modernism.* Westport, Conn.: Greenwood Press, 2003.

Poulet, George. *Proustian Space.* Translated by Elliott Coleman. Baltimore: Johns Hopkins University Press, 1977.

Quinones, Ricardo J. *Mapping Modernism: Time and Development.* Princeton, N.J.: Princeton University Press, 1985.

Rainey, Lawrence. *Institutions of Modernism: Literary Elites and Public Culture.* New Haven, Conn.: Yale University Press, 1998.

Richards, Ivor. *Principles of Literary Criticism.* New York: Harcourt, Brace, 1930.

Ryan, Judith. *Vanishing Subject: Early Psychology and Literary Modernism.* Chicago: University of Chicago Press, 1991.

Schnapp, Jeffrey, and Matthew Tiews, eds. *Crowds.* Palo Alto, Calif.: Stanford University Press, 2006.

Schorer, Mark. "Technique as Discovery." *Hudson Review* 1, no. 1 (1948). Reprinted in *Essentials of the Theory of Fiction,* edited by Michael Hoffman and Patrick Murphy. Durham, N.C.: Duke University Press, 1988.

Schorske, Carl. *Fin-de-siècle Vienna: Politics and Culture.* New York: Knopf, 1979.

Shaw, Bernard. *The Perfect Wagnerite.* London: Constable, 1971.

Shirer, William L. *The Rise and Fall of the Third Reich.* New York: Fawcett Crest, 1960.

Strychacz, Thomas. *Modernism, Mass Culture, and Professionalism.* Cambridge: Cambridge University Press, 1993.

Symons, Julian. *Makers of the New: The Revolution in Literature, 1912–1939.* London: Andre Deutsch, 1987.

Sypher, Wylie. *Loss of Self in Modern Literature.* Westport, Conn.: Greenwood Press, 1979.

Tratner, Michael. *Modernism and Mass Politics: Joyce, Woolf, Eliot, Yeats.* Palo Alto, Calif.: Stanford University Press, 1995.

Wald, Alan. *Revolutionary Imagination*. Chapel Hill: University of North Carolina Press, 1983.

Walder, Dennis, ed. *Literature in the Modern World: Critical Essays and Documents*. New York: Oxford University Press, 1990.

Watt, Ian. *The Rise of the Novel: Studies in Defoe, Richardson, and Fielding*. Berkeley and Los Angeles: University of California Press, 1957.

Weir, David. *Decadence and the Making of Modernism*. Amherst: University of Massachusetts Press, 1995.

Weston, Jessie. *From Ritual to Romance*. Garden City, N.Y.: Doubleday, 1957.

Willey, Basil. *Darwin and Butler: Two Versions of Evolution*. London: Chatto and Windus, 1960.

Wolin, Richard. *Walter Benjamin: An Aesthetic of Redemption*. New York: Columbia University Press, 1982.

INDEX

WITHDRAWN

Gramley Library
Salem Academy and College
Winston-Salem, N.C. 27108